EXAMPLES & EXPLANATIONS

Employment
Discrimination

EDITORIAL ADVISORS

Rachel E. Barkow
Segal Family Professor of Regulatory Law and Policy
Faculty Director, Center on the Administration of
Criminal Law
New York University School of Law

Erwin Chemerinsky
Dean and Distinguished Professor of Law
Raymond Pryke Professor of First Amendment Law
University of California, Irvine School of Law

Richard A. Epstein
Laurence A. Tisch Professor of Law
New York University School of Law

EDITORIAL ADVISORS

Rachel E. Barkow
Segal Family Professor of Regulatory Law and Policy
Faculty Director, Center on the Administration of Criminal Law
New York University School of Law

Erwin Chemerinsky
Dean and Distinguished Professor of Law
Raymond Pryke Professor of First Amendment Law
University of California, Irvine School of Law

Richard A. Epstein
Laurence A. Tisch Professor of Law
New York University School of Law
Peter and Kirsten Bedford Senior Fellow
The Hoover Institution
Senior Lecturer in Law
The University of Chicago

Ronald J. Gilson
Charles J. Meyers Professor of Law and Business
Stanford University
Marc and Eva Stern Professor of Law and Business
Columbia Law School

James E. Krier
Earl Warren DeLano Professor of Law
The University of Michigan Law School

Tracey L. Meares
Walton Hale Hamilton Professor of Law
Director, The Justice Collaboratory
Yale Law School

Richard K. Neumann, Jr.
Professor of Law
Maurice A. Deane School of Law at Hofstra University

Robert H. Sitkoff
John L. Gray Professor of Law
Harvard Law School

David Alan Sklansky
Stanley Morrison Professor of Law
Faculty Co-Director, Stanford Criminal Justice Center
Stanford Law School

EXAMPLES&EXPLANATIONS

Employment Discrimination

Third Edition

Joel Wm. Friedman

Jack M. Gordon Professor of Procedural Law
   & Jurisdiction
Tulane Law School

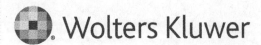 Wolters Kluwer

Copyright © 2017 CCH Incorporated.

Published by Wolters Kluwer in New York.

Wolters Kluwer Legal & Regulatory U.S. serves customers worldwide with CCH, Aspen Publishers, and Kluwer Law International products. (www.WKLegaledu.com)

No part of this publication may be reproduced or transmitted in any form or by any means, electronic or mechanical, including photocopy, recording, or being utilized by any information storage or retrieval system, without written permission from the publisher. For information about permissions or to request permissions online, visit us at www.WKLegaledu.com, or a written request may be faxed to our permissions department at 212-771-0803.

To contact Customer Service, e-mail customer.service@wolterskluwer.com, call 1-800-234-1660, fax 1-800-901-9075, or mail correspondence to:

Wolters Kluwer
Attn: Order Department
PO Box 990
Frederick, MD 21705

Printed in the United States of America.

1 2 3 4 5 6 7 8 9 0

ISBN 978-1-4548-6848-4

Library of Congress Cataloging-in-Publication Data

Names: Friedman, Joel Wm. (Joel William), 1951- author.
Title: Employment discrimination / Joel Wm. Friedman, Jack M. Gordon
   Professor of Procedural Law & Jurisdiction, Tulane Law School.
Description: Third edition. | New York : Wolters Kluwer, 2017. | Series:
   Explanations & examples
Identifiers: LCCN 2017002277 | ISBN 9781454868484
Subjects: LCSH: Discrimination in employment--Law and legislation--United
   States.
Classification: LCC KF3464 .F738 2017 | DDC 344.7301/133--dc23
LC record available at https://lccn.loc.gov/2017002277

About Wolters Kluwer Legal & Regulatory U.S.

Wolters Kluwer Legal & Regulatory U.S. delivers expert content and solutions in the areas of law, corporate compliance, health compliance, reimbursement, and legal education. Its practical solutions help customers successfully navigate the demands of a changing environment to drive their daily activities, enhance decision quality, and inspire confident outcomes.

Serving customers worldwide, its legal and regulatory portfolio includes products under the Aspen Publishers, CCH Incorporated, Kluwer Law International, ftwilliam.com, and MediRegs names. They are regarded as exceptional and trusted resources for general legal and practice-specific knowledge, compliance and risk management, dynamic workflow solutions, and expert commentary.

To Viviane, Alexa,
Chloe, & Max ("The Man")

Summary of Contents

Contents   *xi*

Preface   *xvii*

PART I: PROVING DISCRIMINATION

Chapter 1: Individual Claims of Intentional Discrimination   3

Chapter 2: Systemic Claims of Intentional Discrimination   27

Chapter 3: Non-Intentional Discrimination: Disparate Impact   41

PART II: TITLE VII OF THE 1964 CIVIL RIGHTS ACT

Chapter 4: A General Overview: Proper Plaintiffs, Suable
Defendants, Covered Practices, Exceptions, and
Exemptions   67

Chapter 5: Specific Proof Issues Under Title VII: Defenses, Sexual
Harassment, and Retaliation   93

Chapter 6: Special Issues Involving the Five Protected
Classifications: Race, Color, Religion, Sex, and
National Origin   133

Chapter 7: Enforcement: Procedures   157

Chapter 8: Enforcement: Remedies   199

PART III: OTHER FEDERAL ANTIDISCRIMINATION STATUTES

Chapter 9: The Reconstruction Civil Rights Acts—
42 U.S.C. §§1981, 1983, and 1985—
and the Equal Pay Act   235

Chapter 10: The Age Discrimination in Employment Act 261

Chapter 11: Discrimination on the Basis of Disability 289

Index 329

Contents

Preface   *xvii*

PART I. PROVING DISCRIMINATION

Chapter 1   **Individual Claims of Intentional
                   Discrimination**   **3**

    A. Introduction   3
    B. The Basic Analytical Framework: A Tripartite Formula   4
    C. The Formula in Operation: Proving Pretext   6
    D. An Alternative Evidentiary Approach for Mixed
        Motive Cases   15
    E. After-Acquired Evidence   22
    F. A Quick Word on Affirmative Defenses   25

Chapter 2   **Systemic Claims of Intentional
                   Discrimination**   **27**

    A. Introduction   27
    B. Using Statistics to Establish a Prima Facie Claim
        of Systemic Disparate Treatment: *Teamsters* and
        "The Inexorable Zero"   28
    C. Another Statistical Model for Closer Cases of Systemic
        Disparate Treatment: *Hazelwood*   30
    D. Yet a Third Model of Statistical Analysis for
        Multi-Factored Decisions: *Bazemore*   32
    E. Another Brief Word on Affirmative Defenses   39
    F. And, Finally, This . . .   40

Chapter 3   **Non-Intentional Discrimination:
                   Disparate Impact**   **41**

    A. Introduction   41
    B. Establishing a Prima Facie Case of Impact Discrimination   42

C. Applying Impact Analysis to Multi-factored Decisions and Subjective Criteria 45
D. Defending Impact Claims: An Introduction 54
   1. An Affirmative Defense to Title VII Impact Claims: Job-Relatedness and Business Necessity 54
   2. An Employer's Alternative to Validation: "Norming" or Other Attempts to Avoid the Existence of Disparate Impact 57
E. That's Not All, Folks . . . 62

PART II. TITLE VII OF THE 1964 CIVIL RIGHTS ACT

Chapter 4   A General Overview: Proper Plaintiffs, Suable Defendants, Covered Practices, Exceptions, and Exemptions   67

A. Introduction 67
B. Suable Defendants: Employers 68
C. Suable Defendants: Employment Agencies 72
D. Suable Defendants: Labor Organizations 74
E. Proper Plaintiffs: "Employees" and "Individuals" 76
F. Covered Practices 78
G. Exceptions and Exemptions: Overview 80
H. The Religious Discrimination Exemption for Religious Institutions 81

Chapter 5   Special Proof Issues Under Title VII: Defenses, Sexual Harassment, and Retaliation   93

A. Introduction: The Basic Proof Formulations Redux 93
B. Affirmative Defense to Intentional Discrimination: §703(e)(1) — The BFOQ Defense 94
C. Affirmative Defenses to Impact-Based Discrimination: §703(h) — Bona Fide Seniority or Merit Systems and Professionally Developed Ability Tests 102
D. Sexual Harassment: Is It Actionable Discrimination? 106
E. Sexual Harassment: Is the Defendant Employer Liable? 114
F. Retaliation 121

Chapter 6   **Specific Issues Involving the Five Protected Classifications: Race, Color, Religion, Sex, and National Origin**   **133**

    A. Religion-Based Discrimination and the Duty to Accommodate   133
    B. National Origin-Based Discrimination   138
    C. Discrimination on the Basis of Race and Color   141
    D. Discrimination on the Basis of Sex   142
       1. Introduction   142
       2. The "Sex-Plus" Doctrine   142
       3. Discrimination on the Basis of Pregnancy   144
       4. An Aside: The Family and Medical Leave Act of 1993   148
       5. Discrimination on the Basis of Sexual Orientation   149
       6. Reliance on Sex-Based Actuarial Tables   151

Chapter 7   **Enforcement: Procedures**   **157**

    A. Title VII Procedural Requirements for Nonfederal Employees: Overview   157
    B. The First Step: Federal and State Administrative Charges   158
    C. Determining the Date of Discrimination   169
    D. Individual Suits: Permissible Scope   178
    E. Individual Suits: Preclusive Effect of Administrative and State Court Rulings   179
    F. The Impact of Arbitration Agreements on Litigating Title VII Claims   180
    G. Suits by the EEOC   187
    H. Procedural Requirements for Federal Employees   188
    I. Class Actions: Overview   191
    J. Class Actions: Rule 23 Analysis   192

Chapter 8   **Enforcement: Remedies**   **199**

    A. Overview   199
    B. Equitable Relief   200
       1. Injunctive Relief   200
       2. Back Pay   202
       3. Attorney's Fees   203
    C. Legal Relief   213
       1. Compensatory Relief   213
       2. Punitive Damages   216

3. Cap on Damages 218
4. Taxation of Monetary Damage Awards 219
D. Equitable and Legal Remedies in Cases Involving
Systemic Discrimination 219
E. Affirmative Action 220
1. Overview 220
2. The Constitutional Limits 221
3. Statutory Limits — Title VII Scrutiny of
Affirmative Action 224

PART III. OTHER FEDERAL ANTIDISCRIMINATION STATUTES

Chapter 9   **The Reconstruction Civil Rights Acts —
42 U.S.C. §§1981, 1983, and 1985 —
and the Equal Pay Act**   **235**

A. The Civil Rights Act of 1866 — 42 U.S.C. §1981 235
1. Overview 235
2. Coverage and Substantive Provisions 236
3. Procedures and Remedies 238
B. The Civil Rights Act of 1871, Section One —
42 U.S.C. §1983 244
C. The Civil Rights Act of 1871, Section Two —
42 U.S.C. §1985(3) 250
D. The Equal Pay Act 252
1. Overview 252
2. Coverage and Substantive Provisions 252
3. Relationship to Title VII 255
4. Procedure and Remedies 256

Chapter 10   **The Age Discrimination in Employment Act**   **261**

A. Overview 261
B. Coverage 261
C. The Meaning of Age Discrimination 263
D. Proving and Defending Intentional Age-Based
Discrimination Claims 263
E. Proving and Defending Disparate Impact Claims 273
F. Voluntary and Involuntary Retirement 274

G. Public Employees and Constitutional Challenges
   to Age Discrimination   276
H. Procedure and Remedies for Nonfederal Employees   280
I. Federal Employees   283

Chapter 11   Discrimination on the Basis of Disability   289

A. The Americans with Disabilities Act (ADA)   289
   1. Overview   289
   2. The Meaning of "Disability"   291
      a. "Regarded As"   291
      b. Physical or Mental Impairment   292
      c. Substantially Limiting   293
      d. Major Life Activities   296
   3. The Meaning of "Otherwise Qualified"   302
   4. The Dual Meaning of Discrimination   306
      a. Proving Adverse Action-Based Discrimination:
         Intentional and Disparate Impact Claims and
         Retaliation   306
      b. Causation   308
      c. Associational Discrimination   308
      d. Defending Adverse Action-Based Discrimination
         Claims   309
         i.   Direct Threat   309
         ii. Bona Fide Insurance Plans   310
         iii. Job-Relatedness and Business Necessity   311
         iv. Religious Entities   311
      e. The Duty to Accommodate   314
         i. A Few Words About Genetic Testing   319
         ii. Drug Testing and Other Medical Examinations   320
   5. Procedures and Remedies   324
B. The Federal Rehabilitation Act of 1973   325
C. Constitutional Claims   326

Index   329

C. Public Employees and Constitutional Challenges to Age Discrimination 279

II. Executive and Legislative Branch Federal Employees 280

2. Federal Employees 281

Chapter 11   Discrimination on the Basis of Disability   285

A. The Americans with Disabilities Act (ADA) 285

Overview 286

The Meaning of "Disability" 291

a. "Regarded As" 291

b. Physical or Mental Impairment 292

c. Substantially Limiting 293

d. Major Life Activities 296

The Meaning of "Otherwise Qualified" 301

The Dual Meaning of Discrimination 302

a. Proving Adverse Action-Based Discrimination: Intentional and Disparate Impact Claims and Retaliation 302

b. Causation 308

c. Associational Discrimination 308

e. Defending a Adverse Action-Based Discrimination Claims 308

E. Direct Threat 309

3. Bona Fide Ineligible Plans 310

B. Global Relevance and Business Necessity 310

D. Religious Entities 311

E. The Duty to Accommodate 314

A Few Words About Genetic Testing 317

d. Drug Testing and Other Medical Examinations 319

C. Procedures and Remedies 321

B. The Federal Rehabilitation Act of 1973 325

Constitutional Claims 326

Preface

Employment discrimination is a subject that nearly everyone is exposed to, directly or indirectly, on a frequent basis. Whether it is from personal knowledge, experiences shared by friends or relatives, or the myriad stories that appear on television and in newspapers, magazines, and other media, there is virtually universal familiarity with this topic. But unlike members of the general public, lawyers and law students are trained to analyze these scenarios through the prism of established legal doctrine. A law school course focusing on employment discrimination, at its most general level of abstraction, examines the extent to which the government should play, and critically assesses the manner in which the government has decided to play, a role in mediating two conflicting principles of public policy: i.e., the traditional, common law-based protection of private property rights and a long-standing commitment to preserving and enforcing civil rights.

Over the years, the ways in which law schools cover the area of labor and employment law have evolved. Nearly all schools have at least one course in this area, and most have more than one. The entire area is composed of three distinct subjects: (1) labor law, which addresses issues concerning the relationship between workers, their employers, and unions; (2) employment discrimination, which focuses solely on the issue of job-based discrimination; and (3) employment law, which deals with those employment-related issues, both statutory and common law, that fall outside the parameters of the first two subjects. The manner in which these three areas are covered varies from school to school. Sometimes two or more of these subjects are combined in one course. Most commonly, however, each subject is addressed separately in a stand-alone course. This book focuses exclusively on employment discrimination law and is intended for use by students who are taking either a course entirely devoted to this subject or a course in which it is an important component.

Whether a law school course focuses entirely or partially on employment discrimination law, the predominant source of legal doctrine in this area is federal legislation. Beginning primarily in the early 1960s (with one important mid-nineteenth-century exception), Congress has chosen to attack the issue of employment discrimination through the enactment of several statutes, each of which addresses a particular form or forms of job bias. Over the past nearly half-century, the courts, and particularly the U.S. Supreme Court, have developed a large body of jurisprudence that interprets the substantive, remedial, and procedural provisions of these enactments. As you will see, much of that case law, particularly in the area of defining how the parties prove and defend against claims of discrimination, is applicable to claims filed under several of these statutes. In response to this development, and consistently with the manner in which these issues are handled in most employment discrimination law casebooks, the initial chapters of this book examine these issues collectively. But there are also many important issues that are treated differently under statutes such as Title VII of the 1964 Civil Rights Act, the Age Discrimination in Employment Act, the Equal Pay Act, and the Americans with Disabilities Act. Accordingly, the subsequent chapters are organized on a statute-by-statute basis.

Where the employer is a governmental entity, grievants also have the possibility of asserting constitutional claims. And so, where appropriate, the constitutional issues, primarily those raised under the Fifth (for federal employers) and Fourteenth (for nonfederal public employers) Amendment guarantees of equal protection and due process, are discussed. Finally, state law also has a role to play, since every state has some form of antidiscrimination statute that encompasses employment-related claims. These are also examined, particularly as they relate to the procedure for bringing employment discrimination claims.

In every chapter of the book, I have attempted to synthesize and explain all of the issues that are commonly examined in a course dealing with employment discrimination law. This includes a detailed parsing of the applicable statutory text, as well as careful summaries and analyses of the relevant case law. But, as you know, the key to success on a law school exam is the ability to spot the legal issues raised in a factual hypothetical, to succinctly state the governing legal principle(s), and to accurately and persuasively apply the applicable doctrine to the relevant facts. To aid you in improving your skill in these areas, I have provided an extensive collection of sample questions in every chapter and subchapter of the book that are expressly designed to accomplish that objective. Like you, I was frequently frustrated by the endless list of unanswered questions in casebooks that provide no insight into solving these problems other than a string of citations to cases that I had neither the time nor the inclination to read. So, after each set of questions, I have written detailed explanations that will focus your attention on the relevant legal issue, provide the governing legal principle, and explain how that doctrine should apply to those facts. To that end, I have fashioned questions of varying level of difficulty and complexity. Some are fairly straightforward, to make sure that you understand the basics. Others are more nuanced and are designed to encourage you to identify the key legal issue at stake and to apply your knowledge of the relevant legal doctrine to a challenging factual pattern in the way that replicates the type of questions that you will find on a final exam. But these questions will only help you improve your skills only if you take the time to read them carefully and give them your full attention. If you approach them with the care that you will devote to your final exam, I am confident that your efforts will be rewarded with increasing confidence in approaching exam questions, as well as an enhanced ability at the skills that you will need for success on the final exam.

I look forward to hearing from you if you have any suggestions, concerns, or corrections for future editions. You can email me at jfriedman@tulane.edu. In the meantime, I wish you the best of luck in this and all your other courses.

June 2017

Joel Wm. Friedman

EXAMPLES&EXPLANATIONS

Employment Discrimination

PART I

Proving Discrimination

Individual Claims of Intentional Discrimination

A. INTRODUCTION

The regulation of the employment relationship to promote equal employment opportunity necessarily involves the interaction between two by now fundamental principles of American jurisprudence: the enforcement of private property rights and the promotion of civil rights and personal dignity. Every course in Employment Discrimination Law necessarily focuses on the extent to which the legal order, through legislation, executive (including administrative agency) action, and judicial opinions, intervenes in the relationship between employer and worker or potential employee in order to balance or accommodate these inevitably competing concepts.

On the federal level, two sources of positive law are relevant to claims of employment discrimination: the U.S. Constitution (principally the equal protection and due process guarantees contained within the Fifth and Fourteenth Amendments) and federal statutes. The Constitution plays a subsidiary role in this context because the state action requirement for claimed violations of these amendments limits their applicability to suits brought by government workers. Similarly, though every state has enacted some form of antidiscrimination statute, the terms of these laws typically mirror the content of the analogous federal statute. Consequently, the focus of virtually all Employment Discrimination Law courses is on federal statutory law.

Congress has enacted a collection of statutes that prohibit discrimination in both the public and private sectors on the basis of a variety of criteria. The most comprehensive federal antidiscrimination statute, Title VII of the

1964 Civil Rights Act, which has been amended on several occasions, prohibits discrimination on the basis of race, color, religion, sex, and national origin with respect to all terms, conditions, and privileges of employment. Prior to 1964, however, Congress did enact legislation that dealt with employment discrimination, but its scope was severely constricted. The Equal Pay Act in 1963 proscribes only sex-based wage discrimination. And as part of the postbellum Reconstruction Era effort to provide substantive rights to newly freed slaves in furtherance of the terms and objectives of the Thirteenth, Fourteenth, and Fifteenth Amendments, Congress passed a collection of related statutes that provide limited protection to victims of certain forms of employment bias. After 1964, three other pieces of legislation, the Age Discrimination in Employment Act (ADEA), the Rehabilitation Act, and the Americans with Disabilities Act (ADA), were enacted to extend the antidiscrimination mandate to decisions based on age and disability.

While each of these federal statutes has generated its own set of substantive, remedial, and procedural questions, they all codify and focus upon a common concept—discrimination. And though the meaning of this term might, at first blush, seem straightforward, it has proved to be anything but that. Not only has the Supreme Court construed that term to encompass two separate analytical doctrines, but its articulation of these two constructs, which evolved over time through a large number of decisions, compelled a dissatisfied Congress to amend these statutes on more than one occasion, precisely and expressly to replace the Court's doctrinal formulation with its own.

We begin with an examination of the most obvious form of discrimination—intentional discrimination, i.e., facially disparate treatment that is motivated by the individual's membership in the proscribed category. And this concept, typically referred to as disparate treatment, is further divided into two subcategories—individual and systemic (pattern or practice) claims. So, first, we turn to the treatment of individual claims of intentional discrimination.

B. THE BASIC ANALYTICAL FRAMEWORK: A TRIPARTITE FORMULA

Although all the major federal civil rights statutes state that employers and other covered entities cannot "discriminate," and even though some of them contain a definition of "discrimination," it still was left up to the Supreme Court to put meat on the bones of these statutory terms in order to provide (1) litigants with meaningful guidance on how to establish or defend against claims of discrimination and (2) the courts with an analytical framework under which to evaluate the evidence tendered by the parties. In employment discrimination suits, as in all civil cases, evidence comes in two flavors: direct and circumstantial. Direct evidence does not require the fact-finder to make any inferences; it is, on its face, evidence that, if believed, establishes a fact in dispute. Circumstantial evidence, on the other hand, is evidence that, even if believed, only establishes a matter in dispute with the aid of an inference or other form of reasoning that links that evidence to the disputed fact. The presentation of a "smoking gun" or other form of direct evidence invariably suffices to establish a prima facie case. The defendant can then attempt to contradict this evidence or assert an affirmative defense to escape liability. In the vast majority of employment discrimination cases, however, the plaintiff relies solely on circumstantial evidence to make its case. And it is for such cases, i.e., where the plaintiff attempts to establish an individual claim of intentional discrimination based upon circumstantial evidence, that the Supreme Court, over a more than 30-year period, has produced a tripartite framework of analysis.

The basic structure of this formulation was set forth initially in McDonnell Douglas Corp. v. Green, 411 U.S. 792 (1973), and modified thereafter in cases such as Texas Department of Community Affairs v. Burdine, 450 U.S. 248 (1981), St. Mary's Honor Center v. Hicks, 509 U.S. 502 (1993), Reeves v. Sanderson Plumbing Products, Inc., 530 U.S. 133 (2000), and Ash v. Tyson Foods, Inc., 546 U.S. 454 (2006). The product of this jurisprudential evolution is a three-stage analysis that was designed to be flexible enough to adapt to the particular facts of any individual case. Under step one, in order to establish a prima facie case, the plaintiff bears the "not onerous" (in the Court's words) burden of proving, by a preponderance of the evidence, that s/he (1) applied for (2) an available employment opportunity (3) for which s/he was qualified (4) but did not receive (5) under circumstances that give rise to an inference of unlawful discrimination. Note, then, that a plaintiff can establish a prima facie claim without offering any evidence of the defendant's intention since, in nearly all cases, the courts view the fifth requirement as redundant of the other four, i.e., that the rejection of a qualified candidate for an available position gives rise to an inference of unlawful discrimination. So, although the plaintiff can, and will, if possible, offer more than the minimum necessary to establish a prima facie claim, evidence of discriminatory intent is not required to meet the plaintiff's initial burden.

If the plaintiff sustains this burden, the establishment of a prima facie case generates a rebuttable presumption that the reason for the plaintiff's rejection was unlawful discrimination. Where this occurs, the case proceeds to stage two. The defendant then must carry the burden of producing evidence (but not the burden of persuasion) of some legitimate, nondiscriminatory explanation for its decision in order to rebut the presumption produced by the prima facie showing. If the defendant fails to come forward with any such evidence, the plaintiff is entitled to judgment as a matter of law since no relevant issue of fact remains. But where, as is likely, the defendant meets this minimal burden of production, the presumption is rebutted ("drops from the case") and the case proceeds to the third and final stage.

At this third stage, the defendant has offered a nondiscriminatory explanation and the presumption of discrimination generated by the plaintiff's prima facie evidence has been eliminated. In the absence of any presumption of discriminatory intent, the plaintiff retains the burden of persuading the fact-finder that the defendant's explanation was not the real reason for the challenged decision but, instead, was merely a pretext for the real reason—intentional discrimination. And the plaintiff can do this in one of two ways. It can attempt to convince the fact-finder that discrimination was the motive either (a) directly by offering evidence of that motivation or (b) indirectly by establishing that the defendant's asserted justification is not believable.

C. THE FORMULA IN OPERATION: PROVING PRETEXT

As the Supreme Court acknowledged in *Burdine*, the plaintiff's task of establishing a prima facie case is not onerous. Neither is the defendant's burden of coming forward with admissible, believable evidence of a nondiscriminatory explanation for its actions. Consequently, the overwhelming majority of litigated individual claims of intentional discrimination come down to the third stage of the formulation, i.e., whether the trier of fact believes the plaintiff or the defendant as to the one and only reason behind the employer's decision. Post-*Burdine*, this so-called "pretext" phase of the analysis was interpreted differently by various federal appellate courts. The major difference revolved around that language in *Burdine* referring to the "indirect" method of proving pretext. Specifically, the circuit courts could not agree on whether it was sufficient for the plaintiff to disprove the defendant's proffered explanation or whether it was essential also to offer some evidence indicating that the plaintiff's explanation—discrimination—was the true reason for the defendant's decision. In *St. Mary's*, the Court sought to resolve the controversy by declaring that once the plaintiff offered evidence that disputed the veracity of the defendant's explanation, i.e., created a genuine issue of fact as to the truth of that explanation, the fact-finder was permitted, though not required, to find in favor of the plaintiff. In other words, the jury (jury trials were available under the Equal Pay Act from its enactment in 1963; they became available in Title VII and ADA claims of intentional discrimination as a result of the passage of the Civil Rights Act of 1991 and in all ADEA cases via a 1978 amendment to that statute) could rely on the facts that established the prima facie case, plus its disbelief of the defendant's explanation as the basis for inferring that the challenged decision was the product of intentional discrimination. But the jury also could find in favor of the defendant in that same situation. The key part of the ruling, then, was that the issue was left up to the jury. Or, to put it another way, it was error to grant judgment as a matter of law to either party where the defendant had offered evidence of a nondiscriminatory explanation and the plaintiff had offered evidence from which a jury could disbelieve the defendant's proffered explanation.

The impact of the ruling in *St. Mary's*, however, was tempered by the Court's subsequent opinion in *Reeves*, a case brought under the ADEA. There, the Court ruled that a plaintiff might not always defeat a defense motion for judgment as a matter of law simply by offering evidence that created an issue of fact as to the credibility of the defendant's asserted explanation. Sometimes, it declared, more evidence is necessary to allow the case to go to the jury. The Court offered (a potentially non-exhaustive list of) two scenarios under which an employer could be entitled to judgment as a matter of law, even when the plaintiff had offered evidence challenging the believability of the employer's explanation: (1) the so-called "lurking in the record" situation where the record conclusively revealed a nondiscriminatory explanation that had not been asserted by the defense; and (2) the situation in which the plaintiff's evidence produced only a "weak" issue of fact on the believability of the defendant's explanation *and* the record contained abundant and uncontroverted evidence that no discrimination had occurred.

A common method utilized by plaintiffs to establish pretext is the introduction of evidence that other similarly situated workers also were subjected to the discriminatory conduct alleged by the plaintiff. The impact of such testimony, however, is really an evidentiary question and not a matter governed by employment discrimination law. The question under the rules of evidence is whether treatment of third parties is admissible as relevant (i.e., probative of a relevant proposition) to the plaintiff's claim and, if so, whether its probative value is, nevertheless, outweighed by its unfair or prejudicial impact upon the defense. In *Sprint/United Management Co. v. Mendelsohn*, 128 S. Ct. 1140 (2008), the Supreme Court addressed, but did not give a bright-line answer to, this question. It held that the admissibility of "me too" evidence was not properly subject to a *per se* approach. Rather, the determination of whether such evidence is probative and/or prejudicial is a fact-intensive matter to be resolved on an *ad hoc* basis by the trial judge subject only to an abuse of discretion standard on review.

Another way in which plaintiffs seek to establish the pretextual nature of the defendant's explanation is by offering evidence that they are more qualified than the candidate that received the employment opportunity that was denied to the plaintiff. But a mere demonstration of the plaintiff's marginally superior qualifications typically is not sufficient to establish pretext. The lower courts require a very substantial comparative difference. Many, though not all, of the circuits used to characterize the requisite level of comparative superiority as a differential that was so apparent as "virtually to jump off the page and slap you in the face." In *Ash v. Tyson Foods, Inc.*, 546 U.S. 454 (2006), the Supreme Court repudiated this standard as "unhelpful and imprecise" and instructed the lower courts to produce an alternative that "would better ensure that trial courts reach consistent results." The courts thereafter have filled this instructional vacuum by requiring that the disparity be of such significance that no reasonable and impartial decision-maker would have chosen the candidate selected over the plaintiff.

McDonnell Douglas/Burdine (Single Motive) Proof Framework

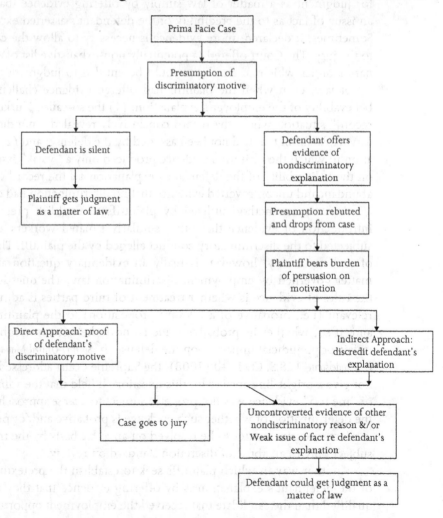

Examples

Damn Yankees

1. Josephine Hardy had been employed as the chief financial officer for Boston Harbor Seafood (BHS) for more than 15 years when the company, located in the heart of Boston, was purchased by Beale Z. ("Bub") Applegate, a multi-millionaire who had been a devout Boston Red Sox fan since childhood. Shortly after purchasing the company, Applegate invited all of the members of his senior staff to attend a Sunday afternoon Red Sox game against the Los Angeles Angels at his suite at the Red Sox's stadium, Fenway Park. Hardy declined the invitation. Applegate was infuriated when he learned that Hardy had chosen not to attend the game because she was a lifelong New York Yankees fan and Red Sox hater who would never attend a Red Sox game unless it was against the Yankees. Three days after that game, Applegate called Hardy into his office to inform her that she was being demoted to the position of filing clerk in the mailroom with a considerable reduction in salary and other benefits. Hardy filed suit against BHS under Title VII alleging that she had been demoted because she was a woman. She testified on direct examination that her personnel file boasted countless letters of commendation and consistently excellent job performance evaluations accumulated over more than 15 years of service, which, she maintained, demonstrated both her loyalty to the company and her trustworthiness and competence to oversee its finances. The defense never sought to contradict this testimony during its cross-examination of Hardy or of any of her other witnesses. At the end of the presentation of Hardy's case in chief, BHS moved for entry of judgment as a matter of law on the ground that Hardy had not established a prima facie claim of sex-based discrimination. How should the court rule on this motion?
2. Would it have made a difference to the court's resolution of the motion for judgment as a matter of law if Hardy had admitted on cross-examination that she had been replaced as CFO by the woman who had served as her deputy?
3. Assume that the trial court denied BHS's motion for judgment as a matter of law. During the presentation of BHS's defense case, Applegate testified that "I need my CFO to be someone who shares my devotion to the Red Sox. I could never hire anyone who is a Yankee lover and Sox hater." At the end of the presentation of BHS's defense case, Hardy moved for judgment as a matter of law. How should the court rule?
4. Suppose that in addition to all the previously discussed testimony, Hardy offered testimony from Lola Taylor, a female who worked in the marketing department, that she had also been demoted because of her sex. In response, BHS offers testimony from two other female former

employees that their demotions were justified and not the result of sex discrimination. Each side objects to the introduction of the other party's evidence. The trial court overruled both objections and admitted all of this evidence. If either side loses the case and appeals the trial judge's evidentiary rulings, how should the appellate court rule?

Anything You Can Do, I Can Do Better

1. Annie O. Klee, a skilled craftsperson employed by Buffalo Bill Rifle Company, was denied a promotion to departmental supervisor. The promotion was given to her colleague, Frank Butler. Annie filed suit under Title VII alleging that she was denied the promotion because of her sex. In support of this claim, she offers evidence that she was better qualified for the position than Butler because of her greater seniority and superior annual performance evaluations. At the close of the plaintiff's evidence, the trial court denied a defense motion for judgment as a matter of law. The case went to the jury, and the jury returned a verdict in favor of the plaintiff. The defense then renewed its motion for judgment as a matter of law. This time, the trial court granted the motion. After noting that the plaintiff had established a prima facie claim and that the defense had offered a nondiscriminatory explanation that was uncontroverted by the plaintiff, the court based its ruling on the ground that the plaintiff's evidence of her superior qualifications was insufficient as a matter of law to establish pretext. With respect to this latter ruling, the trial court added that pretext can be established through comparing qualifications only when "the disparity in qualifications is so apparent as virtually to jump off the page and slap you in the face." The plaintiff appealed the trial court's judgment. How should the appellate court rule?

2. In response to Annie's evidence of her superior qualifications, the company maintained that it chose Butler because Annie recently had demonstrated a lack of commitment to her job as evidenced by increased absenteeism and lateness over the preceding 12 months. Annie proffered evidence that she had been absent and late a total of four times over that period and that two other workers in other departments with worse records of absence and lateness had been promoted to supervisor. Although the company insists that Butler was chosen over Annie solely because of her decreasing level of commitment, the uncontradicted testimony of several other witnesses established that every single person who had been promoted over the past five years, including Butler, was a member of the family that owned Buffalo Bill. At the end of the trial, the company moved for judgment as a matter of law. How should the court rule?

Anything You Can Do, I Can Do, Too

1. After William Portnoy, an African American male, was denied a promotion that subsequently was given to James Cobb, a Caucasian male, he brought a Title VII claim of race discrimination against his employer. At trial, he offered evidence that he was just as qualified for the position as Cobb. At the close of the plaintiff's evidence, the defendant moved for judgment as a matter of law on the ground that Portnoy had failed to establish the qualifications element of the prima facie case by failing to prove that he was better qualified than Cobb. How should the court rule?

Explanations

Damn Yankees

1. The court should deny the defense motion on the ground that the plaintiff has established all the elements of her prima facie case. In order to establish a prima facie case, the plaintiff need only establish that she was qualified for the position from which she was demoted and that the position remained available after she was demoted. She is not required to offer any evidence of the reason for her demotion. And although the formula set forth in McDonnell Douglas also refers to proof of circumstances that give rise to an inference of discrimination, the courts invariably do not regard this as an independent element of the prima facie case. Rather, they typically find it redundant of the other factors, i.e., that evidence establishing the other elements also constitutes circumstances that give rise to an inference of discrimination. So, the only conceivable issue in this example is whether or not the plaintiff has established that she was qualified. The circuit courts have not agreed on whether a discharged or demoted plaintiff must establish that she was performing her original job satisfactorily or whether it is sufficient to prove that she satisfied that position's eligibility requirements. But in this case, it would appear that the plaintiff met both of these standards. The undisputed testimony is that she performed more than adequately in her job. And even if the defendant had offered evidence to contradict her testimony of job qualifications, the courts limit their assessment of the qualifications element of the prima facie case solely to the plaintiff's evidence. The evaluation of any testimony to the contrary offered by the defense occurs at the third and final (pretext) phase of the analysis. Consequently, Hardy has established a prima facie claim of discrimination that generates a presumption that her demotion was the product of unlawful sex discrimination. If defendant BHS is silent in the face of this presumption,

i.e., does not come forward with any evidence of a nondiscriminatory explanation for her demotion, Hardy will be entitled to judgment as a matter of law. But before we get to that issue, which is the focus of the third example in this sportive quartet, we need to assess the significance, if any, of the evidence discussed in the second example.

2. The introduction of this evidence should not change the result; the defense motion should still be denied. The question here is whether evidence that the plaintiff was replaced by someone of her own sex group is fatal to the court's conclusion that the plaintiff's evidence established circumstances that give rise to an inference of discrimination. By and large, the lower courts agree that a plaintiff does not have to establish that the person who obtained the employment opportunity that s/he sought was a non-member of her protected category. Of course, such evidence, when available, will bolster the plaintiff's circumstantial case. But the fact that the plaintiff was rejected in favor of another member of her protected class is not fatal *per se* to defeating a defense motion alleging failure to establish a prima facie case. Thus, motion for judgment as a matter of law at this stage of the proceedings would be improper.

3. The plaintiff's motion for judgment as a matter of law should be denied. The issue here is whether or not the defendant has offered evidence that creates a genuine issue of fact as to whether its decision was the product of a legitimate, nondiscriminatory reason. All that is required is that the reason be legitimate and nondiscriminatory; it does not have to be intelligent, morally meaningful, or even sensible. It simply has to be nondiscriminatory. And though devotion to a baseball team may appear to be irrelevant to the job performance of a CFO, such relevance is beside the point. As long as the jury could believe that the defendant was motivated by this reason, which is a nondiscriminatory reason, the jury is entitled to consider that fact and then choose to believe the defendant or not. Note that, as here, where the plaintiff has not offered any evidence of a discriminatory motivation, even if the jury disbelieves the defendant's explanation, under St. Mary's, the trier of fact is free to infer or not to infer the existence of a discriminatory explanation, i.e., it can render a verdict in favor of either party. Of course, the fact that the reason sounds inane might very well convince the jury that this was a pretext for a discriminatory reason. But that is for the jury to resolve. Accordingly, no judgment as a matter of law is made for this plaintiff.

4. Either party's appeal of the evidentiary ruling should be denied unless the appellate court believes, which is unlikely, that the trial court abused its discretion in admitting the evidence. The testimony by a co-employee that, just like the plaintiff, she was the victim of a sex-based demotion decision raises the evidentiary question of the admissibility of so-called "me too" evidence. Similarly, the evidence offered by BHS that the

demotion of two other females was not sex-based is, in effect, an example of "me not-too" evidence that, presumably, should be treated the same as "me too" evidence. This problem is really a question of evidence and not employment discrimination law. The initial evidentiary issue is whether this evidence meets the relevance standard (under Federal Rule of Evidence 401) for admissibility, i.e., is it probative of a material proposition? But even if the evidence meets that requirement for admission, it still could be excluded (under Federal Rule of Evidence 403), in the discretion of the trial judge, if its prejudicial impact on the opposing side substantially outweighs its probative value. The Supreme Court addressed this question in *Sprint*, where it held that the admissibility of such "me too" evidence was not properly subject to a *per se* rule of admissibility or inadmissibility. Rather, the Court explained, the Rules 401 and 403 calculations were fact-intensive, context-specific assessments that had to be made by the trial court on an *ad hoc* basis subject only to an abuse of discretion standard of review on appeal; the appellate court is not to engage in its own evaluation of these factors. Consequently, the trial court's determinations of probativity and its balance of probativity against prejudice should be sustained on appeal unless the appellate court believes that these rulings constituted an abuse of discretion.

Anything You Can Do, I Can Do Better

1. The appellate court should reverse and remand the case for new trial. The plaintiff attempted to establish pretext through evidence that her qualifications were superior to those of the chosen applicant. In *Ash*, the Supreme Court expressly rejected the "jump and slap" standard applied by the appellate court therein and the trial court in this example. The Court said that this standard was unhelpful and remanded for development of a more workable standard. Thereafter, the courts have responded to this challenge by applying a standard that requires that the degree of superiority of plaintiff's qualifications be such that no reasonable and impartial decision-maker would have chosen the candidate who had been selected over the plaintiff. So, here the appellate court should reverse the trial court's judgment for the defendant and remand for trial under this or some comparable standard.

2. The court should grant the motion. The plaintiff has established a prima facie case, the defendant has offered a nondiscriminatory explanation, and the plaintiff has offered evidence challenging the veracity of that proffered explanation (absences and lateness demonstrative of diminished job commitment). The question here is whether the plaintiff can defeat the defense motion for judgment as a matter of law and get to the jury on the question of pretext. Clearly, the plaintiff is attempting to prove pretext through the "indirect" alternative mentioned in *Burdine*. In

St. Mary's, the Court held that if the jury disbelieves the defense explanation, it is permitted (though not required) to infer from that plus the evidence that established the prima facie case that the defense explanation was a pretext for a discriminatory motive. This suggested that it was sufficient for the plaintiff to get to the jury, i.e., to defeat a defense motion for judgment as a matter of law, by offering evidence that put the credibility of the defense explanation in dispute so that the jury could be given the opportunity to disbelieve the defense and find that the explanation was pretext for discrimination. But in *Sanderson*, albeit a case brought under the ADEA, the Court refined its ruling in *St. Mary's* to state that a plaintiff will not always be successful in defeating a defense motion for judgment as a matter of law merely by creating a factual issue as to the believability of the defense's nondiscriminatory explanation. It offered two scenarios in which doing so would not be sufficient to defeat such a defense motion. One of those stated alternatives is the so-called "lurking in the record" situation, where the record conclusively revealed a nondiscriminatory explanation that had not been asserted by the defense. Here, although the plaintiff has offered evidence that, at a minimum, creates an issue of fact as to the believability of the defense's nondiscriminatory explanation, other uncontroverted evidence reveals another nondiscriminatory explanation — nepotism. Accordingly, under *Sanderson*, which has been applied to Title VII cases, because of the presence of this uncontradicted evidence of a nondiscriminatory explanation, the court could and should grant the defense motion for judgment as a matter of law, even though the plaintiff did offer evidence from which the jury could have disbelieved the defendant's "official" explanation of unacceptable absence and lateness.

Anything You Can Do, I Can Do, Too

1. The motion should be denied. The question here is whether the plaintiff must establish that s/he is better qualified than the chosen candidate in order to meet the qualifications component of the prima facie case. The short answer is no; the courts only require the plaintiff to establish that s/he is qualified in terms of meeting the employer's stated qualifications. In *Patterson v. McLean Credit Union*, 491 U.S. 164 (1989), the Court held that it was an error for the trial court to instruct the jury in an action brought under the 1866 Civil Rights Act (42 U.S.C. §1981) that in order to establish pretext under the *McDonnell Douglas* framework (that, it stated, governed §1981 claims), the plaintiff had to establish that he was better qualified than the chosen candidate. Most circuit courts have construed the ruling in *Patterson* also to mean that a plaintiff does not have to establish her superior qualifications in order to meet the qualifications

element of the prima facie case. Consequently, the defendant's motion should be denied.

D. AN ALTERNATIVE EVIDENTIARY APPROACH FOR MIXED MOTIVE CASES

The *McDonnell Douglas/Burdine* formula is premised on the theory that the trier of fact is attempting to divine the reason behind the defendant's challenged conduct. It presumes that the essential question in the case is whether the employer's action was the result of discrimination or of something else. For example, the Court's description of the plaintiff's ultimate burden of persuasion is couched in terms of establishing that the defendant's tendered explanation is a pretext for "the true reason." But actions are often the product of multiple factors. In *Price Waterhouse v. Hopkins*, 490 U.S. 228 (1989), the Supreme Court confected an alternative evidentiary structure for cases involving decisions grounded upon both legitimate and illegitimate considerations. There, a plurality of the Court declared that plaintiffs could establish a prima facie case by proving that sex or any of the other four forbidden classifications was a motivating factor behind the challenged employer action. It added, however, that upon such a showing, the employer could escape liability completely by asserting and proving (by a preponderance of the evidence) a "same decision" affirmative defense, i.e., that it would have reached the same decision in the absence of the proscribed consideration. Justice O'Connor wrote a concurring opinion agreeing with this mixed motive analysis but limiting it to cases where the plaintiff had offered "direct" evidence of discrimination. Consequently, a majority of the Court agreed in principle with the mixed motive framework.

The ruling in *Price Waterhouse* was the subject of significant controversy and ultimately was one of the reasons why Congress passed the Civil Rights Act of 1991. This Act, *inter alia*, amended Title VII by codifying the *Price Waterhouse* ruling concerning the prima facie case. But it also reversed the *Price Waterhouse* Court's treatment of the "same decision" defense by limiting its impact to the issue of remedies. Specifically, new subsection (m) of §703 states that a plaintiff can establish a violation by proving that race, sex, etc., was a motivating factor for the challenged employment practice, even when another factor also motivated that decision. But newly added language to §706(g)(2) provides that where the plaintiff establishes discrimination pursuant to §703(m) and the defense proves that it would have taken the same decision in the absence of that unlawful motivating factor, the court may only grant declaratory and injunctive relief and attorney's fees, and cannot award positive relief such as damages or orders of reinstatement, promotion, and the like. Thus, Congress reversed that portion of *Price Waterhouse* that made the same decision defense an affirmative defense to liability.

After the enactment of the 1991 Civil Rights Act, a question arose as to whether the mixed motive theory of *Price Waterhouse* was limited, as suggested in Justice O'Connor's concurrence, to cases involving "direct" evidence of discrimination. The Court answered this question directly in *Desert Palace, Inc. v. Costa*, 539 U.S. 90 (2003), where it held that in the absence of any statutory reference to a heightened evidentiary standard for mixed motive cases, this analysis was available in cases where the plaintiff's demonstration of discrimination was based on either direct or circumstantial evidence.

Mixed Motive Proof Framework

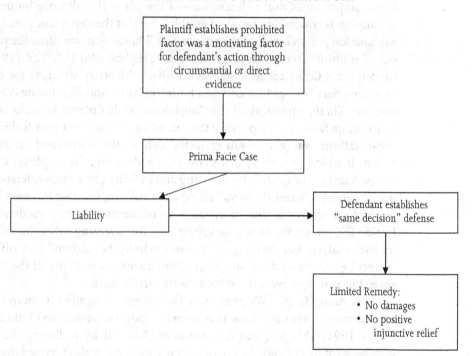

Examples

No Harm, No Foul

1. During his interview for a marketing position with Sterling Cooper, an advertising firm in New York City, Don Draper was asked by Roger Sterling, the firm's senior partner in charge of hiring, whether he would be willing to play on the firm's basketball team in the highly competitive New York Advertising Firm Basketball League. Don, who stood 6'8", told Roger that although he had played in high school and in college, he

no longer was interested in competitive sports and preferred to spend his spare time reading and writing poetry. When Don was not hired, he filed a Title VII action alleging sex-based discrimination. Neither party requested a jury trial. During the bench trial, Don offered a copy of the interview form that Roger had filled out and circulated to the other partners at the firm's hiring meeting. The form included these two comments made by Roger: (1) "Don seems to be a capable guy but almost all of our clients sell products geared to stay-at-home moms, and we really should hire a woman who can better understand and relate to our target audience. So, let's pass on Don"; and (2) "I would not hire Don even if he were a woman. Being a team player is an essential qualification for working at Sterling Cooper, and even though I made it clear to Don that playing on our basketball team was important to the firm, he made it clear that he would not play on that team." Solely on the basis of this evaluation by their senior partner, the committee members voted unanimously not to offer the job to Don. The firm did not assert a §703(e) defense. How should the trial judge decide this case?

2. What if the interview form that Roger had filled out about Don contained only these two statements: (1) "I must admit that I am a bit concerned that this otherwise interesting candidate prefers writing poetry to playing basketball. Because this causes me to wonder what kind of a man he is and, therefore, whether he would be a good fit for our office, we should not hire him"; and (2) "During the interview, Don mentioned that he did not have any pets. We must never hire anyone whose love for animals is not manifested by the presence of a friendly dog or cat in the home." Assume once again that the committee voted unanimously not to hire Don based exclusively on Roger's assessment. If Don's Title VII sex discrimination claim goes to trial, who should win and why?

3. After 20 years of employment as a sales associate with Wunder Bread, Inc., Charles St. Clair applied for a promotion to regional sales manager. The other candidate, Sam Poston, had worked at Wunder for ten years as a sales associate. When Sam, a Caucasian employee, received the promotion, Charles, an African American, filed a Title VII suit alleging that he had been denied the promotion because of his race. At trial, Charles offered proof that there had never been an African American regional sales manager at Wunder and that each of the preceding ten promotions in other departments of the company had been awarded to Caucasian employees. The company offered uncontradicted evidence that Sam got the promotion because he was engaged to the daughter of Marvin Wunder, the owner of the company. At the end of the trial, Sam objected to Charles's request that the trial judge give the jury a mixed motive instruction requiring the defense to prove that it would have promoted Sam in the absence of any consideration of Charles's race in order limit its liability. How should the court rule on Sam's objection?

4. As a consequence of the downturn in the national economy, World's Best Wrestling (WBW), a sports agency that arranged and promoted heavyweight wrestling matches, was forced to eliminate many of its entry level positions. Juan Oliva was one of ten employees who lost their jobs because of this reduction in force. He filed a Title VII action alleging that he had been chosen for termination because of his national origin. During discovery, the attorneys for WBW discovered that Juan had been taking bribes from the managers of a handful of wrestlers to arrange for these managers' clients to be chosen to participate in some of its highest paid and most heavily promoted wrestling matches. At the end of the trial, Oliva objected to WBW's request that the trial court give the jury a mixed motive instruction. How should the court rule on Oliva's objection?

Cats and Rubbers

1. Poussin Butes was employed by Rub Our Stamps, Inc., a rare stamp dealer, for ten years in its sales department. During the first nine years, his supervisor, Polly Anna, gave Butes outstanding annual evaluations. But when Polly retired, she was replaced by Simon DeGree. Unbeknownst to Cheshire ("Paw") Katz, the longtime owner and president of Rub Our Stamps, DeGree harbored violently racist attitudes. Katz was unaware that DeGree had demonstrated his hostility to Butes and several other African American male employees on multiple occasions. As part of his campaign to have Butes terminated, DeGree submitted a totally fabricated and harshly negative annual evaluation of Butes that included a recommendation that Butes be discharged. Katz did not know anything about Butes. In fact, he had never met Butes. But based solely on DeGree's evaluation and recommendation, Katz terminated Butes. Butes filed a Title VII action claiming that he was discharged because of his race. All of the above stated facts were established at trial. Neither party asked for a jury trial. How should the trial judge decide the case?

2. Suppose that DeGree pursued that same course of conduct with respect to Sidney Feline, another African American salesperson. After Katz read DeGree's racially motivated negative job evaluation of Feline, which also recommended Feline's discharge, Katz pulled Feline's personnel file, which included Feline's time sheets. Katz's review of the timesheets revealed that Feline was habitually late in reporting to work and often left the office before the official quitting time. As a result of this information, Katz discharged Feline. Feline then brought a Title VII suit against the company, alleging that his discharge was the product of racial discrimination on the part of DeGree. All of the above stated facts were established at trial. Neither party asked for a jury trial. How should the trial judge decide the case?

Explanations

No Harm, No Foul

1. The court should issue a judgment in favor of Don but limit his remedy to a declaratory judgment, an injunction, and attorney's fees. The firm should not be ordered to hire Don, and he should be denied back pay and any form of compensatory or punitive damages. This is a classic mixed motives case. Pursuant to the language of §703(m), Don has established a prima facie case that his sex was a motivating factor behind the decision not to hire him. He offered direct evidence of this in the form of Roger's statement in the interview form to the effect that the clients preferred the presence of a female in this position. Plus, the facts indicate that the firm relied on this statement in making the decision not to offer Don the job. And although customer preference normally is not accepted as a BFOQ (bona fide occupational qualification) under §703(e), whether or not it could be successfully invoked as an absolute defense to liability in this case is mooted by the fact that the firm did not assert this (waivable) defense. So, under the jurisprudence of *Price Waterhouse* as codified by Congress in 1991 through the addition of §703(m) to Title VII, the plaintiff will win on the issue of liability. However, in accordance with §706(g)(2)(B), the plaintiff's remedy will be limited to certain forms of equitable relief where the defendant persuades the fact-finder by a preponderance of the evidence that it would have reached that same decision in the absence of its unlawful consideration of sex. Remember that such an alternative explanation can be inane, mystical, based on the laws of chance, or any other seemingly irrelevant justification; it simply needs to be nondiscriminatory. Here, the firm's desire to have its new employee play on the basketball team may or may not be relevant to his job performance or other measure of value. But there is nothing that suggests that it is founded upon consideration of his sex, including his failure to conform to a sex stereotype. Thus, it is a nondiscriminatory explanation. Since Roger's statement indicates that this was an independent basis for his recommendation to reject Don's candidacy, and the facts state that the firm's decision was based entirely on Roger's evaluation, the defense has carried its burden of persuasion on this affirmative defense. And since, per §706(g)(2)(B), this "same decision" defense goes only to limit the plaintiff's recovery and not to the issue of liability, the court may grant declaratory relief, attorney's fees, costs, and injunctive relief other than an order requiring hiring. It cannot award compensatory or punitive damages.
2. The result should be the same as in the preceding example. The only difference between these two examples is that Don's evidence of sex discrimination here takes the form of direct evidence indicating that the

adverse recommendation is based on Don's failure to conform to Roger's sex-stereotyped expectations of a successful employee. The firm's reliance on Roger's statement that Don's penchant for poetry causes concern "over what kind of a man" Don is constitutes sufficient evidence of reliance on a sex stereotype to fit within that portion of the Supreme Court's ruling in Price Waterhouse that was left untouched by the 1991 Civil Rights Act. In Price Waterhouse, the Court said that taking adverse action because of the plaintiff's failure to conform to a sex stereotype is a form of sex-based conduct. Accordingly, since Don has established that sex was a motivating factor in his rejection, he has established liability under §703(m). But Roger's seemingly inane concern over Don's failure to have a pet also constitutes a nondiscriminatory reason for the firm's decision, and the facts indicate that Don would have been rejected on that basis even if he had not been a poetry lover. Consequently, the firm has sustained its burden of persuasion on the same decision defense. So, under §706(g)(2)(B), Don's recovery will be limited to declaratory relief, attorney's fees and costs, and an injunction not including an order of instatement. He also will be precluded from recovering damages.

3. The court should overrule Sam's objection and give the jury the mixed motive instruction. The basis for Sam's objection would be that the plaintiff is not entitled to a mixed motive instruction because he offered only circumstantial, and not direct, evidence that race was a motivating factor in the promotion decision. But in Desert Palace, the Supreme Court held that §703(m) does not contain any express reference to a heightened evidentiary standard and that in the absence of such language (which does exist in some other statutes), the default rule that material issues in civil cases can be proven by either direct or circumstantial evidence was applicable. Thus, as long as the plaintiff offers evidence, either direct or circumstantial, from which a jury could believe, by a preponderance of the evidence, that race was a motivating factor for the challenged decision, the plaintiff is entitled to a mixed motive instruction. Charles satisfied that standard by offering circumstantial evidence of (1) the absence of other African American regional sales managers and (2) the pattern of prior promotion decisions throughout the company being awarded solely to Caucasian employees. So, Charles gets his mixed motive instruction.

4. The court should uphold the objection and refuse to give a mixed motive instruction. A mixed motive instruction is only available where the defendant has offered some evidence from which a reasonable jury could believe that the defendant would have reached the same decision, wholly apart from any forbidden consideration of the plaintiff's national origin, sex, etc. Here, the defense has offered evidence of damaging information that it obtained about the plaintiff after he had been

discharged. Such after-acquired evidence is not probative of the employer's motivation for the termination since it concerns information that the company did not have when it discharged the plaintiff. Consequently, this is not a mixed motive case, and giving such an instruction would be improper.

Cats and Rubbers

1. The court should issue a judgment in favor of the plaintiff. The issue here is whether discriminatory intent has to be established on the part of the actual decision-maker or whether it is sufficient to establish that the decision was made on the basis of information provided by an intermediary who was motivated by racial bias. Such cases are referred to as either "cat's paw" or "rubber stamp" cases. The idea is that if an unbiased decision-maker is duped into making a discriminatory decision by a prejudiced subordinate, i.e., the actual decision-maker is the dupe or cat's paw of the biased individual (or the decision-maker is viewed as merely rubber stamping the biased judgment of the subordinate), the bias of the subordinate is imputed to the actual decision-maker, and the employer is held liable. The decision-maker is viewed as the conduit of the subordinate's prejudice, and his personal innocence does not spare the company from liability. In *Staub v. Proctor Hospital*, 131 S. Ct. 1186, 179 L. Ed. 2d 144 (2011), the Supreme Court addressed this scenario in a non–Title VII case but one arising under a statute that the Court stated was "very similar to Title VII." The Court rejected the defense contention that the fact of an independent investigation by the actual decision-maker was sufficient to immunize the employer from liability for the discriminatorily motivated actions of the plaintiff's supervisors. Instead, the Court ruled that as long as the plaintiff could establish that his supervisor acted with discriminatory animus *and* that the supervisor committed that act with the intention of causing the plaintiff's discharge and that the supervisor's action was in fact a cause of the termination (by showing that this information was considered by the actual decision-maker without any determination of whether the adverse action was independently justified), the employer will be liable despite the fact that the actual decision-maker conducted an independent investigation. And this analysis subsequently has been adopted by the lower courts in Title VII cases. Here, the actual decision-maker, Katz, did not even know the plaintiff's race. Nor was there any evidence that Katz based his decision on his own racial prejudice. Rather, he just served as the conduit for the patently discriminatory action of DeGree, the plaintiff's supervisor. The facts strongly indicate that DeGree wrote this negative evaluation for the purpose of causing Katz's discharge and that the actual decision-maker made no attempt to corroborate it. This is a classic example of a cat's paw

case. Consequently, the employer will be held liable, and so the court should enter judgment for the plaintiff.

2. The court should issue judgment in favor of the defense. Here again, the plaintiff has been the victim of racial discrimination by his supervisor. But in this case, the discriminatory actions of the supervisor will not be imputed to the actual decision-maker, and so the company will avoid liability. Whether they use the "cat's paw" or "rubber stamp" terminology, the appellate courts agree that where the actual decision-maker conducted an independent investigation and did not rely perfunctorily on the input from the biased subordinate, the subordinate's discriminatory motive is not imputed to the decision-maker. And since the evidence here demonstrates that the judgment by the decision-maker was the product of an independent investigation that yielded a nondiscriminatory basis for the discharge—habitual lateness and early departure—the court should issue judgment in favor of the defense.

E. AFTER-ACQUIRED EVIDENCE

A separate evidentiary issue is raised when the employer seeks to offer evidence of plaintiff misconduct that would justify the challenged employment practice but that was not uncovered by the employer until after it took the challenged action. These scenarios typically occur when the employer discovers such evidence as part of the discovery process triggered by the plaintiff filing suit. The issue is whether such evidence is admissible (on relevance grounds) and, if so, to which material issue in the case. In *McKennon v. Nashville Banner Publishing Co.*, 513 U.S. 352 (1995), an ADEA case whose holding has been applied uniformly by the courts to Title VII actions, the Supreme Court ruled that since such evidence was not known to the employer at the time of the challenged employment practice, it could not have been a factor in arriving at the challenged decision at the time it was made. Consequently, as it does not help prove the employer's motive, this evidence is inadmissible on the issue of liability and does not render the case eligible for mixed motive analysis. However, the *McKennon* Court also held that in recognition of the statutory interest in preserving a degree of employer prerogative, the equitable concern for assessing the parties' relative moral entitlements, and the practicality that requiring the employer to reinstate or promote someone who could then lawfully be discharged on the basis of the uncovered misconduct would be inequitable and pointless, the evidence was admissible in determining the appropriate remedy. And that is true even if the information would not have been obtained in the absence of litigation. As a general rule in discharge cases, the Court declared, where the defense establishes (burden of persuasion) that the wrongdoing was of a nature that the employer would have terminated the plaintiff on that ground alone, reinstatement and front pay are not appropriate remedies. On the other hand, absent extraordinary circumstances, back pay ordinarily would be available from the time of the discharge to the time of discovery of the after-acquired evidence.

Examples

Better Late Than Never?

1. Wendy Darling was discharged by Pan Flutes, Inc., a music store. She filed an age discrimination claim, alleging that she was terminated because of her age. One day prior to Wendy's discharge, a co-employee overheard a discussion at a management meeting where the company president, Cap Tenhook, said "We need some new blood here. It is time to put Wendy out to pasture and to replace her with a much younger person." When defense counsel took Wendy's deposition, she revealed that she had been stealing small flutes from the store and giving them to needy children in her neighborhood. Pan Flutes has a zero-tolerance policy mandating dismissal for any employee who engages in criminal activity of any kind. All of these facts come to light during the trial. How should the case be decided?

2. Suzanne Sophone, a technician employed for five years by a telephone repair company, was discharged three months after a new employee was hired to be her supervisor. Suzanne was discharged at the urging of this new supervisor, who frequently used racial epithets in Suzanne's presence when no other employees were around to hear his racist rants. Suzanne filed a Title VII action, alleging that she had been discharged because of her race. During the trial, the company's human relations director learned that Suzanne had been parking her car in the customer parking lot even though all employees, including Suzanne, had been informed that, if possible, the company preferred them to park in a separate lot so that nearby spaces would always be available for customers. Assuming the jury finds that Suzanne's discharge was the result of racial bias, and that she frequently parked in the customer parking lot, what remedy should the trial judge order?

3. Barry Star, a paralegal, was discharged by his law firm. In keeping with its longstanding tradition, the firm allowed Star to continue to use a spare office in the building as his base of operations during his search for another job. During that period, Star stole confidential client documents in the hope of bringing these clients to his subsequent employer. The firm's personnel policy provides that unauthorized tampering with confidential client communications is cause for immediate and mandatory

discharge. Star filed suit under Title VII, claiming that he was terminated because of his race. Star objected to the firm's introduction of evidence of Star's pilfering of confidential client documents. How should the court rule on the objection?

Explanations

Better Late Than Never?

1. The plaintiff will win the case but will not be reinstated. But she should receive back pay from the date of her discharge until the day the company discovered that she had been stealing its flutes. This is an obvious instance of the use of after-acquired evidence, i.e., evidence of wrongdoing that would justify the employer's termination decision acquired after the employer made that decision. Under the rule in *McKennon*, the evidence is not relevant to the issue of liability since it does not help prove the employer's motive at the time it decided to terminate Wendy. Thus, since this does not provide the employer with a lawful motive for the discharge, this case cannot be evaluated as a mixed motive case. Rather, the plaintiff's direct evidence of an age-based motive for the discharge establishes the violation of the ADEA. However, under *McKennon*, the after-acquired evidence is admissible for purposes of limiting the remedy made available to the plaintiff if the company can prove that the misconduct (here, stealing) was sufficiently serious to justify, in and of itself, the plaintiff's discharge. This will be easy to prove here since Pan Flutes has a zero-tolerance policy in place that mandates dismissal for anyone who engages in criminal behavior. Thus, in the absence of any extraordinary circumstances that would justify deviating from the default rule, the plaintiff will win the case, but her relief will be limited to back pay from the date of discrimination to the date of discovery of the stealing.

2. Gwen's recovery should not be limited by the fact of this after-acquired evidence. The court should award her the full range of remedies based on the jury's finding of racial discrimination, including reinstatement with full back pay (or front pay if a position is not available). This is a case where the employer has after-acquired evidence of employee misconduct. The evidence does not go to liability and, in this case, should not be used to limit the plaintiff's recovery. Under the ruling by the Supreme Court in *McKennon*, relief should be limited in discharge cases based on the presence of after-acquired evidence of employee misconduct only where the misconduct is of a sufficiently severe degree that the employer would have discharged the employee solely on the basis of this behavior. Here, the employer does not have a rule forbidding employee use of the customer parking lot, nor does it indicate that any

consequences will flow from parking in the customer lot. Rather, it just requests the employees not use the lot when and if it is possible to do so. Thus, the employer cannot sustain its burden of persuading the trier of fact that the employee's actions constitute misconduct of such a degree that would justify, let alone mandate, discharge on that ground alone.

3. The court should grant the objection and rule that the evidence is inadmissible. This situation is different from the standard case of after-acquired evidence in that this evidence, which was acquired after the challenged employment decision, also concerns misconduct that occurred after the challenged employment decision. Most courts refer to this as "after-after acquired evidence." They generally rule that the causal link between the postdecision misconduct and the challenged decision is so attenuated that evidence of such misconduct is not admissible and, therefore, should have no impact on the issues of liability or damages.

F. A QUICK WORD ON AFFIRMATIVE DEFENSES

This chapter has focused on the meaning of discrimination and the roles assigned to the parties in proving and denying individual claims of intentional bias. Where, however, the plaintiff has established the existence of intentional discrimination, the defendant still has the opportunity to avoid liability because of the availability, under all of the major federal antidiscrimination statutes, of one or more affirmative defenses. All affirmative defenses are, by nature, explanations or justifications. They are not denials of the plaintiff's claim (here, of discrimination) but rather explanations or justifications that the law has recognized as a basis for escaping liability. Consequently, since they do not define or shape the meaning of discrimination but rather, where available, provide defendants with an authorized excuse for engaging in otherwise proscribed discrimination, and because their invocation often raises unique issues associated with the differing factual contexts governed by the various antidiscrimination statues, they will be examined separately in the chapters that are devoted to each of the major federal antidiscrimination statutes.

Systemic Claims of Intentional Discrimination

A. INTRODUCTION

Not all claims of intentional discrimination (*aka* disparate treatment) involve challenges to employment decisions that affect an individual employee or a discrete group of workers. Frequently, employers adopt broadly based policies that affect large categories or classes of employees. In addressing the unique issues raised by alleged instances of systemic disparate treatment, the Supreme Court has developed an analytical structure that resembles, but does not replicate, the framework governing individual claims of intentional discrimination. This chapter focuses on the manner in which systemic claims of intentional discrimination are handled.

The essence of a claim of systemic discrimination is that the employer has engaged in a pattern or practice of conduct, such as the implementation of a general policy or collection of policies, that repeatedly, regularly, and purposefully discriminates against members of a protected category in the aggregate. Individual claims of intentional discrimination, by way of comparison, challenge isolated decisions targeted at a single individual or discrete number of individuals because of membership in a protected class.

Claims of systemic intentional discrimination typically are brought either by a group of joined plaintiffs, as class actions, or by the government in what are called "pattern or practice" cases. (Under Title VII, for example, the Equal Employment Opportunity Commission [EEOC] is authorized to bring pattern or practice claims against private sector employers and the attorney general is authorized to bring such claims against public sector employers.) As in cases alleging individual disparate treatment, claims of systemic intentional discrimination can be established through either direct or circumstantial evidence, or a combination of the two. So, for example, sometimes a claim of systemic disparate treatment is based on the facially discriminatory content of a policy or series of policies. In such cases, this direct evidence of the express use of race or sex or some other prohibited factor establishes liability, and the defendant is left only with an applicable affirmative defense such as the existence of a bona fide occupational qualification (BFOQ) or a voluntary affirmative action plan. Thus, in *Dothard v. Rawlinson*, 433 U.S. 321 (1977), as one example, where the State of Alabama explicitly excluded all women from being employed in contact positions in its all-male maximum security institutions, this part of the case turned solely on whether sex was a bona fide occupational qualification for that job.

But more commonly, plaintiffs in systemic discrimination cases rely on circumstantial evidence to establish the employer's general pattern or practice of discriminating against all members of their protected class. In such cases, the same evidentiary structure that we already examined in connection with claims of individual intentional discrimination applies. The plaintiff bears the burden of proving the existence of discrimination by a preponderance of the evidence. To do so, it must establish a prima facie case. The defendant can, of course, offer evidence to deny the existence of a prima facie case. But where the court determines that the plaintiff has established a prima facie claim, the defendant then bears the burden of producing evidence of a nondiscriminatory reason behind its challenged policies. The case then turns on whether the plaintiff can persuade the trier of fact that the employer implemented a discriminatory practice or policy.

The most regularly used (though not the only) form of circumstantial evidence in cases alleging systemic disparate treatment is statistical data demonstrating the "observed" representation of members of the plaintiff group in the employer's workforce that is then compared with statistical data of the level of representation that would be "expected" in the absence of discrimination. The use of statistical evidence presents unique interpretive issues that the Supreme Court has attempted to address in several important cases. Let's turn now to that analysis.

B. USING STATISTICS TO ESTABLISH A PRIMA FACIE CLAIM OF SYSTEMIC DISPARATE TREATMENT: *TEAMSTERS* AND "THE INEXORABLE ZERO"

In most instances, plaintiffs in systemic discrimination cases offer statistical evidence as circumstantial proof of the employer's intent to discriminate against the members of a protected group. In *International Brotherhood of Teamsters v. U.S.*, 431 U.S. 324 (1977), the Supreme Court relied on probability theory to explain how statistical data could be used to establish a prima facie case of systemic disparate treatment. There, the EEOC filed a Title VII suit against a shipping company with terminals located throughout the United States, alleging that the defendant had engaged in a pattern or practice of discriminating against minorities in hiring, promotion, and transfer to a high-paying job category (line driver). The Court explained that since this was a claim of systemic (pattern or practice) discrimination, the plaintiff had to establish that discrimination was the company's standard operating procedure rather than an isolated or sporadic occurrence. And the government sustained its burden of persuasion, the Court declared, by introducing statistical evidence comparing the percentage of minorities employed as line drivers (zero African Americans prior to the commencement of the suit) with the percentage of minority workers in the general population of the locales in which the defendant had its terminals.

Rejecting the defendant's claim that statistical evidence alone could not establish a prima facie case, the Court held that a statistically significant demonstration of a longstanding and gross disparity between the observed racial composition of a defendant's workforce and the racial composition one would expect in the absence of discrimination was probative of a pattern of purposeful discrimination and would generate an inference of intentional discrimination. And, the Court continued, the "expected" racial composition that would emerge from a nondiscriminatory environment can be established through statistical evidence of the percentage of the relevant minority group in the general population of the surrounding communities. The relevance of general population statistics was based on the premise that, over time, nondiscriminatory hiring practices ordinarily will result in a workforce more or less representative of the racial composition of the population from which employees are hired.

But the *Teamsters* Court also noted that the probative value of such statistical evidence could be diminished by considerations such as a small sample size or evidence demonstrating that the general population figures might not accurately reflect the pool of qualified applicants (a point reaffirmed in the Court's subsequent opinion in *Hazelwood*). It also declared that once the plaintiff established a prima facie case through evidence of workplace disparities, the defendant must be given the chance to demonstrate that the discriminatory pattern was a product of pre-Act hiring and not post-Act discrimination.

C. ANOTHER STATISTICAL MODEL FOR CLOSER CASES OF SYSTEMIC DISPARATE TREATMENT: *HAZELWOOD*

The fact that the defendant in *Teamsters* had employed zero African Americans as line drivers in communities with large minority populations made it pretty easy for the court to infer the defendant's discriminatory motivation from the plaintiff's statistical evidence. In *Hazelwood School District v. U.S.*, 433 U.S. 299 (1977), however, the Court was confronted with evidence of a less compelling disparity. Accordingly, it offered a more nuanced approach to statistical proof of discrimination in cases involving substantially less dramatic racial imbalances.

There, the U.S. Attorney General brought a pattern or practice suit under Title VII against a suburban county school district outside St. Louis, Missouri. The district had employed no African American teachers prior to 1969. This number increased slightly over the succeeding years so that although the African American composition of the district's total workforce was only 1.8 percent, 3.7 percent of its most recently hired teachers (between 1972 and 1974) were African Americans. The Court noted that prior to 1972, Title VII did not apply to public employers like the defendant school district. Consequently, it held that the circuit court had erred in disregarding the post-Act hiring statistics by focusing exclusively on the "snapshot" of the entire workforce as the basis for calculating the "observed" racial composition comparator.

Although African Americans constituted only 5.7 percent of the qualified teacher population of the defendant school district, 15.4 percent of all qualified teachers in the city of St. Louis and its surrounding county were African American. Without deciding which of these population measures of the "expected" racial composition of the employer's workforce should be compared to the "observed" composition (this was left for the trial court on remand), the Court stated that whatever population statistic was used as the estimation of the expected presence of minority workers absent discrimination, the courts should employ standard deviation analysis (a method of calculating the likelihood that the difference between the predicted and actual outcome is the product of chance) to measure the significance of the disparity between that and the defendant's workforce racial composition. Under standard deviation analysis, when the actual outcome (here, the racial composition of the employer's recently hired or total workforce) is more than two standard deviations from the expected outcome (here, the racial composition of the relevant population), the disparity between these two variables is deemed to be statistically significant, i.e., there is a 5 percent

Hazelwood-style Statistical Proof of Systemic Intentional Discrimination

chance or less that the disparity is simply the product of chance. Under these circumstances, the underrepresentation cannot be explained as a product of chance or random selection. Thus, in the absence of an alternative explanation, it is proper to allow the trier of fact to infer that the disparity was the consequence of the employer's unlawful motive. Or, to put it another way, such a statistically significant showing establishes a prima facie case.

As part of its order remanding the case to determine the appropriate population group to compare to the employer's workforce, the Court reiterated that it had relied on general population statistics as a comparator in *Teamsters* because the job in question in that case required skills (ability to drive a truck) that were available throughout the general population. But where, as in the instant case, special qualifications were required for the job at issue, it was appropriate to restrict that comparator to qualified members of the population. The Court also advised the trial court on remand, however, that it should determine whether competent proof of applicant flow data, i.e., the actual percentage of African American applicants for teaching positions (as opposed to the percentage of African Americans in the qualified population) was available and, if so, to evaluate whether that was a more appropriate comparator population pool in determining whether or not the plaintiff had established a prima facie claim.

31

D. YET A THIRD MODEL OF STATISTICAL ANALYSIS FOR MULTI-FACTORED DECISIONS: *BAZEMORE*

Both *Teamsters* and *Hazelwood* involved the use of statistics in cases where the issue was whether the employer's policy was racially motivated or not. And the Court in both of these cases relied on what is called binomial distribution analysis. Binomial distribution means that the evaluator focuses on the connection between two factors. In those cases, the Court assessed the relationship between the race of the employer's workforce and some segment of a geographically relevant population. But as we already have seen, some decisions can be the product of a multiplicity of factors. In systemic discrimination cases involving these kinds of decisions, the object is to isolate and measure the effect of each of these various factors, including chance, on the challenged policy or policies. To accomplish this, the Court has sanctioned the use of a different kind of statistical analysis called multiple regression. In *Bazemore v. Friday*, 478 U.S. 385 (1986), a pattern or practice case in which the plaintiff claimed that salaries were based on race, the defense denied this and maintained that its salaries were determined by several other factors—education, tenure, job title, and performance. The Court unanimously endorsed the utilization of regression analysis to sort through these various factors and to determine whether a particular factor (in this case, race) had a statistically significant impact on the company's salary decisions and, therefore, whether the plaintiff had established a prima facie claim of systemic intentional discrimination.

Examples

You Can't Eat Atmosphere

1. Seymour Eatmore recently opened a new restaurant called "TASEE: The Authentic Szechuan Eating Experience." TASEE provides authentic Szechuan cuisine in an environment designed to replicate the Sichuan region of southwestern China. In pursuit of that objective, Eatmore adopted a policy of hiring only individuals of Chinese heritage for each and every job at the restaurant. Chef Boy R. Dee, an American of Italian ancestry, graduated from the Cordon Blue School of Szechuan Cuisine in China and was executive chef at a variety of Szechuan eateries located in the Sichuan region of China for more than 20 years before he decided to return to the United States. His application for the position of executive chef at TASEE was rejected pursuant to the restaurant's Chinese ancestry requirement. He filed a class action Title VII suit against TASEE, alleging

that he and all other persons of non-Chinese ancestry were being discriminated against by TASEE on the basis of their national origin. How should this case be analyzed?

2. After the tremendous success he enjoyed at TASEE, Seymour decided to expand his operations by opening another restaurant in his home town of Dallas, Texas. His concept was to offer an all-meat menu featuring prime cut steaks called the "Cattle Call." Because he believed that the concept would appeal mostly to male customers, Seymour initially adopted a policy of hiring only female servers during the first six months of the Dallas restaurant's operation. At the end of that six-month trial period, that official policy was revoked. Nevertheless, the restaurant's employment records reveal that over the entire five years of its existence, the Cattle Call never employed a male server. Survae Voo, a male of French ancestry, had 15 years of experience as a server at a variety of restaurants in Dallas. At the end of his job interview at the Cattle Call, Voo was informed that he would not be hired. Voo brought a Title VII class action against the Cattle Call, alleging a pattern or practice of sex discrimination in hiring for server positions, and relied completely on the restaurant's employment records to establish his case. TASEE filed a motion for judgment as a matter of law based on the plaintiff's failure to establish a prima facie claim. How should the court rule on this motion?

3. With business booming at the Cattle Call, Seymour decided to enlarge the restaurant by adding an additional dining room. This required him to increase the number of servers from 20 to 25. Although all of the Cattle Call servers were women throughout its first five years of existence, two of the five newly hired members of the expanded wait staff were men. When Survae Voo's application for a server position was rejected, he brought a class action alleging that TASEE engaged in a pattern or practice of national origin discrimination in hiring servers. In support of his case, Voo offered evidence of the company's history of never hiring male servers. During cross-examination of one of Voo's witnesses, the defense established that two of the most recently hired five servers were men. At the end of the presentation of the plaintiff's case, the defense filed a motion for judgment as a matter of law on the ground that the plaintiff had failed to establish a prima facie case. How should the court rule?

Determining the Appropriate Comparator Populations

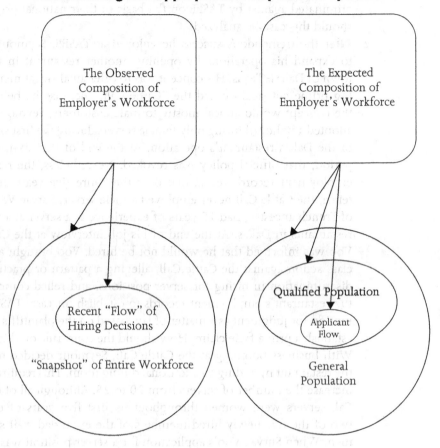

Down the Drain

1. Plumb Right, Inc. (PRI) is a family-owned plumbing installation and repair shop with four locations in the city of Miami, Florida, that employs 100 licensed plumbers. PRI has been in business since 1985. After being rejected for employment with PRI, licensed plumber Walter Tite, an African American male, brought a Title VII class action against PRI, alleging that it was engaged in a pattern or practice of racial discrimination in hiring plumbers. At trial, the plaintiff established that PRI employed six African American plumbers and that African Americans accounted for 48 percent of the adult population of the city of Miami. During its cross-examination of the plaintiff's witnesses, the defense established that according to data reported by the state plumber licensing board, 8 percent of all licensed plumbers in Miami were African American. At the end of the presentation of the plaintiff's case, the defense moved for judgment as a matter of law on the ground that the plaintiff had not established a prima facie case of racial discrimination. How should the court rule on this motion?

2. Let's stick with this same example but add one fact. Although African Americans represented only 8 percent of the total number of licensed plumbers residing in the city of Miami, African Americans comprised 39 percent of licensed plumbers residing in the three surrounding counties. How, if at all, should that affect the court's disposition of the defense motion for judgment as a matter of law?

3. Now suppose the evidence established that although African Americans comprised 39 percent of all the licensed plumbers in greater Miami and the surrounding area, only 5 percent of all applicants for plumbing positions with PRI were African Americans. The defense claims that its low proportion of African American employees is a product of the low number of applications from members of this group and not from any discriminatory intention on its part. How should the court rule on the defense motion for judgment as a matter of law on the ground that the plaintiff had not established a prima facie claim?

Explanations

You Can't Eat Atmosphere

1. The employer here has a facially discriminatory policy based on ancestry/national origin. Accordingly, the plaintiff has clearly established a prima facie claim of systemic intentional discrimination under Title VII without the need for any statistical evidence. Thus, the only remaining issue is whether or not the defendant can establish an affirmative defense. The only conceivably relevant such defense is the bona fide occupational qualification (BFOQ) defense set forth in §703(e) of Title VII. That provision permits an employer to discriminate on the basis of sex, religion, or national origin (but not color or race), when membership in one of these classifications is a BFOQ reasonably necessary to the normal operation of the defendant's particular basis. Although we will discuss the BFOQ defense in more detail a bit later, it is sufficient right now to note that in a case like this, the BFOQ defense would be based on a claim of either customer preference or authenticity. Generally, the courts do not accept customer preference as a BFOQ since catering to such preferences tends to reinforce or perpetuate the kind of bias that the statute was intended to eradicate. And although authenticity has been recognized as a BFOQ, the issue here would be whether individuals occupying any, let alone all, of the jobs at this restaurant must be of Chinese ancestry in order to promote TASEE's image as a restaurant serving authentic Szechuan cuisine in an authentic environment. For example, those jobs that do not involve contact with the customers presumably do not require visual authenticity. If the chef is not seen by the clientele, then, presumably, the relevant job requirement is whether that

chef can cook authentic Szechuan cuisine and not whether her ancestors came from China. On the other hand, the situation with servers, who deal directly with the customers, may be different. A few courts and the EEOC have recognized a BFOQ in situations when it comes to employees in high customer-contact positions.

2. This motion should be denied. In this situation, in contrast to the preceding example, the defendant no longer relies upon a facially discriminatory hiring policy. So the issue becomes whether or not the plaintiff Voo has made a sufficient statistical showing of sex discrimination to establish a prima facie claim of systemic intentional discrimination. As in *Teamsters*, the plaintiff has demonstrated the "inexorable zero" in terms of the number of men on its wait staff. Since the job of server, like that of truck driver in *Teamsters*, is not an occupation that requires a skill set that is found in a limited percentage of the general population, the fact that there are zero men employed in the position of server would be sufficient, without more, to establish a prima facie claim of systemic intentional discrimination. So the defense motion should be denied.

3. This motion should also be denied, but for a different reason. These facts now resemble *Hazelwood* as opposed to *Teamsters* in the sense that the defendant's exclusion of males is not absolute, i.e., this is not a case of the "inexorable zero." *Hazelwood* teaches that the court is to assess the disparity between the gender composition of the actual workforce with that of the labor pool available to the employer, i.e., to compare the observed and expected gender composition of the employer's workforce. With respect to the first comparator, the composition of the employer's workforce, the issue here is whether the appropriate statistic is the "snapshot" statistic of the employer's overall workforce at one specific moment in time irrespective of when they were hired—with 8 percent (2 out of 25) of all servers being men—or the population of most recently hired individuals—of which 40 percent (2 out of 5) were men. In *Hazelwood*, the Court noted that prior to 1972, Title VII did not apply to public employers like the defendant school district. Consequently, it held that the circuit court had erred in disregarding the post-Act hiring statistics by focusing exclusively on the "snapshot" of the entire workforce as the basis for calculating the "observed" racial composition comparator. But in the instant situation, since there was no important change in the law, such as a relevant amendment to Title VII during the period in question, the courts typically will rely on the snapshot statistics and not the "flow" statistics of the employer's most recent hiring experience. Consequently, the remaining question is whether the 8 percent representation of men on the employer's server staff is a gross disparity from the percentage of men that would be expected to be hired as servers in the absence of discrimination. Since the position of server does not require skills that are

possessed by only a limited segment of the general population, the gender composition of the employer's workforce composition will be compared to the gender composition of the general population. Presuming that the latter is close to 50/50, the 8 percent utilization would constitute the type of longstanding and gross disparity required by the Court in *Teamsters* and *Hazelwood*. So the court should deny the defense motion for judgment as a matter of law.

Down the Drain

1. The pivotal issue in this example is whether the "expected" racial composition of the defendant's workforce that is compared to the "observed" racial composition of the employer's workforce should be measured by general population statistics or a subset of that population restricted to qualified members of the general population. The observed racial composition of the employer's workforce is 6 percent African American. When that is compared to the 48 percent of African Americans in the general adult population, the disparity would appear to meet the *Teamsters* and *Hazelwood* requirement of a longstanding and gross racial disparity sufficient to establish a prima facie case of systemic intentional discrimination. But if that 6 percent figure is compared to the 8 percent figure that represents the percentage of qualified (i.e., licensed) African Americans in the general population, the disparity is not only dramatically reduced, it virtually disappears. In *Teamsters*, the Court relied on general population statistics as the measure of the "expected" racial composition comparator. But the Court also acknowledged in that case that figures for the general population might not accurately reflect the pool of qualified job applicants where the jobs in question required skills that were not typically present in members of the general population. And in *Hazelwood*, the Court expressly noted that the use of general population statistics was proper in *Teamsters* because the job skill required was present in, or readily acquirable by, members of the general population. But where a job requires special qualifications, the *Hazelwood* Court added, comparisons to the general population may have little probative value, and the court will need to look instead to that subset of the general population that possesses the relevant job qualifications. In order to obtain a plumbing license, an individual must demonstrate knowledge and skills not present in the general population. Thus, general population statistics are not really probative of the existence of a pattern of discrimination, and the court will compare the observed racial composition of the employer's workforce with the expected composition as reflected in the population of qualified individuals in the relevant geographical area. Here, that translates to a workforce consisting of 6 percent African Americans and a qualified population of 8 percent African Americans.

2. Systemic Claims of Intentional Discrimination

When the court evaluates these numbers according to standard deviation analysis under the binomial distribution tool of statistical theory, it is extremely unlikely that this underrepresentation is sufficiently stark to meet the "longstanding and gross disparity" standard articulated in *Teamsters* and *Hazelwood*. Consequently, the plaintiff has not established a prima facie case of systemic intentional discrimination, and the court should grant the defense motion for judgment as a matter of law.

2. The motion should be denied. The appropriate "qualified" population for measuring an employer's "expected" racial composition is not always determined solely by a job skills–related filter. Sometimes the determination of this qualified pool must take into account the geographical area from which the employer reasonably can be expected to draw employees. Depending upon such factors as the employer's size or the nature of the job in question, including, *inter alia*, its attractiveness, associated benefits, and requisite skill level, an employer might be expected to draw employees from a larger geographical region than its immediate environs. This was an issue that the *Hazelwood* Court declined to resolve, leaving it for determination on remand. And it is the issue presented by this example. Because plumbers are highly skilled and relatively highly paid, it would not be surprising that a court would expect a company, particularly one with multiple locations in a large metropolitan area, to look outside the city confines for such employees. Consequently, the court should use the qualified population of the surrounding counties as the comparator to the observed racial composition of the employer's workforce. When one compares the defendant's 6 percent employment figure for African American plumbers to the 39 percent availability of African American licensed plumbers in the surrounding counties, standard deviation analysis is likely to produce a conclusion that this disparity is not attributable to chance or random selection and that it is sufficiently "gross" and longstanding (the company has been in business for 24 years) to establish a prima facie case. So, the defense motion should be denied.

3. This is the closest call of these three examples. The issue here is whether "applicant flow" data, rather than the entire qualified population pool, is the proper measure of the "expected" composition of the employer's workforce. The use of "applicant flow" data has been approved by many lower courts, particularly when the job in question requires a high skill level and the applicant data is statistically significant in terms of sample size and other related factors. In fact, although the Court in *Hazelwood* did not require the government to use applicant flow statistics to establish its prima facie case, it did note that such data, if available and probative, could rebut the inference of discrimination produced by the prima facie showing. However, the probative value of applicant flow statistics

will be diminished where the plaintiff establishes that qualified members of the plaintiff class were discouraged from applying because of the employer's discriminatory reputation based on its traditional use of employment criteria that excluded members of the plaintiff class. On the other hand, where the employer can establish that it had undertaken specific efforts to recruit applicants from the plaintiff class, this will enhance the probativity of its applicant flow statistics. And where the observed racial composition of the workforce is comparable to the composition of the applicant pool, the courts are prepared to find that the defense has rebutted the inference of discrimination that flowed from the plaintiff's statistical showing of disparity between the observed workforce and the qualified population. Here, African Americans constituted 6 percent of the employer's workforce and only 5 percent of the qualified applicant pool. Assuming the absence of evidence that the defendant's reputation for discriminating chilled applications from individuals who felt it would be futile to apply, the applicant flow data is likely to be viewed as statistically reliable and, if so, the absence of any meaningful disparity would defeat the plaintiff's effort at establishing a prima facie case. So, under these circumstances, the motion will be granted.

E. ANOTHER BRIEF WORD ON AFFIRMATIVE DEFENSES

This chapter has focused on the meaning of discrimination and the roles assigned to the parties in proving and denying systemic claims of intentional bias. Where, however, the plaintiff has established the existence of such systemic discrimination, the defendant still has the opportunity to avoid liability because of the availability, under all of the major federal antidiscrimination statutes, of one or more affirmative defenses. All affirmative defenses are, by nature, explanations or justifications. They are not denials of the plaintiff's claim (here, of discrimination) but rather explanations or justifications that the law has recognized as a basis for escaping liability. Consequently, since they do not define or shape the meaning of discrimination but rather, where available, provide defendants with an authorized excuse for engaging in otherwise proscribed discrimination, and because their invocation often raises unique issues associated with the differing factual contexts governed by the various antidiscrimination statutes, they will be examined separately in the chapters that are devoted to each of the major federal antidiscrimination statutes.

F. AND, FINALLY, THIS . . .

Where the plaintiff has established the existence of systemic intentional discrimination, and the defendant has not successfully established the existence of a recognized affirmative defense, the defendant will be adjudged to be in violation of the governing law. But that is not where the matter ends. It is one thing to establish the existence of a pattern of unlawful discrimination against a particular group. It is quite another to determine which individual members of that group are entitled to relief as a result of that group-based finding. Consequently, as envisioned by the Court in *Teamsters*, systemic discrimination cases are divided into liability and remedial stages. Although the issue of individual relief will be addressed in greater detail in the remedies sections of the chapters devoted to each of the federal antidiscrimination statutes, here is a brief summary of the relevant legal principles.

First, the finding of systemic discrimination (the "liability phase") generates a *rebuttable* presumption that every member of the protected group who actually applied for an employment opportunity and was the victim of an adverse decision during the relevant time frame suffered that adverse result because of his or her membership in that group. In other words, all employment decisions of the type found to be a part of the employer's systemic pattern of discrimination are *rebuttably* presumed to have been the product of an unlawful motive. Consequently, upon a finding of liability, as explained by the Court in *Teamsters*, the trial court typically will convene a separate proceeding to determine the scope of individual relief. At this second stage (the "remedial phase"), the plaintiff (the government in a pattern or practice case) need establish only that the specific individual in question applied for some term or condition of employment that she did not receive. This, according to *Teamsters*, imposes upon the defendant the burden of *persuading* the trier of fact that the adverse decision was the product of a nondiscriminatory reason. Such reasons include the unavailability of the position sought by any particular plaintiff, the plaintiff's lack of qualifications, or the fact that the preferred candidate was more qualified than the plaintiff. Finally, relief may also be obtained by protected class members who never applied for a position during the relevant time period, but only if they can sustain the difficult burden of proving that they were minimally qualified for the position *and* that they would have applied but for their reasonable belief that applying would be futile because of the employer's discriminatory reputation.

Non-Intentional Discrimination: Disparate Impact

A. INTRODUCTION

Although it certainly was the focal point of Title VII as originally enacted in 1964, intentional discrimination is not the only form of unlawful job bias. In *Griggs v. Duke Power Co.*, 401 U.S. 424 (1971), the Supreme Court held that Title VII's ban on employment-related discrimination extended to the utilization of facially neutral criteria that

- produce a disparate exclusionary impact upon a protected group; and
- are not shown to be related to job performance or supported by business necessity
- irrespective of the employer's lack of discriminatory intent.

The *Griggs* Court further noted that its ruling was consistent with §703(h) of Title VII, which expressly permits employers to base decisions on the results of "any professionally developed ability test," but only, as that provision states, where the test or reliance on the test is not "designed, intended or used to discriminate." A facially neutral employment criterion that produces a disparate exclusionary impact and that is not shown to "bear a demonstrable relationship to successful performance of the jobs for which it was used," the Court explained, falls outside the safe harbor of §703(h) because it is being "used" to discriminate.

For many years, the ruling in *Griggs* was criticized as a judicial invention unsupported either textually or by any evidence of congressional intention to proscribe the use of facially neutral policies. But Congress ultimately mooted that controversy when it amended Title VII in 1991 to insert a provision expressly codifying the *Griggs* impact doctrine. Impact-based claims also are cognizable under both the Americans with Disabilities Act (ADA) and the Age Discrimination in Employment Act (ADEA), the former by express statutory provision and the latter by way of the Supreme Court's construction of that statute in *Smith v. City of Jackson*, 544 U.S. 228 (2005). Impact analysis is not applicable, however, to suits brought under either the U.S. Constitution (alleging violations of its equal protection and due process guarantees) or the 1866 Civil Rights Act codified at 42 U.S.C. §1981.

The manner in which the prima facie case is established in an impact-based claim is highly reminiscent of the statistical methodology employed in a circumstantial evidence-based claim of systemic intentional discrimination. In both of these situations, the plaintiff relies on statistical evidence of the effect of an employer's policies on a protected classification. But whereas the statistical impact is used as the basis for inferring discriminatory motive in cases alleging systemic intentional discrimination, the disparate exclusionary effect, in and of itself, establishes the unlawful discrimination in impact cases, subject to the defendant's proof that the impact-generating device is sufficiently job-related to justify its implementation notwithstanding that impact. Nevertheless, while the method of proving the prima facie cases in these two types of claims is comparable, as we will see later, the affirmative defense available in impact cases is quite separate and distinct from the affirmative defense associated with claims of systemic intentional discrimination. Let's start, though, with an examination of the method of proving a prima facie claim of impact-based discrimination.

B. ESTABLISHING A PRIMA FACIE CASE OF IMPACT DISCRIMINATION

In *Griggs*, the Supreme Court held that a plaintiff could establish a prima facie claim of discrimination under Title VII by proving that a facially neutral requirement produced a disparate exclusionary impact upon members of a protected class. In that case, after the enactment of Title VII, the employer required all new job applicants for positions in those departments that previously had been restricted to white employees, regardless of race, to possess a high school diploma and to pass a standardized aptitude test. As a consequence of these new policies, very few African Americans were able either to transfer into or to be hired into these previously all-white departments. The plaintiffs demonstrated that although 34 percent of the white residents of the defendant's home state of North Carolina possessed high school diplomas, only 12 percent of African American North Carolinians had high school degrees. Similarly, only 6 percent of African American test-takers passed the aptitude test, compared to a 58 percent passage rate by white applicants. This racial disparity in the success rate on the employer's facially neutral job qualifications was sufficient, per se, to establish a prima facie violation of Title VII, irrespective of both the company's reason for adopting those eligibility requirements and its lack of direct responsibility for those comparatively lower passage rates.

As a result of the ruling in *Griggs*, a plaintiff could establish a prima facie claim of impact discrimination simply by demonstrating that the employer's facially neutral (applies to all individuals regardless of race, age, disability, sex, etc.) criterion or criteria produced a statistically significant disparate impact on members of a protected classification. And this doctrine has been applied in a myriad of settings, including instances where the employer utilizes a facially neutral criterion whose disparate exclusionary impact is the result of factors outside any human or societal control. For example, in *Dothard v. Rawlinson*, 433 U.S. 321 (1977), the State of Alabama imposed minimum height and weight requirements for law enforcement positions. Since the proportion of women nationwide who could meet this standard was significantly less than the percentage of men nationwide who could satisfy those requirements (the trial court had found that the minimum height requirement operated to exclude 33 percent of adult women while excluding less than 2 percent of adult men and that the minimum weight requirement excluded 22 percent of adult women and 2 percent of adult men), the Court relied on *Griggs* to conclude that the plaintiffs had established a prima facie violation even though, unlike the situation in *Griggs*, these sex-linked height and weight differences could not conceivably be traced to individual or societal discrimination.

Any controversy over whether or not the impact theory introduced in *Griggs* and reaffirmed in *Dothard* was based on a fair and proper construction of either the text of Title VII or of the legislative intent behind its enactment was mooted by the enactment of the 1991 Civil Rights Act. Among the many changes to various federal antidiscrimination statutes contained within this statute was an amendment adding new §703(k)(1)(A)(i) to Title VII. This provision codifies the *Griggs* formulation of the prima facie case by allowing a "complaining party" to demonstrate that a "particular employment practice" causes a "disparate impact" on the basis of any of the five proscribed classifications. And although all of the pre-1991 Supreme Court cases applying impact analysis involved claims of adverse impact brought by members of racial/ethnic minorities or women, the lower courts have relied on the text of §703(k)(1)(A)(i), making impact claims available to any "complaining party" as justification for ruling that impact claims can be asserted by white or male plaintiffs.

The use of statistical evidence to establish disparate impact raises several important and complicated issues. Among them are questions concerning the proper measure of statistical significance that we previously encountered in connection with the plaintiff's reliance, in cases alleging systemic intentional discrimination, on circumstantial evidence in the form of a statistical disparity between the demographic composition of the employer's observed and expected (in the absence of discrimination) workforce. In *Griggs* and *Dothard*, the Court compared the racial impact of the challenged facially neutral criteria on members of the general population (statewide in *Griggs* and nationwide in *Dothard*). In each of these cases, the Court assumed that these large population pools did not differ markedly from the more local pool from which the defendant could be expected to draw its employees. On the other hand, in *New York City Transit Authority v. Beazer*, 440 U.S. 568 (1979), the Supreme Court renounced the lower courts' reliance on general citywide population statistics, insisting that this data was not probative of the alleged racial impact of the employer's blanket policy excluding all former heroin addicts receiving methadone treatment from employment because it did not focus either on the more limited populations of otherwise qualified individuals or actual job applicants.

These cases can be reconciled in much the same manner as was discussed in connection with the use of statistics to establish a prima facie case of systemic intentional discrimination. Where the general population is an accurate mirror of the employer's workforce, as in *Griggs* and *Dothard*, reliance on the impact of a facially neutral requirement on the general population is sufficient to establish a prima facie claim of impact discrimination. But where the general population is not an accurate reflection of the employer's workforce, either because of the nature of the jobs in question or because of the nature of the pool of likely applicants, then, as in *Beazer*, evidence of the impact of the challenged facially neutral practice on the general population will not be sufficient. Another example of the latter scenario occurred in *Espinoza v. Farah Manufacturing Co.*, 414 U.S. 86 (1973), where the employer refused to employ anyone who was not an American citizen. Although this citizenship requirement clearly would disparately exclude American citizens of Mexican ancestry on a nationwide, or even a regional or local basis, the Court found that the plaintiff could not establish a prima facie claim of impact-based national origin discrimination because American citizens of Mexican national origin constituted more than 95 percent of the defendant employer's workforce. Obviously, therefore, the more narrowly tailored the population group used by the plaintiff to establish impact, the more likely the plaintiff will succeed in establishing a prima facie case of impact-based discrimination.

Assuming you have determined the appropriate population upon which the impact of the employer's criterion is measured, how much of an impact is necessary or sufficient to establish a prima facie case? In other words, how disproportionate must the impact be to establish a prima facie case? The Supreme Court never has put its imprimatur on any particular quantum of impact. And Congress did not define the "disparate impact" that is outlawed by §703(k)(1)(A)(i). Nevertheless, some courts look to, as a rule of thumb, the "four-fifths rule" set forth in the Uniform Guidelines on Employee Selection Procedures promulgated by the Equal Employment Opportunity Commission (EEOC). Under this rule, one compares the success rate on the challenged practice of the two comparator groups. If the success rate of the lower scoring group is at least 80 percent as high as the success rate of the other group, the differential impact is not deemed to be sufficiently adverse to establish a prima facie claim of impact-based discrimination. But even those courts that consider the four-fifths rule recognize that its probativity is greatly diminished if the operative sample size is small. For this and other reasons, many courts apply the same statistical tools—standard deviation and multiple regression analysis—to disparate impact cases that they use when evaluating statistical data tendered in systemic disparate treatment cases.

C. APPLYING IMPACT ANALYSIS TO MULTI-FACTORED DECISIONS AND SUBJECTIVE CRITERIA

In cases like *Griggs* or *Dothard*, other than choosing the proper population pool and setting the bar for sufficiently disparate impact, it is a relatively straightforward matter for the plaintiff to establish the success rate of the two comparator populations because the employer in such cases is relying on a discrete set of neutral criteria, and failure to meet any single criterion is an absolute bar to employment. Thus, in such cases, the pass/fail rate of groups in these criteria can easily be quantified, as can the impact of failure on disqualification for employment. The situation is more complex, however, when an employer uses multiple selection criteria and where failure on no single factor is an absolute disqualifier. But the 1991 Civil Rights Act expressly addresses this problem. One of its amendments to Title VII, found at §703(k)(1)(A)(i), states that a complaining party must establish that "a particular employment practice" produced a disparate impact. This means that it will not suffice for the plaintiff to merely point to a disproportionate exclusion of minorities or women on the employer's workforce, i.e., a malproportioned "bottom line." Rather, the plaintiff must establish the impact of a specific employment criterion or practice on members of his or her protected group. However, Congress also created an exception to this rule when it amended Title VII through the enactment of the 1991 Civil Rights Act. Section 703(k)(1)(B) provides an exception to the requirement that the plaintiff point with specificity to the particular employment practice alleged to have caused the disparate impact where the components of the employer's decision-making process are not "capable of separation." In such a case, the plaintiff need only establish the impact of the entire process taken as a whole, i.e., through evidence of an imbalance on the employer's bottom line. The most obvious example of an instance where the employer's selection process is not capable of separation is where the employer relies on a series of factors, no one of which is dispositive or disqualifying, but where performance on every criterion is assessed, and the employer bases the ultimate decision on a holistic evaluation of performance on all of these factors.

Yet while evidence of an unbalanced bottom line can establish unlawful impact where the employer's multi-component selection process is not capable of separation, the converse is not true. The presence of a balanced bottom line will not insulate an employer from an impact-based challenge where the plaintiff can establish that one or more of the defendant's specific selection criteria produced an adverse impact on a protected group. In *Connecticut v. Teal*, 457 U.S. 440 (1982), the employer required candidates for promotion to pass a written examination. The passage rate for black candidates was only 68 percent as high as the passage rate for white candidates. In making promotions from the list of test passers, the employer took other affirmative steps to ensure that that it would promote a significant number of minority workers. Consequently, it emerged from the entire process with a racially balanced bottom line. But the Court held that these bottom line statistics did not preclude those African American employees who were barred from consideration for promotion from establishing a prima facie case based upon the disparate impact of the written examination on their candidacies for promotion.

Impact analysis is not limited to cases like *Griggs, Dothard, Beazer, Espinoza,* and *Teal* that involve the use of objective selection devices. Subjective considerations, such as interviews or letters of recommendation, also are subject to impact theory challenge. For example, in *Watson v. Fort Worth Bank & Trust,* 487 U.S. 977 (1988), the Court unanimously held that a *Griggs*-based Title VII claim could be asserted to challenge promotions based on the subjective assessment of candidates by their supervisors. If *Griggs* were limited to cases involving objective criteria, the Court reasoned, employers would be encouraged to replace objective criteria with subjective criteria that could produce the same kind of arbitrary barriers to employment opportunity that the *Griggs* impact theory was designed to eliminate. And though a portion of the opinion in *Watson* (addressing the nature of the defense response to an impact claim) was reversed by Congress in the 1991 Civil Rights Act, this statute left the Court's ruling concerning the availability of impact challenge to subjective criteria untouched. Moreover, the text of §703(k)(1)(A)(i), which refers to "a" particular employment practice, contains no express limitation to objective criteria, thereby supporting the Court's antecedent ruling in *Watson*.

Examples

The Not-So-Friendly Skies?

1. Going Airlines, Inc., an airplane manufacturer, needed to replace its vice president in charge of development. The person in this position is in charge of the team that designs all of the airplanes that the company will offer to build for its customers. Consequently, one of the non-waivable requirements for this position is possession of a Ph.D. degree in physics. Going insists that the only reason for this requirement is that it is essential to enable the job holder to perform the central function of the position. It also maintains that it would be delighted to hire a qualified minority group member or woman for the position. The attorney for Charley Lindberger, an African American whose application for this position was denied solely because he did not possess a Ph.D. in physics, has discovered that 3 percent of all physics Ph.D. degrees awarded annually in the United States for each of the past 20 years have been received by African Americans. Additionally, 0.01 percent of all adult African Americans in the United States possess a Ph.D. in physics, whereas 1 percent of all adult white American residents possess that academic degree. Is this a sufficient basis upon which Charley's attorney can state and establish a Title VII claim of race-based discrimination against Going?

2. With the advent of fees imposed for checking luggage, Trans-National Airlines (TNA) has discovered that an overwhelming percentage of its passengers now are carrying their bags onto the plane to store them in the overhead compartments. As a consequence of this, flight attendants are increasingly being asked to help passengers lift the bags into the compartments. In response, TNA now requires each applicant for flight attendant positions to demonstrate that they can lift a 75-pound weight over her or his head. Both Steward Tress, a male applicant, and Alice B. Toteless, a female applicant, were denied employment as flight attendants by TNA for failure to pass the weightlifting test. Alice has retained you to represent her in her a Title VII suit against TNA alleging sex discrimination. You have discovered that 70 percent of all men and 30 percent of all women in the U.S. can pass a 75-pound weightlifting test. TNA insists that it has no interest in discriminating against either men

47

or women and substantiates that claim by proving that 50 of the 100 flight attendants hired by TNA since implementation of the weightlifting requirement are women. How should the trial court rule on the defense motion for judgment as a matter of law on the ground that the plaintiff has failed to establish a prima facie case?

3. Steward Tress was denied employment as a flight attendant by TNA for failing the weightlifting standard and wants to bring an impact-based sex discrimination claim against TNA. His attorney has discovered that 70 percent of all men and 30 percent of all women in the United States can pass a 75-pound weightlifting test. How should the trial judge rule on a defense motion to dismiss the complaint for failure to state a claim upon which relief can be granted?

4. Steward Tress was denied employment as a flight attendant by TNA and wants to bring an impact-based sex discrimination claim against TNA. The only evidence that Tress's attorney has unearthed is that TNA's employment records reveal that only two of TNA's 100 flight attendants are men, even though men constitute 50 percent of the population in all locations from which TNA could be expected to draw flight attendants. How should the trial judge rule on a defense motion for judgment as a matter of law on the ground that the plaintiff has failed to establish a prima facie case?

Explanations

The Not-So-Friendly Skies?

1. This is a case well suited to a *Griggs*-styled claim of disparate impact. The employer is utilizing a facially neutral employment criterion (all candidates must meet its physics Ph.D. requirement) that the plaintiff's attorney should allege produces a disparate impact on the basis of race. The combination of the facts that African Americans constitute only 3 percent of the qualified population for this highly skilled position and that the percentage of whites with the degree is 100 times as great as the percentage of African Americans possessing a physics Ph.D. is a sufficient demonstration of the requirement's disparate impact to state and establish a prima facie claim. It will then be up to the defendant to assert and to prove that the criterion is job-related and supported by business necessity. The fact that TNA does not intend to discriminate on the basis of race is an irrelevant response to the plaintiff's impact-based claim since the essence of such a claim, as explained in *Griggs* and its progeny, is that it focuses on the impact of a facially neutral requirement and not the discriminatory intention (or lack thereof) behind its creation or utilization.

2. The motion should be denied. The attorney should assert a *Griggs*-styled disparate impact claim. The defendant employs a facially neutral weight-lifting requirement that can be shown to have a statistically significant disparate impact on female candidates. Since this is a job that does not require unusual skills that are not commonly found in the general population, it is sufficient for the plaintiff to rely on general population statistics to compare the success rate of men versus women with respect to this specific job requirement. Nationwide, 70 percent of men can pass the test as compared to 30 percent of women who can do the same. Under the "four-fifths" standard, the pass rate for women is substantially less than four-fifths of the pass rate for men (four-fifths of 70% would be 56%; the female pass rate of 30% is barely more than two-fifths as high as the male pass rate). This statistical proof of disparate impact is sufficient, *per se*, to establish a prima facie claim of sex discrimination. The fact that the employer does not intend to discriminate against women is not fatal to the plaintiff's claim since evidence of the defendant's lack of discriminatory motive is irrelevant when the plaintiff is asserting an impact-based claim. Nor is the fact that the cause of the impact upon women cannot be linked to prior discriminatory action by this defendant or by anyone else. Any sufficiently disparate impact, whether or not it is caused by factors within human or societal control, generates a prima facie claim under Title VII. Finally, the fact that half of all employees hired after implementation of the weightlifting rule are women demonstrates only that the defendant has a gender-proportional "bottom line." But it does not insulate it from Title VII liability. As the Supreme Court ruled in *Teal*, the absence of a sex-based or racially malproportioned workforce does not preclude the plaintiff from establishing an impact-based claim where the plaintiff can demonstrate that a particular employment practice (here, the weightlifting requirement) disproportionately excludes females from consideration for employment. So, the plaintiff can establish a prima facie case, and the defense motion should be denied.

3. This motion should be granted. Here, the issue is whether or not the plaintiff can state an impact-based claim when he is denied employment pursuant to an employment requirement that generates a disparate impact on the basis of sex but where he is not a member of the sex classification that is disproportionately excluded by that requirement. The short answer to this question is no; he cannot assert a claim under these circumstances. The plaintiff asserting an impact claim must be a member of the disparately excluded group. Consequently, the court should grant the defense motion and dismiss the complaint for failure to state a prima facie case.

4. The motion should be granted. The problem here is, in part, the flip side of an issue raised in Example #2. Here, the only evidence of impact

that the plaintiff is offering is the lack of proportionate representation of males in the employer's workforce, i.e., the "bottom line" statistic. The 1991 Civil Rights Act expressly addressed this problem when it amended Title VII by adding §703(k)(1)(A)(i), which states that a complaining party must establish that "a particular employment practice" produced a disparate impact. Accordingly, it is not sufficient for the plaintiff to merely point to a disproportionate exclusion of members of his sex classification on the employer's workforce, i.e., a malproportioned "bottom line." Rather, the plaintiff must establish the impact of a specific employment criterion or practice on members of his protected group. Here, the plaintiff has not pointed to any specific employment practice that produced a sex-based disparate impact. And though §703(k)(1)(B) provides an exception to this evidentiary requirement where an employer uses a multi-factor selection process and the components of the employer's decision-making process are not "capable of separation," Steward has not made such an allegation or showing here. So, the defense should be granted judgment as a matter of law dismissing the complaint for failure to establish a prima facie case.

Examples

Way Down Yonder . . .

1. Scripts R Us, a local New Orleans chain of pharmacies, is constantly hiring pharmacists to staff its stores. Scripts requires all of its pharmacists to be residents of the city of New Orleans and to have obtained a B.S. degree in pharmacy from an accredited college program. The single largest undergraduate program offering a bachelor's degree in pharmacy is located in New Orleans at a traditionally African American educational institution. As a consequence, 5 percent of the African American residents of New Orleans possess this degree, while only 2 percent of the white residents of New Orleans possess this academic degree. It is also true, however, that less than one-tenth of 1 percent of the adult African American population of the United States possesses this degree. Diz Penser, an African American who had just moved from his native city of Memphis to New Orleans, heard that Scripts was looking for pharmacists and applied for the job. Diz was rejected because he did not have the required bachelor's degree. He filed a Title VII race discrimination claim, alleging that the degree requirement created a disparate impact on the basis of race. How should the trial court rule on the defense motion for judgment as a matter of law on the ground that the plaintiff has not established a prima facie claim?

2. Blew By You (BBY), a blown glass manufacturer located in New Orleans, employs more than 100 individuals in its factory and retail outlet. Its

unique service is that it allows customers to create their own glassware after some rudimentary glass blowing training. When a supervisory position became available in the company's marketing department, Linda Wrongstad, a BBY employee with 20 years of seniority, applied for the job. BBY's corporate policy required all otherwise qualified applicants for supervisory positions to undergo a job interview conducted by a committee of three BBY supervisors. Wrongstad was denied the promotion on the ground that she received an unfavorable review from the interview committee. All of BBY's supervisors are male, and no female applicant for a supervisory position has ever received a favorable review from an interview committee. Sixty percent of all male applicants for supervisory positions passed the interview criterion. How should the trial court rule on the defense motion to dismiss Wrongstad's Title VII claim of sex-based disparate impact for failure to state a claim upon which relief can be granted?

3. Crescent City Marine (CCM) is a New Orleans company that employs longshore workers whose job requires them to load and unload cargo from ships after they arrive in the New Orleans port. Because this job also requires these workers to move cargo from place to place on forklifts and other trucks, no one is employed by CCM as a longshoreman unless he or she possesses a truck driver's license. Only those applicants for longshore positions who possess a truck driver's license are then subjected to the final two stages of the selection procedure. These candidates are required to undergo a personal interview and to submit letters of recommendation in support of their candidacy. A group of CCM executives conduct all interviews and assess all letters of recommendation. They give each candidate a score on the interview and on the content of the letters of recommendation. The individuals with the highest combined scores are placed in a priority list. When jobs became vacant, they are awarded to applicants on the basis of their place on the priority list. Steph O. Dorr applied for a longshore job with CCM, but her application was rejected because she did not possess a truck driver's license. Four percent of adult females in Louisiana and New Orleans possess a truck driver's license, while 20 percent of adult males in Louisiana and New Orleans have such a license. (These percentages mirror the national population figures.) CCM maintains that its commitment to equal opportunity is well demonstrated by the fact that 49 of its 100 longshore workers are women. What will Steph have to prove in order to establish a prima facie case of impact-based sex discrimination under Title VII?

4. Let's change the facts from the preceding example just a bit. Suppose, instead, that CCM merely preferred applicants to have a regular driver's license and that it interviewed all job applicants and required all applicants to submit letters of recommendation. Further assume that it accorded a

score to each of these three criteria (possession of license, job interview, and letters of recommendation) and then used the combined score as the sole basis for placing applicants on a priority list, according to whose rank it hired all longshore workers. Finally, according to CCM's employment records, 6 percent of its 100 longshore workers are female. How should the court rule on the defense motion for judgment as a matter of law as to Steph's Title VII impact-based claim of sex discrimination on the ground that the plaintiff failed to establish a prima facie case?

Explanations

Way Down Yonder . . .

1. The court should grant the motion. The question here is whether or not the plaintiff has established that the degree requirement produces a disparate impact on the basis of race. And this, in turn, raises the issue of whether the impact should be assessed by looking to its effect on a nationwide or local population. Because this is a local concern that is committed to hiring only local residents, it is likely that the court will focus on the impact of the degree requirement on the local population from which the company is most likely to draw applicants and employees. As it turns out, the local population does not mirror the nationwide population in the relevant regard of the percentage of individuals who possess the required degree. Consequently, the fact that the degree requirement does produce a disparate impact on African Americans if you look at nationwide population statistics will not be determinative. Rather, the court will look to the impact on the local population from which this employer is likely to draw its applicants and employees. And in this population, the percentage of African Americans who can satisfy this requirement is actually greater than the number of whites in the local area who possess this degree. As a result, the plaintiff will be unable to establish the requisite disparate impact, and the court should grant the defense motion for judgment as a matter of law.

2. The defense motion should be denied. The issue in this example is whether a disparate impact claim can be based on the impact of a purely subjective criterion such as success on a job interview. In *Watson v. Fort Worth Bank*, the Supreme Court ruled unanimously that disparate impact claims can be based on the effect of a subjective, as well as an objective, criterion. And although the 1991 Civil Rights Act amendments to Title VII reversed a portion of the Court's ruling in *Watson*, the amendments did not address that part of *Watson* that expanded the application of impact analysis to the use of subjective criteria. Moreover, the text of §703(k)(1)(A)(i), which refers to "a" particular employment practice, contains no express limitation to objective criteria, thereby supporting the

Court's antecedent ruling in *Watson*. So, the plaintiff can state an impact-based claim challenging the use of a subjective employment criterion such as a job interview. And the facts of this example suggest that the plaintiff will be able to prove the existence of that disparate impact since the success rate of female applicants on the job interview was zero, compared to a 60 percent success rate on this criterion experienced by male candidates.

3. Steph can establish an impact claim despite the fact that the employer uses a couple of subjective hiring criteria and notwithstanding that the employer's "bottom line" is sex-balanced since almost half of its long-shore workers are females. First, as the Supreme Court noted in *Watson*, a ruling that was left unchanged by the passage of the 1991 Civil Rights Act amendments to Title VII, *Griggs*-styled impact theory is applicable to subjective as well as objective employment criteria. So, the fact that the employer uses job interviews and evaluates the content of letters of recommendation is not a bar to a disparate impact claim. Second, as the Supreme Court held in *Teal*, the fact that an employer's workforce is racially or sexually balanced does not insulate it from liability under a disparate impact challenge to its employment policies where the plaintiff can point to a specific employment criterion that produces an adverse impact on the group of which the plaintiff is a member. Here, the truck driver's license requirement can be met by only 4 percent of women but by 20 percent of men. This means that the success rate for women as to this requirement is only 20 percent as high as the success rate for men. And because this is a job that does not require special skills possessed by a small portion of the population, it is appropriate to look to the passage rate of females in the general population. Moreover, as that passage rate is the same for the local, state, and national populations, there is no issue here of which population area to utilize as the statistical base for measuring impact. This differential is sufficient, *per se*, to establish a prima facie case of impact discrimination. Finally, the court will not look to the bottom line here because, although the employer uses a multi-factor selection process, the impact of at least one of the individual components of that process—the license requirement—can be quantitatively assessed, since failing this standard automatically eliminates a candidate from further consideration. Consequently, this is not one of those cases that fits within the exception of §703(k)(1)(B) that permits reliance on bottom line statistics when the employer uses a multi-factor selection process whose components are not capable of separation. Thus, the plaintiff can establish a prima facie claim by focusing on the evidence of the disparate impact on women of the truck driver's license requirement.

4. Under these changed facts, the court should deny the defense motion to dismiss the case for failure to state a claim. Here, the employer relies on a combination of scores assigned to each of its three (two subjective)

criteria. It bases its employment decisions on the combined score received by each candidate. Consequently, it is impossible to determine the impact of any one of these criteria on job applicants. This, in turn, means that the elements of the employer's multi-factor selection process are not capable of separation, i.e., their individual impact on a candidate's success or failure cannot be measured. Thus, per §703(k)(1)(B) of Title VII, a provision added by the 1991 Civil Rights Act, the plaintiff can point, and the court can look, to the employer's bottom line to determine whether the entire selection process, viewed as one entity, generated a disparate impact upon women. Since only 6 percent of its longshore workers are women, and women constitute approximately half of any general population, the plaintiff has established a prima facie case of disparate impact, and so the defense motion should be denied.

D. DEFENDING IMPACT CLAIMS: AN INTRODUCTION

When the plaintiff asserts a disparate impact-based claim of discrimination, the defendant can attempt to deny the existence of a prima facie case by either challenging the plaintiff's statistical evidence or by offering its own data to demonstrate the absence of a statistically significant disparate impact. But even failing this, the plaintiff's establishment of a prima facie case does not mean that the plaintiff always will win the case. The Supreme Court has recognized the existence of an affirmative defense to impact claims under all of the federal antidiscrimination statutes. Yet, although the method of proving a prima facie case of disparate impact is the same under all of these statutes, the nature of the affirmative defense varies from statute to statute. So, this chapter focuses on the most commonly employed affirmative defense—job-relatedness and business necessity—as applied in Title VII cases. The way in which this and other affirmative defenses are asserted under the other federal antidiscrimination statutes will be examined in the chapters dealing with each of those separate statutes.

I. An Affirmative Defense to Title VII Impact Claims: Job-Relatedness and Business Necessity

Beginning with *Griggs* and continuing in cases including *Albemarle Paper Co. v. Moody*, 422 U.S. 405 (1975), the Supreme Court recognized an affirmative defense to impact claims brought under Title VII. As the Court declared

3. Non-Intentional Discrimination: Disparate Impact

in *Griggs*, "the touchstone is business necessity. If an employment practice which operates to exclude [African Americans] cannot be shown to be related to job performance, the prohibited is prohibited." In *Albemarle*, the Court read *Griggs* to impose upon the defendant the burden of persuasion as to this issue. It also expanded upon the nature of evidence that would be required to satisfy this defense. The Court adopted the language of EEOC guidelines that required the defendant to "validate" any scored test that produced a disparate impact.

These guidelines require the defendant to establish, by professionally acceptable methods, that the selection test is "predictive of or significantly correlated with" important components of the job for which that test is being used as an evaluative device. And the guidelines recognize three alternative methods of validation: content validation, criterion validation, and construct validation. A content validity study is appropriate when the employer relies upon a selection device that purports to measure skills or abilities deemed necessary for successful job performance. Such a selection device will be content validated if its proponent demonstrates that it accurately measures that skill and also that such skill is actually essential to perform the job for which the test is used. Criterion validity, on the other hand, is used in connection with a selection device that does not focus directly on any particular job performance-predictive skill, ability, or trait. Criterion validation is shown through empirical data demonstrating that success on the test is positively correlated to successful job performance. Finally, construct validity analysis is used where a test is designed to measure or identify the existence of abstract qualities such as psychological, personality, or character traits. This form of validation study assesses whether or not the selection device accurately measures "construct" (personality, character, psychological) traits that are shown to be positively correlated with those work behaviors that are required for successful job performance.

The ruling in *Albemarle* went beyond describing the nature of the defense that could justify the use of an impact-creating facially neutral selection device. The Court also announced that even where the defendant sustained its burden of proving this job-relatedness/business necessity defense, the plaintiff still could prevail if it established that a less discriminatory (in terms of impact) alternative selection device would also serve the employer's legitimate interest in selecting competent workers.

For more than two decades after the release of the opinions in *Griggs* and *Albemarle*, the courts consistently held that job-relatedness/business necessity was an affirmative defense as to which the defendant bore the burden of persuasion. But in a pair of cases, *Watson v. Fort Worth Bank & Trust*, 487 U.S. 977 (1988), and *Wards Cove Packing Co., Inc. v. Atonio*, 490 U.S. 642 (1989), the Court (by plurality decision in *Watson* and majority opinion in *Wards Cove*) dramatically altered this jurisprudence by ruling that the defendant's burden was only that of *coming forward* with evidence that the challenged practice served, in a significant way, its *legitimate* employment goals. Moreover, the Court in both of these cases also constricted the availability of the plaintiff's "less discriminatory alternative" rebuttal by demanding that the plaintiff establish that the alternative practice was "equally effective" in meeting the employer's needs as the challenged device and declaring that the cost of, or other burdens associated with, the alternative device were relevant to this "equally effective" calculation.

Congress responded directly to, *inter alia*, these two opinions by enacting the 1991 Civil Rights Act, a statute that amended various provisions of several federal antidiscrimination statutes. These amendments were designed to return the law to its pre-*Watson* and pre-*Wards Cove* content. Specifically, §703(k)(1)(A)(i) expressly imposes upon defendants the burden of persuading the trier of fact as to the justification for using an impact-creating device. (The text requires the defendant to "demonstrate" job-relatedness and business necessity, and §701(m) defines "demonstrate" as encompassing both the burdens of production and persuasion.) As to the nature of that justification, the statute mirrors the Court's ruling in *Griggs* to the extent that it refers to *both* job-relatedness *and* business necessity. Section 703(k)(1)(A)(i) requires the defendant to demonstrate that the challenged practice "is job related for the position in question and consistent with business necessity." Thus, the text of this provision indicates that the defendant must establish both prongs of the defense in order to avoid liability. Moreover, Congress also took the unusual step of limiting the sources that could be relied upon by the courts to provide content to the meaning of "job-relatedness" and "business necessity." Section 105(b) of the 1991 Act directs the courts to consider nothing other than a specific interpretative memorandum in giving meaning to those terms. And that memorandum, in turn, tersely declares that this pair of terms is "intended to reflect the concepts enunciated by the Supreme Court in *Griggs* and in the other Supreme Court decisions prior to *Wards Cove*."

With respect to the "less discriminatory alternative" phase of this tripartite analysis, §703(k)(1)(A)(ii) provides that the plaintiff can prevail if it establishes that a less discriminatory alternative practice existed and the defendant "refuses" to adopt it. And the type of evidence necessary to establish the existence of a less discriminatory alternative practice is to be governed by "the law" that existed the day before the ruling in *Wards Cove*. Although most courts have reasoned that Congress intended to reinstate the *Albemarle* formulation of the rebuttal, this issue is a bit muddled by the fact that the plurality opinion in *Watson* employed the same "equal effectiveness" standard that was adopted nearly one full year later by a majority in *Wards Cove*. And so, the *Watson* standard could remain in effect if the content of its plurality opinion is deemed to constitute "the law" extant on the day before the ruling in *Wards Cove*.

Proving and Defending Disparate Impact Claims

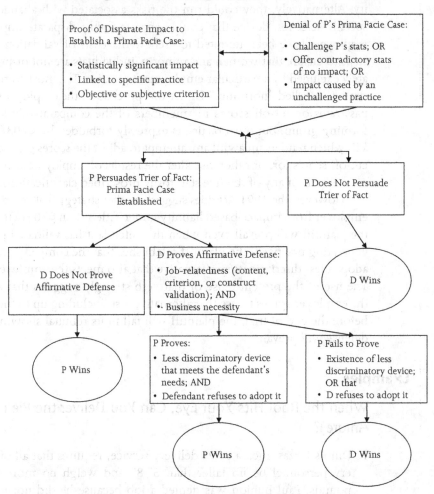

2. An Employer's Alternative to Validation: "Norming" or Other Attempts to Avoid the Existence of Disparate Impact

The Supreme Court's ruling in *Albemarle* and its progeny, together with the codification of this doctrine in the 1991 Civil Rights Act, placed many employers in what they saw as an impossible situation. On the one hand, if they choose to select employees based on some facially neutral criteria, they run the risk that these devices will produce a disparate impact upon a protected classification, and where this happens, they will have to absorb the time and expense of validating their devices in order to avoid Title VII liability. Alternatively, they could run the risks associated with abandoning any specific selection device that could generate such a disparate impact. Some employers have been tempted to eschew the costs of validation by taking steps to ensure that women and minority individuals are not disproportionately excluded by a particular employment practice. The most common such strategy is called "norming." Under this procedure, the employer sets lower pass rates or cut-off scores for members of the comparatively lower performing group. But this practice is expressly forbidden by §703(l) of Title VII, which renders unlawful any attempt to adjust the scores of, use different cut-off scores for, or otherwise alter the results of employment-related tests on the basis of any of the five statutorily proscribed classifications.

However, the 1991 Act does suggest another strategy that could shield the employer from impact-based liability under Title VII. In §703(k)(1)(A)(ii), the plaintiff will prevail even when the defendant has validated its impact-generating practice if the plaintiff establishes that the company "refuses" to adopt a less discriminatory alternative that also meets the employer's needs. The use of the present tense of that verb strongly suggests that as long as the employer agrees to use that alternative test, including up to the moment before the end of trial, the plaintiff will fail in its rebuttal showing and the defense will prevail.

Examples

When the Roof Hits Your Eye, Can You Deliver the Pie (That's Amore)?

1. Dino's Pizzas, Inc., a pizza delivery service, requires that all of its delivery personnel be no taller than 5' 8" and weigh no more than 200 pounds. Paul Bunion was denied a job because he did not meet these requirements. So, he brought a Title VII action against Dino's alleging sex-based discrimination. The plaintiff has uncontroverted evidence that the percentage of men who meet this set of requirements is significantly lower than the percentage of women (in any relevant population) that satisfy this standard. The employer has offered discovery evidence that (1) all of its delivery personnel are required to make deliveries by driving company-owned cars to the destination address; (2) it purchased a fleet of sub-compact cars for all deliveries because of their comparatively low purchase price, reduced anticipated maintenance expense, and more environmentally friendly operation; and (3) drivers taller than 5' 8" cannot comfortably fit in the driver's seat, and drivers weighing more than 200 pounds will add significantly to the cost of operating and maintaining these cars. The plaintiff has tendered discovery evidence

that all of these cars have 6' 2" of headroom and come with heavy duty suspension that would permit individuals taller than 5' 8" and weighing more than 200 pounds to comfortably and efficiently drive these cars. How should the trial court rule on the defense pretrial motion for summary judgment?

2. Dino's Authentic Ristorante, a chain of Italian restaurants, specializes in "traditional Italian-style hand-tossed pizzas." All of the chefs in all of its restaurants are required to be able to prepare all the dishes on the menu, including the pizzas. Accordingly, Dino's requires that all chef applicants demonstrate that they are able to lift a 30-pound weight above their shoulders and hold the weight in the air for ten seconds. Jeannie Martin was denied employment as a chef because she was unable to satisfy this weightlifting requirement. She brought an action against Dino's under Title VII alleging sex-based discrimination. At trial, the plaintiff offered uncontroverted evidence that the percentage of women (in all relevant populations) that could meet this requirement was substantially lower than the percentage of men who could satisfy this standard. The defense offered evidence that (1) its chefs are called upon to prepare up to 100 pizzas per night; (2) the dough for each of these pizzas has to be thrown into the air three times by each chef; and (3) the weightlifting requirement is necessary to determine whether the chef applicant will have the arm strength needed to meet the challenge of throwing as many as 100 pizza doughs into the air three times each. The plaintiff offered no evidence to contradict this testimony. But the plaintiff did offer evidence that many restaurants used an automated device that stretches pizza dough in a manner that renders the dough indistinguishable in every respect from dough that has been hand-tossed in the air. And though the user of this device must have a high level of manual dexterity, the plaintiff contends that the employer could require applicants to pass one of several available manual dexterity tests that would not generate a disparate impact on women as a class. Who should win the case?

3. Tin Men, Inc., a manufacturing concern that produces tin products, including pie shells, requires all of the workers in its factory to wear air filtration masks to shield them from the quasi-toxic fumes that are produced during its production processes. It also requires all such employees to have no facial hair of any kind so that the masks will make a tight seal on their faces and adequately protect them from the fumes. Frank Elbaum, an African American male with years of experience working in tin manufacturing plants, was denied employment by Tin Men because he did not comply with its no facial hair requirement. He brought a Title VII claim against Tin Men, alleging that he had been discriminated against on the basis of his race. At trial, Elbaum offered uncontradicted evidence that African Americans are disproportionately excluded from

employment eligibility because African Americans disproportionately are afflicted, as is he, with a bacterial disorder called pseudofolliculitis barbae (PFB) that causes men's faces to become infected when they shave. Tin Men offered evidence that its production processes release quasi-toxic fumes into the air and that it was essential to job safety for the men to wear air filtration masks and that its masks will not make a tight and effective seal if the wearer has facial hair. Toward the end of the trial, Elbaum introduced testimony from Whizzer Dovoz, an engineer, who reported that he recently had invented a new kind of air filtration mask that could be worn safely and effectively by individuals with facial hair. Three weeks later, on the day before closing arguments were completed, Cowerd Lee Lion, the defense attorney, announced to the court that Tin Men had replaced its filtration masks with the one mentioned by Whizzer Dovoz and would no longer implement its no facial hair policy. How should the court rule on the defendant's motion for judgment as a matter of law?

4. Dino's Authentic Ristorante, a chain of Italian restaurants, specializes in "traditional Italian-style hand-tossed pizzas." All of the chefs in all of its restaurants are required to be able to prepare all the dishes on the menu, including the pizzas. Accordingly, Dino's requires that all chef applicants demonstrate how many of these pizza doughs they can throw into the air and catch in 30 seconds. But Dino's management is keenly aware that women constitute a majority of their clientele, and they do not want to do anything to offend this important client base. So, to ensure that its customers can see that a significant number of Dino's chefs, who are visible to the customers behind glass windows, are women, female chef applicants are only required to toss five pizza doughs into the air to pass the test, while male applicants are required to toss 15 doughs into the air to pass that same test. Jerry Lou Esch was denied employment as a chef by Dino's because he did not pass the pizza-tossing test. He brought a Title VII claim against Dino's, alleging that he had been the victim of sex discrimination. How should the court rule on the case?

Explanations

When the Roof Hits Your Eye, Can You Deliver the Pie (That's Amore)?

1. The court should deny the defense motion for summary judgment because the plaintiff has created, at a minimum, a genuine issue of fact as to whether the job requirements are justified under the statutory job-relatedness and business necessity defense, an issue as to which the defense bears the burden of persuasion. The plaintiff clearly has established a

prima facie claim of disparate impact. Pursuant to §703(k)(1)(A)(i) of Title VII, the defendant bears the burden of persuading the trier of fact (which will be the judge in this case because Title VII only provides for the right to jury trial with respect to claims of intentional discrimination) that the impact-creating standard (here, maximum height and weight) is both job-related and consistent with business necessity. The defendant has certainly come forward with evidence of job-relatedness and business necessity, but the plaintiff has offered evidence challenging the existence of job-relatedness and business necessity. If this case were to go to trial, the judge would have to determine whether or not the defendant's evidence is convincing under the preponderance of evidence standard. But since the question here asked whether or not the defense could obtain summary judgment on a pretrial motion, the court would only grant the motion if it could determine, before either party actually offered evidence at trial, that the defendant had established both parts of this affirmative defense as a matter of law. There clearly is a genuine issue of fact as to parts of the affirmative defense at this stage of the proceedings, and so the motion for summary judgment will be denied.

2. The defense should win because it has established job-relatedness and business necessity and the plaintiff has not rebutted this defense by proving that a less discriminatory alternative method of preparing dough exists that would meet the defendant's needs and that the defendant refuses to adopt that less discriminatory method. The plaintiff's uncontradicted evidence has established a prima facie case of sex-based disparate impact caused by this facially neutral weightlifting requirement. And the defense has offered uncontradicted evidence that the requirement is both job-related and consistent with the necessities of its business. Ordinarily, this would mean that the defendant would win. But §703(k)(1)(A)(ii) of Title VII provides that the plaintiff can prevail if it establishes that a less discriminatory alternative practice existed that meets the employer's legitimate business needs and that the defendant "refuses" to adopt it. Here, the plaintiff has offered evidence of a less discriminatory practice—a manual dexterity test—that, it maintains, would both fulfill the defendant's objectives and avoid the disparate impact of the weightlifting test. The question, then, is whether the less discriminatory alternative would meet the defendant's needs. The 1991 amendments to Title VII instruct the court to apply the definition of this standard as it existed prior to the ruling in *Wards Cove* that had required the plaintiff to show that the alternative was "equally effective" as the challenged selection criterion. So, the issue here would be whether the dexterity test meets the employer's needs, even if not as perfectly as the weightlifting requirement. The relatively easy answer to this is no. Even if dexterity is an accurate measure of ability to use the dough-stretching

machine, the use of a machine to stretch the dough changes the nature of the plaintiff's product from its publicized "hand-tossed" quality. Thus, the court would not conclude that this less discriminatory test meets the employer's needs. Consequently, it is unnecessary also to determine whether or not the employer refuses to adopt that test. The defendant should win the case.

3. The court should grant the defense motion for judgment as a matter of law. The plaintiff has established a prima facie case of disparate impact caused by this facially (in terms of race) neutral requirement. But the defense also has established that its no facial hair policy is job-related and consistent with business necessity. The issue here is whether the plaintiff can rebut that defense by proving the existence of a less discriminatory alternative that meets the employer's needs and that the employer "refuses" to adopt, as set forth in §703(k)(1)(A)(ii) of Title VII. Although there is little case law on this latter issue, the fact that the statute uses the present tense of the verb "refuses" strongly suggests that the plaintiff must establish that the defendant previously refused and continues, to the present moment, to refuse to adopt the proposed less discriminatory alternative. Here, the defendant, albeit at the last moment but, nevertheless, before the end of the trial, has agreed to adopt the less discriminatory alternative. Thus, the court should rule that the plaintiff has failed to prove that the defendant "refuses" to adopt the less discriminatory alternative and, therefore, the defense motion for judgment as a matter of law should be granted.

4. The court will rule in favor of the plaintiff. The employer's use of a sex-differentiated passage rate on an otherwise facially neutral test in order to avoid that test's potentially disparate impact on a protected class is a form of "norming" that is expressly prohibited by Title VII. Under §703(l), it is an unlawful employment practice for an employer to use different cut-off scores for an employment-related test on the basis of sex. So, the plaintiff will win this one.

E. THAT'S NOT ALL, FOLKS . . .

Disparate impact claims can be asserted under Title VII, the ADEA, and the ADA. They are not available, however, when the plaintiff is bringing a constitutional challenge to an employer's decision or when suit is filed under §1981. But where impact analysis is available, the method by which a plaintiff establishes a prima facie case does not vary depending upon the statutory basis for the claim. But that is not also true when it comes to the various affirmative defenses (such as bona fide seniority systems, merit-based plans, or various employee benefit plans) available under these different statutes. Consequently, we examine in more detail the unique aspects of defensive pleading in impact claims associated with each of these statutes in the separate chapters specifically devoted to issues arising under each separate statute. The first such statute will be Title VII, to which we now direct our attention.

PART II

Title VII of the
1964 Civil Rights Act

A General Overview: Proper Plaintiffs, Suable Defendants, Covered Practices, Exceptions, and Exemptions

A. INTRODUCTION

In 1964, Congress passed an omnibus Civil Rights Act that outlawed discrimination on the basis of a collection of classifications in several different sectors of American society. The statute is divided into Titles, each of which deals with a particular target of discrimination. Title VII addresses discrimination in employment and is, by far, the most highly litigated of all the federal antidiscrimination statutes. It is a lengthy and complex enactment that initially was drafted in very broad terms and has been amended many times over the succeeding decades in response to both jurisprudential developments and other events. In this chapter, we examine the myriad of interpretative issues that have arisen in connection with the basic coverage provisions of Title VII.

Most broadly stated, Title VII prohibits public and private sector employers, labor unions, and employment agencies from discriminating on the basis of race, color, religion, national origin, and sex with respect to all terms and conditions of employment. Its most significant substantive terms are found at §§701-704. Section 701 contains the statute's various definitions provisions, several of which are the result of amendments enacted by Congress in response to interpretations of extant text by the Supreme Court. Nearly all of the exemptions from coverage, including exceptions to the categories of covered entities, as well as to the proscribed classifications of discrimination and the types of covered employment-related decisions, are catalogued in §702. The general antidiscrimination mandate, as well as the statutory affirmative defenses, are located at §703. A separate and independent form of discrimination—retaliation for engaging in either of two categories of protected conduct—is prohibited by §704. Finally, a complex of procedural requirements and remedial provisions are set forth in §706. We will begin with an examination of the three groups of covered entities—employers, labor organizations (unions), and employment agencies.

B. SUABLE DEFENDANTS: EMPLOYERS

There are three categories of entities subject to Title VII's antidiscrimination command: employers, labor unions, and employment agencies. Section 703(a) makes it an unlawful employment practice for an "employer" to discriminate with respect to terms and conditions of employment on the basis of five proscribed classifications (race, color, religion, national origin, and sex). Section 701(b) defines employers in intentionally expansive terms, reflective of Congress's general desire to make the terms of Title VII broadly applicable. A "statutory employer" is defined as (a) a "person" (b) engaged in an industry affecting commerce (c) who has employed at least 15 "employees" for 20 weeks (they need not be consecutive) during the current or preceding calendar year. The combination of §701(a)'s broad definition of "person" to encompass virtually every organizational structure designed to further a business objective and the expansive judicial interpretation of the scope of the Commerce Clause means that the only significant limitation on the scope of the covered class of employers is the minimum employee requirement. Title VII also applies to federal, state, and local government employers. Although the definition of "employer" excludes the federal government, a separate provision, §717, extends the protection of Title VII to nearly all federal government workers.

Title VII applies only to employers who employ at least 15 "employees" each working day for at least 20 weeks during the current or preceding calendar year. In unenlightening, if not tautological, fashion, §701(f) defines "employee" as a person employed by an employer. But this provision also expressly excludes elected state or local government officials, their legal advisors and members of their personal staff, and appointed public officials with policy-making authority who are not subject to civil service laws. Any individual falling within this limited group of exceptions is not counted when determining whether the employing entity is a statutory employer. This distinction was expressly codified into the statute via §321 of the Government Employee Rights Act (GERA). This statute, which expanded the protections of Title VII previously afforded federal government workers, expressly extends statutory coverage to all but elected officials.

In the absence of a meaningful statutory definition of "employee," the courts have fashioned a totality of the circumstances test that focuses on the functions performed rather than the title given to an individual. Not surprisingly, former employees and job applicants fall within the meaning of this term. Professional workers are covered unless they are deemed to possess an ownership interest in the organization. Thus, bona fide partners of a business organized as a partnership do not fall within the definition of employee based on an *ad hoc* assessment of their (1) degree of participation in the firm's profits and losses; (2) exposure to liability; (3) extent of capital investment in the firm; (4) extent of ownership of firm assets; and (5) voting rights. In *Clackamas Gastroenterology Associates v. Wells*, 538 U.S. 440 (2003) (a case brought under the Americans with Disabilities Act but where the Court noted that the test for determining the meaning of "employee" would extend to Title VII cases), the Supreme Court relied on common-law agency doctrine, whose touchstone is the degree of control that the principal exercises over the agent. Thus, in the corporate context, courts are instructed to examine, *inter alia*, whether the defendant has the power to hire and fire the individual in question, the degree of supervision exerted over the individual's work performance, and the extent to which the individual reports to someone else in the administrative hierarchy.

All of the minimum 15 employees must be employed for each working day in at least 20 weeks during the preceding or current (vis-à-vis the date of the alleged discrimination) year. In *Walters v. Metropolitan Educational Enterprises, Inc.*, 519 U.S. 202 (1997), the Supreme Court unanimously adopted a bright-line rule for determining whether an individual was working on any particular day. The key factor, the Court held, is whether an employment relationship exists, and not whether the individual is actually at work or being compensated on any discrete day. And the existence of that relationship is demonstrated by the presence of the individual's name on the company's payroll. Thus, as long as the individual's name remains on the payroll, she is counted as an employee, regardless of whether she is on paid or unpaid leave, working part-time, or otherwise absent from the workplace. However, the payroll rule adopted in *Walters* has been construed by the lower courts to exclude uncompensated individuals, such as volunteers or interns, from counting toward the numerosity requirement.

Warning: Common Pitfalls

1. The definition of "employee" contained in §701(f) is only relevant for the purpose of determining whether a defendant meets the minimum employee requirement for being deemed a statutory "employer." It says nothing about whether or not such an individual is entitled to the

protections against discrimination afforded by Title VII. The antidiscrimination requirement codified at §703 protects "individuals," not just "employees," from discrimination. Thus, the fact that an individual falls within some of the exceptions to the definition of employee contained in §701(f), including unpaid volunteers, matters only with respect to determining whether the defendant is a statutory employer. If the defendant is a covered employer, these non- "employees" can bring cognizable claims of race, etc., discrimination under Title VII.

2. Title VII cases often are decided on the issues unrelated to the merits of the plaintiff's claim. One such threshold issue is whether the defendant meets the 15 employee requirement for being deemed a statutory employer. This question is properly raised via a motion to dismiss for failure to state a claim under Federal Rule of Civil Procedure 12(b)(6). As the Supreme Court held in *Arbaugh v. Y&H Corp.*, 546 U.S. 500 (2006), this is not a jurisdictional objection assertable via motion under Rule 12(b)(1) to dismiss for lack of subject matter jurisdiction. This distinction is much more than a nitpicking technicality. Subject matter jurisdiction objections can never be waived and are thus assertable by the parties or by the court *sua sponte* at any time. But since workforce numerosity is deemed a nonjurisdictional requirement, any attempt to dismiss on this ground must be timely filed or the objection is waived.

Examples

You Can Check In Any Time You Like, But You Can Never Leave

1. Glenn Fry filed suit under Title VII against the Hotel California, alleging that she had been denied a position as the hotel's night manager because of her sex. The hotel, a small establishment on a dark desert highway, employed only ten workers. It is, however, a wholly owned subsidiary of Eagle Enterprises, a corporation with more than 10,000 employees. How should the trial court rule on the defense motion to dismiss on the ground that it is not a statutory employer?

2. Suppose that Eagle Enterprises had purchased the Hotel California only *after* Fry had filed her Title VII suit against the hotel. If Fry amended her complaint to substitute Eagle for the hotel, could she state a cognizable claim against Eagle?

3. What if Joe Walsh Enterprises, Inc. (JWE), a corporation with thousands of employees nationwide, developed a chain of Hotel California locations throughout the United States. Could Dan Hendley, who was discharged after serving as the wine captain of the Hotel California in Champagne, Illinois, since 1969, state a Title VII race discrimination claim against JWE?

4. Mercedes Bends filed a Title VII sexual harassment claim alleging that her Tiffany-twisted supervisor and several pretty mean co-employees, whom she previously called friends, surrounded her in the courtyard and made obscene gestures, stabbed her with their steely knives, and touched her in inappropriate ways because of her sex. Can she state a Title VII claim against the supervisor and/or the co-employees?

Explanations

You Can Check In Any Time You Like, But You Can Never Leave

1. The motion should be granted. The issue here is whether the minimum employee requirement is assessed by looking only to the number of workers employed by a wholly owned subsidiary or whether the court will also look to the number of workers employed by the parent company under the theory that the parent and subsidiary are one integrated employer. Most, though not all, federal circuit courts employ a multi-factor test (borrowed from cases arising under the federal labor relations statute) in order to resolve whether two nominally distinct companies should be treated as a single integrated employer for minimum employee size purposes. Under this prevailing view, the courts assess the degree of (1) interrelated operations; (2) common management; (3) centralized control of labor relations; and (4) common ownership. While not individually conclusive, heaviest emphasis is placed on the third factor, control over the subsidiary's essential employment decisions—hiring, firing, and supervision of employees. The court will only look to the parent when it determines that the parent exercises more than the level of control normally invoked by a parent corporation that is separate and apart from the subsidiary corporate entity.

2. Perhaps. In contrast to the prior example, this scenario raises the issue of successor (rather than parent/sub) liability. The few cases on this subject have invoked labor law doctrine under which the courts undertake an *ad hoc* evaluation of such factors as (1) whether the successor had notice of the charge; (2) the predecessor's ability to provide relief; (3) whether the successor retains the predecessor's plant, work force, jobs, working conditions, machinery, methods of production, or business identity; and (4) whether the successor produces the same product. The courts utilize these factors in order to balance the interests of the aggrieved in obtaining meaningful relief and the owners' interests in rearranging their businesses. Of course, the successor can minimize, if not eliminate, its exposure by including an indemnification clause in the purchase agreement.

71

3. No. This example asks whether an aggrieved employee of an individual franchise can sue the franchisor under Title VII. Once again, this will come down to a question of control. Typically, the franchisor does not retain control over labor management issues at the local franchise level. And assuming this is the case with respect to the Champagne location, the franchisor JWE will not be viewed as Hendley's statutory employer. Thus, the suit will be dismissed.

4. No. Title VII claims can only be brought against a statutory employer. And although the definition of "employer" set forth at §701(b) includes "any agent" of an entity that meets the general definition, the courts uniformly have ruled that this "agent" terminology was intended by Congress only to serve as the basis for vicarious liability for the employing entity under Title VII and not to subject individual agents to suit in his or her individual capacity under that statute. This, however, would not prevent the plaintiff from filing some non–Title VII claim, such as a tort claim for battery or infliction of emotional distress, against the individual actors.

C. SUABLE DEFENDANTS: EMPLOYMENT AGENCIES

Section 703(b) prohibits employment agencies from discriminating in referral or in any other manner against any individual on the basis of race, color, religion, sex, or national origin. Employment agencies are defined in §701(c) as organizations that (a) regularly undertake (b) with or without compensation (c) to either (1) procure employees for an employer or (2) procure employment opportunities to work for an employer. The key component of this definition is the "regularly procuring" element. Section 703(b) was intended to apply to companies like "temp" agencies whose primary function is to provide workers for employers. It does not apply to newspapers who publish job opening advertisements because the papers do not actively and regularly procure workers for employers. Note also that the word "employer" in this context takes on the meaning ascribed in §701(b), i.e., an entity with at least 15 employees. Consequently, unless an employment agency procures workers for at least one statutory employer, i.e., one client with 15 or more employees, the agency will not meet the statutory definition. But if it does, it will be a covered entity and can be sued by one of its clients, even if that particular client is not a statutory employer. Finally, keep in mind that an employment agency may also qualify as a statutory employer and be subject to suit by any of its employees for discriminating against them with respect to their terms or conditions of employment as long as the agency employs at least 15 workers.

Examples

I Fought the Law . . . And the Law Won

1. Bobby Fuller, a third-year law student, claims that he was denied the opportunity to interview with a variety of law firms because his law school did nothing to bar firms from refusing to interview African Americans. He brought a Title VII claim in federal district court against the school's placement office. How should the trial court rule on the defense Rule 12(b)(6) motion for dismissal for failure to state a claim upon which relief can be granted?
2. Upon graduation from law school, Bobby Fuller took the state bar exam. After learning that he failed the exam, Fuller brought a Title VII claim in federal district court against the State Board of Bar Examiners, alleging that it was an employment agency and that its racially biased examination discriminated against him on the basis of race. How should the trial court rule on the defense Rule 12(b)(6) motion for dismissal for failure to state a claim upon which relief can be granted?

Nannygate

1. Two college students formed "Super Sitters," a company that, for a fee, refers a trained and qualified babysitter to any parent from its roster of 11 qualified sitters. When Super Sitters refused to refer Biffy Lee Jones, a trained and qualified babysitter, to any of its clients, Biffy filed a Title VII claim of racial discrimination against Super Sitters. How should the trial court rule on the defendant's motion to dismiss for failure to state a claim upon which relief can be granted?

Explanations

I Fought The Law . . . And the Law Won

1. The motion should be granted. In the few such cases that have been reported, the courts have held that law school placement offices meet the statutory definition of employment agency. But this means only that the office cannot discriminate in the way that it operates, i.e., in terms of the various ways in which it deals with the students that it is helping to place with employers. But the courts also have held that such an office is not liable for the discriminatory practices of those employers who use its facilities and services. Thus, it is not under any obligation to monitor the employment policy of recruiting employers. That role, the courts reason, has been delegated to the Equal Employment Opportunity Commission (EEOC) and the courts. Thus, since the plaintiff challenged

the office's refusal to sanction discriminating employers, the defendant will be entitled to judgment as a matter of law, not because it is not a statutory employment agency, but because the plaintiff has not stated a claim upon which relief can be granted. So, the complaint should be dismissed.

2. The motion should be granted. The state bar is not an employment agency. It is a licensing agency, but it does not take affirmative steps to procure or refer employees for specific employers. So, the motion will be granted and the case will be dismissed.

Nannygate

1. The motion will be granted. Super Sitters is neither a statutory employer nor an employment agency. Even if the babysitters on its roster are its employees and not independent contractors, which is unlikely, it has only 11 such babysitters and so does not satisfy the minimum employee requirement for eligibility as a statutory employer under §701(b). It also does not qualify as an employment agency under §701(c) because it does not procure employees for any statutory employer. The parents to whom it refers the babysitters are not statutory employers. Thus, the motion will be granted and the complaint will be dismissed.

D. SUABLE DEFENDANTS: LABOR ORGANIZATIONS

It is unlawful under §703(c) for a labor organization, i.e., union, to discriminate in membership, referral for employment, or in any other manner that would tend to deprive any individual of employment opportunities on the basis of the five proscribed classifications. Section 701(d) defines labor organization to include any form of association, group, or committee in which employees participate that is either a certified or otherwise recognized bargaining representative that deals with a (statutory) employer (in the public or private sector) with respect to terms and conditions of employment and that is engaged in an industry affecting commerce. The definition also extends to an affiliate of a body that represents or is seeking to represent employees of a statutory employer, which means that the statute covers national and international unions as well as their local chapters. Any such organization also must either have 15 or more members or operate a hiring hall that procures employees for an employer. And note, as with employment agencies, that a union can also qualify as a statutory employer and be subject to suit by its employees if it employs at least 15 workers.

Examples

Prescription Love?

1. Wayne Coin, a registered pharmacist, filed a Title VII action in federal district court against Local 7 of the International Drug Store Workers Union (IDSWU), alleging that he was denied membership because of his race. Local 7 represents all ten workers employed by each of the 12 Flaming Lips Pharmacies located in Asbury Park, New Jersey. How should the trial court rule on the defense Rule 12(b)(6) motion for dismissal for failure to state a claim upon which relief can be granted?

2. Michael Ivenz, one of nine office workers employed by Local 8 of the International Pharmaceutical Workers Union, was discharged. The union claims he was fired for not doing his work, for disturbing his co-workers by playing his guitar in the workplace, and for wandering around for quite a while. In order to send a message that the union could understand, Michael filed a Title VII action in federal district court against Local 8, alleging that he had been discharged because of his sex. Local 8 represents all 20 workers employed by the Flaming Lips Pharmacy in Philadelphia. How should the trial court rule on the defense Rule 12(b)(6) motion for dismissal for failure to state a claim upon which relief can be granted?

Explanations

Prescription Love?

1. The motion will be granted. In order to meet the statutory definition of labor organization, the union must be the bargaining representative for workers employed by at least one statutory employer. Each of the pharmacies that this local union deals with in this example has only ten employees. Thus, no single pharmacy is a statutory employer. Consequently, the union does not meet the statutory definition of labor organization, and the motion to dismiss will be granted. The fact that the local union has over 100 members is not sufficient to meet the statutory definition; it also must deal with at least one statutory employer.

2. The motion should be granted. Here, Local 8 is a statutory labor organization because it represents the workers of a statutory employer, i.e., the pharmacy employing 20 workers in Philadelphia. But the plaintiff is suing Local 8 only in its capacity as his employer. Thus, his claim is brought under §703(a) rather than §703(c). This, in turn, means that the union must qualify as a statutory employer. But since the union employs only nine workers, it does not meet the minimum employee

requirement set forth in §701(b). Thus, it is not a statutory employer, and the court will grant the defense motion and dismiss the complaint.

E. PROPER PLAINTIFFS: "EMPLOYEES" AND "INDIVIDUALS"

All three of the substantive provisions of Title VII—§§703(a), (b), and (c)—prohibit discrimination against "any individual" on the basis of any of the five proscribed classifications. The most significant interpretive issue raised by the use of this term arises in connection with claims filed under §703(a). Specifically, since Title VII prohibits employers from discriminating against any "individual" rather than against any "employee," what is the scope of the protected plaintiff class? Obviously, since the statute prohibits, *inter alia*, discriminatory discharges, refusals to hire, and retaliation, former employees (as in *Robinson v. Shell Oil Co.*, 519 U.S. 337 (1997)) and applicants for employment have been held to fall within the protected class. The state of the law is a bit murky with respect to the applicability of the statute to someone who does not have an existing, former, or potential employment relationship with the defendant. The courts agree that the defendant must be a statutory employer. But whether the defendant must be the plaintiff's statutory employer remains unresolved. Thus, for example, the courts have not determined whether a present, former, or prospective employee of statutory employer A can bring a Title VII action under §703(a) against statutory employer B (who is not the plaintiff's employer) alleging that B's discriminatory conduct interfered in some way with the plaintiff's employment relationship with A.

Examples

What's Up Doc?

1. Dr. Rajab ("Bugs") Bunnee, an orthopedic surgeon operating out of his own private office, enjoyed surgical privileges at Datsall Folks Hospital in Detroit, Michigan, until January 1, 2010, when the hospital revoked his privileges. The hospital employs hundreds of workers. Dr. Bunnee filed a Title VII action against the hospital, alleging that his privileges had been revoked by the hospital because of his national origin. How should the trial court rule on the hospital's motion to dismiss for failure to state a claim upon which relief can be granted?

2. Dr. Rajab ("Bugs") Bunnee, an orthopedic surgeon operating out of his own private office, enjoyed surgical privileges at Datsall Folks Hospital

in Detroit, Michigan, until January 1, 2010, when the hospital revoked his privileges. Datsall employs hundreds of workers. As a result of this decision, Dr. Bunnee could no longer perform at the best equipped hospital in town. Within a few months, Dr. Bunnee had lost so many patients that he was compelled to close his office and look for employment as a staff surgeon. His application for employment with Elmer Fund Memorial Hospital in Ann Arbor, Michigan, was rejected when that hospital learned that Datsall Folks Hospital had revoked Dr. Bunnee's surgical privileges. Shortly thereafter, Dr. Bunnee brought suit against Datsall Folks Hospital, alleging that his privileges had been revoked because of his national origin. How should the trial court rule on the hospital's motion to dismiss the complaint for failure to state a claim upon which relief can be granted?

Explanations

What's Up Doc?

1. The motion will be granted. The plaintiff is filing a §703(a) claim against the hospital. And although the hospital is a statutory employer (since it employs more than 15 workers), is it the plaintiff's employer? The facts indicate that the doctor operates out of his own office, and there is no suggestion that the hospital exerts any control over the manner in which the doctor performs his functions when he exercises his surgical privileges. Thus, it is clear that Dr. Bunnee is an independent contractor and not an employee of the defendant hospital. The only remaining issue is whether Dr. Bunnee could claim that the defendant statutory employer is interfering with his employment opportunities with another statutory employer. The courts have not resolved whether a Title VII plaintiff can state a claim under these circumstances. But it turns out that this does not matter under the facts of this example. While the revocation of Dr. Bunnee's surgical privileges has affected his ability to retain patients, none of these patients is a statutory employer. Even if it were assumed, contrary to fact, that patients exercise the degree of control over their doctor that would allow the doctor to be classified as an employee rather than as an independent contractor, the fact of the matter is that no patient would meet the statutory definition of employer since the patient would not satisfy the 15 employee requirement. Consequently, Dr. Bunnee cannot state a claim against the hospital under §703(a), and so the motion will be granted and the complaint will be dismissed.

2. The motion should be denied. This is a more difficult case than the prior example. Here again, the defendant is a statutory employer. But it is also not the plaintiff's employer since he is, vis-à-vis this hospital, an independent contractor for the reasons previously mentioned. But the difference in this example is that the plaintiff is alleging that a statutory

employer who is not his employer is nevertheless interfering with his employment opportunities with another statutory employer. Since Elmer Fund Hospital has more than 15 employees, it is a statutory employer. The few cases that have ruled on this issue conclude that a plaintiff can state a §703(a) claim against a statutory employer who is not his employer where that plaintiff alleges that the defendant interfered with the plaintiff's employment opportunities with a different statutory employer. So, the court should deny the motion.

F. COVERED PRACTICES

Section 703(a) prohibits covered employers from discriminating with respect to any term, condition, or privilege of employment. The broad language with which this provision was drafted reflects Congress's intention to bring the widest possible range of employment-related decisions within its non-discrimination mandate. In *Hishon v. King & Spalding*, 467 U.S. 69 (1984), the Supreme Court held that in appropriate circumstances a law firm's decision as to whether to make an associate attorney a partner could qualify as a statutorily covered employment practice, even if attaining partnership (i.e., ownership) status would remove the attorney from the category of employee. If the contract between the law firm and the associates expressly provided for partnership consideration, that promise consisted a "term or condition" of employment. But the Court also declared that even if the firm had no contractual obligation to consider the associates for partnership, if such consideration was "part and parcel" of their employment relationship, such as where the lure of partnership consideration was used to induce attorneys to join the firm, or where the firm regularly considered associates for partnership, that practice would constitute a "privilege" of employment. Consequently, the Court ruled, the employer had to make the partnership decision in a nondiscriminatory fashion or face liability under §703(a). The issue of whether the employer's action constitutes a sufficiently adverse action to fall within the statutory ban on retaliation or sexual harassment will be examined separately in connection with our discussion of those specific topics.

Examples

To Be or Not To Be

1. Ham Lett, a partner in the law firm of Elsinore & Castle, met with representatives of the firm of Dane & Dane to discuss the possibility of his coming over to their firm as a full partner. Ultimately, Dane & Dane

agreed to hire Lett, but only as an associate. He filed a Title VII action against Dane & Dane, claiming that they refused to grant him partnership status because of his national origin. How should the trial court rule on the defendant's motion to dismiss for failure to state a claim upon which relief can be granted?

2. Honey Bee, Inc., a honey manufacturing and bottling company, restricts the sale of its corporate stock to employees of Danish ancestry. When Rosen Krantz, a Honey Bee employee of German ancestry, was denied the opportunity to purchase stock in the company, he filed a Title VII action against it, alleging that he had been discriminated against on the basis of his national origin. How should the trial court rule on the company's motion to dismiss the complaint for failure to state a claim upon which relief can be granted?

Explanations

To Be or Not To Be

1. The motion will be granted. The defendant's decision to not hire Lett *as a partner* in the firm does not involve a term, condition, or privilege of employment. This case is distinguishable from the ruling in *Hishon* because the Court based its ruling on the assumption that the partnership decision was made in the context of an incumbent associate attorney who either enjoyed a contractual or non-contractual right to partnership consideration. But since Lett is employed as an attorney with another firm and is seeking a lateral move to partnership status, he enjoys no contractual or non-contractual right to partnership consideration by the defendant. Thus, the decision to grant him partnership status would not constitute a term, condition, or privilege of his employment with the defendant. As a result, the motion will be granted and the complaint dismissed.

2. The motion should be granted. The question here is whether the opportunity to purchase stock in the defendant corporation is a term, condition, or privilege of employment. Since the ownership of stock is not a requirement of employment, and since stock ownership does not provide a worker with any additional employment benefit, such as increased salary or seniority, the only way that stock ownership could be viewed as a covered practice is if ownership was deemed, à la *Hishon*, to be "part and parcel" of the employment relationship. Unlike partnership consideration in *Hishon*, however, the employer here did not make stock ownership generally available to its employees. Nor is there any evidence that it used stock ownership as an inducement to lure workers into its employ. Consequently, the opportunity to purchase corporate stock would not be

deemed a term, condition, or privilege of employment. Accordingly, the motion will be granted and the complaint will be dismissed.

G. EXCEPTIONS AND EXEMPTIONS: OVERVIEW

Title VII contains both complete and partial exceptions to the categories of entities that are subject to its nondiscrimination requirement, as well as limitations on the expanse of this requirement. Some of these are found in its definitional provisions, some in its substantive antidiscrimination provision, and others in a section devoted specifically to exemptions.

The definition of employer in §701(b) expressly excludes from coverage the federal government (although §717 extends the same protection against discrimination that is enjoyed by private sector workers to nearly all federal employees), Indian tribes, and "bona fide private membership clubs" that are not subject to federal taxation. Section 703(e)(2) exempts educational institutions that are affiliated with pervasively religious organizations from the statutory duty not to discriminate on the basis of religion. And any business or enterprise located on or near an Indian reservation is permitted by §703(i) to give publicly announced preferential treatment to an Indian living on or near a reservation. Rarely invoked exceptions for discrimination taken against any member of the U.S. Communist Party or of any Communist front organization and against any individual who does not possess requisite national security clearance are found at §§703(f) and (g), respectively.

The other exemptions are codified at §702, some portions of which relate to the rights enjoyed by aliens and the extraterritorial effect of Title VII with respect to American workers. Under §702(a), Title VII has no extraterritorial application to aliens since it provides that *aliens* employed *outside* the United States are excluded from coverage under Title VII. In *Espinoza v. Farah Mfg. Co.*, 414 U.S. 86 (1973), however, the Supreme Court declared that aliens employed *within* the United States are protected against the five types of discrimination prohibited by Title VII. Section 702(b) limits the extraterritorial application of Title VII to American employees. Under §701(f), a U.S. citizen employed in a foreign country is a covered "employee." But under §702(b), discriminating against such an "employee" outside the United States is prohibited by Title VII *unless* compliance with Title VII would cause that employer to violate the domestic law in the country in which it is located. Finally, per §702(c)(2), discrimination against American citizens employed overseas by *foreign* employers is not covered under Title VII *unless* that foreign-incorporated corporation is controlled by an American employer. And §702(c)(3) sets forth four criteria by which American control over a foreign corporation is to be determined — (1) interrelation of operations; (2) common management; (3) centralized control over labor relations; and (4) common ownership or financial control of both entities.

Section 702(a) also contains an exemption for pervasively religious organizations. It permits such entities to discriminate against any individual on the basis of religion without regard to whether that individual is connected to the organization's religious activities.

Finally, in *Sumitomo Shoji, American, Inc. v. Avigliano*, 457 U.S. 176 (1982), the Supreme Court recognized a non-statutory exception for entities exempted from the coverage of Title VII by the express terms of an extant treaty between the United States and a foreign nation (usually authorizing citizenship-based hiring of executive personnel).

Most of the litigation concerning the meaning and scope of these exceptions, however, has focused on the limited right to discriminate on the basis of religion that is granted to religious organizations by §702.

H. THE RELIGIOUS DISCRIMINATION EXEMPTION FOR RELIGIOUS INSTITUTIONS

Title VII contains two express exemptions from the obligation not to discriminate on the basis of religion. Pervasively religious organizations are accorded such an exemption by §702(a), while educational entities that are affiliated with a pervasively religious organization, but that are not sufficiently religious in nature themselves to fall within the §702(a) exemption, are covered by §703(e)(2). Several interpretive issues have arisen in connection with these provisions. Additionally, the meaning of these statutory exemptions must be construed in light of the terms of the two religion clauses (Establishment and Free Exercise) of the First Amendment, which impose both obligations and restrictions on governmental action relevant to religious belief and practice. For example, by allowing religious institutions, but not their secular counterparts, to discriminate on the basis of religion, has Congress overstepped the limitations on its power contained in the Establishment Clause of the First Amendment in an attempt to promote the objectives of the Free Exercise Clause? Alternatively, by subjecting religious institutions to the statutory ban on discrimination based on race, color, national origin, and sex, has Congress so entangled itself with the workings of religious entities as to violate either of the First Amendment religion clauses?

Both §§702(a) and 703(e)(2) provide a partial exemption from Title VII's ban on employment discrimination. The entities covered by these two sections are relieved only from the obligation not to discriminate on the basis of religion. However, both provisions allow these entities to discriminate on the basis of religion with respect to the employment of all individuals, i.e., regardless of whether or not that individual is connected in any way to the entity's religious activities. This raised the question of whether the First Amendment permitted Congress to pass legislation that permits religious, but not secular, institutions to discriminate on the basis of religion against purely secular employees. In *Corporation of Presiding Bishop of the Church of Jesus Christ of Latter-Day Saints v. Amos*, 483 U.S. 327 (1987), the Supreme Court addressed the question of whether providing only religious entities with an exemption from the nondiscrimination requirement violated the Establishment Clause of the First Amendment. In an opinion of limited application, the Court held only that the §702 exemption was not unconstitutional as applied to the activities of a religious institution's non-profit activities (a gymnasium in *Amos*). Three separate concurring opinions in *Amos* suggested that the disposition of the constitutional challenge might have been different if the religious organization had been engaging in a for-profit activity.

The fact that §§702(a) and 703(e)(2) do not insulate religious entities from Title VII's ban on discrimination on the basis of race, color, national origin, and sex raised another constitutional concern. Could subjecting religious organizations to Title VII–generated investigations so entangle the government in their operations as to violate the terms of either of the religion clauses of the First Amendment? In response to these constitutional concerns, the federal circuit courts uniformly read into Title VII a "ministerial exception" that totally exempted all decisions made by a "church" that concerned the employment of a "minister" from challenge under Title VII. Although the circuits could not agree on whether this exemption was mandated by either the Free Exercise or Establishment Clause of the First Amendment, or both, they did recognize that any application of Title VII to decisions concerning the employment relationship between a "church" and its "ministers" would violate either or both of the religion clauses. And though there was rarely litigation on whether a particular defendant constituted a "church" within the meaning of this exemption, there was a significant divergence between the circuits in determining when a particular individual was a "minister" for purposes of insulating the church employer's decision from Title VII scrutiny.

The Supreme Court finally addressed the scope and nature of the ministerial exemption, albeit in a case brought under the Americans with Disabilities Act (ADA), in *Hosanna-Tabor Evangelical Lutheran Church and School v. E.E.O.C.*, 132 S. Ct. 694 (2012). In *Hosanna-Tabor*, the Supreme Court unanimously recognized the existence of the ministerial exception, stating that it was mandated by both religion clauses of the First Amendment in order to prevent the government from interfering with the employment relationship between a religious institution and its ministers. Although the instant suit was brought under the ADA, the Court announced in broad terms that any employment discrimination statute would be unconstitutional to the extent it attempted to regulate in any way a "church's" employment relationship with any of its "ministers." And although all the Justices joined in the unanimous opinion authored by Chief Justice Roberts, there were concurring opinions written by Justices Thomas and Alito (who was joined by Justice Kagan) that sought to offer a different approach toward determining when a particular individual qualified as a "minister" when a defendant sought to invoke this blanket exemption from statutory coverage.

In his opinion for the Court, the Chief Justice stated that the Court was "reluctant . . . to adopt a rigid formula for deciding when an employee qualifies as a minister." It was sufficient, he continued, to conclude that this employee fell within the ministerial exception. That determination, in turn, was based on the Court's assessment of several factors: (1) the church held the employee out as a minister by giving her the title "Minister of Religion, Commissioned"; (2) she was tasked with performing her job "according to the Word of God" and the standards of the Lutheran Church as drawn from sacred scriptures; (3) she was granted the title of minister by the congregation after a significant degree of religious training followed by a formal commissioning process culminating in election by the congregation; (4) she had held herself out as a minister by claiming a special housing allowance on her tax return that was available only to employees who earn compensation in the exercise of the ministry; and (5) her job duties reflected a role in conveying the Church's message and carrying out its religious mission of transmitting the faith to the next generation in that she taught religion classes, led the students in daily prayers, and occasionally led chapel services. Based on all of these factors, and in the face of a finding that the employee's religious duties consumed only 45 minutes of each workday and that the rest of her day was devoted to teaching secular subjects, the Court concluded that she was a minister covered by the exemption. Though none of these factors was individually dispositive, each one was relevant to making the ministerial determination. Moreover, the Court rejected the Sixth Circuit's conclusion that the fact that these same functions were performed by lay teachers automatically precluded the employee from being designated a minister. Similarly, it rejected the EEOC's claim that the ministerial exception should be restricted to individuals who perform exclusively religious functions, noting that most, if not all, clergy perform a mix of duties, including secular ones. The Court also noted that its ruling applied only to suits brought under employment discrimination statutes. It left for another day the question of whether a ministerial exception should be recognized in employment-related breach-of-contract or tort actions by employees against religious institutions. Finally, it added, by way of footnote, that the ministerial exception was a waivable affirmative defense and not a (nonwaivable) jurisdictional bar to suit.

In a concurring opinion, Justice Thomas took a narrower view of the Court's proper role in the ministerial designation process. To give full effect to the religion clauses, he maintained, the courts should defer to the religious organization's good faith determination of who qualifies as its minister. If the courts could second-guess a religious entity's determination of who was one of its ministers, he reasoned, that organization's constitutional right to choose its own ministers without governmental interference would be hollow. Moreover, he added, the determination of who is a minister was itself a religious question that needed to be within the sole province of the religious institution. Since, in his view, the defendant sincerely considered the employee to be a minister, that was enough for him to invoke the ministerial exception. Justice Alito, joined by Justice Kagan, offered a third approach. Their primary concern was based on the use of the word "minister" to define those employees subject to the exemption because that precise designation, although used by many Protestant denominations to refer to members of their clergy, was not employed by other religious groups such as Catholics, Jews, Muslims, Hindus, and Buddhists. Additionally, they were concerned that the term might encompass a requirement of ordination, a concept or practice that was not a prerequisite to being a member of the clergy of many religions. So they proposed that the courts undertake a functional, rather than titular analysis of the employee in question to determine whether or not that person was subject to the exemption. For Justices Alito and Kagan, in order to maintain the constitutionally mandated autonomy of religious institutions, the key question was whether the individuals performed important functions in worship services and in the performance of religious ceremonies and rituals and whether they were entrusted with teaching the tenets of the faith to the next generation. Neither a ministerial title nor ordination, while relevant to making that determination, they declared, was either necessary or sufficient to resolution of the functional analysis. Based on this approach, these two Justices agreed that the teacher was an employee as to whom the exemption applied.

Title VII Coverage

1. Suable Defendant

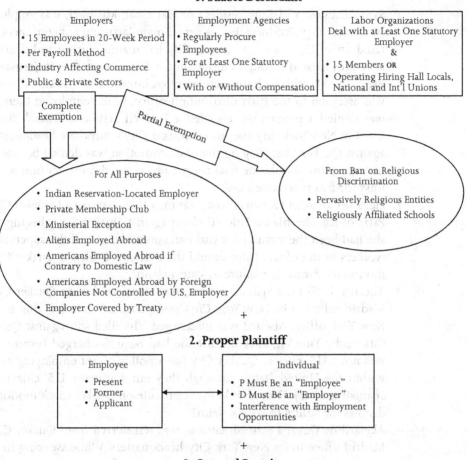

Employers	Employment Agencies	Labor Organizations
• 15 Employees in 20-Week Period	• Regularly Procure	Deal with at Least One Statutory Employer
• Per Payroll Method	• Employees	&
• Industry Affecting Commerce	• For at Least One Statutory Employer	• 15 Members OR
• Public & Private Sectors	• With or Without Compensation	• Operating Hiring Hall Locals, National and Int'l Unions

Complete Exemption

Partial Exemption

For All Purposes

- Indian Reservation-Located Employer
- Private Membership Club
- Ministerial Exception
- Aliens Employed Abroad
- Americans Employed Abroad if Contrary to Domestic Law
- Americans Employed Abroad by Foreign Companies Not Controlled by U.S. Employer
- Employer Covered by Treaty

From Ban on Religious Discrimination

- Pervasively Religious Entities
- Religiously Affiliated Schools

+

2. Proper Plaintiff

Employee	Individual
• Present	• P Must Be an "Employee"
• Former	• D Must Be an "Employer"
• Applicant	• Interference with Employment Opportunities

+

3. Covered Practice

- Terms or
- Conditions or
- Privileges of Employment that are Part and Parcel of Employment Relationship

Examples

Innocence Abroad

1. Sam Clemens, a lifelong resident of Hannibal, Missouri, was employed by Quaker City Products, Inc., a cereal manufacturing concern incorporated under Delaware law. Quaker City has manufacturing and distribution sites located throughout the United States, as well as in Jerusalem, Paris, and Madrid. Each such site employs hundreds of workers. Clemens was assigned to the Paris distribution office. While employed there, he was denied a promotion. He filed a Title VII action in federal district court in New York City, the site of Quaker City's corporate headquarters, against Quaker City, alleging that the promotion was denied because of his race. How should the trial court rule on the defense motion to dismiss for failure to state a claim?

2. Heloise Canard, a French citizen, was the office manager of Quaker City's Paris office. She filed a Title VII claim against Quaker City alleging that she had been the victim of sexual harassment by one of the supervisory workers in the office. How should the trial court rule on Quaker City's motion to dismiss for failure to state a claim?

3. Abelard de Goya, a Spanish citizen, was transferred from Quaker City's Madrid office to its New York City headquarters. While working in the New York office, Abelard was discharged. She filed suit against Quaker City under Title VII, alleging that she had been discharged because she was not a U.S. citizen. Quaker City has a policy of not employing aliens within the United States, although they employ many U.S. citizens of Spanish ancestry. How should the court rule on Quaker City's motion to dismiss for failure to state a claim?

4. Abelard de Goya, a Spanish citizen, was transferred from Quaker City's Madrid office to its New York City headquarters. While working in the New York office, Abelard was discharged. She filed suit against Quaker City under Title VII, alleging that she had been discharged because of her sex. How should the court rule on Quaker City's motion to dismiss for failure to state a claim upon which relief can be granted?

5. Holly Land, a lifelong resident of New York City, quit her job and moved her family to London, England, where she obtained an advertising position with the *London Observer*. When her application for promotion to Director of Advertising was rejected, Land filed a Title VII claim in federal district court in New York City against the *London Observer*, alleging that she had been discriminated against because of her sex. How should the trial court rule on the *Observer*'s motion to dismiss for failure to state a claim?

4. A General Overview

A Matter of Faith?

1. Thomas Payne, a proofreader of advertisements printed in a church-owned and -operated monthly newsletter, was discharged when the church discovered that he had converted to another religion. Payne filed a Title VII action against the church, claiming that he had been discriminated against on the basis of religion. How should the court rule on the church's motion to dismiss the complaint?

2. Suppose that Payne's Title VII claim alleges that he was discharged because of his race. How should the court rule on the church's motion to dismiss the complaint?

3. Agnes Nostick, the only female mathematics professor at Righteous University, an institution offering undergraduate and graduate degrees in secular areas of study, which is a wholly owned subsidiary of the Church of the Biblical Revelation, was denied tenure. She brought suit under Title VII against the university, alleging that she had been denied tenure because of her sex. How should the court rule on the university's motion to dismiss the complaint for failure to state a claim upon which relief can be granted?

4. Suppose that all tenure and promotion decisions made at Righteous University had to be approved by the Board of Elders of the Church of Biblical Revelation and that Agnes had filed her sex discrimination claim against the church instead of the university. How should the court rule on the defense motion to dismiss for failure to state a claim?

5. What if Prof. Nostick was a professor of theology at the religious seminary operated by the Church of Biblical Revelation and she brought a Title VII action against the church alleging that the decision to deny her tenure, which was approved by the church's Board of Elders, was based solely on her sex. How should the court rule on the defense motion to dismiss the complaint for failure to state a claim?

6. An ordained female associate minister brought a Title VII action against her church, alleging that she was paid less than the church's other associate minister, a male, solely because of her sex. She also alleges that this pay disparity is not mandated, justified, or explained by the church's religious belief, practice, or doctrine. How should the court rule on the church's motion to dismiss for failure to state a claim upon which relief can be granted?

7. A member of the clergy alleges that he was denied employment by a church solely because of his race, even though the church represented in all of its publications and job advertisements that it was an equal opportunity employer. How should the court rule on the church's motion to dismiss the clergyman's Title VII claim alleging that he had been denied employment because of his race?

8. Jane Rowe was employed as a bookkeeper by her local Catholic church. Jane, who is Catholic and a member of the church, was discharged when she informed her supervisor that she had an abortion, a practice that is inconsistent with the church's religious precepts. She filed a Title VII claim against the church, alleging that she had been discriminated against on the basis of religion. How should the court rule on the church's motion to dismiss for failure to state a claim upon which relief can be granted?

Explanations

Innocence Abroad

1. The motion will be denied. The issue here is whether Title VII applies to a U.S. citizen employed abroad by a U.S.-incorporated employer. The answer is yes, unless, per §702(b), enforcement of Title VII would require the employer to violate the domestic law of the foreign country in which it is located. In the absence of evidence that French law would be violated by enforcing Title VII, the plaintiff Clemens can state a claim against his U.S.-incorporated employer since he is a U.S. citizen.

2. The motion will be granted. The plaintiff is an alien employed by a U.S. employer operating outside the United States. Pursuant to the exemption contained in §702(a), a U.S. employer is not subject to suit under Title VII by an alien employed outside the United States. Consequently, this motion will be granted and the complaint will be dismissed.

3. The motion will be granted. The plaintiff is an alien who is employed within the United States by a U.S. employer. The Supreme Court held in *Espinoza v. Farah Mfg.* that aliens employed within the United States are covered by Title VII. However, they are only covered against the forms of discrimination prohibited by Title VII, and this statute prohibits discrimination only on the basis of race, color, religion, sex, and national origin. Here, the plaintiff is not alleging that she was discriminated against because she is a Latina or because she or her ancestors came from Spain. And the facts demonstrate that the defendant employs U.S. citizens of Spanish ancestry. The plaintiff has alleged that she was discharged because of her lack of American citizenship. In *Espinoza*, the Court held that alienage (i.e., lack of U.S. citizenship) discrimination is not a proscribed basis of classification under Title VII. Thus, the complaint fails to state a cognizable claim and will be dismissed.

4. The motion will be denied. The plaintiff is an alien who is employed within the United States by a U.S. employer. The Supreme Court held in *Espinoza v. Farah Mfg.* that aliens employed within the United States are covered by Title VII. Since Abelard is claiming sex-based discrimination, she can state a claim under Title VII. Thus, the defense motion will be denied.

5. The motion will be granted. The plaintiff is a U.S. citizen employed outside the United States by a foreign employer, the *Observer*. Pursuant to §702(c)(2), Title VII does not apply to an American employed outside the United States by a foreign entity unless that foreign entity is controlled by an American statutory employer. In the absence of any evidence that the *London Observer* is owned or managed (the criteria for control under §702(c)(3)) by an American statutory employer, the exemption in §702(c)(2) applies, and so the defense motion will be granted and the complaint will be dismissed.

A Matter of Faith?

1. The motion will be granted. The issue here is whether either of the exemptions from the prohibition against religious discrimination applies. Obviously, the publisher is not an educational institution, so §703(e) is inapplicable. But the exemption in §702(a) applies to pervasively religious organizations. And the facts indicate that the newsletter is owned and operated by the church and that the defendant is, in fact, the church. So, the church clearly is covered by §702(a). That provision renders the church immune from Title VII claims alleging religious discrimination. And it applies to claims by all employees, regardless of whether the employee has any connection to the religious organization's religious activities. So, the fact that Tom is a proofreader with respect to advertisements, i.e., that he has a purely secular job, is irrelevant. What is important is that the plaintiff is alleging discrimination on the basis of religion. Consequently, the motion will be granted and the case will be dismissed.

2. The motion will be denied. Once again, the plaintiff has sued the church, and so it enjoys partial immunity from Title VII challenges under §702(a). But that provision only immunizes the church from allegations of religion-based discrimination. Here, the plaintiff is alleging racial discrimination. However, the defendant is a church, and churches are entitled to complete immunity from Title VII with respect to any employment decision relating to a "minister." But does this non-statutory "ministerial exception" apply here? The answer is no. Although the defendant is a "church," the plaintiff is not a "minister," because his primary job duties are not important to the church's spiritual or pastoral mission.

3. The motion will be denied. The defendant university, as a wholly owned subsidiary of a pervasively religious organization, is subject to the §703(e)(2) exemption. But this exemption is limited to claims of religious discrimination. Since the plaintiff has alleged racial discrimination, the exemption does not apply, and so the university's motion will be denied. Additionally, since the university offers primarily secular education, it would not fall within the §702(a) exemption for pervasively

89

religious organizations. Finally, the "ministerial exception" would not apply because the university is not a "church" and the plaintiff, a mathematics professor, is not a "minister" since her primary functions are not essential to the church's spiritual or pastoral mission. So, the defense motion will be denied.

4. The motion will be denied. Here, the plaintiff is suing the church and not the university. That means that the defendant is covered by the §702(a) exemption. But since that provision only covers claims of religious discrimination and this plaintiff is alleging sex-based discrimination, this statutory exemption does not apply. Additionally, the non-statutory ministerial exception does not apply. Although the defendant is a "church," the plaintiff, a mathematics professor, does not meet the definition of "minister" since her primary functions are not essential to the church's spiritual or pastoral mission. So, the defense motion will be denied.

5. The motion will be granted. Here, the plaintiff is bringing a sex discrimination claim against a religious organization. So, the §702(a) exemption does not apply. But the defendant is a church, and the plaintiff, a professor of theology at the church's seminary, would fit within the definition of "minister," so that the non-statutory "ministerial exception" to Title VII would apply. Although she is not an ordained individual, that is not necessary. As the Supreme Court majority noted in *Hosanna-Tabor*, the test for coverage within this exception is a multi-factor analysis that includes the plaintiff's title and an examination of whether the plaintiff's primary duties are important to the church's spiritual or pastoral mission. That test would be met here. Consequently, the exception applies, and so the motion will be granted and her complaint will be dismissed.

6. The motion will be granted. The only issue here is whether the non-statutory "ministerial exception" applies to employment decisions made by a church concerning a minister when that decision is totally unrelated to religious practice, belief, or doctrine. The Supreme Court broadly affirmed in *Hosanna-Tabor* that the application of any employment discrimination statute to regulate the employment relationship between a church and its minister in any way violated both religion clauses of the First Amendment. Thus, as long as the decision relates to the "selection" of a minister by a church, the religion clauses of the First Amendment preclude the application of Title VII to that decision, irrespective of whether the decision is religiously motivated. So, the motion will be granted and the complaint will be dismissed. A few courts have said that the ministerial exception does not apply to Title VII claims brought against churches by ministers where the minister asserts a hostile environment form of sexual harassment on the ground that this does not involve the "selection" of a minister. But discrimination in compensation, as alleged in this example, would fit clearly within the ministerial exception.

7. The motion will be granted. Since the defendant is a church and the plaintiff is a minister and the decision affects the selection of a minister, the constitutionally derived ministerial exception will not permit the application of Title VII to this decision. The issue here is whether the church will be deemed to have waived the non-statutory ministerial exception because of its public pronouncements that it is an equal opportunity employer. The answer is no; this constitutionally based ministerial exception is not waivable. So, the motion will be granted and the complaint will be dismissed.

8. The motion will be granted. Section 702(a) provides that Title VII shall not apply to religious institutions with respect to the employment of "individuals of a particular religion." Here, the plaintiff was not discharged for failure to be a member of the church's religious denomination. Rather, she was discharged because she engaged in conduct that the church maintains is inconsistent with its religious precepts. The courts have construed §702(a) to apply to such situations. The courts reason that because a contrary ruling would raise difficult issues under the religion clauses of the First Amendment, an entity covered by §702(a) is permitted to discriminate against individuals whose beliefs and conduct are inconsistent with its religious precepts, even if such individuals are members of the religious organization's denomination.

Special Proof Issues Under Title VII: Defenses, Sexual Harassment, and Retaliation

A. INTRODUCTION: THE BASIC PROOF FORMULATIONS REDUX

Chapters 1 and 2 of Part I explored the basic evidentiary framework that governs the proof and defense of claims of individual and systemic intentional discrimination under Title VII. As you will recall, Title VII plaintiffs relying on circumstantial evidence to establish individual claims of intentional discrimination need to establish the elements of a prima facie case that, if proved, give rise to a presumption of discrimination that the defendant can rebut by coming forward with evidence of a legitimate, nondiscriminatory reason for its challenged decision. If this presumption is rebutted, it then remains the plaintiff's burden to persuade the trier of fact that the defendant's asserted nondiscriminatory reason is a pretext for the defendant's true, discriminatory motivation. We also saw that where the facts suggest that both a discriminatory and nondiscriminatory explanation contributed to the defendant's challenged practice, the plaintiff will establish liability by proving that any one of the proscribed categories was a motivating factor for the employer's decision, but the employer can limit the plaintiff's recovery by proving that it would have reached the same decision in the absence of the statutorily forbidden consideration. Finally, recall that under the after-acquired evidence doctrine, the plaintiff's recovery can be limited in those circumstances where the defendant obtained evidence after the date of the alleged discriminatory act that justifies the action previously taken against the plaintiff.

As noted in Chapter 2 of Part I, claims of systemic intentional discrimination follow the same general analytic pattern that governs claims of individual intentional discrimination. But the statistical data relied on in such cases as the predominant form of circumstantial evidence to establish the existence of a pattern or practice of discrimination can take a variety of forms, all of which were explored in that chapter.

Chapter 3 of Part I explained that where the plaintiff alleges that the defendant's reliance on a facially neutral criterion generated a disparate impact upon a statutorily protected group of which the plaintiff is a member, the defendant can escape liability by establishing that the criterion is both job-related and consistent with business necessity. If the defendant sustains its burden or persuasion as to this affirmative defense, the plaintiff can still prevail if it can establish that the employer refuses to adopt another neutral criterion that also meets its needs but that generates a lesser disparate impact upon the plaintiff's protected group.

Affirmative defenses are not limited, however, to claims of impact discrimination. Title VII, like the other federal antidiscrimination statutes, contains affirmative defenses to claims of intentional as well as impact-based discrimination. Because these defenses have distinctive application to Title VII, they were not explored in Chapters 1 and 2. They are one of the three subjects of this chapter. The other two portions of this chapter address two specific forms of intentional discrimination, each of which has generated its own unique evidentiary structure — sexual harassment claims brought under §703(a) and retaliation claims brought under §704(a). We turn first to the statutory defenses to intentional discrimination claims codified in Title VII.

B. AFFIRMATIVE DEFENSE TO INTENTIONAL DISCRIMINATION: §703(e)(1) — THE BFOQ DEFENSE

Section 703(e)(1) provides a defense to claims of intentional discrimination in hiring (but not in post-hiring terms and conditions of employment, including discharge) on the basis of sex, religion, and national origin (but not race and color) where the employer can persuade the trier of fact that membership in one of these three protected classes is a (a) bona fide occupational qualification (BFOQ) or requirement that is (b) reasonably necessary (c) to the normal operation (d) of the defendant's particular business. The existence of this BFOQ defense reflects Congress's determination that, on occasion, sex, religion, or national origin does matter, i.e., employers can rely on membership in these groups in making certain employment-related decisions. But, as with all affirmative defenses, the Supreme Court also has noted on numerous occasions that this grant of immunity should be narrowly construed so as to avoid wholesale evisceration of the statutory mandate of nondiscrimination. It is critical to remember that the BFOQ defense is associated exclusively with claims of intentional discrimination. It arises only when the defendant admits that it is explicitly relying on consideration of sex, religion, or national origin, but seeks to justify that decision on the ground that membership in a particular class is reasonably necessary to the normal operation of its business. On the other hand, the combined job-relatedness/business necessity defense is asserted only in response to claims of impact-based discrimination. This analytical dichotomy has been emphasized in several Supreme Court opinions, including *International Union, UAW v. Johnson Controls, Inc.*, 499 U.S. 187 (1991), and was expressly codified into Title VII by the 1991 Civil Rights Act's addition of §703(k)(2), which states that business necessity is unavailable as a defense to claims of intentional discrimination.

The BFOQ defense is most commonly asserted in cases involving allegations of sex-based discrimination. Since religious discrimination most typically would be justified as a BFOQ by religious entities, the safe harbor provided to predominantly religious entities and religiously affiliated educational institutions by §702 and §703(e)(2) has substantially curtailed the use of this defense in cases involving religious discrimination. The BFOQ defense does come into play from time to time in cases involving allegations of national origin discrimination cases. As we will see, these instances typically involve a claim by the defendant that possession of a particular ancestry or heritage is necessary to promote the authenticity of its operations.

The first Supreme Court case invoking the BFOQ defense in a sex discrimination case was *Phillips v. Martin Marietta Co.*, 400 U.S. 542 (1971). After holding that an employer's policy of excluding women (but not men) with pre-school aged children from employment constituted intentional sex discrimination, the Court remanded the case for consideration of whether the employer could establish a BFOQ defense by proving that the existence of conflicting family obligations was more relevant to job performance for women than for men. Although reliance on this "ancient canard" (as characterized by Justice Marshall in his concurring opinion) suggested that the Supreme Court might be receptive to a broad application of the BFOQ defense, subsequent rulings by the Court demonstrate that this defense is very tightly construed.

To successfully invoke the BFOQ defense, the employer must establish two propositions: (1) that all or nearly all members of the excluded sex cannot perform a particular job function (or that it is highly impractical to make individualized determinations of fitness); *and* (2) that this job function is reasonably necessary to the essence of the defendant's business operations. So, for example, where an airline sought to limit employment as flight attendants to women because it believed that its corporate image was based on appealing to the sexual fantasies of a primarily adult male clientele, the BFOQ defense was rejected because the court found that even if only women could perform these functions, these sex-lined duties did not go to the essence of the airline's business of transporting customers efficiently and safely to their chosen destination. Similarly, generalized assertions that making a profit is necessary to the essence of the business plan and that only members of one sex can enhance the company's profitability (i.e., a customer preference–based BFOQ) are deemed insufficient to establish a BFOQ defense. Rather, the courts typically limit the application of the BFOQ defense to instances where discrimination on the basis of sex, religion, or national origin can be justified on grounds of authenticity, privacy, or safety.

One prominent example of the Court's recognition of a safety-based invocation of the BFOQ defense can be found in *Dothard v. Rawlinson*, 433 U.S. 321 (1977). There, the Supreme Court upheld the Alabama state prison system's exclusion of female guards from inmate-contact positions in its sex-segregated, all-male penitentiaries because the "rampant violence" and "jungle atmosphere" prevalent in Alabama prisons, which included the integration of sex offenders and other dangerous inmates into the general population, posed a sufficient threat to the physical security of female guards (as well as to inmates and other prison personnel) to conclude that all or nearly all women would be compromised in their ability to perform the essential job function of maintaining prison security, a job task that was essential to the essence of the prison system's operation. Yet in *Johnson Controls*, the Court unanimously rejected the defendant battery maker's assertion of a BFOQ defense to its policy of excluding fertile women, but not fertile men, from high level lead-exposure jobs. Since the reproductive capacity of fertile men could also be impaired by lead exposure, the exclusion only of fertile women from these jobs was not essential to protecting employee safety. Moreover, to the extent that the fetal protection policy was justified by the employer's desire to protect unconceived children, the Court held that this was neither job-related nor within the essence of the defendant's battery-making business. The *Johnson Controls* Court also repudiated the employer's contention that a BFOQ could be established by showing that employing women was more expensive than employing men. The Court rejected, as a matter of law, the employer's assertion of a cost justification-based BFOQ defense predicated on the argument that the potential of tort liability in claims brought by its female employees for prenatal injury or fetal wrongful death caused by lead exposure made women cost more.

The BFOQ defense also has been sanctioned when the discriminatory policy is justified on the basis of traditional notions of privacy, typically in cases where employees are exposed to persons in various states of undress or to individuals who are engaged in intimate bodily functions. Thus, the defense has been recognized in cases involving the employment of workers in restrooms and locker rooms, and where hospitals restrict employment to female nurses in their labor and delivery departments. The courts justify recognizing the BFOQ defense in this latter category of case because the hospitals' (exclusively) female patients' highly vulnerable conditions justify the presence of only female professionals in this intimate setting and that nurses, unlike most doctors working in these labor and delivery areas, are not chosen by the patient.

Perhaps the most controversial acceptance of the BFOQ defense comes in the context of authenticity-based assertions of this defense. Notwithstanding the fact that men played female and male roles in Shakespeare's day, this defense is invariably accepted in cases involving personnel choices made in the performing arts. The most significant analytic difficulty in applying the BFOQ defense for authenticity purposes is that such cases often involve, explicitly or implicitly, reliance on customer preference. In the abstract, the courts typically reject reliance on customer preference as a basis for invoking the BFOQ defense on the ground that this would directly undermine the stereotype-busting objective of Title VII. For example, in *Fernandez v. Wynn Oil Co.*, 653 F.2d 1273 (9th Cir. 1981), the Ninth Circuit rejected the BFOQ defense raised by an employer that maintained that hiring a female for an international marketing position would significantly impair its extensive business with its Latin American clients who were uncomfortable doing business with women. The court stated that customer preference, as a matter of law, could not render sex a BFOQ. On the other hand, particularly in the national origin-based discrimination context, the Equal Employment Opportunity Commission (EEOC) and a few courts have upheld, on authenticity grounds, policies that restrict employment in ethnic restaurants to members of specified ethnic groups. They also recognize a BFOQ defense to policies that exclude members of one sex from employment in restaurants or lounges whose primary function is to provide sex or vicarious sexual recreation.

Finally, although §703(e)(1) does not include race or color as a permissible basis for a BFOQ, there is a limited context of cases in which the essence of this defense is relied upon, albeit usually under a different name. Whether it is for authenticity purposes in theatrical productions, or for safety or authenticity purposes in connection with undercover law enforcement assignments, the EEOC guidelines do not preclude employers in these very limited circumstances from discriminating on the basis of race or color. But since the BFOQ defense is nominally unavailable, the few cases in which the issue has been confronted use the language of business necessity, even though it is, in terms of analytic purity, inapposite to intentional discrimination claims and conflicts with the 1991 amendment to Title VII that added §703(k)(2), which declares that establishing business necessity cannot be used as a defense to a claim of intentional discrimination.

Title VII Affirmative Defenses

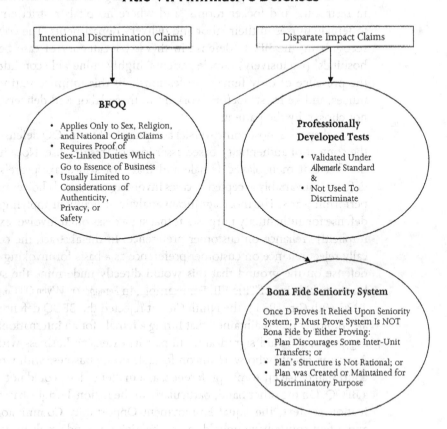

Examples

What Happens in Vegas . . .

1. The Bonanza Inn, Inc. owns and operates a chain of Bonanza Inn gaming establishments throughout Nevada. When it opened its newest Bonanza Inn in Las Vegas, the company announced to great fanfare that all of its croupiers and dealers would be women in an attempt to set itself apart from all the competitor establishments. Joe and Ben Cartwrong, the majority shareholders of Bonanza, had conducted a marketing survey that revealed that 95 percent of all high rollers were adult men and that the presence of female employees at all the gaming tables would increase the casino's daily take by nearly 35 percent, or about $15 million in gross revenue per week. Adam Mada, a 50-year-old male with 15 years

experience as a croupier on the Vegas strip, was denied employment pursuant to this policy and brought a sex discrimination claim under Title VII against the Inn. Adam admitted the accuracy of the casino's marketing study. Bonanza admitted that Adam was rejected because he was a man but filed a motion for judgment as a matter of law. How should the court rule on the motion?

2. The Bonanza Inn located outside Reno contains a casino, restaurant, and brothel. The Inn's brothel is open only to heterosexual male customers desiring the lawful services of female prostitutes. After Roy Coffee was denied employment as a prostitute in the brothel, he filed suit under Title VII against the Inn, alleging that he had been discriminated against on the basis of his sex. The Inn admits that it hires only female prostitutes for its brothel and filed a motion for judgment as a matter of law. How should the court rule on the motion?

3. The Bonanza Inn in Las Vegas employs a large number of parking attendants whose primary job is driving the cars of its clients to the casino parking lot and then retrieving those cars in the quickest possible time when the clients desire to leave. Because quick service is an essential component of the job, the Inn hires only men for this position. The management of the Bonanza Inn believes that women lack the strength and running speed needed to repetitively and quickly run the three block distance from the casino entrance to the parking lot. Kitty Russell brought a Title VII sex discrimination claim against the Inn when she was denied a position as a parking attendant. How should the trial court rule on the defense motion for judgment as a matter of law?

4. The Bonanza Inn in Las Vegas also operated "St. Basil's," an upscale Russian restaurant that was advertised as offering Las Vegas's only "truly and uniquely authentic Russian fine dining experience." When Viktor Romanovsky retired as chef of St. Basil's, the Inn announced that it was looking for "another great Russian chef to replace our world famous Romanovsky and to maintain the authenticity of this award-winning Russian restaurant." Hop Sing, a Chinese-born chef with 15 years of experience in a host of New York restaurants, applied for the job. When he was denied the chef position because he was not of Russian ancestry, Sing filed a national origin claim under Title VII against the Inn. How should the trial court rule on the defendant's motion for judgment as a matter of law?

5. Metro Insurance Brokers, an insurance agency, sells life and medical insurance policies in and around Las Vegas. One of the communities that it services has an overwhelmingly African American population. Metro's insurance salesmen are assigned a particular geographical area to canvas by telephone and door-to-door solicitation. When the agent who had been assigned the predominantly African American neighborhood

retired, Metro announced that it would fill that position with an African American in light of uncontroverted proof that African American insurance agents were vastly more successful in selling insurance policies to other African Americans than were Caucasian insurance agents. Danny McCoy, an experienced white insurance agent applied for this job and was rejected. He filed a Title VII action against Metro, alleging that he had been the victim of race discrimination. Metro admitted that Danny's application had been rejected only because he was white and that it had hired an African American applicant to fill the position because being an African American was a BFOQ for that position. Danny offered no evidence to contradict Metro's proof of the success of black insurance agents in selling policies in predominantly black neighborhoods. How should the trial court rule on the defendant's motion for judgment as a matter of law?

6. Bonanza Inn employs a large number of security officers in its casino. In order to project an image of strength and power to deter criminals and provide its customers with a feeling of comfort, the Inn requires all security officers to be at least 6'5" tall and weigh over 250 pounds. Candy Korn, a 5'6" female who weighed 140 pounds, applied for a security position with the Inn. Even though she previously had served for 15 years with the Las Vegas Police Department, her application was rejected for failure to meet the height and weight requirements. She filed a Title VII claim of sex discrimination against the Inn, alleging that its height and weight requirements created an unlawful disparate impact upon female applicants. In its answer, Bonanza maintained that being a man was a BFOQ for the security job because only men could project the requisite image of strength and power. How should the court rule on the defendant's motion for judgment as a matter of law on its BFOQ defense?

Explanations

What Happens in Vegas . . .

1. The court will deny the motion. The defense has admitted that it engaged in intentional discrimination on the basis of the plaintiff's sex. The issue here is whether the defense is entitled to judgment as a matter of law pursuant to the BFOQ defense codified at §703(e)(1) of Title VII. This is an affirmative defense as to which the defendant bears the burden of persuasion. To meet this burden, the defendant must establish that all or substantially all men are incapable of performing a job function and that this sex-linked job function goes to the essence of the defendant's business. In light of the defense's uncontradicted evidence that nearly all of its high roller customers are men who will be encouraged to gamble, and gamble heavily, at its casino because of the presence of

female croupiers and dealers, the casino will be able to establish the first element of this defense. The question then becomes whether the sex-linked job function of appealing to these desires of male customers goes to the essence of the casino's business. This case is analogous to the airline cases in which the courts rejected the BFOQ defense to policies excluding men from flight attendant positions on the theory that female flight attendants were good for business because they appealed to the fantasies of male customers. The essence of the casino's business, as was true with the airlines, is not catering to sexual fantasies. It is providing gaming activities. Consequently, the BFOQ defense will fail, and the defense motion will be denied.

2. The motion will be granted. Here again, the issue is whether the defense can successfully assert a BFOQ defense. But unlike the prior example, this employer is selling sexual services. Consequently, since it provides prostitution services only to heterosexual male clients, the Inn can establish that only women can perform essential job functions. And since the brothel is in the business of selling sexual services, the sex-linked job functions go to the essence of the Inn's business. Thus, it can successfully assert a BFOQ defense, and the motion will be granted.

3. The motion will be denied. The issue here is whether the employer can justify its admittedly discriminatory decision not to hire Kitty because of her sex. In order to establish a BFOQ, a defendant must establish that (1) all or nearly all members of the excluded sex cannot perform a particular job function (or that it is highly impractical to make individualized determinations of fitness); and (2) that this job function is reasonably necessary to the essence of the defendant's business operations. Running speed is an important job function that goes to the essence of this portion of the defendant's business. But this company is using sex as a proxy for running ability by assuming that all or nearly all women are incapable of repetitively running a long distance in a short amount of time. This is a situation, however, where the relevant job skill is not necessarily sex-linked and where it is practical to make an individualized determination of fitness. The Inn could, for example, require all candidates for parking lot attendant positions to undergo a running test that would establish their fitness for the job. Consequently, the BFOQ defense will not be established in this case, and the defense motion will be denied.

4. The motion should be granted; but this is a close case. One of the limited bases for the successful invocation of the BFOQ defense is where the defendant can demonstrate that membership in a particular sex, religion, or national origin group is necessary for purposes of authenticity. Authenticity goes to the essence of this defendant's operation of a "uniquely authentic Russian" dining establishment. The EEOC and a few courts have recognized that providing an authentic environment is a part of what some restaurants are selling. The question, then, is whether a

chef needs to be Russian in order to provide the restaurant's customers with an authentically Russian eating experience. A chef certainly does not have to be Russian to be able to cook authentic Russian cuisine. Non-Russians can be trained to accomplish that feat. The question, then, is whether there is more to the job of chef than actually cooking or supervising the preparation of food. Where, for example, the face of the chef is seen by the customers, such as where the chef is portrayed in publicity efforts, or where the chef comes out of the kitchen to mingle with customers, or where the chef is visible to customers while working in the kitchen, the restaurant would have a stronger authenticity-based claim that national origin is a BFOQ for this position. But where the identity of the chef is unknown to the public, the argument for a BFOQ is significantly weakened. Here, the restaurant's prior chef was publicly visible and, indeed, famous. This suggests that the chef's persona and identity are an important part of the job, in addition to adding to the restaurant's promise to provide an authentic Russian eating experience. Consequently, the court probably will rule in favor of the defense on the BFOQ defense and, therefore, grant the motion.

5. The motion will be denied. The BFOQ defense of §703(e)(1) is unavailable in cases alleging race or color discrimination. Consequently, it cannot be asserted by the defense in this case, and so the defense motion will be denied.

6. The motion will be denied. The plaintiff has asserted a claim of disparate impact discrimination. The only relevant defense to such claims is the job relatedness and business necessity defense. The BFOQ defense is limited to cases of intentional discrimination. Since the BFOQ defense is inapposite to this plaintiff's claim of impact-based discrimination, the defense motion will be denied.

C. AFFIRMATIVE DEFENSES TO IMPACT-BASED DISCRIMINATION: §703(h) — BONA FIDE SENIORITY OR MERIT SYSTEMS AND PROFESSIONALLY DEVELOPED ABILITY TESTS

In Chapter 3 of Part I, we explored the evolution of one now-statutorily codified affirmative defense to claims of disparate impact discrimination. As explained in that chapter, §703(k)(1)(A) provides that the defendant can respond to a prima facie case of impact-based discrimination by demonstrating that the challenged practice is job-related for the position in question and is consistent with business necessity. But §703(h) also sets forth a trio of affirmative defenses to impact claims.

The testing proviso of §703(h) permits an employer to "act upon" the results of a professionally developed ability test unless the test is being used for the purpose of discriminating on the basis of any of the five statutorily protected classifications. This portion of §703(h) has been folded into the body of law developed by the Supreme Court governing reliance on neutral standards that generate a disparate impact upon a protected group. If the professionally developed test, a facially neutral employment criterion, produces a disparate exclusionary impact and is not validated under the professional validation standards enunciated in *Albemarle*, it is deemed to fall outside the safe harbor of §703(h) because it is being "used" to discriminate.

Section 703(h) also provides immunity for actions taken pursuant to the terms of a "bona fide seniority or merit system," as long as that system is not being used for the purpose of discriminating on any of the five proscribed bases. Since, by definition, seniority systems produce decisions that favor more senior workers, reliance on this facially neutral factor can disproportionately work to the disadvantage of minority and female workers where they historically had been excluded from obtaining employment. But §703(h) shields employers from impact liability when that impact is produced by a "bona fide" seniority system that was not created or used for the purpose of discriminating against protected groups.

In *American Tobacco Co. v. Patterson*, 456 U.S. 63 (1982), the Court construed this seniority proviso of §703(h) to apply not only to seniority systems in existence at the time that Title VII was enacted, but also to subsequently created, revised, and maintained systems. And in *California Brewers Assn. v. Bryant*, 444 U.S. 598 (1980), the Supreme Court declared that a seniority-related regime falls within the meaning of "seniority system" as long as it is regularized (as opposed to the *ad hoc* application of variable standards), defines the factors upon which it relies and how and when they are accumulated, and creates legitimate employee expectations of its applicability. It does not have to be codified in any express contractual undertaking. There is, however, a unique quirk associated with this "defense." In *Pullman-Standard v. Swint*, 456 U.S. 273 (1982), the Court held that where the plaintiff establishes the disparate impact of a facially neutral practice, the employer only needs to prove that the decision was made according to the terms of a seniority system. The burden then falls upon the plaintiff to persuade the trier of fact that the plan is *not* bona fide and, therefore, is not entitled to protection under §703(h). Moreover, as the Supreme Court explained in, among other cases, *International Brotherhood of Teamsters v. U.S.*, 431 U.S. 324 (1977), a seniority system does not relinquish its "bona fide" status merely because it perpetuates the effects of prior (pre- or post-Act) discrimination. Rather, a system will not be deemed to be bona fide only if the plaintiff can establish either (1) that the system does not discourage equally all employees from transferring between seniority units; (2) that the structure of that system (i.e., reliance upon departmental or total employment seniority) is not rational or reflective of industry norms; or (3) that the employer initially developed the system or continued to maintain it for discriminatory motives.

So, for example, a company's pension plan that limited years-of-service seniority credit for individuals who took pregnancy leave prior to the enactment of the 1978 Pregnancy Discrimination Act (PDA) (which made pregnancy-based distinctions a form of unlawful sex-based discrimination under Title VII) while giving full credit for disability leave for all other conditions taken during that same period, the Supreme Court held in *AT&T Corp. v. Hulteen*, 129 S. Ct. 1962 (2009), was still a bona fide system protected by §703(h). The Court reasoned that since discrimination against pregnant workers was not unlawful when the company's calculation of service rule was created, that system could not have been formulated with an intention to discriminate on the basis of sex. Thus, even though the method of calculating years of service produced a current adverse effect on women (through lower pension payments), since that system was not formulated for the purpose of discriminating, the mere fact that it operated to disadvantage employees on the basis of pregnancy/sex did not take it outside the realm of §703(h)-protected bona fide seniority systems. However, if the seniority plan had given less credit to pregnancy-based disability leave taken *after* the enactment of the PDA, such a seniority system would be found to be not bona fide and, therefore, unprotected by §703(h).

Examples

Time Wasn't on Her Side

1. Rolling Skones Co., a pastry manufacturing company with hundreds of workers, had a policy of not employing married females. Bianca Jagged had worked at Skones for ten years before she got married. But when the company learned of Bianca's marriage, she was discharged. Bianca never challenged her discharge. Eight years later, Skones revoked its no-marriage rule for females and Bianca was rehired. Under Skones's contractual seniority plan, any significant break in service with the company resulted in the forfeiture of all theretofore accumulated seniority, and seniority accumulation restarted as of the date of re-employment. When the company had to lay off workers because of the economic downturn, Bianca was among those terminated because of her comparatively low seniority. She filed a Title VII sex discrimination claim against the company alleging that through its use of the break-in-service rule, Skones was perpetuating the effect of its previously unlawful decision to not hire or to fire married women. Skones maintained that Jagged had been

discharged pursuant to the terms of a bona fide seniority system and moved for judgment as a matter of law. How should the trial court rule on that motion?

2. The president of Rolling Skones, Keith Recharged, had unilateral authority to award raises and bonuses to all Skones employees. Recharged typically doled out bonuses during the holiday season and, when times were good, provided employees with raises at the end of the fiscal year. Sometimes Recharged issued the raises and bonuses on the basis of merit, sometimes on the basis of years of service with the company, and sometimes purely on the basis of whether individuals had come to his emotional rescue. Ruby Tuesday filed a Title VII sex discrimination claim against Recharged, claiming that she had been denied bonuses and raises because of her sex. Skones maintained that its bonus and raise decisions were made pursuant to a bona fide seniority system and filed a motion for judgment as a matter of law dismissing Tuesday's complaint. How should the trial court rule on that motion?

Explanations

Time Wasn't on Her Side

1. The motion will be granted. In *United Airlines, Inc. v. Evans*, 431 U.S. 553 (1977), the Supreme Court held that even though this break-in-service component of the company's seniority plan perpetuated the effect of its previously unlawful sex-differentiated no-marriage policy, it was bona fide within the meaning of §703(h) because the plaintiff did not prove that the facially neutral seniority plan was created for the purpose of discriminating. Thus, this plan is a bona fide plan, and the motion will be granted.

2. The motion will be denied. As the Supreme Court held in *California Brewers*, in order to seek shelter under §703(h)'s seniority clause defense, the defendant must establish that the decision was made pursuant to a seniority "system." And to come within the meaning of that term, the system must be regularized and employees must have a reasonable expectation that it will govern certain employment-related decisions. The occasional or intermittent use of seniority does not meet this "regularized" requirement. Here, the company makes *ad hoc* decisions in which seniority is sometimes, but only sometimes, a factor. Thus, this does not qualify as a seniority system, and so the defendant's motion will be denied.

D. SEXUAL HARASSMENT: IS IT ACTIONABLE DISCRIMINATION?

Title VII does not contain any textual provision referring expressly to sexual harassment. Sexual harassment is simply one particular form of sex-based discrimination. As such, sexual harassment violates Title VII only if and when it violates the terms of §703(a), i.e., the plaintiff must establish that the employer has engaged in conduct that discriminates as to her (or his) terms, conditions, or privileges of employment because of her (or his) sex. Sexual harassment actions fall into one of two categories. The first, called a "quid pro quo" claim, consists of an allegation that a supervisor made some demand (typically sexual in nature) and either conditioned an employment opportunity on submission to the demand or threatened the plaintiff with a retaliatory employment-related consequence for failure to accede to this demand. Where the plaintiff alleges either that s/he submitted to this demand under duress or refused to accede and suffered the consequences, this type of harassment claim falls into the quid pro quo category. The other form of harassment action is referred to as a "hostile environment" claim, which the Supreme Court recognized as falling within the purview of Title VII in Meritor Savings Bank, FSB v. Vinson, 477 U.S. 57 (1986). There, the Court declared that action taken against an employee that rendered the workplace hostile or abusive, even if it was unaccompanied by any tangible job loss, such as discharge, denial of promotion, or demotion, affected that employee's terms or conditions of employment. Consequently, the Court ruled, if the action that created this hostile environment was taken because of the plaintiff's sex, the plaintiff could state a claim of actionable discrimination under §703(a). In Meritor and, thereafter, Harris v. Forklift Systems, Inc., 510 U.S. 17 (1993), the Court developed a formula for determining when acts of harassment affected the plaintiff's terms or conditions of employment. The plaintiff must persuade the fact-finder by a preponderance of the evidence that the challenged conduct was (1) severe or pervasive; and (2) unwelcomed; and (3) rendered the plaintiff's working environment both objectively and subjectively hostile/abusive. If the plaintiff establishes this, it must also prove, as in all §703(a) claims, that the conduct was taken because of his or her sex. Let's look at each of these elements one at a time.

The courts have explained that determining whether the challenged conduct was severe or pervasive is based on an assessment of the totality of the circumstances, with focus on (1) the level of offensiveness of the unwelcomed speech or conduct; (2) the frequency of occurrence of such conduct or speech; (3) the length of time over which the alleged harassment occurred; and (4) the context in which the challenged conduct occurred.

Evidence of prior acts of harassment taken against individuals other than the plaintiff is admissible under the Federal Rules of Evidence only to establish the motivation behind the allegedly harassing conduct. It is not admissible to prove the occurrence of the alleged harassment of the plaintiff.

It is not necessary for the plaintiff to offer evidence of tangible psychological or physiological damage caused by the challenged conduct to establish the existence of a hostile or abusive work environment. In *Harris*, the Supreme Court ruled that the conduct must be sufficiently offensive to create an environment that would be viewed by the reasonable person as hostile or abusive by evaluating all the circumstances, including, but not limited to, the impact on the plaintiff's performance and psychological well-being. But in addition to this objective standard, the Court also required the plaintiff to meet a subjective standard relative to hostility — she must prove that she perceived her environment to be hostile or abusive. Some courts, notably the Seventh Circuit, also have ruled that a plaintiff who can establish that action directed at another or others nevertheless rendered her working environment hostile or abusive can state a claim of harassment, at least as long as the plaintiff is a member of the protected classification whose other members were within the "target area" of the alleged harassment. And the Second Circuit has held a female plaintiff who alleged that she was traumatized by learning that other female workers in another department were subjected to harassment outside her presence by someone who was not the plaintiff's supervisor could still state a claim if she could prove that this information polluted her working environment and would have rendered the environment hostile to a reasonable person under these circumstances. With respect to the "unwelcomed" element of the plaintiff's prima facie case, the *Meritor* Court distinguished this concept from voluntariness. The fact that a plaintiff was not compelled to engage in conduct against her will is not a defense to a harassment claim. The issue is not whether the plaintiff engaged in the challenged conduct voluntarily or involuntarily, but whether the plaintiff's actions indicated that the challenged conduct was unwelcomed by her. And, the *Meritor* Court added, evidence of the plaintiff's "sexually provocative speech or dress" is relevant to demonstrating that the challenged conduct was not unwelcomed by her. The Court left it to the discretion of the trial courts under Federal Rule of Evidence 403 to determine in any particular case whether the probative value of such evidence was substantially outweighed by its prejudicial impact upon the plaintiff. But there certainly is no *per se* rule against admissibility of such evidence.

Where a plaintiff has established that the conduct affected her terms or conditions of employment, there remains the essential requirement that she prove that the conduct occurred because of her sex. Sexual harassment is not limited to acts involving sexual activity. The "sexual" in the term "sexual harassment" refers to the fact that the harassment must have occurred because of the plaintiff's sex. So as long as the harassment affects the plaintiff's terms and conditions of employment *and* occurred because of the plaintiff's sex, any behavior, regardless of the presence or absence of sexual overtones, can constitute unlawful harassment.

One commonly litigated aspect of this question occurs in self-styled "same-sex harassment" actions, i.e., where the alleged perpetrator and the victim are members of the same sex. Even though discrimination on the basis of sexual orientation, *per se*, is not included within Title VII's prohibition against discrimination on the basis of sex, the Supreme Court, in *Oncale v. Sundowner Offshore Services, Inc.*, 523 U.S. 75 (1998), held that same-sex harassment cases are not, *per se*, outside the scope of Title VII. The Court held that as long as the plaintiff can establish that the alleged harassment occurred because of his or her sex, i.e., it would not have happened to a member of the opposite sex, then the plaintiff can state a claim. Determining whether this is the case, the Court added, is a question of fact that often is resolved by inferences derived from circumstantial evidence. Sexual harassment occurs, the Court explained, either because of sexual desire or sex group–based animus on the part of the alleged perpetrator. And where the plaintiff alleges that the harassment occurred because of sexual desire, the sexual orientation of the perpetrator can be relevant in determining whether an inference of such sexual desire–based causation is appropriate. For example, where the perpetrator is a gay male and the victim/plaintiff is a male, the Court stated, it would be permissible to infer that the harassment occurred because of sexual desire, just as the same inference was permissible where the perpetrator was a heterosexual male and the victim was a female.

The causation issue also arises in so-called "paramour" cases, where the plaintiff suffered some adverse action at the hands of someone with whom the plaintiff previously had shared a consensual romantic or intimate relationship. Although the circuit courts are not united on this issue, the prevailing view is that the plaintiff in such instances cannot state a harassment claim under Title VII on the theory that the challenged conduct was not taken because of the plaintiff's sex but in response to the termination of the relationship or personal animosity.

Since unlawful harassment can take the form of conduct and/or speech where the claim challenges only harassing speech, an issue arises as to whether the application of Title VII in this context conflicts with the free speech provision of the First Amendment. The few lower courts that have addressed this issue have agreed that the application of Title VII to speech-based harassment is not unconstitutional.

Examples

Rocking the Boat

1. Julie McCoy worked on the assembly line of We Love Boats, Inc. (WLB), a shipbuilding company. Her supervisor, Merrill Stubble, twice made extremely offensive sexually based remarks about Julie's anatomy and his desire for contact with it in front of the entire work crew on Julie's late night shift. He also attempted to put his arms around her on one such occasion. Although McCoy had informed Stubble that she did not appreciate the first comment, and that it had greatly unnerved her and made it difficult for her to look her colleagues in the eye, that did not stop him from repeating it one more time. Julie filed a Title VII sex discrimination suit against WLB, alleging that she had been the subject of sexual harassment. WLB filed a motion to dismiss on the ground that the plaintiff has not established a prima facie claim of actionable discrimination under Title VII. How should the court rule?

2. Suppose that the Julie McCoy case goes to the jury and the jury believed that McCoy was so deeply distressed by the remarks that she found it hard to return to work. But also suppose that the jury concluded that McCoy had seriously overreacted to what they all believe was a minor source of unpleasantness. How should this latter determination affect their verdict, if at all?

3. In the trial of her Title VII action against WLB, McCoy admitted on cross-examination that she had laughed off the remarks and conduct by Stubble, that she always thought he was kidding, and that the two had remained friends after these incidents. But McCoy also offered the testimony of all 11 other female employees of WLB, all of whom testified that they would have been outraged, distressed, and depressed if such remarks had been directed at them. At the end of the plaintiff's case, WLB moved for judgment as a matter of law. How should the trial court rule on the motion?

4. Anna Bricker, another employee of We Love Boats, Inc., filed a Title VII sex discrimination suit against WLB. She alleged that her supervisor, Isaac Washington, pushed her to the ground on several occasions and threatened her with other acts of physical violence if she did not quit working at the shipyard because Washington believed that it was bad luck for women to work on ships or in any place where ships were constructed. She also alleged that she had complained on several occasions to Washington that she did not appreciate being subjected to that conduct. WLB filed a motion to dismiss for failure to state a claim upon which relief could be granted. Its motion is based on the ground that the complaint did not allege the commission of any sexually related conduct, such as demands for sexual favors or inappropriate sexual remarks. How should the court rule on the motion?

5. Burl Smith, a welder employed by We Love Boats, Inc., filed a Title VII sex discrimination suit against WLB. In his complaint, Burl alleged that he had been subjected to a barrage of sexually demeaning remarks by his supervisor, Vicki Stubble, and that Ms. Stubble had also touched him in inappropriate ways on a dozen occasions. Smith testified that as a result of this series of events, he found it extremely difficult to come to work and to perform his job. Several other employees offered corroborating testimony about the conduct of Ms. Stubble and indicated that they would have found such conduct deeply disturbing had it been directed at them. At the end of the presentation of the plaintiff's case, WLB filed a motion for judgment as a matter of law on Smith's hostile environment claim on the ground that Smith had offered no evidence that the alleged conduct by Ms. Stubble had caused any psychological or physiological injury. How should the trial court rule on the motion?

6. Julie McCoy, an assembly line worker at We Love Boats, Inc., filed a Title VII claim against WLB, alleging that she had been the victim of sexual harassment. At trial, she offered evidence that her male supervisor, Merrill Stubble, frequently distributed and showed pornographic photos and movies and discussed lewd forms of sexual behavior in the plaintiff's presence. During its cross-examination of the plaintiff, defense counsel got the plaintiff to admit that she had posed nude for two commercial magazines at the magazines' studios. At the end of the presentation of the plaintiff's case, WLB moved for judgment as a matter of law on the ground that the plaintiff did not establish a prima facie claim since the evidence of her posing nude for magazines demonstrated that she had welcomed the challenged conduct. How should the trial court rule on this motion?

7. Anna Bricker worked in a different part of the We Love Boats factory than Julie McCoy and reported to a different supervisor than McCoy. But when she heard that McCoy's supervisor had demanded sexual favors from McCoy on several occasions, had made repeated lewd references to McCoy's sexuality, and had touched McCoy in a sexual way on multiple occasions, Bricker filed a Title VII sex discrimination suit against WLB, claiming that her working environment had been made hostile and abusive as a result of this conduct by Stubble. How should the court rule on WLB's motion to dismiss for failure to state a claim upon which relief can be granted?

8. Anna Bricker applied for a promotion at We Love Boats. The WLB officer in charge of personnel decisions rejected Anna's application and promoted a co-worker, Julie McCoy, with whom the vice president was having a consensual sexual relationship. Bricker filed a Title VII suit against WLB alleging that she had been denied the promotion because of her sex. At trial, the plaintiff testified that she was furious when she was not chosen and that she thought it was totally unprofessional to

base promotion decisions on a personal relationship. But she offered no evidence of the decision's impact on her ability to work at WLB. At the end of the plaintiff's case, the defense moved for judgment as a matter of law. How should the trial court rule on this motion?

9. Julie McCoy and Dennis Johnson, WLB's vice-president for personnel relations, engaged in a consensual intimate relationship for five years until McCoy terminated the relationship. One week thereafter, disgruntled and hurt by that decision, Johnson discharged McCoy. She filed a Title VII action against WLB, alleging that she had been terminated because of her sex. WLB filed a motion to dismiss for failure to state a claim upon which relief can be granted. How should the trial court rule on the motion?

Explanations

Rocking the Boat

1. The motion should be denied, but it is close to a toss-up. The plaintiff is attempting to assert a hostile environment for a sexual harassment claim. As the *Meritor* Court set forth, in order to state a prima facie claim of hostile environment–based sexual harassment, the plaintiff must allege that she was subjected to (a) severe and pervasive conduct (b) that created an abusive or hostile environment for her and for the reasonable person (c) that was unwelcomed by her. Here, the plaintiff has alleged two instances of inappropriate speech and one instance of attempted offensive touching. The first question is whether or not this meets the "severe or pervasive" standard. Although this criterion is stated in the disjunctive, the courts inevitably apply a sliding scale approach, i.e., the more offensive (severe) the conduct, the less frequently (pervasive) it will have to have occurred. These acts are inappropriate but may not be viewed as extremely severe in nature. And the fact that the remarks occurred twice and the attempted touching only once may or may not be enough to meet the severe or pervasive standard. On the other hand, there is evidence that the plaintiff's environment was rendered hostile and that she communicated to her supervisor that his remarks were unwelcomed. So, the court will probably deny the motion and let the case go to the jury to decide on these issues and whether a reasonable person would have found the environment to have been made hostile or abusive in light of these remarks and actions by the supervisor. So, the motion should probably be denied.

2. The jury could issue a verdict in favor of the defendant. To establish the existence of actionable harassment, the plaintiff must convince the trier of fact, by a preponderance of the evidence, that she found that her working environment had been rendered hostile or abusive as a consequence of

the challenged conduct. But the plaintiff also must convince the jury that a reasonable person under all the circumstances would have found that environment to have been rendered hostile or abusive. So, the plaintiff must prove the existence of a hostile environment by both a subjective and objective standard. McCoy clearly has established the subjective component. But if the jury determines that a reasonable person under all these circumstances would not have found that the remarks and conduct created a hostile or abusive environment, it must render judgment for the defense. So, if the jury makes that objective assessment based on its determination that she was a "thin-skinned plaintiff" who overreacted to a minor situation, it will issue a verdict in favor of the defendant, because the plaintiff will not have established the existence of actionable harassment.

3. The court will grant the defense motion. To establish the existence of actionable hostile environment–based sexual harassment, the plaintiff must establish both that she personally found the environment to have been made hostile and that a reasonable person would share in that reaction. The evidence from the other female workers may very well convince the jury that a reasonable worker would have found that the challenged remarks and conduct rendered the plaintiff's working environment hostile or abusive. But the plaintiff's concessions on cross-examination demonstrate that she did not feel that her environment had become hostile. Thus, she has failed to establish an essential element of her prima facie case, and the court will grant the defendant's motion for judgment as a matter of law and dismiss the case.

4. The court will deny the motion. Sexual harassment claims are another form of sex discrimination claim founded upon a violation of §703(a). As such, they require the plaintiff to establish, inter alia, that the challenged conduct was taken because of the plaintiff's sex. In addition, the plaintiff must prove that the conduct was severe or pervasive conduct that was unwelcomed and that rendered the working environment both objectively and subjectively hostile. But the conduct need not be sexual in nature. If the plaintiff alleges all these elements of the prima facie claim, as well as alleges that the conduct occurred because of her sex, the plaintiff can state a prima facie case. The facts here indicate that she has alleged the existence of all the requite elements of a claim of sexual harassment founded upon a hostile working environment. So, the motion will be denied.

5. The motion will be denied. Although the plaintiff must establish the creation of a hostile or abusive environment, from both a subjective and objective perspective, the Supreme Court held in Harris that a plaintiff does not have to offer evidence of tangible psychological or physiological damage caused by the challenged conduct to establish the existence of a hostile or abusive work environment. Thus, since this is the basis of the defense motion, it will be denied.

6. The motion will be denied. The issue here is whether the plaintiff's decision to pose nude in a location off company premises during her non-working time demonstrates that she welcomed the otherwise offensive conduct and speech to which she was subjected while on the job. The few cases in which this issue has been raised, such as *Burns v. McGregor Electronic Industries, Inc.*, 989 F.2d 959 (8th Cir. 1993), have held that off-duty participation in the taking of pornographic photos does not demonstrate the plaintiff's welcoming of or acquiescence to sexually offensive conduct on the job. Although the plaintiff bears the burden of persuading the trier of fact, by a preponderance of the evidence, that she communicated that the challenged conduct was unwelcomed, posing for nude photos during her non-working time at a non-working location is not probative of whether she welcomed the challenged conduct. Thus, since the defense motion was predicated solely on the premise that posing nude demonstrated that the challenged conduct was welcomed, that motion will be denied.

7. The court will grant the motion. A plaintiff who was not a subject of the allegedly harassing conduct can state a claim if that plaintiff can establish that her working environment had been rendered hostile or abusive by the challenged conduct (from both a subjective and objective perspective). But where the courts have allowed bystanders (to the harassment) to assert such claims, they typically have limited it to situations where the plaintiff was in the "target area" of the harassment. And by this the courts mean either that the plaintiff was a member of the group that was vilified by the challenged conduct or that the plaintiff was present in the work area where the conduct, albeit targeted at some other particular person, occurred. Here, the plaintiff worked in a completely different portion of the factory, was not present when this conduct occurred, and is not under the supervision of the alleged harasser. Additionally, the alleged harassment was directed individually at the plaintiff and did not target women as a group, as would be the case, for example, where the harassment involved the distribution of pornographic photos depicting women in degrading fashion or remarks making sexually offensive reference to women. Consequently, based on these facts, the motion will be granted and the complaint will be dismissed.

8. The motion will be granted. Since the vice president did not make any sexual demands of the plaintiff, this case would be analyzed as stating a claim of hostile environment form of sexual harassment. In the few cases on this point, the courts have focused on the impact on the plaintiff's working environment and not the nature of the consensual relationship that created the challenged conduct. In these cases, the courts have found that the existence of the consensual sexual relationship did not create a sufficiently oppressive working environment either because the

two partners to that relationship had not flaunted the romantic nature of their relationship or because there was no evidence that this kind of relationship was prevalent at the company. They conclude that even though it may be unfair and/or unprofessional, a decision-making supervisor can show favoritism to a paramour without instilling the workplace with an oppressive sexual atmosphere. Since the plaintiff offered no evidence that she found her environment to be rendered hostile or abusive, the court will grant the motion and issue judgment in favor of the defense.

9. This motion probably will be granted, although a minority of jurisdictions would deny the motion. Although the courts are divided on this question, the prevailing view is that decisions based on the termination of a consensual relationship are not based on the plaintiff's sex but on the basis of the failed relationship and the contempt that flows from that fact. The minority view, however, rejects the purported dichotomy between sex and a romantic relationship gone sour. These courts state that since it is probable that the relationship would never have commenced if the plaintiff had been of the opposite sex, the victim's sex is inextricably linked to the decision to retaliate. Thus, they conclude, it is proper in such cases to allow the jury to infer that the decision was motivated by the victim's sex. But under the present majority view, the motion will be granted and the complaint will be dismissed.

E. SEXUAL HARASSMENT: IS THE DEFENDANT EMPLOYER LIABLE?

As previously mentioned, even though §701(b) defines "employer" to include "any agent of such person," the lower courts uniformly agree that a Title VII plaintiff can sue only her employer and not any agent employed by that employer. This is of particular moment in sexual harassment cases since the allegedly unlawful harassment was engaged in by an individual or individuals, none of whom can be sued by the plaintiff under Title VII. (The plaintiff could bring some other claims against the individuals, such as tort claims for battery, assault, or infliction of emotional distress.) Thus, assuming the plaintiff has established actionable harassment, the court then must examine whether the defendant employer is to be saddled with liability for actions taken by individuals in its employ.

The first question to ask in examining the issue of employer liability is whether the alleged harasser was a supervisor or a co-employee. The Supreme Court has only decided cases involving supervisorial harassment. In Meritor, since the Court remanded the case for a determination of whether or not the plaintiff could prove the existence of actionable harassment, it offered limited direction on the issue of employer liability. It only went so far as to say that Congress intended for the courts to look to common-law agency doctrine for guidance on this question. Subsequently, in a pair of companion cases—*Burlington Industries, Inc. v. Ellerth*, 524 U.S. 742 (1998), and *Faragher v. City of Boca Raton*, 524 U.S. 775 (1998)—the Court provided a more definitive standard for assessing employer liability in cases involving harassment by a supervisor. To determine the standard of employer liability in cases of alleged supervisorial harassment (i.e., where the perpetrator had supervisory authority over the plaintiff), the critical factor is whether or not the harassment resulted in a "tangible employment action." Where the supervisorial harassment did result in a tangible employment action (i.e., a *quid pro quo* case), the employer is absolutely liable, i.e., the plaintiff does not have to prove employer negligence and the employer has no defense. But where the supervisorial harassment does not result in a tangible employment action (i.e., a hostile environment case), the employer will be held strictly liable in the sense that the plaintiff does not have to prove employer negligence, but the employer can escape liability if it establishes both components of the affirmative defense created in *Burlington*. The employer will win the case if it can prove *both* that (1) it acted reasonably in preventing and promptly correcting acts of sexual harassment; and (2) the plaintiff acted unreasonably by failing to utilize these preventive or corrective opportunities or otherwise to avoid harm. Normally, the Court explained, proof that the employer promulgated and distributed an effective anti-harassment policy containing an enforcement mechanism will satisfy the "preventing" component of the first element of the defense. With respect to proving that it acted reasonably to "promptly correct" harassing behavior, the prevailing rule is that the defendant must establish that its response was reasonably calculated to end the charged harassment. A minority of circuits go further and require proof that the defendant's response is likely to dissuade others potential harassers from engaging in such unlawful activity. With respect to the second element of the defense, proof that the plaintiff failed to use that mechanism ordinarily will suffice to establish the second element of the affirmative defense. However, if the plaintiff can establish that it would have been futile to invoke the company's anti-harassment process, e.g., because the person in charge of that process was the alleged harasser, or because prior claims of harassment were not seriously investigated by the employer, the plaintiff's failure to utilize the anti-harassment mechanism will not be enough to establish the affirmative defense.

The question of whether or not supervisorial harassment resulted in a tangible employment action is, therefore, a critical matter since it will determine whether or not the employer can take advantage of the *Burlington* affirmative defense. The *Burlington* Court defined a "tangible employment practice" as "a significant change in employment status, such as hiring, firing, failing to promote, reassignment with significantly different responsibilities, or a decision causing a significant change in benefits." In *Pennsylvania State Police v. Suders*, 542 U.S. 129 (2004), for example, a female employee who had not filed a complaint under the employer's anti-harassment policy alleged that acts of supervisory harassment forced her to resign from her position. Since the employer could establish both elements of its affirmative defense, the critical issue in the case was whether her allegation that she had been constructively discharged (compelled to resign under circumstances that would have impelled any reasonable employee to resign) satisfied the requirement of a tangible employment action. The Supreme Court ruled that a constructive discharge, even where it could be established, did not constitute a tangible employment action because it was not an affirmative action by the employer. Unless the plaintiff could prove on remand that the harassment had produced some other tangible employment action—such as a demotion, undesirable reassignment, loss of pay, or other tangible employment opportunity—that ultimately forced her to resign, the plaintiff could not establish the existence of a tangible employment action, and the employer would be able to assert its affirmative defense. On the other hand, submission to a supervisor's threat conditioning continued employment on acceding to the supervisor's sexual demand has been held to constitute a tangible employment action that precludes the assertion of the *Burlington* affirmative defense.

Although the Supreme Court has not weighed in on the standard for employer liability in cases where the perpetrator is a co-employee of the plaintiff, it has endorsed the uniform position taken by the circuit courts. In *Vance v. Ball State University*, 133 S. Ct. 2434 (2013), the Supreme Court addressed the other question left unanswered in *Burlington* and *Faragher*—that is, who qualifies as a "supervisor" when determining employer liability in a sexual harassment case. In *Vance*, the Court explained that the standard for determining employer liability depends upon whether the alleged harasser is a "supervisor" or a "co-employee" because, it noted, where the harasser is only a co-employee, the employer will be liable only if the plaintiff proves that the employer was negligent in controlling working conditions. Since, by definition, one co-employee, unlike a supervisor, has not been delegated authority over another co-employee by the employer, the plaintiff must prove that the employer was negligent in order to subject the employer to liability for the acts of its harassing employees. This, in turn, requires the plaintiff to establish that the employer (1) knew or should have known of the harassing conduct and (2) failed to take prompt and appropriate remedial action.

Consequently, it is critical to resolution of the employer liability issue in a sexual harassment claim to determine whether or not the alleged harasser was a "supervisor." In *Vance*, a 5-4 decision, the majority ruled that an employee is a "supervisor" for these purposes only when he or she was empowered by the employer to take tangible employment actions against the alleged victim. In so ruling, the Court expressly rejected what it termed the "nebulous" standard employed by the EEOC and some federal

circuits that tied supervisory status simply to the ability to exercise significant direction over another worker's daily work. Although the majority
acknowledged that "supervisor" has varying meanings both in colloquial
usage and in the law, it criticized the EEOC's "open-ended" standard as
making supervisory status determinations dependent upon a highly case-
specific evaluation of numerous factors rather than the more "easily workable" tangible employment-based standard that it chose to adopt. Under its
chosen definition, the majority insisted, supervisory status typically could
and would be resolved as a matter of law prior to trial, thereby simplifying
the task of the jury at trial. Moreover, in response to the dissenters' claim
that an employee possessing the power to direct another worker's tasks was
capable of creating a hostile working environment, the majority noted that
the same could be said of co-workers. Finally, the majority emphasized
that its ruling did not leave workers unprotected against harassment by
co-workers who possess the authority to create a hostile environment by
assigning them unpleasant tasks. It simply requires such plaintiffs to prove
employer negligence to recover under Title VII.

Sexual Harassment Claims

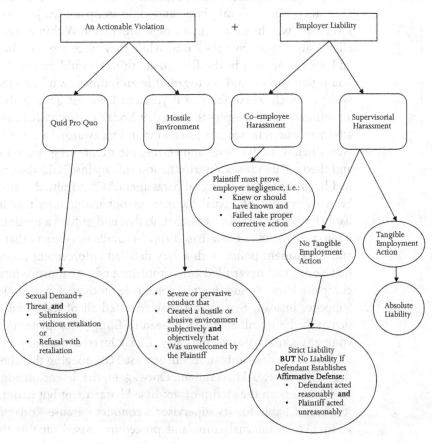

Recall that the judicially created "ministerial exception" provides pervasively religious organizations with immunity from suit under Title VII in cases involving the selection of a "minister" by a "church." In *Elvig v. Calvin Presbyterian Church*, 375 F.3d 951 (9th Cir. 2004), a female associate pastor filed a Title VII claim against her employer church, alleging that she had been sexually harassed by the pastor, her supervisor. The Ninth Circuit ruled that to the extent that the plaintiff alleged that the harassment produced a hostile working environment and not any tangible employment action, the ministerial exception did not immunize the church defendant from her suit because the case did not involve the "selection" of a minister by a church.

Finally, although the overwhelming majority of harassment cases allege sex-based harassment, a plaintiff also can state a claim under Title VII alleging harassment based on race, religion, or national origin.

Examples

Some Kodak Moments

1. Emily Kodak had been employed for ten years as a cable installer for That's Our Line (TOL), a local phone and cable company. On January 1, 2010, John Daly was hired as Emily's new supervisor. Within a month thereafter, Daly repeatedly told Emily, while they were together in the office and sometimes out in the field, that "things would go much better for you if you and I could get together in an intimate way" and that "things will get much worse for you if you and I do not get together soon in an intimate way." Despite the fact that Kodak consistently rebuffed these advances, she retained her job and even was awarded a raise and bonus. Nevertheless, Kodak never appreciated the attentions given to her by Daly and filed a Title VII sex discrimination suit against TOL, alleging that she had been the victim of sexual harassment. TOL admitted that Kodak had been the victim of sexual harassment but maintained that it was not liable for the supervisor's conduct. To that end, it filed a motion for judgment as a matter of law based on the undisputed facts that it had an anti-harassment policy with a very detailed enforcement procedure and that Kodak had never filed any complaint under that procedure with the company. How should the trial court rule on the defense motion?

2. Suppose, instead, that after Kodak rebuffed all of Daly's advances and demands, he terminated her. Instead of filing a complaining under the company's anti-harassment policy, Kodak hired an attorney and brought a Title VII sex discrimination suit against TOL, alleging that she had been the victim of sexual harassment. Once again, the defendant admitted that Kodak had been the victim of sex-based harassment but maintained that it was not liable for its supervisor's conduct because Kodak had failed to invoke its internal complaint procedure. Based on this theory, the

defense moved for judgment as a matter of law. How should the trial court rule on that motion?

3. Arlene Kodak Francisco, Emily Kodak's sister and a member of That's Our Line's public relations department, worked under the supervision of department head Benny Surf. On at least three occasions, Surf cornered Francisco in the staff lounge and told her that "things would go much better for you if you and I could get together in an intimate way" and that "things will get much worse for you if you and I do not get together soon in an intimate way." In fear of losing her job, Francisco agreed to Surf's demand. As a result, she was not discharged. Francisco filed a Title VII sex discrimination suit against TOL, claiming that she had been subjected to sexual harassment. TOL admitted that Francisco had been the victim of sex-based harassment but maintained that it was not liable for its supervisor's conduct because Francisco had failed to invoke its internal complaint procedure. Based on this theory, the defense moved for judgment as a matter of law. How should the trial court rule on that motion?

4. After resisting her supervisor's sexual propositions for weeks, Emily Kodak determined that her working environment had become absolutely insufferable even though the supervisor, John Daly, never followed through on his threats to retaliate for failing to meet his demands. Unable to take the strain of working under these conditions, Kodak resigned. She then filed suit against the company, TOL, under Title VII, claiming that she had been the victim of sexual harassment that resulted in her constructive discharge. TOL admits that Kodak was sexually harassed, and Kodak admits that she never filed a complaint under the company's extensive and previously effective anti-harassment policy. On the basis of Kodak's admissions, TOL filed a motion for judgment as a matter of law on the ground that it could not be held liable for the acts of its supervisor, John Daly. How should the court rule on this motion?

5. Benny Surf was the supervisor of all employees in TOL's public relations department, including Henry Lessgan and Arlene Francisco. From the moment he joined the staff at TOL, Lessgan began a campaign of directing sexual innuendos, insults, and other degrading remarks at Francisco in the staff lounge during coffee break times when some of the other departmental workers were present. After several unsuccessful attempts by Francisco to convince Lessgan to cease making these remarks, Francisco filed a Title VII sex discrimination action against TOL. Francisco admitted that neither she nor any other employee ever complained to anyone (other than to Lessgan) about this behavior, and that Lessgan was very careful to make the remarks only when Surf and all other supervisors were not present in the staff lounge. TOL admitted that Francisco was subjected to sexual harassment but filed a motion for judgment as a matter of law on the ground that it was not liable for the actions of Lessgan. How should the trial court rule on the motion?

Explanations

Some Kodak Moments

1. The motion will be granted. Since this is a case of supervisory harassment and the employer has admitted the existence of harassment, the issue is one of employer liability. Under the Supreme Court's ruling in *Burlington*, the first issue to ask when assessing employer liability in a case involving supervisorial harassment is whether the harassment resulted in a tangible employment action. Although the supervisor made sexual demands, the supervisor did not take any retaliatory action, and the plaintiff refused to submit to his demands. These two facts produce two consequences. First, this would be viewed as a hostile environment and not a *quid pro quo* claim. Second, the harassment did not result in a tangible employment action. Under *Burlington*, this, in turn, means that although the plaintiff does not have to prove negligence on the employer's part, i.e., there is a strict liability standard for employer liability, the absence of a tangible employment action means that the employer can assert its two-part affirmative defense. And the facts indicate that the employer acted reasonably in having an enforceable anti-harassment policy and that the plaintiff acted unreasonably in failing to utilize it. So, the employer's motion for judgment as a matter of law will be granted.

2. The motion will be denied. This is a clear case of *quid pro quo* harassment because the supervisor made a sex-based threat, the plaintiff failed to submit, and the supervisor took retaliatory action — discharge — which constitutes a tangible employment action. Consequently, under *Burlington*, the employer is absolutely liable, and the affirmative defense used in the prior example is not available. As a result, the fact that the plaintiff did not invoke the internal machinery is irrelevant and the defense motion will be denied.

3. The motion will be denied. This is a case of *quid pro quo* harassment. Where a supervisor makes a sexual demand upon a subordinate employee and the employee submits to that demand for fear of suffering an adverse employment consequence, the courts hold that this constitutes *quid pro quo* harassment and that the harassment has resulted in a tangible employment action. This is true notwithstanding that the supervisor did not invoke the threatened retaliation because of the plaintiff's submission to his demands. Submission to a supervisor's threat conditioning continued employment on acceding to that supervisor's sexual demand has been held to constitute a tangible employment action that precludes the assertion of the *Burlington* affirmative defense. Since this supervisorial harassment resulted in a tangible employment action, the employer is absolutely liable and cannot invoke the *Burlington* affirmative defense. So, the fact that the plaintiff did not invoke the internal machinery is irrelevant, and the defendant's motion will be denied.

4. The motion will be granted. The issue here is whether or not a constructive discharge constitutes a tangible employment action. The Supreme Court held in *Suders* that a constructive discharge does not constitute a tangible employment action because the affirmative action — termination of employment — was taken by the plaintiff and not by the defendant. Thus, the employer can assert its *Burlington* affirmative defense. And based on the plaintiff's admissions, it will be successful in asserting that defense. Consequently, the court will grant the employer's motion for judgment as a matter of law.

5. The court will grant the motion. This is a case involving the question of employer liability for acts of co-employee harassment. Although the Supreme Court has never ruled on employer liability for co-employee harassment, the lower courts agree that, unlike cases of supervisorial harassment, a plaintiff in a co-employee harassment case must prove that the employer was negligent in order to subject the employer to liability. This means that the plaintiff must prove that the employer knew or should have known of the harassing conduct *and* that it failed to take prompt and appropriate remedial action. Based on the facts that neither the plaintiff nor any other employee ever informed any company official of the harassing conduct, and that the offending remarks were made in the absence of any supervisory employees, the plaintiff will be unable to establish that the employer knew or should have known of the harassing conduct. Consequently, the employer cannot be held liable for the acts of its nonsupervisory employee, and the motion will be granted.

F. RETALIATION

In addition to the antidiscrimination provision codified at §703, Title VII, like the Age Discrimination in Employment Act (ADEA) and the Americans with Disabilities Act (ADA), contains a separate provision outlawing certain types of retaliation. (As we will see, 42 U.S.C. §1981 does not contain an express anti-retaliation provision, but one has been read into it by the Supreme Court.) Section 704(a) prohibits covered entities from retaliating against anyone who has either (a) *participated* in some formal Title VII–related enforcement proceeding or (b) *opposed*, in some informal manner, an employment practice made unlawful by Title VII. The evidentiary framework for §704(a) claims tracks the tripartite *McDonnell Douglas/Burdine* formula governing intentional claims under §703. To state a prima facie claim under §704(a), the plaintiff must establish all of these three elements: (1) that she engaged in either protected "participation" or "opposition" conduct; (2) that she was subjected to some adverse action; and (3) that there is a causal connection between the protected conduct and the adverse action. If these elements are established, the defendant bears the burden of coming forward with evidence of a nondiscriminatory reason to rebut the presumption of a retaliatory motive generated by the prima facie case. If that is done, the burden of persuasion rests with the plaintiff to convince the trier of fact that the defendant's asserted explanation is a pretext for a retaliatory motive.

With respect to the first of these three elements, it is important to determine not only whether the plaintiff engaged in protected conduct but which form of protected conduct. In order to qualify as a protected act of "participation," the plaintiff must have been involved in some way in a Title VII enforcement proceeding. This includes not only the filing of an EEOC charge or lawsuit but also participating or refusing to participate as a witness in such a proceeding. Presently, the circuit courts are divided as to whether a person who is involved in an employer-initiated internal investigation is engaging in an act of participation. Some circuits apply the term to employer-instigated investigations that were the product of an EEOC filing; some also extend it to employer-initiated investigations that ultimately lead to an EEOC filing. Others have concluded that Congress intended to include only unlawful employment practice investigations carried on by the EEOC or its designated representative and not an employer's in-house investigation. Although the issue was raised in *Crawford v. Metropolitan Government of Nashville and Davidson County*, 129 S. Ct. 846 (2009), the Supreme Court declined to answer this question, focusing instead on the plaintiff's alternate pleading that he had been retaliated against for engaging in opposition activity. What is clear, however, is that the participation must involve some form of proceeding to enforce Title VII, including involvement in state administrative proceedings that were commenced as a prerequisite to filing a federal charge with the EEOC. Thus, a plaintiff who is retaliated against for filing a claim of age or disability discrimination would not have a claim under §704 since that person would not have participated in a proceeding, as the text requires, "under this Title." What is also clear, perhaps more importantly, is the consequence of labeling protected conduct as participation. All but one (the Seventh) circuit agree that individuals who engage in participation, as opposed to acts of opposition, enjoy absolute immunity from retaliation taken in response to the participation. Thus, regardless of the *bona fides* of the act of participation, including the invidious bringing of baseless charges solely for the purpose of harassing, intimidating, defaming, or otherwise damaging the employer, the conduct is protected, and any retaliatory response will violate Title VII.

The scope of the category of protected opposition conduct, on the other hand, is circumscribed. The courts uniformly agree that this form of unofficial, informal protest is protected only if the actor reasonably believes that he is opposing conduct that is proscribed by Title VII. So, while the plaintiff does not have to prove that the challenged conduct is unlawful, she does have to prove that she had a reasonable belief that it was unlawful. This means that a plaintiff will be protected when the opposition conduct was based on a *reasonably* mistaken belief (a reasonable mistake of law or fact) that the protested conduct was unlawful. In *Crawford*, the Supreme Court unanimously ruled that the lower court had erred in requiring opposition conduct to be either repetitive or actively initiated by the plaintiff. There, as part of an employer-initiated investigation into allegations of sexual harassment, the plaintiff had responded to an investigator's questions by stating that the supervisor in question had engaged in multiple acts of harassment. After the employer decided to take no action against that supervisor, it terminated the plaintiff and two other accusers. The Court endorsed the EEOC's view that the definition of opposition was satisfied where the plaintiff communicated to her employer a belief that the employer had engaged in unlawful discrimination unless the context indicated that the speaker did not actually find the conduct in question to be offensive. And the form of the opposition activity can remove it from the category of protected conduct, such as where the conduct is independently unlawful, such as criminal or tortious conduct, or is insubordinate or otherwise harmful to the employer's legitimate interests.

A Title VII plaintiff asserting a retaliation claim also must establish that he suffered some adverse action. In *Burlington Northern & Santa Fe Railway Co. v. White*, 548 U.S. 53 (2006), the Court held the retaliatory response does not have to be employment-related to fit within the terms of §704(a). Although §703(a) expressly refers to terms and conditions of employment, §704(a) prohibits conduct that "discriminates against" a person engaged in protected activity. In light of this textual differentiation, and the Court's determination that employers can retaliate effectively by taking actions not directly related to employment by harming the plaintiff outside the workplace, the Court concluded that the appropriate test is whether or not a reasonable employee would have found the employer's response "materially adverse" and not a "petty slight or minor annoyance" resulting in "trivial harms." And, the Court also explained, the "materially adverse" standard is to be judged from an objective perspective, i.e., a response is materially adverse if it "might well have" dissuaded a reasonable worker in light of all the surrounding circumstances from engaging in §704(a)-protected activity.

Although §704(a) prohibits retaliation against any "employee or applicant," in *Robinson v. Shell Oil Co.*, 519 U.S. 337 (1997), the Supreme Court unanimously held that this provision extends to retaliation against former employees taken during or after their term of employment. To exclude former employees, the Court reasoned, would preclude victims of retaliatory discharges from stating a claim for relief and also would allow the threat of post-employment retaliation to discourage victims of discrimination from challenging unlawful conduct.

But the circuit courts were split on the question of whether the anti-retaliation provision of §704(a) encompassed so-called third-party retaliation claims. Such claims arise when the victim of the reprisal is not the person who engaged in the protected act of "participation" or "opposition." Rather, the employer attempts to punish an employee who engaged in protected activity by taking adverse action against someone close to that individual. The Supreme Court resolved this conflict and ruled that third-party harassment claims are cognizable under §704(a).

In *Thompson v. North American Stainless, LP*, 131 S. Ct. 863 (2011), a male employee was fired after his fiancée, a co-employee, had filed a sex discrimination charge against the employer with the EEOC. The discharged male employee filed a §704(a) Title VII retaliation claim against the employer alleging that it had discharged him in retaliation for the filing of an EEOC charge against that employer by her. The trial court granted summary judgment to the employer, concluding that this plaintiff could not state a claim under §704 since the anti-retaliation provision did not permit third-party retaliation claims, i.e., that a §704(a) plaintiff had to be the person who had engaged in statutorily protected "participation" or "opposition" conduct. The Sixth Circuit panel reversed the trial court, but the trial judge's ruling was later affirmed by a 10-6 vote of the *en banc* court, which agreed that a person who did not engage in statutorily protected "participation" or "opposition" could not state a claim of retaliation under §704(a). An eight-member Supreme Court (Justice Kagan did not participate in the case) unanimously reversed the *en banc* court and held that this plaintiff could state a claim under §704.

In an opinion by Justice Scalia, the Court set forth a two-part analysis for deciding whether the plaintiff could state a claim. First, it had to determine whether the discharge of the plaintiff violated Title VII in any way. If so, then it had to examine whether this plaintiff—an individual who had not engaged in statutorily protected "participation" or "opposition"—could bring a retaliation claim under Title VII. As to the first question, the Court relied on the broad interpretation of §704(a) that it had announced in *Burlington Northern & Santa Fe Railway v. White*, 548 U.S. 53 (2006). In *Burlington*, the Court had held that §704(a) extended to claims where the alleged reprisal was not employment related. It construed §704 as extending to any employer response that "might well have dissuaded a reasonable worker" from engaging in statutorily protected conduct. And the discharge of one's fiancé, the Court reasoned, would generate such a chilling effect on a reasonable employee. And though the Court noted that there was a difficult line-drawing problem associated with recognizing this form of third-party harassment claim (i.e., where the retaliation plaintiff had engaged in protected conduct but where the employer's retaliatory response was taken against some third party), the Court determined that the problems associated with making such *ad hoc* decisions did not justify a categorical exclusion of all third-party reprisal claims under §704(a). There was no textual justification, the Court continued, for excluding third-party harassment situations from the chilling effect standard set forth in *Burlington*. However, the Court declined the opportunity to identify a fixed class of relationships that would meet the *Burlington* chilling effect standard. Instead, it acknowledged that firing a close family member would "almost always" meet the *Burlington* standard but that a milder reprisal taken against an acquaintance "will almost never do so." Beyond that, however, the Court was "reluctant to generalize." Given the broad array of contexts in which retaliation could occur, the Court concluded, it was inappropriate to establish a bright-line rule other than to say that the standard for judging harm must be "objective" in order to avoid unfair discrepancies that would result if the courts attempted to assess each plaintiff's subjective feelings.

Having determined that third-party harassment claims were cognizable under Title VII, the Court then turned to the question of whether this plaintiff could assert such a claim under Title VII. To answer this question, the Court examined §706(f)(1), which provides for a private right of action "by the person claiming to be aggrieved." The Court rejected the plaintiff's contention, which had been adopted by the Sixth Circuit *en banc*, that this statutory standard simply reiterated the minimal Article III standing requirement that a plaintiff allege an actual injury caused by the defendant that was remediable by a court. To apply that minimal standard, the Court explained, would create such "absurd consequences" as allowing a stockholder to sue a company for discriminatorily firing a valuable employee by establishing that the discharge caused the value of his stock to decrease. But the Court also rejected the defense argument that the statutory "person aggrieved" standard limited a retaliation claim to someone who had engaged in statutorily protected "participation" or "opposition." If Congress had wanted to so limit the availability of a civil action, the Court continued, it "would more naturally" have used "person claiming to have been discriminated against" than "person claiming to be aggrieved" language.

So instead of either of those standards, the Court adopted the "zone of interests" standard that it previously had read into language in the Administrative Procedure Act that authorized suit by a person "adversely affected or aggrieved." Under this standard, the putative plaintiff must establish that he or she is asserting an interest that is "arguably sought to be protected" by Title VII. Then, applying that standard to the instant case, the Court found that the discharged plaintiff fell within the zone of interests protected by Title VII because (1) he was an employee and Title VII was

enacted to protect employees from unlawful acts by their employer, and
(2) he was not an accidental victim ("collateral damage") of the employer's unlawfully retaliatory act because injuring him was the employer's
intended method of punishing the plaintiff's fiancée for filing an EEOC sex
discrimination charge against it.

Post-*Thompson*, many questions arose as to the intended scope of now-
cognizable "third-party retaliation" claims. For example, suppose that plaintiff Eric's fiancée, Miriam, had worked for a company other than Stainless
and that she had filed a sex discrimination charge against her employer,
Apex Construction. Suppose also that it turned out that the supervisor whom
she had charged with engaging in sex discrimination had an uncle who
worked for Stainless. Finally, imagine that when Miriam's supervisor told
his uncle that Miriam had filed a charge naming him as the perpetrator, the
uncle convinced Eric's supervisor to fire Eric. Could Eric state a §704(a)
claim against Stainless? In *Underwood v. Dept. of Financial Services State of Florida*,
2013 WL 1760623 (11th Cir. 2013) (unpublished), the Eleventh Circuit
upheld the trial court's issuance of summary judgment in favor of the defendant. Rejecting the plaintiff's contention that his claim fell squarely within
the ruling in *Thompson*, the Eleventh Circuit panel, in an unpublished opinion,
ruled that the plaintiff could not state a claim under §704(a) because the
defendant employer did not retaliate against the person who engaged in the
protected conduct. After finding that the employer who had been the subject
of the underlying charge was a separate employer from the defendant named
in the plaintiff's §704(a) charge (the two employers were separate agencies
of the State of Florida), the court construed the *Thompson* Court's reliance on
Burlington Northern as requiring it to assess the impact of the retaliatory act on
the person who filed the underlying charge. As far as the Eleventh Circuit was
concerned, "the retaliatory action must be against an employee who engaged
in protected conduct." And since the defendant was not the employer of the
person who had engaged in §704(a)-protected activity, the appellate panel
concluded, this employer could not be said to have retaliated against her.
The fact that it retaliated against someone else, the court reasoned, did not
meet the *Burlington Northern* standard. Having determined that the plaintiff's
claim did not fall within the scope of §704(a), the panel declared that it was
unnecessary to consider the standing question of whether the plaintiff fell
within the zone of interests protected by Title VII.

Finally, with respect to the issue of causation, the Supreme Court, in
University of Texas Southwestern Medical Center v. Nassar, 133 S. Ct. 2517 (2013),
another 5-4 decision, ruled that §704(a) retaliation cases were not susceptible to mixed motive analysis. In other words, a Title VII plaintiff claiming
retaliation under §704(a), unlike a Title VII plaintiff alleging a claim of status-based discrimination under §703(a), has to meet a "but-for" causation
standard. In reaching this decision, the Court majority employed the same
analysis it had relied on four years earlier in *Gross v. FBL Financial Services, Inc.*,

557 U.S. 167 (2009) (see Chapter 10, Section D). Once again, the majority reasoned that since the plaintiff's portion of mixed motive analysis originally enunciated by the Supreme Court in *Price Waterhouse v. Hopkins*, 490 U.S. 228 (1989) (see Chapter 1, Section D), had been codified in §703 (specifically, §703(m)), and not also in §704, by the 1991 Civil Rights Act, this reflected the legislature's deliberate intention to limit the availability of the mixed motive causation standard to claims brought under §703. Moreover, the majority pointed to the fact that the text of the mixed motive provision in §703(m) refers only to status-based unlawful employment practices and does not mention retaliation. Accordingly, the Court ruled that retaliation claims brought under §704(a) of Title VII, like claims of age discrimination filed under the ADEA, were subject only to a but-for causation standard.

In attempting to prove causation, the plaintiff can rely on direct or circumstantial evidence. Frequently, plaintiffs rely on the temporal proximity of the protected conduct and the adverse action as some circumstantial evidence of causation. Obviously, the closer the temporal connection, the stronger the inference of causation. But the courts are split on whether close temporal proximity *alone* is sufficient to establish causation. (Although the Supreme Court, in *Clark County School District v. Breeden*, 532 U.S. 268 (2001), noted that some circuit courts have accepted mere temporal proximity as sufficient evidence of causation, it declined to comment on the correctness of those decisions.) On the other hand, proof of employer knowledge that the plaintiff engaged in protected conduct is necessary to establish that the adverse action was taken because of the involvement in protected activity.

Retaliation — §704(a)

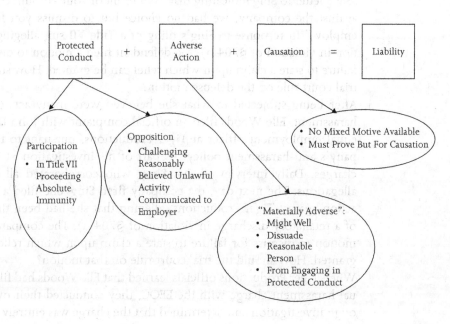

| Protected Conduct | + | Adverse Action | + | Causation | = | Liability |

Participation
- In Title VII Proceeding Absolute Immunity

Opposition
- Challenging Reasonably Believed Unlawful Activity
- Communicated to Employer

- No Mixed Motive Available
- Must Prove But For Causation

"Materially Adverse":
- Might Well
- Dissuade
- Reasonable Person
- From Engaging in Protected Conduct

Examples

The Lady and the Tiger

1. Elle Woods, a production assistant with Tiger Productions, a production firm specializing in television commercials, filed an EEOC charge, alleging that she had been the victim of sexual harassment by her supervisor in violation of Title VII. For several months prior to and after the filing of that charge, Elle had received multiple disciplinary warnings for excessive absenteeism and tardiness. Three months after filing her harassment charge, Elle was told that she had been fired. After satisfying all procedural requirements, Elle filed a Title VII suit in federal court, alleging that she had been discharged in retaliation for filing the sexual harassment charge with the EEOC. During the presentation of the defense case, the company president admitted that he knew of and had been troubled by Elle's harassment charge prior to the time he decided to discharge her. But he also testified that even if the fact of the EEOC filing had played a role in his decision, he also had concluded that she needed to be discharged because of her unacceptably high rate of absenteeism and tardiness. The plaintiff did not dispute any of this testimony. At the end of the presentation of evidence, the defendant moved for judgment as a matter of law. How should the trial court rule on this motion?

2. Samantha "D.J." Sing, a 60-year-old actor employed by Tiger Productions who specialized in portraying disc jockeys, filed suit against Tiger, alleging that she had been denied a role in one of its commercials because the producers thought that she was too old for the part. One week after receiving a copy of Sing's complaint, the company president, L.N. Nordgreen, sent a letter to Sing indicating that "as a result of your unfounded charges against the company, we had no choice but to dismiss you from our employ." In response to Sing's filing of a Title VII suit alleging retaliation in violation of §704(a), the defendant filed a motion to dismiss for failure to state a claim upon which relief can be granted. How should the trial court rule on the defense motion?

3. After being subjected to what she believed were many acts of sexual harassment, Elle Woods filed an official complaint with John Daily, the equal employment officer at Tiger Productions, pursuant to the company's anti-harassment policy. As part of his investigation of Woods's charges, Daily interviewed D.J. Sing, who corroborated all of Elle's allegations. The next day, the company fired Sing. She filed a Title VII action against Tiger Productions, alleging that she had been the victim of a retaliatory discharge in violation of §704(a). The company filed a motion to dismiss for failure to state a claim upon which relief can be granted. How should the trial court rule on that motion?

4. When Tiger Productions officials learned that Elle Woods had filed a sexual harassment charge with the EEOC, they conducted their own thorough investigation and determined that the charge was entirely baseless.

Several of Elle's co-employees also reported to the company's investigator that Elle had admitted that she had made up the entire charge because she wanted to humiliate the company publicly because she thought it was making horrible commercials. This prompted the company to file a defamation action against Elle in state court. In response to that suit, Elle filed a Title VII suit against Tiger Productions, alleging that its filing of the defamation action against her constituted unlawful retaliation in violation of §704(a). The company subsequently filed a motion to dismiss for failure to state a claim upon which relief can be granted. How should the trial court rule on the company's motion?

5. After D.J. Sing heard that her co-employee, Elle Woods, had filed a sexual harassment charge with the EEOC against her supervisor at Tiger Productions, Sing wrote a letter to the editor of the local newspaper criticizing her employer for tolerating a working environment in which female employees were subjected to unlawful acts of sexual harassment by their supervisors. Her letter was published, and when company president L.N. Nordgreen read the article, she instructed her vice president for human resources to discharge Sing. Sing then filed a Title VII action against Tiger Productions, alleging that she had been discharged in retaliation for writing the letter to the newspaper. After Sing's discharge, bur prior to her filing of her retaliation suit, the EEOC dismissed Woods's harassment charge on the ground that it found no reasonable cause to believe that a violation had occurred. Tiger Productions filed a motion to dismiss for failure to state a claim upon which relief can be granted. How should the trial court rule on that motion?

6. D.J. Sing's sister, Phyllis Nickelson, worked in the post-production department at Tiger Productions. After Nickelson filed her third sex discrimination charge with the EEOC, all of which were dismissed as non-meritorious, the company fired Sing. Sing then filed a Title VII action against Tiger Productions, alleging that she had been the victim of a retaliatory discharge in violation of §704(a). How should the trial court rule on the company's motion to dismiss for failure to state a claim upon which relief can be granted?

Explanations

The Lady and the Tiger

1. The court will grant the motion. The undisputed facts indicate that the company had dual motives for discharging the plaintiff—retaliation for filing an EEOC charge (which is protected participation conduct) and excessive absenteeism and tardiness. Although the Supreme Court has not ruled on this issue, the prevailing view among those circuit courts is that mixed motive analysis is available for retaliation claims. This then raises the issue of whether the impact of the same decision defense goes

to the issue of liability, as initially declared by the Supreme Court in *Price Waterhouse*, or whether the change to the mixed motive doctrine effected by the 1991 Civil Rights Act—limiting the impact of the same decision defense to the issue of remedies—applies to retaliation claims. The prevailing view is that because the mixed motive provisions codified in Title VII by the 1991 Act refer only to claims brought under §703, these provisions do not apply to §704(a) retaliation claims. Thus, the courts conclude, mixed motive analysis in retaliation claims is governed by the doctrine set forth in *Price Waterhouse*. This, in turn, means that the employer's same decision defense is a complete defense to liability. And since the undisputed evidence is that the plaintiff would have been fired for absenteeism and tardiness irrespective of her filing that harassment charge with the EEOC, this same decision defense insulates the defendant from liability, and so its motion will be granted.

2. The court will grant the motion. Section 704(a) of Title VII requires that the participation constitute involvement in a proceeding brought under "this" Title, i.e., involvement in some Title VII proceeding. The plaintiff had filed an age discrimination charge, which is not covered by Title VII. Thus, since the allegedly motivating cause of the retaliation was the filing of an age discrimination charge under the ADEA and not Title VII, the plaintiff cannot state a claim under §704(a), and so the court will grant the motion. The fact that the defendant maintained that the ADEA charge was non-meritorious is irrelevant to a retaliation claim based on participation.

3. The motion will be denied. The issue here is whether involvement in an employer-initiated internal investigation of a matter that has not been the subject of any official Title VII proceeding constitutes protected participation or opposition conduct under §704(a). This was precisely the issue before the Supreme Court in *Crawford*. There, the Court declined to rule on whether or not participation in an employer-initiated investigation that was not linked to an official Title VII enforcement proceeding constitutes participation within the meaning of §704(a). The lower courts have split on this question. Some have concluded that participation is limited to involvement in an official Title VII enforcement proceeding. Others have extended the meaning of participation to involvement in employer-initiated internal investigations, but only when that investigation was prompted by the filing of an EEOC charge. Here, the employer conducted an investigation in the absence of any pending or threatened EEOC charge. Consequently, the plaintiff will not be found to have engaged in a protected act of participation. However, the *Crawford* Court also held that involvement in an employer-initiated investigation could constitute protected opposition conduct, rejecting the defendant's argument that opposition conduct had to be either

repetitive or plaintiff-initiated. Consequently, the plaintiff's response to the employer-initiated questioning will be considered opposition conduct since it meets the *Crawford* standard of communicating the plaintiff's belief to the employer that the employer has engaged in unlawful discrimination (here, harassment). And since the plaintiff has alleged protected opposition conduct, an adverse action (discharge), and causation, she has stated a claim under §704(a), and the company's motion will be denied.

4. The motion should be denied. Here, the issue is whether the plaintiff has suffered an adverse action in response to her act of participation. In *Burlington Northern*, the Court held that the employer's retaliatory response does not have to be employment-related to constitute an adverse action for purposes of §704(a). Rather, the test is whether that response would discourage a reasonable person under all the same circumstances from engaging in protected conduct. Thus, the question here is whether the filing of a defamation action would be discouraging to the reasonable employee. Most courts probably would conclude that the *Burlington Northern* test is satisfied under these circumstances and, therefore, that this constitutes an adverse action. Since the plaintiff has alleged that this action was prompted by her protected participation activity of filing a harassment charge, she has stated a claim. And since the plaintiff engaged in participation, the fact that her charge was baseless and ill-motivated does not remove it from the protection of §704(a). Therefore, the motion will be denied.

5. The motion should be denied, although it is a close call. Here, the plaintiff has engaged in a classic form of opposition activity, i.e., an informal protest against what she believed was unlawful conduct by her employer. But opposition conduct is only protected activity under §704(a) if the actor harbors a reasonable belief that she is indeed complaining about activity that is made unlawful by Title VII. This means, however, that the plaintiff's opposition conduct will be protected even if she is wrong about the lawfulness of the protested employer conduct, if that mistake is a reasonable mistake of law or fact. So, the fact that the EEOC determined that the sexual harassment charge that prompted the plaintiff's letter was baseless is not fatal to her claim, particularly since this occurred *after* she wrote the letter and after it was published. Under these circumstances, and even though there is no suggestion that the plaintiff did anything to independently corroborate the truth of the harassment allegation contained in Elle's EEOC charge, a court probably would conclude that even if the plaintiff was mistaken about either the facts (what the supervisor did or did not do) or the law (whether the conduct amounted to unlawful harassment), that was a reasonable mistake. Finally, though the form of the opposition activity can remove it from the category of protected

conduct, writing a letter is not unlawful and would not be deemed so destructive of the employer's legitimate interests to remove it from protection under §704(a). Accordingly, the plaintiff has alleged that she engaged in protected opposition conduct, that she suffered an adverse action (discharge), and that there was a causal link between these two events. Therefore, she has stated a claim of retaliation, and the defense motion will be denied.

6. This motion probably will be denied. In *Thompson*, the Supreme Court recognized the existence of a third-party retaliation claim but did not define which relationships would qualify for such a claim. But since the adverse action here was a discharge and since the plaintiff is the brother of the person who engaged in the protected act of participation, it is likely that the courts would find this relationship sufficiently close to fall within the holding of *Thompson*. Accordingly, the plaintiff will be allowed to pursue this claim and so the defense motion should be denied.

Specific Issues Involving the Five Protected Classifications: Race, Color, Religion, Sex, and National Origin

A. RELIGION-BASED DISCRIMINATION AND THE DUTY TO ACCOMMODATE

Among the amendments to Title VII, enacted in 1972, was a provision expanding upon the statutory prohibition against discrimination on the basis of religion. In 1972, Congress added a new definitional provision to §701 that, for the first time, defined religion. The text of §701(j) requires employers to "reasonably accommodate" an employee or prospective employee's religious observance, practice, or belief, unless the employer demonstrates that doing so would impose an "undue hardship" on the conduct of its business. In Trans World Airlines, Inc. v. Hardison, 432 U.S. 63 (1977), the Supreme Court issued an extremely restrictive interpretation of the duty to accommodate. Hardison involved an employee whose religious convictions prevented him from working on the Sabbath day. But pursuant to the terms of a collective bargaining agreement between the airline and the union that represented its workers, shift assignments were based on seniority. And Hardison had insufficient seniority to obtain a non-Saturday shift. Moreover, although the union unsuccessfully attempted to find a worker who would voluntary swap shifts with Hardison, it was unwilling to allow the employer to violate the terms of that contractual seniority provision. Hardison was discharged when he refused to work on a Saturday after the parties could not agree on an accommodation. The Supreme

Court offered three reasons for its determination that the employer had not violated its statutory duty to make a reasonable accommodation. First, it ruled, the duty to accommodate did not require an employer to violate the terms of an otherwise valid collective bargaining agreement, particularly a seniority provision. Second, the duty to accommodate did not mandate "unequal treatment" in the sense of requiring the employer to provide a benefit to one employee because of his religious observance that it would deny to another employee who did not possess such a religious conviction or belief. Finally, the Court added that an accommodation would impose an undue hardship upon the employer if it required that employer to bear more than a "*de minimis*" cost. Although the Court did not make any reference to this factor, it is likely that the Court's narrow interpretation of the duty to accommodate religious beliefs was a response to the potential First Amendment Establishment Clause problem associated with governmental mandate of religion-based decision-making. For that reason, perhaps, the constitutionality of §701(j) uniformly has been upheld by the lower courts.

In addition to the statutory definition, the cases inform us that religion or religious belief includes moral or ethical values that occupy a place in someone's life akin to theistic belief, including atheism's commitment to an absence of religious belief.

Traditionally, post-Hardison, the courts required the plaintiff alleging failure to meet the statutory duty to accommodate to establish that he or she adhered to a religious belief or practice that was in conflict with a term or condition of employment, that the employee requested an accommodation, and that the employer continued to enforce that term of employment. At that point, the courts ruled, the burden shifts to the employer to persuade the fact-finder that it made a good faith effort to accommodate and either that it did make a reasonable accommodation or that it was unable to reasonably accommodate without an undue hardship.

But in *EEOC v. Abercrombie & Fitch Stores, Inc.*, 135 S. Ct. 2028 (2015), the Court examined the question of whether the plaintiff must affirmatively inform the employer of a religious mandate that requires an accommodation or whether it is sufficient if the employer has indirect notice of the need for an accommodation. In that case, the plaintiff, a Muslim woman, had been denied employment by the defendant company because the headscarf that she wore in compliance with her religion's requirements conflicted with the company's "Look Policy." This company policy prohibited employees from wearing "caps" (a term undefined by the policy) as not in compliance with Abercrombie's desired image. The plaintiff wore a headscarf during her job interview. The interviewer rated her as qualified, but informed also her supervisor of the fact that the plaintiff had worn a headscarf during the interview and that the interviewer believed that that plaintiff wore the headscarf because of her faith. The plaintiff was not hired. The Supreme Court ruled that an applicant asserting a claim of religious discrimination under Title VII only needs to establish that the need for an accommodation was a motivating factor in the employer's decision not to hire her. Since, the Court explained, the essence of any intentional discrimination (as opposed to disproportionate impact) claim is the allegation that the employer took an action in order to discriminate, which in this context means the desire to avoid the statutory duty to accommodate, if the employer acts for the purpose of avoiding an accommodation, it has violated Title VII even if it has only an unsubstantiated suspicion that an accommodation would actually be needed. It is the desire to avoid accommodation, rather than concrete knowledge that the plaintiff wants or needs an accommodation, that constitutes unlawful religion-based discrimination. Accordingly, as long as the plaintiff can prove that his or her religious practice was factored into the decision-making process, the plaintiff can establish a prima facie case.

Additionally, in *Ansonia Board of Education v. Philbrook*, 479 U.S. 60 (1986), the Supreme Court ruled that the duty to accommodate is satisfied as long as the employer makes a reasonable accommodation; the employer does not have to implement the most reasonable or desirable (to the plaintiff) accommodation. So, for example, the employer's decision to provide unpaid leave for religious observance when the plaintiff had requested paid leave typically would be viewed as a reasonable accommodation. Additionally, subsequent circuit court cases reveal that in order to be deemed reasonable, a proposed accommodation does not always have to completely eliminate the religious conflict. A partial elimination of the conflict could be reasonable, for example, when completely eliminating the conflict would impose an undue hardship upon the employer.

Although §701(j) expressly imposes the duty to accommodate solely upon an "employer," the lower courts uniformly apply that duty to unions and, *Hardison* notwithstanding, require unions to offer substituted payment accommodations to members whose religious views prohibit them from being required to pay dues (tithes) to non-religious entities, even where the cost to the union in lost dues could be described as greater than *de minimis*. The courts also recognize the availability of a claim of religion-based harassment, subject to the same proof formula applied to claims of sex- or race-based harassment. Finally, as the duty to accommodate is a component of the duty not to discriminate on the basis of religion, religious organizations that are exempted from the duty not to discriminate on the basis of religion by either §§702(a) or 703(e)(2) are similarly relieved from the duty to accommodate.

Examples

Of Mice and Men

1. Lennie Small, president of Computer Peripherals, Inc., a deeply religious man who believed in daily Bible readings, held a mandatory prayer session at the beginning of every work day. George Milton, an avowed atheist, refused to attend the prayer sessions and requested an accommodation that would excuse him from attending these sessions. Small denied the request on the ground that granting it would so deeply offend his own religious convictions that he could not bear the spiritual cost that this accommodation would impose upon him. Milton filed a Title VII action against Computer Peripherals, alleging that he had been discriminated against on the basis of his religion as a consequence of Small's refusal to accommodate him. On the basis of these undisputed facts, the company filed a motion for judgment as a matter of law on the ground that making this accommodation would impose an undue hardship. How should the court rule on this motion?

2. Candy Kane complained to her supervisor at Computer Peripherals that nearly all of her co-workers constantly used profane language and engaged in vulgar conduct in the workplace, which deeply offended her sincerely held religious beliefs and values. When the company ignored her concerns, she brought a Title VII action against it, alleging that she had been the victim of religious discrimination. The company filed a motion to dismiss for failure to state a claim upon which relief can be granted. How should the trial court rule on that motion?

3. Jamaal Carlson, a devout Muslim, was employed as a janitor by the St. Stephens Baptist Church. Carlson had a small office/changing room in the church basement. He had attached several images of the prophet Mohammed on the walls and had pasted a small star and crescent on the mouse attached to his laptop computer. When church authorities demanded that he remove these religious images and objects, Carlson refused and thereafter was discharged. Carlson filed a Title VII action against the church alleging that by refusing to accommodate his religious beliefs, the church had discriminated against him on the basis of his religion. The church filed a motion to dismiss for failure to state a claim upon which relief can be granted. How should the trial court rule on that motion?

Explanations

Of Mice and Men

1. The court will deny the motion. Section 701(j) requires an employer to make a reasonable accommodation unless it would impose an undue hardship on the conduct of the employer's *business*. Here, the defense is claiming that the proposed accommodation would unduly burden the religious values of its president. There is no evidence that the accommodation would have any impact on the company's business, only a spiritual hardship upon its president. Moreover, even if the company had alleged that excusing one employee from the mandatory prayer sessions would impose a spiritual hardship upon the company, the cases indicate that the defendant would have to link such a spiritual hardship to a demonstrable adverse impact upon the company's economic well-being. Finally, the fact that the plaintiff is an atheist does not exempt him from the coverage of §701(j). The courts uniformly hold that atheism fits within the statutory definition of religion. Thus, as there is no evidence that this accommodation would negatively impact the company's economic well-being, the company has not established undue hardship as a matter of law, and so the court will deny this motion.

2. The motion will be granted. Here, the issue is whether the plaintiff can state a claim of religion-based harassment. The courts recognize the availability of such a claim and impose the same evidentiary standard used in race- and sex-based harassment cases. Consequently, to establish a prima facie case, the plaintiff would have to allege and prove that the conduct was sufficiently severe or pervasive to create an abusive or hostile environment to her and to a reasonable person and that the conduct was both unwelcomed by her and undertaken because of her religion. Even if these facts meet the severe or pervasive standard sufficient to create an objectively and subjectively hostile environment, and though the plaintiff has alleged that the conduct was unwelcomed by her, the plaintiff has not alleged that the conduct was undertaken by the co-employees because of her religion. Consequently, her claim would fail, and the court would grant the motion to dismiss.

3. The motion will be granted. The church enjoys an exemption from the statutory duty not to discriminate on the basis of religion per §702(a). Consequently, it also has no duty to accommodate any employee's religious beliefs. Therefore, the motion will be granted.

B. NATIONAL ORIGIN–BASED DISCRIMINATION

There is no definition of "national origin" contained in Title VII. Nor is there any meaningful amount of legislative history addressing this topic. In *Espinoza v. Farah Manufacturing Co.*, 414 U.S. 86 (1973), the Supreme Court declared that Congress intended for this term to refer to the country of origin of the plaintiff and/or his or her ancestors. But, the Court added, "national origin" did not embrace discrimination on the basis of alienage, i.e., lack of U.S. citizenship. Thus, the Court held, Farah Manufacturing could lawfully limit employment to U.S. citizens, and the plaintiff, a Mexican national who was lawfully residing in the United States, could not state a claim of either intentional or disparate impact discrimination on the basis of national origin since over 96 percent of Farah's employees were of Mexican ancestry. Note, however, that although an alien cannot state a Title VII claim challenging a decision based on her lack of U.S. citizenship, since Title VII protects "individuals," an alien can state a claim for discrimination on the basis of any of the five enumerated classifications. So, for example, if an employer refused to hire aliens from European countries but employed aliens from Asian nations, the excluded individuals could assert a national origin–based claim.

Some interpretive issues have arisen concerning the meaning of "national origin." For example, it extends to countries that no longer exist as geopolitical entities at the time of litigation on the theory that national origin–based animus can persist after the changing of traditional political structures and boundaries. Affiliation with any particular Native American tribe is deemed to be a matter of national origin because these tribes historically were considered to be nations by the American government. Ethnic groups whose members come from a variety of different countries, such as Arabs, Hispanics, and Cajuns, have been held to constitute a national origin within the meaning of Title VII. And national origin, like beauty, is deemed to be in the eye of the beholder in the sense that what is important to a claim of intentional discrimination based on national origin is whether the decision-maker believed the plaintiff to have a particular national ancestry.

The employment of undocumented aliens, however, raises different issues. The Immigration Reform and Control Act of 1986 (IRCA), 8 U.S.C. §1324a, prohibits the employment and job referral of undocumented (lacking authorization for either permanent residence or employment) aliens and requires employers, unions, and employment agencies to demand the presentation of specifically prescribed forms of documentation verifying an individual's lawful status. And this statute has been construed to mean that an undocumented alien is not entitled to the protections of Title VII because the IRCA renders the undocumented person ineligible for employment. At the same time, however, the IRCA prohibits employers with more than three employees from discriminating against documented alien workers on the basis of national origin or citizenship, except where such discrimination by a public employer is permitted or required by law, or where a lawfully resident alien is competing against an "equally qualified" American citizen. The IRCA also contains an anti-retaliation provision comparable to §704(a) of Title VII.

Some of the most challenging issues relating to national origin discrimination arise in contexts where the employer's facially neutral policy is alleged to produce a disparate impact on persons based on their national origin or where the defendant asserts that national origin is a bona fide occupational qualification. For example, employers that forbid their multilingual employees from speaking Spanish on the job unless they are communicating with a customer could be said to have a disparate impact on persons who come from Spanish-speaking countries. Although the circuit courts do not adhere to a uniform position, the prevailing view is to reject such claims on the ground that these facially neutral English-only rules (the rules are applied to all employees regardless of ancestry) only impact the multilingual workers' desire to speak in their native language, an interest, the courts conclude, that is neither immutable nor statutorily protected and, therefore, one to which impact analysis should not apply. A majority of the circuits that have ruled on the matter also reject the plaintiffs' claims that such rules create a national origin–based hostile working environment. On the other hand, where an employer rejects an applicant because of his foreign accent, the courts typically find that the plaintiff has stated a prima facie claim of intentional national origin discrimination, and the case boils down to whether or not the employer can establish that the absence of that sort of accent is a bona fide occupational qualification (BFOQ) and not merely the product of a distaste for foreign accents on the part of the company, its employees, or its clients.

As is true when the BFOQ defense is asserted in cases alleging intentional discrimination on the basis of sex or religion, §703(e)(1) is very narrowly construed in cases involving claims of national origin bias. As discussed in Chapter 5, the BFOQ defense is most commonly raised in cases where the defendant claims that possession of a particular ancestry is necessary to promote the authenticity of its operations, such as cases involving persons employed as chefs or in customer-contact positions in ethnic restaurants.

Examples

Fur and Away

1. Amanda Hite-Jones, a British subject who was lawfully admitted for permanent residence in the United States and who possessed work authorization, applied for employment with America Furs, Inc. (AFI), a manufacturer and retailer of fake furs that proudly advertised that all of

its employees were American citizens. Pursuant to its American citizens–only policy, AFI rejected Amanda's application. In its rejection letter, the company noted that it was impressed by Hite-Jones and would employ her if and when she became a U.S. citizen. The letter noted that several AFI employees were Americans of English ancestry and that the company would be happy to add to that number. Nevertheless, Amanda filed suit against AFI under Title VII, alleging that its decision discriminated against her on the basis of her national origin. How should the trial court rule on AFI's motion to dismiss her complaint for failure to state a claim upon which relief can be granted?

2. If you were the lawyer for Hite-Jones, what advice would you offer to enhance her ability to successfully challenge the company's decision to reject her application for employment?

3. Suppose that Amanda Hite-Jones was an American citizen but that her application for employment with AFI was rejected because the hiring official believed that Hite-Jones was of Iraqi ancestry and that hiring such a person would be terrible for employee morale and customer relations. Assume also that it turned out that Hite-Jones was of German ancestry and that the company employed many German Americans. If Hite-Jones filed a Title VII suit alleging national origin–based discrimination, how should the trial court rule on the company's motion to dismiss for failure to state a claim upon which relief can be granted?

Explanations

Fur and Away

1. The motion will be granted. In *Espinoza*, the Supreme Court made it clear that Title VII's prohibition against discrimination on the basis of national origin does not encompass discrimination on the basis of citizenship. The fact that the company employs Americans of British ancestry also demonstrates that citizenship is not being used as a pretext for national origin–based discrimination. Thus, Amanda cannot state a claim of intentional discrimination on the basis of national origin. She could state a disparate impact–based claim if she could proffer evidence that the company's citizenship requirement had a disparate impact on U.S. citizens with British ancestry. But the facts indicate that the company employs American citizens of British ancestry, and so that impact claim also would fail. Thus, the court will grant the defense motion and dismiss this Title VII claim.

2. You should advise her to file a claim under the IRCA. As an authorized alien, i.e., a lawfully permanent resident alien who has work authorization, she is protected by the IRCA against discrimination on the basis of citizenship, a level of protection that is not afforded by Title VII. She will

be able to state a claim under the IRCA for citizenship discrimination and will win unless the company can prove that it rejected her in favor of an equally qualified American citizen.

3. The motion will be denied. Assuming that the American citizen plaintiff can prove that she was rejected for employment because the company official believed her to be of Iraqi ancestry, the fact that she actually is a German American would not preclude her from stating a claim of national origin discrimination. The relevant question in such a claim of intentional discrimination on the basis of national origin is whether the decision-maker believed the plaintiff to be of a particular national origin, not whether that belief was factual. Consequently, the plaintiff can state a claim and the defense motion to dismiss will be denied.

C. DISCRIMINATION ON THE BASIS OF RACE AND COLOR

The fact that §703(a) prohibits discrimination on the basis of both race and color certainly suggests that Congress did not intend for these two terms to be coterminous. Yet, although there is a substantial amount of scholarship addressing the complex question of the meaning of race, and though this issue was addressed by the Supreme Court in a case filed under 42 U.S.C. §1981, one of the Reconstruction Civil Rights Acts, the Supreme Court never has defined the term for Title VII purposes. However, in *McDonald v. Santa Fe Trail Transportation Co.*, 427 U.S. 273 (1976), the Court ruled that a Title VII claim of racial discrimination can be filed by a member of any race, be it a majority or minority racial group.

It is important to determine whether a plaintiff's claim is race- or national origin–based because the BFOQ defense is not available in race or color cases, but can be asserted in response to a charge of national origin discrimination. The few cases involving charges of color discrimination involve claims by a dark-skinned person that she or he was discriminated against in favor of a light-skinned person of the same racial group, or vice versa. One interesting interpretive question has arisen in cases where the employer discriminates against individuals who are engaged in an inter-racial relationship. In these cases, the employer employs members of all races but will not hire or retain a member of any race who is involved in an interracial relationship. Of the few circuits that have examined this issue, a majority conclude that the plaintiff can state a claim of race-based discrimination under these circumstances. They conclude that since race is at the heart of the employer's policy, the plaintiff's race was a factor in the decision and, therefore, she can state a claim of racial discrimination. The minority view is that as long as the employer applies this ban on interracial relationships to members of all races, the plaintiff cannot establish that she is being discriminated against on the basis of her race.

D. DISCRIMINATION ON THE BASIS OF SEX

I. Introduction

Of the five forbidden bases of classification under Title VII, the one that has generated the widest array of interpretive questions is the prohibition against discrimination on the basis of sex. The meaning of "because of . . . sex"—text that was added to the bill on the day before its enactment by a member of the U.S. House of Representatives in a desperate attempt to derail passage of the entire statute—has arisen in connection with challenges to employer policies that discriminate on the basis of pregnancy, grooming standards, harassment, sexual orientation, and longevity. We shall address each of these issues in turn.

Before turning to these specific issues concerning the meaning of sex discrimination, a quick general reminder about sexual harassment claims. Under Title VII, charges of sexual harassment are treated like all other claims of sex-based discrimination in the sense that the plaintiff always must establish that s/he was subjected to the allegedly harassing conduct because of his or her sex. Turn back to Chapter 5 for a discussion of what constitutes actionable harassment, regardless of whether it is sex-, race-, or national origin–based. Later in this chapter, however, we examine issues that have arisen with respect to whether or not harassment occurred "because of sex" within the meaning of Title VII.

2. The "Sex-Plus" Doctrine

In a series of cases involving employment policies that excluded some, but not all, men or women, the courts developed a "sex-plus" theory to explain their rulings. The doctrine can be traced to the Supreme Court's decision in *Phillips v. Martin Marietta Corp.*, 400 U.S. 542 (1971), although the Court never actually used that term nor did it invoke the doctrine associated with it. In *Phillips*, the defendant would not hire or retain women with pre-school aged children. It did not, however, restrict the employment of men with such children. In a brief per curiam opinion, the Court unanimously agreed that this policy facially discriminated on the basis of sex since it imposed a requirement—no pre-school aged children—on females that it did not impose on males. The fact that the employer did not preclude all females from employment was irrelevant; it was enough that the employer applied "one hiring policy for women and another for men." Having concluded that the plaintiff established a prima facie claim of intentional discrimination, the Court, over the objection of Justice Marshall, remanded the case for determination of whether the company could establish that sex was a BFOQ based on its assertion that female, but not male, employees with pre-school aged children bore conflicting family obligations that would detract from their job performance.

In a flood of post-*Phillips* cases, the circuit courts developed the "sex-plus" framework for analyzing employer policies that discriminated against a subset of one of the two sex groups, i.e., on the basis of "sex plus" a facially neutral qualification. Most of these cases arose in the context of sex-differentiated grooming codes or other requirements relating to an individual's appearance or manner of presentation. All of these cases, like *Phillips*, involved a sex-differentiated policy in the sense that men and women were subjected to different standards or a single standard was applied only to members of one sex. Although the *Phillips* Court had ruled that the pre-school aged children standard constituted intentional sex-based discrimination on its face, the circuit courts have sought to limit the ruling in *Phillips* by adding a component to that ruling that was never mentioned by the *Phillips* Court. Specifically, in an attempt to distinguish the ruling in *Phillips* from their handling of grooming code cases, the circuit courts confected the "sex-plus" theory. Under this doctrine, the fact that the policy is sex-differentiated does not, by itself, establish a prima facie case. Rather, evidence that the employer has implemented a sex-differentiated employment policy will establish a prima facie case of sex-based discrimination only if the plaintiff also demonstrates that the "plus" factor that is applied to members of only one sex affects either an immutable characteristic or a fundamental right. Under this theory, the no-pre-school aged children policy of *Phillips* can be explained on the ground that the plus factor—having pre-school aged children—affected the fundamentally protected right to bear and raise children. In comparison, the courts routinely uphold grooming codes that, for example, impose different hair length, weight, uniform (as long as both sexes are required to wear some kind of uniform; an employer rule that required only women to wear a uniform has been struck down as facially discriminatory on the basis of sex), or marital status requirements on male and female employees on the ground that none of these factors affects an immutable characteristic or a fundamentally protected right.

More recently, some circuits have amended the sex-plus doctrine by replacing the immutability or fundamental right requirement with an examination of whether compliance with the "plus" requirement would impose an "undue burden" on women or men. In *Jesperson v. Harrah's Operating Co., Inc.*, 444 F.3d 1104 (9th Cir. 2006) (*en banc*), the entire Ninth Circuit found that the fact that the employer implemented a sex-differentiated grooming and appearance code (by requiring women to wear makeup and prohibiting men from doing the same) did not *per se* establish a prima facie claim of sex discrimination. It required evidence that the policy imposed an undue burden on women as a group and found that the plaintiff had not offered sufficient evidence to establish such an undue burden, rejecting the plaintiff's request that it take judicial notice of the fact that makeup costs money and takes time to apply.

In applying this sex-plus theory, the circuit courts have rejected the plaintiffs' claim that sex-differentiated policies are predicated upon and perpetuate a stereotyped view of women and, therefore, constitute the form of sex-based discrimination recognized by the Supreme Court in *Price Waterhouse*. They hold that stereotype analysis is simply inapplicable to grooming/appearance code cases. The Ninth Circuit's *en banc* ruling in *Jesperson* constitutes a limited exception to this general pattern. There, the court held that sex-stereotyping analysis could be applied in grooming/appearance code cases, but only where the plaintiff also could establish that the policy was adopted with an intention either to compel women to adhere to stereotyped expectations or to objectify women as sexual objects.

3. Discrimination on the Basis of Pregnancy

With sex-plus theory firmly entrenched in Title VII jurisprudence, the Supreme Court eventually had to determine whether, and to what extent, that doctrine was relevant to employer policies that discriminated against pregnant workers and job applicants. In *General Electric Co. v. Gilbert*, 429 U.S. 125 (1976), the Court ruled that a private employer's non-occupational disability plan that covered all conditions other than pregnancy did not discriminate against its female employees on the basis of their sex in violation of Title VII. The Court rested this ruling on its determination that the monetary value of the comprehensive-save-for-pregnancy benefit package that was provided to female employees was comparable to the fully comprehensive policy that was made available to the company's male employees. The following year, in *Nashville Gas Co. v. Satty*, 434 U.S. 136 (1977), the Court limited the impact of its ruling in *General Electric* in a case involving a non-occupational disability policy that (1) provided paid leave for all disabling conditions other than pregnancy (pregnant workers could take an unpaid leave of absence), and (2) required pregnant workers to forfeit accumulated job seniority upon returning to work after childbirth while permitting full retention of accumulated seniority for individuals who took disability-based leave for any other reason. Adhering to *General Electric*, the Court found that the sick leave portion of the disability policy did not discriminate on the basis of sex because the total value of the disability policies provided to men and women was the same. However, the Court also ruled that although the seniority policy was sex-neutral on its face, it had a disparate impact on women because denial of seniority imposed a burden on (pregnant) women that men did not suffer. In the Court's view, denying women the benefit of paid leave was distinguishable from burdening them with a loss of seniority. Both of these rulings were highly controversial and led ultimately to Congress's enactment of the Pregnancy Discrimination Act of 1978 (PDA). This statute added a new sub-section (k) to §701, the definitions provision of Title VII, expressly defining sex discrimination to include distinctions based on pregnancy.

Thus, under §701(k), the pregnancy-based distinction found in General Electric's disability policy would constitute sex-based discrimination within the meaning of Title VII. And in *Newport News Shipbuilding & Dry Dock Co. v. EEOC*, 462 U.S. 669 (1983), the Supreme Court ruled that this amendment also prohibited an employer from providing less favorable pregnancy-based health benefits to employee spouses than it did for all other spousal health benefits contained in the company's employee benefit package. But in *AT&T Corp. v. Hulteen*, 129 S. Ct. 1962 (2009), the Supreme Court ruled that a pension plan that provided limited years-of-service credit for individuals who took pregnancy leave prior to the enactment of the PDA while giving full credit for disability leaves taken during that same period for any other reason did not constitute sex-based discrimination in violation of Title VII. Section 703(h) of Title VII protects the employer from liability for sex-based benefit differentials that are produced by a bona fide seniority system unless those differentials are found to have been the result of an intention to discriminate. The Court reasoned that since pregnancy-based discrimination was lawful prior to the enactment of the PDA, the limitation on pregnancy leaves taken during that pre-PDA period could not have been intended by the company to violate Title VII. Thus, under these circumstances, the fact that the seniority system operated to the disadvantage of employees on the basis of pregnancy did not render it unlawful. In response to the enactment of the PDA, employers were required either to eliminate their disability and health benefit packages entirely or to amend them to treat pregnancy the same as other covered conditions. This led to an interesting question concerning the lawfulness of benefit packages that provided very limited benefits for all covered conditions. While facially neutral, an issue was raised whether a particularly short period of paid or even unpaid leave for all conditions might create an unlawfully disparate impact on women because pregnancy was more likely to require a longer period of leave than many, if not most, other covered conditions. The courts, however, have not been receptive to this impact-based claim, primarily because they construe the "equal treatment" language of the second clause of §701(k) (requiring pregnant workers to be treated the same as other persons similarly able or unable to work) as reflecting congressional intent to codify only an equal treatment (and, therefore, not a disparate impact) theory of pregnancy discrimination. And despite the fact that the codification of impact analysis in Title VII as a consequence of the 1991 Civil Rights Act amendments does not expressly exclude (or include) pregnancy claims from the coverage of that provision, a majority of the circuits continue not to recognize the applicability of impact analysis in cases alleging discrimination on the basis of pregnancy.

But the California legislature did address this concern when it enacted a statute requiring employers covered by Title VII to provide only pregnant workers with up to four months of unpaid disability leave as well as the right to return to that or a substantially similar job. In *California Federal Savings & Loan Assn. v. Guerra*, 479 U.S. 272 (1987), the Supreme Court held that this preferential-to-pregnancy benefit did not violate the portion of §701(k) that required pregnant workers to be treated "the same for all employment-related purposes" as nonpregnant employees. Since the PDA's legislative history reflected Congress's intention to enhance the ability of women to fully participate in the workforce without sacrificing their participation in family life, the Court concluded that the PDA was intended to create only a minimum level of protection for pregnant workers that could be enhanced by state legislation. Thus, it held, although Title VII did not require such accommodation/preferential-to-pregnancy benefits, this form of preferential treatment of pregnancy did not constitute sex-based discrimination forbidden by §§701(k) or 703(a).

Having determined in *Guerra* that the provision in §701(k) requiring that pregnant employees be treated the same for employment-related purposes as nonpregnant workers did not prevent states from enacting laws mandating preferential-to-pregnancy benefits, the Supreme Court inevitably had to determine whether that same provision also meant that pregnant employees must be provided every employment benefit that is accorded to any other category of employee. This issue was resolved in *Young v. United Parcel Service, Inc.*, 135 S. Ct. 1338 (2015). There, the employer required all drivers to manipulate packages weighing up to 70 pounds and to assist in moving packages weighing up to 150 pounds. Additionally, the governing collective bargaining agreement provided for temporary alternative work for workers who were unable to perform normal work assignments because of an on-the-job injury. Pursuant to that obligation, the company offered light duty work to employees (1) who were either injured on the job or (2) who suffered from any permanent impairment cognizable under the Americans with Disabilities Act (ADA). But it did not extend this option for light duty work to any female worker whose limitation arose solely as a result of her pregnancy. The plaintiffs argued that the PDA required that pregnant workers be granted "most favored nation" status, i.e., that any benefit allotted to any other group also had to be extended to pregnant workers. The company, on the other hand, argued that since its light duty accommodation was denied to all individuals whose disability was the result of a nonoccupational occurrence and which was not a disability covered by the ADA, it was not discriminating against pregnant workers. The Supreme Court took a middle position. It rejected the plaintiff's contention that the PDA granted pregnant workers a "most-favored-nation" status. But it also concluded that the fact that the employer's accommodation was denied to both pregnant and nonpregnant workers with a nonoccupational disability that was not protected by the ADA did not immunize the employer from liability. Rather, it said, the plaintiff could prevail if it could establish that the employer's policy imposed a significant burden on pregnant workers by offering evidence that the employer accommodated a large percentage (but not all) of its nonpregnant workers while not accommodating a large percentage of pregnant workers. Section 701(k) defines "because of sex" to include because of pregnancy, childbirth, "or related medical conditions." A denial of requests for leave or other benefits on the basis of such pregnancy-related behaviors as breastfeeding has been held not to fall within this definition. But the circuit courts have disagreed on whether a denial of benefits on the basis of infertility falls within the meaning of the amendment. Some circuits hold that since both men and women can suffer from infertility, fertility-based distinctions are not a form of intentional discrimination on the basis of sex. And some courts also have rejected the assertion that since women undergo a majority of fertility treatments, a policy that denies leave or other benefits to infertile workers creates a disparate impact upon women. On the other hand, at least one circuit has held that denying a female worker's request for leave in order to undergo in vitro fertilization constituted sex-based discrimination since this surgical procedure is performed only on women. A female worker who was discharged for having an abortion was held to be able to state a cognizable claim of sex discrimination under Title VII on the ground that an abortion is a "related medical condition" within the meaning of §701(k). However, §701(k) expressly states that although an employer is permitted to include abortion coverage within its health benefits plan, it is not required to do so, except that where the life of the mother is endangered by carrying the pregnancy to term, the abortion would have to be covered to the same degree as other conditions.

In *International Union, U.A.W. v. Johnson Controls*, 499 U.S. 187 (1991), the Court ruled that an employer policy prohibiting fertile women, but not fertile men, from holding lead-exposure jobs was facially discriminatory on the basis of sex for two separate reasons. First, the policy applied only to women. And second, classifying employees on the basis of potential for pregnancy fell within the meaning of §701(k)'s definition of sex-based discrimination.

Keep in mind that pregnancy-based discrimination, like all other forms of intentional sex-based discrimination, is subject to the BFOQ defense. And the same is true of the job-relatedness/business necessity defense with respect to claims alleging disparate impact on pregnant workers.

4. An Aside: The Family and Medical Leave Act of 1993

Some issues concerning the rights of male and female workers to leave for child-rearing have been addressed by Congress through the enactment of the Family and Medical Leave Act of 1993 (FMLA), 29 U.S.C. §§2601 et seq. Employers with more than 50 employees must provide eligible employees, male and female, with up to 12 weeks of unpaid leave in any 12-month period to provide infant care (after childbirth or adoption) or to provide care for a child, spouse, or parent suffering from a "serious health condition." It also requires employers to provide unpaid leave to an employee when it is prompted by that employee's own illness, although the employer can require that the employee exhaust accrued paid leave before requesting unpaid family leave.

This statute expressly covers state and local governmental workers and provides them with a cause of action for monetary damages. In *Nevada Dept. of Human Resources v. Hibbs*, 538 U.S. 721 (2003), the Supreme Court resolved a conflict among the circuits by upholding the constitutionality of this portion of the Act as it applied to the provision requiring unpaid leave to take care of a family member with a serious health condition. Applying the bipartite "congruence and proportionality" standard it previously announced in cases challenging Congress's abrogation of state sovereign immunity, the Court held that this enactment (1) contained a legislative record revealing a pattern of state unconstitutional gender-based conduct and (2) exhibited congruence and proportionality between the injury to be prevented or remedied and the means adopted to that end. Accordingly, it ruled that Congress had constitutionally abrogated sovereign immunity pursuant to its authority under §5 of the Fourteenth Amendment. However, in *Coleman v. Court of Appeals of Maryland*, 132 S. Ct. 1327 (2012), a five-member majority of the Court agreed that the FMLA's self-care provision did not validly abrogate the state's immunity from suit for damages in federal court and struck it down. A four-member plurality held that this provision failed to meet the "congruence and proportionality" test. The plurality reasoned that in contrast to the family-care provision of the FMLA, the self-care provision was not passed in response to a well-documented pattern of state constitutional violations accompanied by a remedy drawn in narrow terms to address or prevent those violations. The plurality also rejected the argument that the self-care provision was such a necessary adjunct to the family-care provision that it should fall within the holding in *Hibbs*. Justice Scalia provided the fifth vote to strike down this portion of the FMLA. He reiterated his objection to the use of the "congruence and proportionality" test, and reasserted that the proper approach was to ask whether the conduct that the statute in question forbade violated the Fourteenth Amendment. Since it was manifest to him that failing to grant state employees leave for the purpose of self-care did not violate the Fourteenth Amendment, the remedies provision had to fall.

5. Discrimination on the Basis of Sexual Orientation

Although the Supreme Court has never ruled directly on this issue, the lower courts unanimously agree that the prohibition against discrimination on the basis of "sex" does not extend to discrimination on the basis of sexual orientation *per se* or, for that matter, on the basis of other forms of gender identity, such as where the plaintiff is bisexual, transsexual, or a transvestite. Over the five decades since Title VII was enacted, a variety of bills have been offered to either amend Title VII or to enact a free-standing statute that would prohibit discrimination on the basis of sexual orientation, but these efforts have not succeeded. Thus, unless and until proposed legislation such as the pending Employment Nondiscrimination Act (ENDA) is enacted, private sector employers who discriminate expressly on the basis of sexual orientation will not be subject to liability under Title VII. More than a score of state legislatures have enacted laws that prohibit sexual orientation–based discrimination in, *inter alia*, employment, and these statutes typically apply to both the public and private sectors.

Policies implemented by public employers that discriminate on the basis of sexual orientation are subject to federal constitutional challenge under the equal protection and due process guarantees of the Fifth and Fourteenth Amendments, the free speech and association provisions of the First Amendment, and the constitutional right to privacy. But the case law demonstrates that these challenges are rarely successful. Equal protection challenges to sexual orientation classifications are subjected to the most lenient form of rational basis scrutiny, in which the courts almost always determine that a rational basis supports the government's use of sexual orientation as a factor in decision-making. First Amendment challenges fail whenever the government employer bases its decision on either actually engaging in homosexual activity or making declarations of status that are deemed to reveal the propensity or intent to do so (as exemplified by the military's "don't ask, don't tell" policy that has been regularly upheld by the courts) on the ground that this Amendment applies only to government regulation of speech and not of conduct. Privacy and due process challenges also are unsuccessful either on the ground that the privacy interest protects only against government interference with consensual sexual conduct

149

within the confine of one's home, or because the government's decision is found to sufficiently promote an important governmental interest.

The absence of sexual orientation from the list of Title VII's prohibited classifications, however, has not totally eliminated Title VII from consideration in employment discrimination cases involving gay persons and individuals with other gender identities. First, applying a sexual orientation requirement only to male or female applicants or employees would constitute unlawful sex-based discrimination. But even in cases involving the facially neutral application of an anti-homosexuality policy, the courts increasingly are becoming receptive to claims predicated on the sex-stereotyping theory of sex discrimination first recognized by the Supreme Court in *Price Waterhouse*. Where a complaint avoids alleging discrimination on the basis of sexual orientation *per se* (i.e., the mere fact of the plaintiff's sexual orientation) but, instead, alleges discrimination on the basis of sex in the form of adverse action prompted by the plaintiff's failure to conform to the employer's stereotyped version of how a man or woman should act or present himself or herself, several courts have recognized the existence of a cognizable cause of action and denied defense motions testing the legal sufficiency of such claims. However, when it comes to ruling on the merits, most courts uphold the employer's action on the ground that they are unable to separate the plaintiff's claim of sex stereotyping from the defense argument that its decision was based on the plaintiff's sexual orientation.

The issue of sexual orientation also arises in cases of so-called "same sex" sexual harassment, i.e., where the alleged perpetrator and victim are members of the same sex. In *Oncale v. Sundowner Offshore Services, Inc.*, 523 U.S. 75 (1998), the Supreme Court unanimously reversed the Fifth Circuit's blanket ruling that a male plaintiff who alleged that he had been harassed by other male employees could not state a cognizable claim under Title VII because Title VII did not prohibit discrimination on the basis of sexual orientation. The Supreme Court ruled that the relevant issue in all harassment cases, regardless of the sexual identity of the harasser and victim, is whether the harassment occurred because of the plaintiff's sex. The fact that both the harasser and victim are men, the Court reasoned, was not automatically fatal to such a claim. Sexual harassment, the Court explained, can occur because of sexual desire or as the result of hostility toward the presence of men or women in the workplace, and either motivation very well could be present in a same-sex harassment situation. One method of proving sex-linked causation is to offer comparative evidence of the harasser's treatment of men and women. (This was unavailable to the plaintiff in *Oncale* because he worked in a single-sex workplace.) Alternatively, evidence that the same-sex supervisor was gay can be the basis of an inference that the plaintiff would not have been the target of the harasser's sexually oriented advances had the plaintiff been a member of the opposite sex. In that instance, although the sexual orientation of the harasser is relevant, it is relevant only in determining whether the plaintiff was harassed because of his sex. However, since the sexual orientation of the victim is irrelevant to this calculation, the plaintiff is not alleging that he was harassed because of his sexual orientation. On the other hand, in a few cases involving an allegedly bisexual supervisor who harassed both men and women, the courts have held that a plaintiff cannot establish that the harassment happened because of the plaintiff's sex unless the nature of the harassment was itself gender-focused or more degrading to members of one sex. Finally, same-sex harassment cases are also subject to the sex-stereotyping theory of sex discrimination, i.e., where the plaintiff alleges that s/he was subjected to harassment for failing to conform to a gendered stereotype.

6. Reliance on Sex-Based Actuarial Tables

Like pregnancy, longevity is another manifestation of a difference between the sexes. Although longevity, unlike pregnancy, is not necessarily a function of biological differentiation, it remains a demonstrably sex-linked characteristic. Consequently, when employers seek to discriminate in the distribution of job benefits on the basis of sex-based actuarial tables that verify assumptions about the average lifespan of men and women, the courts have had to determine whether reliance on these actuarial tables operates as a proxy for unlawful sex-based discrimination. In *Los Angeles Dept. of Water & Power v. Manhart*, 435 U.S. 702 (1978), the Supreme Court held that requiring female employees to make larger contributions to a pension fund than male employees in order to receive the same monthly benefits after retirement constituted sex discrimination in violation of Title VII. The Court rejected the employer's argument that the contributions differential was justified by the actuarially verifiable assumption that the average female employee would live longer and, therefore, receive more post-retirement payments than the average male employee. Even though the Court acknowledged that women as a class outlived men as a class, it ruled that Title VII required employers to treat employees on an individual basis and not on the basis of their membership in a gender group. Thus, the use of sex-segregated actuarial tables violated Title VII's ban on sex discrimination regardless of whether those tables accurately predicted the comparatively greater longevity of women as a class. And in *Arizona Governing Committee v. Norris*, 463 U.S. 1073 (1983), the Court extended this analysis to the pay-out stage of a retirement plan. The *Norris* court struck down as unlawful sex discrimination violative of Title VII a state employer's deferred compensation plan that relied on sex-based mortality tables in setting the level of benefits to be received by employees who elected to receive the deferred compensation in the form of post-retirement monthly annuities. Under this plan, males received larger monthly payments than females who deferred the same amount of compensation and who retired at the same age, based on the assumption that women would live longer and, therefore, receive more monthly post-retirement payments. But since the plan treated individual women differently than individual similarly situated men (i.e., with equal amount of deferred compensation and the same retirement age), the Court held that the employer had discriminated against these women on the basis of their sex.

Examples

A Whale of a Story

1. Moby Dicks, Inc. (MDI), a private investigating firm, employs 30 private investigators and 50 support personnel. The company follows a strict policy of requiring all of its male investigators to have short, cropped hair so that they can easily wear wigs and other disguises in the conduct of their sensitive investigations. When Johnny ("Captain") Ahab initially was hired by MDI, he complied with the company's hair-length policy. But over the years, as he became more and more intensely driven to find a missing high stakes gambler who had failed to make good on a large debt owed to a Las Vegas casino, Ahab chose to ignore this and other personal grooming habits and refused the instructions of his supervisor, Orfan Ishmael, to cut his hair. After refusing a direct order from Ishmael to cut his hair, Ahab was discharged for failure to abide by the company's hair-length policy. He filed a Title VII action against MDI, alleging that he had been discriminatorily terminated because of his sex, even though he admitted that the policy was implemented for the reason stated in that policy. The company filed a motion to dismiss the complaint for failure to state a claim upon which relief can be granted. How should the trial court rule on this motion?

2. Moby Dicks, Inc. (MDI) has a comprehensive health insurance plan that provides coverage for all medical expenses incurred by an employee on behalf of that employee and his or her spouse. The plan also provides coverage for the children of all MDI employees, subject to one exception. Children up to the age of 20 were covered for all medical expenses except those relating to pregnancy. After clerical employee Jo Jo Starbuck's daughter became pregnant, Starbuck applied for reimbursement of her daughter's medical expenses. When the company refused to cover the costs associated with the daughter's pregnancy, Starbuck filed a Title VII action, alleging that she had been discriminated against on the basis of her sex. How should the trial court rule on MDI's motion to

dismiss the complaint for failure to state a claim upon which relief can be granted?

3. Marie Queequeg had been employed as an investigator with Moby Dicks, Inc. (MDI) for 13 years before she became pregnant. On the day that she learned that she was two weeks pregnant, Queequeg shared this news only with her closest friend and co-worker, Jane Stubb. One week after telling Stubb of her pregnancy, Queequeg received a letter from her supervisor, Ike Tashtego, informing Queequeg that she had been discharged. Tashtego had been on vacation for the month prior to the day he wrote the letter. Feeling like she had been struck by a harpoon, Queequeg filed a sex-discrimination claim under Title VII against MDI, alleging that she had been discharged because of her pregnancy. In conjunction with its motion for summary judgment, the company submitted an affidavit from Stubb averring that she never informed anyone at MDI of Queequeg's pregnancy. The plaintiff offered no affidavits or other discovery documents in response to the defense motion. How should the court rule on the defense motion for summary judgment?

4. Moby Dicks, Inc. (MDI) offers health insurance to all of its employees. The plan is funded by contributions from the company and participating workers. The plan is comprehensive and covers all medical costs incurred by its employees. It does not include spousal or dependent child coverage. Relying on its actuarial tables, the insurance company charges MDI a higher premium for covering female workers because the tables demonstrate that the average woman incurs higher medical expenses than the average man, regardless of age. As a result, the company requires all participating female employees to pay a set monthly premium that is $100 more than the monthly premium charged to participating male employees. Trudy Flask, a female MDI employee who elected to participate in the plan, filed a Title VII action against MDI, alleging that by requiring participating female employees to pay a higher monthly premium, the company was discriminating against them on the basis of their sex. How should the trial court rule on MDI's motion to dismiss the complaint for failure to state a claim upon which relief can be granted?

5. Parsi Fedallah, a male investigator employed by Moby Dicks, Inc. (MDI), was subjected to a barrage of remarks from his male supervisor and male co-workers, including statements that "you walk and talk like a girl, so you really must be a girl," "I hope I never have a son who acts like you," and "go and get us some coffee like a good girl." After the last such occasion, Fedallah's supervisor, Ulysses Pequod, called him into his office and said, "Look Fedallah, things are just not working out here for you. I can't send a guy who talks and walks like you do out on a case involving rough and tough characters. So I am afraid that you are fired." Fedallah filed a Title VII action against MDI, alleging that he had been discharged

because of his sex, citing all of the above stated facts in support of his claim. In response, the company filed a motion to dismiss the complaint for failure to state a claim upon which relief can be granted. How should the trial court rule on that motion?

Explanations

A Whale of a Story

1. The court will grant the motion. Here, the company has a sex-differentiated policy in that it requires only male investigators to have short, cropped hair. But since the company is not discriminating overtly against all male employees, the courts would treat this as a "sex-plus" case. This means that the fact that the employer enforced a sex-differentiated policy would not, by itself, suffice to establish a prima facie case of sex-based discrimination. Rather, relying on the Supreme Court's ruling in Phillips, the courts would inquire as to whether the "plus" characteristic — here, hair length — was either immutable or a fundamentally protected right. In all the cases in which grooming codes related to hair length have been challenged, the courts have determined that hair-length restrictions do not affect either an immutable characteristic or a fundamental right. Additionally, all but one of the circuit courts expressly refuse to apply Price Waterhouse sex-stereotyped analysis to grooming code cases. And though the Ninth Circuit has deviated from this pattern, it will only recognize a sex-stereotype claim in a grooming code case when the plaintiff can establish that the grooming code was implemented for the purpose either of enforcing a sex stereotype or to demean the plaintiff's gender group. But the complaint acknowledges that the policy was implemented for a different purpose, and so the courts will conclude that the plaintiff cannot state a claim of sex-based discrimination and it will grant the company's motion.

2. The court will grant the motion. Although §701(k) defines discrimination on the basis of sex to include discrimination on the basis of pregnancy, the question here is whether the plaintiff is being discriminated against on the basis of her sex. In Newport News, the Supreme Court ruled that a company that provides comprehensive coverage for the spouses of female employee, but does not include pregnancy coverage for the spouses of male employees, does discriminate on the basis of sex with respect to a term or condition of employment (fringe benefit of spousal coverage) of male employees. But the Court also noted, albeit in dictum, that limiting pregnancy coverage for children would not violate Title VII's ban on sex discrimination since both male and female employees could have a pregnant child whose coverage would be limited. Since that is what is

happening here, the plaintiff does not have a cognizable claim of sex discrimination, and the motion to dismiss will be granted.

3. The court will grant the motion. Where the plaintiff alleges that she was the victim of pregnancy discrimination, she must prove that the adverse action occurred because of her pregnancy. And to establish causation, the courts require that the plaintiff establish that the employer knew of her pregnancy at the time of the adverse action. Sometimes that can occur by common eyesight. But particularly where the alleged adverse action occurred very early in the pregnancy, when there is no visual evidence of the pregnancy, the courts require other evidence that the employer knew of the pregnancy. Here, the adverse action occurred only three weeks after the beginning of the pregnancy, and so the supervisor could not have visually determined the existence of the pregnancy, particularly because he had not even seen the plaintiff after she became pregnant since he had been on vacation until the day he wrote the letter of discharge. And the defense has submitted an uncontradicted affidavit that establishes a lack of knowledge on the company's part. Accordingly, the court will find that the plaintiff has not established causation as a matter of law and will grant the defense motion.

4. The court will deny the motion. In *Manhart*, the Supreme Court held that even when a company's differential benefit is based on an actuarially verifiable assumption that the cost of providing that benefit is greater to women as a class than to men as a class, such differential treatment constitutes unlawful discrimination on the basis of sex because Title VII requires each individual to be treated without regard to his or her membership in a gender group. Moreover, the fact that this is a non-mandatory term or condition of employment is irrelevant to that determination. By making all participating women pay higher insurance premiums than all participating men because of a statistically demonstrable difference in the cost of providing that benefit to women as a class, the employer, per *Manhart*, is discriminating against each individual woman on the basis of her sex. Accordingly, the plaintiff can state a claim of sex discrimination under Title VII, and the court will deny the defense motion to dismiss.

5. The court should deny the motion. The issue here is whether the court will view the plaintiff's complaint as stating a claim of discrimination on the basis of sex or on the basis of sexual orientation. If the court construes the complaint to assert a claim of discrimination on the basis of sexual orientation, the complaint will be dismissed for failure to state a cognizable claim since Title VII does not prohibit discrimination based expressly on sexual orientation. However, on the face of the complaint, the plaintiff has alleged sex-based discrimination. And the factual allegations, which are taken as true for the purposes of ruling on a Rule 12(b)(6) motion to dismiss for failure to *state* a claim, indicate that the

plaintiff is alleging that he was fired because of the way in which he behaved or presented himself, i.e., for failing to conform to the company's stereotyped view of how a man should present himself. In light of that, the court should deny the motion. Applying the teachings of *Price Waterhouse*, the court should conclude that the plaintiff has at least stated a claim of sex stereotyping that, under *Price Waterhouse*, is a form of sex discrimination. Accordingly, the court should deny the defense motion.

Enforcement: Procedures

A. TITLE VII PROCEDURAL REQUIREMENTS FOR NONFEDERAL EMPLOYEES: OVERVIEW

When Congress enacted Title VII, it designed a complex of procedural requirements designed to accomplish several objectives. Among the most prominent was a desire to confect an administrative system that would encourage the resolution of employment discrimination disputes at the state and federal administrative level so as not to overburden the federal courts with the task of resolving the anticipated flood of discrimination suits filed under this law, thereby promoting both administrative enforcement and federal-state comity. To accomplish this, however, the statute erects a maze of state and federal administrative prerequisites to filing suit that does not necessarily operate to promote these intended or desired objectives. This pattern was followed, with some modifications, in the subsequently enacted Age Discrimination in Employment Act (ADEA) and the Americans with Disabilities Act (ADA). So, once you are familiar with the enforcement regime that was created for Title VII, you already understand most of what you need to know about the procedural requirements governing claims brought under these other two statutes. To the extent that there are some meaningful differences between the requirements imposed in the ADEA and ADA, and there are a few, they will be discussed in the chapters devoted expressly to each of those enactments.

In Title VII, Congress created the Equal Employment Opportunity Commission (EEOC), a federal agency tasked with interpreting and, to a limited degree, enforcing the terms of the statute. Although, as we will see, the EEOC is responsible for investigating and adjudicating discrimination charges, Congress chose not to provide it with any cease-and-desist power or other authority to require a covered entity to comply with the statute. It is only authorized to issue interpretive guidelines, investigate alleged violations, determine whether or not reasonable cause exists to believe that a violation occurs, attempt voluntary compliance, or bring suit against a union, employment agency, or private sector employer. And because §717 of Title VII provides a separate enforcement mechanism for federal government workers, that scheme will be examined separately in this chapter.

B. THE FIRST STEP: FEDERAL AND STATE ADMINISTRATIVE CHARGES

The enforcement of Title VII commences with the filing of a "charge" alleging a statutory violation (an "unlawful employment practice"). Per §706(b), that charge can be filed by either the aggrieved, by some third person or entity "on behalf" of the aggrieved, or by a member of the EEOC. In order to preserve one's right to file suit under Title VII, there are a host of steps one must invoke. Notice that the operative word here is "invoke." Oftentimes in administrative law, we talk in terms of "exhaustion" of administrative remedies. That is not the case under Title VII. Although Congress erected these administrative prerequisites to encourage state and federal administrative disposition of discrimination charges, the fact of the matter is that the statute only requires a person to invoke these administrative remedies as a prerequisite to filing suit under Title VII. An aggrieved individual who is intent on filing suit is not required to exhaust any administrative proceeding to the point of completion.

If the alleged violation occurred in the overwhelming majority of states that have both a state or local law (hereinafter referred to collectively as state law) that prohibits the alleged unlawful employment practice and a state or local agency (hereinafter referred to collectively as state agency or state authority) authorized to grant or seek relief from such a practice (called a "deferral state"), the first step that a Title VII grievant must take, per §706(c), is to file a charge of discrimination alleging a violation of that state law with the state enforcing authority. The grievant can choose to let that process play out until its conclusion, with the possibility of appealing that administrative decision through the state court system as a method of enforcing his or her state statutory rights. But in order to preserve the right to pursue relief under Title VII, §706(c) requires only that the grievant file the state law-based charge with the state enforcing agency and wait a minimum of 60 days, unless the state agency proceedings have terminated before the end of that period. After the 60-day period has expired, or after state agency proceedings have terminated, whichever comes first, the grievant is entitled to take the next required step — the filing of a discrimination charge with the EEOC.

Section 706(b) requires that the EEOC charge be made under oath and in writing. The EEOC historically has provided a charge form designed to be filled out by a lay individual at an agency office. And the Supreme Court has issued a couple of opinions that are intended to ease the pleading burden on lay grievants. For example, in *Federal Express Corp. v. Holowecki*, 128 S. Ct. 1147 (2008), a case brought under the ADEA and not Title VII, the Supreme Court upheld the reasonableness of the position codified in the EEOC's guidelines that a document (such as a letter or an intake questionnaire filled out at an EEOC office) meets the statutory requirement of a "charge" as long as it alleges a covered act of discrimination and the name of the responding party in a manner and form that reasonably can be construed to request agency action and appropriate relief. However, language in the opinion cautioned workers and their attorneys not to assume that this decision would extend to charges filed under Title VII. That issue remains in doubt. Also, several years prior to its ruling in *Holowecki*, the Court, in *Edelman v. Lynchburg College*, 535 U.S. 928 (2002), upheld the reasonableness of an EEOC regulation that permitted charges to be amended to cure technical defects or omissions, such as the absence of a verification (oath) and, most importantly, provided that the date of the amendment related back to the date of the original filing. The *Edelman* Court ruled that the defect in a timely filed, but unverified charge was cured by the filing of an amended, verified charge that had been filed no more than 300 days after the alleged unlawful employment practice. This "relation back" rule, however, would not apply to amendments that involve substantive changes to the grievant's allegations, such as newly asserted theories for relief or newly sought remedies.

Section 706(e)(1) mandates that the EEOC charge must be filed no later than 300 days after the occurrence of the alleged unlawful employment practice or 30 days after state agency proceedings have terminated, whichever comes first. Thus, absent a quick termination of state proceedings, the combination of the requirements that the EEOC charge must be filed no later than 300 days after the alleged act of discrimination, and no sooner than 60 days after the filing of a charge under state law with the state enforcing entity, means that to preserve her Title VII right of action, the grievant must file with the state enforcement agency no later than 240 days after the alleged act of discrimination. Again, this time frame only applies to a grievant who wants to preserve his right to file suit under Title VII. Title VII does not contain any limitations period governing the filing of a state law charge of discrimination with the state enforcing agency that could affect the continued viability of the state law claim. That is governed by state law.

Conversely, compliance with the state limitations period is not a prerequisite to preserving one's right to file suit under Title VII. In *EEOC v. Commercial Office Products Co.*, 486 U.S. 107 (1988), the Supreme Court ruled that a charging party was entitled to the full 300-day filing period in a deferral state irrespective of whether the claimant's state law charge had been timely filed under state law. The only requirement, as noted by the Court in *Mohasco Corp. v. Silver*, 447 U.S. 807 (1980), is that the state charge be filed with the state agency within 240 days after the alleged unlawful employment practice so that the charging party can wait the required 60 days and still file with the EEOC within its 300-day window.

In order to simplify the charge filing process, the EEOC adopted a "deferral" policy, approved by the Supreme Court in *Love v. Pullman*, 404 U.S. 522 (1972), under which a grievant who files an EEOC charge without initially proceeding with a state law claim will not have that EEOC charge dismissed. Instead, the Commission will refer that charge to the appropriate state agency and defer any further action on its own until the 60-day period has expired. Additionally, many states have entered into a "work sharing agreement" with the EEOC under which both the EEOC and state authority designate the other as its agent for receipt of charges so that a charge received by one partner to the agreement is deemed received by the other. Moreover, these agreements typically provide that the state entity can waive its right to process such a charge referred to it by the EEOC, which has the effect of permitting the federal agency to process the charge without waiting for the §706(c) 60-day period to expire. And many such agreements have an automatic waiver provision, which means that as soon as the charge is filed with the EEOC, the EEOC can begin processing it without going through the motions of referring it back to the state authority. It also means that the grievant need not file with the state agency within 240 days of the unlawful practice, but, instead, has a full 300 days within which to take the initial step of filing a charge with the federal agency. Work sharing agreements were approved by the Supreme Court in *Commercial Office Products*.

On the other hand, if the alleged unlawful employment practice occurs in the few non-deferral states, i.e., those without a state antidiscrimination law and enforcing entity, §706(b) requires the grievant to begin the process by filing a charge with the EEOC within 180 days of the alleged unlawful employment practice.

The timely filing of an EEOC charge is not, however, an inviolable jurisdictional prerequisite to filing suit. In *Zipes v. Trans World Airlines, Inc.*, 455 U.S. 385 (1982), the Supreme Court ruled that the filing period requirement was non-jurisdictional and, therefore, like a statute of limitations or other procedural condition to filing suit, a claim of untimely filing is an affirmative defense that is subject to waiver (i.e., through non-assertion by the defendant), estoppel, and equitable tolling. For example, the courts have tolled the limitations period where (1) the charging party timely filed a charge with the wrong state or federal agency; (2) the EEOC or a state agency misled the charging party concerning the governing time limits; (3) the employer has not complied with its statutory obligation to post notice of its employees' statutory rights and remedies; and (4) the defendant engaged in misrepresentation, intimidation, or other conduct designed to, or which reasonably could be expected to, delay filing with the EEOC. And in *Crown, Cork & Seal Co. v. Parker*, 462 U.S. 345 (1983), the Supreme Court held that the filing of a class action operates to toll the limitations period for filing of charges by class members if the class action is dismissed. On the other hand, in *Int'l Union of Electrical, Radio & Machine Workers, Local 790 v. Robbins & Myers, Inc.*, 429 U.S. 229 (1976), the Supreme Court declared that pursuing some separate, non–Title VII remedy, such as a grievance, does not toll the period within which the EEOC charge must be filed.

Once a charge has been filed with the EEOC, §706(b) requires the EEOC to notify the responding party within ten days and begin its investigation. The Commission can either dismiss the charge for lack of jurisdiction, dismiss the charge based on its determination that there is no reasonable cause to believe that a violation has occurred, or make a finding that reasonable cause does exist to believe that a violation occurred. If the EEOC makes a "reasonable cause" determination, it attempts to obtain voluntary compliance by the responding party through conference, conciliation, and persuasion. In making these reasonable cause determinations, the EEOC is required by §706(b) to give "substantial weight" to any findings previously made by the state enforcing authority.

Although Title VII vested the EEOC with substantial discretion over how to fulfill this statutory obligation to conciliate, the Supreme Court has ruled that the courts have the power to review, to a limited degree, whether or not the Commission has complied with this duty. In *Mach Mining, LLC v. E.E.O.C.*, 135 S. Ct. 1645 (2015), a unanimous Supreme Court ruled that the duty to conciliate includes, at a minimum, the obligation to (1) communicate the nature of the plaintiff's claim to the defendant and (2) engage the employer in either written or oral discussion in order to give the defendant an opportunity to remedy the allegedly discriminatory practice through voluntary compliance. But in reviewing whether or not the Commission has met that standard, courts are to impose a limited scope of review. The role of the courts is limited to verifying the Commission's claim that it actually tried to conciliate. To that end, a sworn affidavit from the agency stating that it performed these tasks will usually suffice. But if the employer provides credible evidence that the agency did not provide the requisite information about the charge or did not attempt to engage in a discussion about conciliating the claim, the court must conduct sufficient fact-finding to resolve that factual question. Beyond that, however, the choice of the methods by which it chooses to conciliate, or the extent of that effort, is left solely to the discretion of the agency.

If within 30 days after a charge has been filed with the EEOC, the Commission has not obtained an acceptable conciliation agreement, it can file suit against a nongovernmental respondent on behalf of the aggrieved or a larger category of individuals. That same suit-filing authority is assigned to the U.S. Attorney General where the respondent is a governmental entity. But, per §706(f)(1), the filing of suit by the EEOC or Attorney General terminates the individual grievant's right to bring her own suit, although the grievant retains the right to intervene in the EEOC action. But where suit has not been filed by the EEOC, §706(f)(1) requires that 180 days after the filing of an EEOC charge, the Commission must notify the aggrieved of its right to bring suit. That same section also provides that suit must be filed no later than 90 days after the "giving" of such notice. The lower courts have construed this latter requirement to mean that the 90-day clock begins on the day the right to sue notice arrives at the claimant's address of record and not the day it was issued. Generally, the circuit courts deem the date of arrival to be the date of actual receipt by the grievant. But sometimes it is impossible to determine precisely the date upon which the claimant actually received the notice, and the circuit courts have not agreed on how to handle such cases. The prevailing rule relies on a rebuttable presumption that receipt occurred three days after the issuance date. A minority of jurisdictions, however, has adopted a five-day rule. And where a dispute exists as to whether, as opposed to when, the right to sue notice was received, the courts apply a "mailbox presumption" commonly used in other forms of civil litigation. Under this rule, proof that the letter was transmitted to the postal service creates a rebuttable presumption that it reached its listed destination and was received by the addressee. Finally, although the circuit courts are willing, in exceptional circumstances, to toll the 90-day limitation period for equitable reasons, in Irwin v. *Veterans Administration*, 498 U.S. 89 (1990), the Court declined to toll the 90-day limit in a case where the right to sue letter was sent to the grievant's attorney while the attorney was out of the country and where the attorney did not learn of the letter until his return, by which time the 90-day limit had expired.

Notwithstanding the express language of §706(f)(1) requiring the EEOC to issue a right to sue letter no later than 180 days after a charge is filed, EEOC regulations require the issuance of a notice of right to sue only when the agency has terminated its proceedings, or at the request of the charging party at the conclusion of the 180-day period. This was done to permit the EEOC to continue to investigate and seek conciliation in cases after the 180-day period had elapsed. This policy was tacitly approved by the Supreme Court in *Occidental Life Ins. Co. v. EEOC*, 432 U.S. 355 (1977). And though some grievants choose this route and only file suit after the EEOC has unsuccessfully (from the grievant's perspective) completed its proceedings (which could be years after the charge was filed) and transmitted the notice of right to sue, there is a risk associated with this strategy. In *Cleveland Newspaper Guild, Local 1 v. Plain Dealer Publishing Co.*, 839 F.2d 1147 (6th Cir. 1988) (en banc), *cert. denied*, 488 U.S. 899 (1988), the plaintiff did not file suit until it received a notice of right to sue more than ten years after the filing of the EEOC charge because it had taken that long for the EEOC to investigate, adjudicate, and complete unsuccessful conciliation efforts. The *en banc* Sixth Circuit upheld the trial court's grant of a defense motion for summary judgment. The courts invoked the doctrine of laches to contract the statutory limitations period for filing suit, ruling that the defendant had been prejudiced by the union's unexplained ten-year delay in filing suit. In so ruling, the courts rejected the union's argument that it was entitled to wait out the EEOC process before filing suit. EEOC regulations also permit the issuance of a notice of right to sue prior to the expiration of the 180-day period where the agency's district director determines that it is probable that the commission will not be able to complete its proceedings within that period of time. The circuit courts currently are split on whether the agency is authorized to promulgate and enforce such a rule.

Title VII Filing Requirements in Non-deferral State

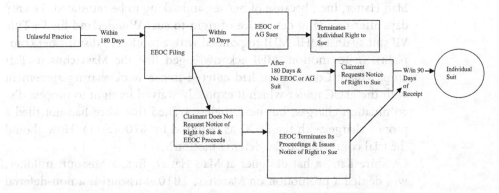

Title VII Filing Requirements in Deferral State

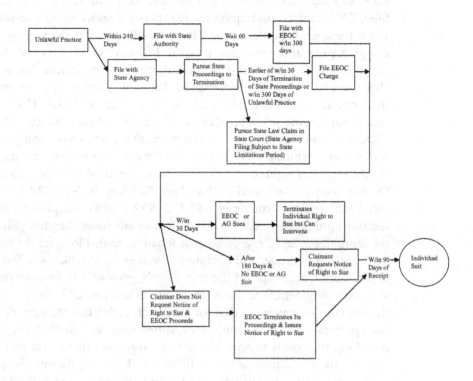

Examples

The White Rabbit's Lament

1. Alice N. Wunderland was terminated by her employer, Mad Hatter, Inc. (MHI), a milliner located in Boston. Within a month of receiving word of her discharge, Alice mailed a verified letter to the local branch of the EEOC, complaining that she had been unlawfully fired by her employer, Mad Hatter, Inc., because of her sex and asking to be reinstated. Twenty days after receiving her notice of right to sue, Wunderland filed a Title VII suit against MHI. MHI responded with a motion to dismiss her complaint. In its motion, MHI acknowledged that the Massachusetts Fair Employment Commission had entered into a work sharing agreement with the EEOC under which it expressly waived its right to process discrimination charges, but nevertheless argued that Alice had not filed a proper charge with the EEOC as required by §706(e)(1). How should the trial court rule on the defense motion?

2. Cheshire Katz, a hat designer at Mad Hatter, Inc., a Missouri milliner, was denied a promotion on March 1, 2010. Missouri is a non-deferral state. Katz filed a sex discrimination charge with the EEOC on August 1,

2010, but neglected to sign and verify it. On November 1, 2010, Katz filed an amended charge that was identical in every way to the original charge except that it was signed and verified. After receiving a notice of right to sue, Katz filed a Title VII action against MHI. MHI subsequently filed a motion to dismiss the complaint on the ground that Katz had failed to timely file a proper charge with the EEOC. How should the court rule on that motion?

3. Bill DeLizard was informed that he had been demoted by his New York employer, Mad Hatters, Inc. (MHI), on January 1, 2010. He challenged that decision by filing sex discrimination charges with the New York Fair Employment Commission on July 1, 2010, and with the EEOC on October 1, 2010. The New York State Antidiscrimination Act requires an aggrieved individual to file a charge of discrimination with the New York Fair Employment Commission within 90 days of the unlawful employment practice. After the state commission dismissed his charge, DeLizard filed suit in New York state court under the state antidiscrimination statute. MHI filed a motion to dismiss that action on the ground that it was barred by the plaintiff's failure to file a timely charge with the New York Fair Employment Commission. How should the trial court rule on that motion?

4. Bill DeLizard was informed that he had been demoted by his New York employer, Mad Hatters, Inc. (MHI), on January 1, 2010. He challenged that decision by filing sex discrimination charges with the New York Fair Employment Commission on July 1, 2010, and with the EEOC on October 1, 2010. The New York State Antidiscrimination Act requires an aggrieved individual to file a charge of discrimination with the New York Fair Employment Commission within 90 days of the unlawful employment practice. Two weeks after receiving a notice of right to sue from the EEOC, DeLizard filed a Title VII action against MHI, alleging that he had been demoted because of his sex. MHI filed a motion to dismiss his complaint on the ground that it was barred by his untimely filing with the state agency. How should the trial court rule on this motion?

5. Mack Turtle was notified that he had been discharged by Mad Hatters, Inc. (MHI), a New York milliner, on January 1, 2010. He challenged that decision by filing a sex discrimination charge, alleging a violation of the New York Antidiscrimination Act, with the New York Fair Employment Commission (which has not entered into a work sharing agreement with the EEOC) 280 days later. Fifteen days later, he received a letter from the state agency announcing that it had dismissed his claim as nonmeritorious. Three days after receiving this letter, Turtle filed a sex discrimination charge with the EEOC. Two weeks after receiving a notice of right to sue from the EEOC, Turtle filed a Title VII action against MHI, alleging that he had been discharged because of his sex. MHI filed a motion to

dismiss the complaint on the ground that it was barred by Turtle's failure to wait 60 days after his state agency filing before filing his charge with the EEOC, as required by §706(c). How should the court rule on this motion?

6. Charles Dodgson was a hat maker employed by Mad Hatter, Inc. (MHI) of Boston. All MHI employees were represented by a union, and MHI and the union had entered into a collective bargaining agreement that contained its own antidiscrimination clause and another clause that required all contractual disputes to be resolved through the contractually created grievance process. After being notified on January 1, 2010, that he had been discharged, Dodgson had his union representative file a grievance on Dodgson's behalf. The grievance process did not produce a final result until October 1, 2010, at which time Dodgson learned that the employer had finally denied his grievance. Massachusetts is a non-deferral state. On October 5, 2010, Dodgson filed a sex discrimination charge with the EEOC, alleging that he had been terminated because of his sex. Dodgson filed a Title VII action against MHI two weeks after receiving a notice of right to sue from the EEOC, alleging that he had been discharged because of his sex. MHI filed a motion to dismiss the complaint on the ground that suit was barred by Dodgson's failure to timely file his EEOC charge. How should the trial court rule on this motion?

7. Queenie Hartz filed a sex discrimination charge with the EEOC against her employer, Mad Hatters, Inc. (MHI), one year after she was notified that she had been discharged. Two weeks after the EEOC dismissed her charge and sent her a notice of her right to sue, Hartz filed a Title VII suit against MHI and received a judgment in her favor. On appeal, MHI argued that the judgment should be reversed because the plaintiff's EEOC charge was not timely filed. How should the appellate court rule?

8. Queenie Hartz filed an EEOC charge against her employer, Mad Hatters, Inc. (MHI), alleging that she had been the victim of sexual harassment. The charge was filed within 100 days of the allegedly harassing conduct. After investigating the claim and finding reasonable cause to believe a violation had occurred, the EEOC terminated its unsuccessful efforts to obtain voluntary compliance on March 1, 2010. It sent a letter via certified mail informing Queenie of these facts and notifying her of her right to bring suit against MHI on April 1, 2010. Queenie had started a sightseeing tour of Asia on March 29, 2010, and did not return home until August 1, 2010. Upon returning home, she discovered the letter from the EEOC and had her attorney file a Title VII sex discrimination suit against MHI on August 5, 2010. MHI filed a motion to dismiss her Title VII complaint as untimely filed. How should the trial court rule on the motion?

Explanations

The White Rabbit's Lament

1. The court should deny the motion. Since the state has entered into a work sharing agreement with the EEOC in which it waived its right to process discrimination charges, Alice's document was timely filed with the EEOC since it was mailed within one month of the allegedly discriminatory discharge. The issue here simply is whether the letter that she sent meets the §706(e)(1) requirement that she timely file a "charge" with the EEOC. In *Holowecki*, the Supreme Court endorsed the EEOC's broad definition of that term, which recognizes any document that alleges a form of proscribed discrimination and names the employer in a manner and form that reasonably can be construed to request agency action and appropriate relief. This letter meets that standard. However, there is one catch. *Holowecki* was an age discrimination case, and the Court expressly cautioned that its decision should not be presumed to extend to charges filed under Title VII. Thus, it remains to be seen whether the lower courts will do so. But in light of the Court's general pattern of endorsing the EEOC's relaxed pleading requirements for lay persons in connection with the filing of EEOC charges under Title VII, it is likely that the ruling in *Holowecki* will be extended to Title VII cases. If so, this motion will be denied.

2. The court will deny the motion. Since the denial of promotion occurred in a non-deferral state, Katz was required by §706(e)(1) to file his charge with the EEOC no later than 180 days from the date of that decision. He did that. But the charge was not formally sufficient since it was unsigned and not verified. But Katz cured those technical defects when he filed an amended charge. And even though that amended charge was filed more than 180 days after the denial of the promotion, the Supreme Court ruled in *Edelman* that amended charges to cure technical defects relate back to the date of the original charge. This "relation back" rule would apply here, and so the amended charge was timely filed. Thus, the defendant's motion will be denied.

3. The court will grant the motion. The key fact here is that the plaintiff filed suit in state court alleging a violation of the state statute. In such a situation, if state law, as here, requires timely invocation of the relevant state administrative remedy, timeliness is defined by state law. The governing state statute here provided a short 90-day filing period with the state agency. The plaintiff filed with the state agency on July 1, i.e., six months (about 180 days) after he was notified of his demotion. Thus, his state administrative filing was untimely under state law, and this will bar his pursuit of the state law claim in state court. So, the trial court will grant the defense motion.

4. The court will deny the motion. It is true that the plaintiff did not file his state charge within the limitations period set by state law. But that limitations period only affects the viability of his state law claim; it does not affect his pursuit of a Title VII claim. In *Commercial Office Products*, the Supreme Court ruled that compliance with the state limitations period is not a prerequisite to preserving one's right to file suit under Title VII. A charging party is entitled to the full 300-day period for filing with the EEOC in a deferral state irrespective of whether the claimant's state law charge has been filed with the state enforcement agency within the state law limitations period. So, since the plaintiff satisfied the key requirements of §§706(c) and (e)(1) — he filed with the state agency, waited at least 60 days (here it was three months or about 90 days after the state filing), and then filed with the EEOC within 300 days of the unlawful practice (here it was nine months or about 270 days after the demotion) — his EEOC charge was timely filed. So, the court will deny this motion.

5. The court will deny this motion. In the absence, as here, of a work sharing agreement between the state and federal agencies, §706(c) does require a claimant to wait 60 days after the filing of a state charge in a deferral state before filing with the EEOC *unless* the state proceedings have been earlier terminated. If the state agency terminates its proceedings before that 60-day waiting period has expired, the claimant can immediately file with the EEOC. In fact, §706(e)(1) requires that in such a situation the claimant must file with the EEOC within 30 days after receiving notice of the termination of the state or local agency proceedings or within 300 days of the unlawful practice, whichever comes first. Here, the state agency terminated its proceedings before the expiration of the 60-day waiting period, which turned out to be 295 days after the unlawful practice. This meant that Turtle had to file his EEOC charge within the next five days to comply with the 300-day EEOC filing deadline in a deferral state. And he did so, filing only three days after receiving notice of the termination of state agency proceedings. He also filed suit two weeks after receiving his notice of right to sue, which is well within the statutory 90-day filing period. So, both his EEOC charge and suit were timely filed and, therefore, the court will deny the defendant's motion to dismiss.

6. The court will grant the motion. Since the unlawful practice occurred in a non-deferral state, the grievant must file his EEOC charge within 180 days of his notification of that decision. Dodgson filed his EEOC charge nine months, or about 270 days after he was notified of his discharge. In *Edelman*, the Supreme Court held that the pursuit of a contractual grievance does not toll the period within which the grievant's EEOC charge must be filed. Thus, Dodgson erred by waiting for his grievance to be

resolved before filing his EEOC charge, and his Title VII suit will be dismissed because of his untimely filed EEOC charge.

7. The appellate court will deny the appeal and uphold the judgment. In *Zipes*, the Supreme Court held that a timely filed EEOC charge was not a jurisdictional prerequisite to suit, but only a procedural precondition that can be waived like other affirmative defenses. By failing to timely challenge the EEOC filing at the trial court level, the defendant has waived this affirmative defense and cannot assert it, for the first time, on appeal. Consequently, the appeal will be denied and the trial court's judgment will be affirmed.

8. The court will grant the motion. Section 706(f)(1) requires a claimant to file suit under Title VII within 90 days after receipt of the EEOC's notice of right to sue. The lower courts have construed this latter requirement to mean that the 90-day clock begins on the day the right to sue notice arrives at the claimant's address of record and not the day it was issued. But the date of receipt does not mean the date on which the claimant actually read the notice of right to sue. If the defendant could not establish the precise date of receipt, i.e., arrival of the notice at the listed address, the courts would employ a presumption that it arrived within three to five days of its issuance. In any event, the courts would not toll the limitations period for the period that the plaintiff was out of the country and, therefore, unable to read the notice. In *Irwin*, for example, the Supreme Court refused to toll the 90-day limit where suit was filed more than 90 days after the letter was received by, although not read by, the claimant's attorney because that attorney had been out of the country when the letter was received. Since the notice of right to sue was issued on April 1, it will be presumed to have been received three to five days thereafter. But since suit was not filed until August 5, i.e., four months or about 120 days after receipt of the notice of right to sue, the complaint will be time barred, and so the defense motion will be granted.

C. DETERMINING THE DATE OF DISCRIMINATION

Section 706(e)(1) requires that an EEOC charge must be filed either within 180 (in a non-deferral state) or 300 (in a deferral state) days "after the alleged unlawful employment practice has occurred." This language was construed by the Supreme Court in *Delaware State College v. Ricks*, 449 U.S. 250 (1980), to mean that the charging period commences on the date that the grievant was notified of the decision. In some cases, the grievant will be notified of the decision after it was made, and in some cases, notice will occur prior to the effective date of the decision. In either case, the limitations period will begin to run from the date of notification, not the date the decision was made or the date on which it became effective. Thus, in *Chardon v. Fernandez*, 454 U.S. 6 (1981), a case filed under §1983, the Supreme Court, relying on *Ricks*, held that a discharge occurs on the date the decision to terminate is communicated to the employee and not the actual date of that discharge.

The process of determining when a "decision" has been communicated has raised several difficult interpretive questions. One occurs when a decision is the product of a multistage process that involves the consideration of recommendations and preliminary decisions by multiple levels of a hierarchical structure. In *Ricks*, for example, the plaintiff's denial of tenure went through several internal stages, including the right to appeal or file a grievance from the decision. In determining when the "decision" was made and communicated, the Court distinguished between tentative decisions or recommendations from a subordinate unit in the decision-making process and the employer's final or official decision. It held that notification of the decision by the highest authority within the defendant university was the act that commenced the running of the limitations period, and that the opportunity for and pendency of an appeal or grievance from an official decision was only an attempt to alter or remedy that decision; it did not extend the date of the decision. Similarly, where a worker becomes aware of discriminatory animus in the decision-making process before the final decision is made and communicated, the circuit courts agree that the limitations period does not begin until the date the grievant was notified of the final decision.

Another important interpretive question arises when a decision produces a subsequent effect. In *Ricks*, pursuant to the defendant's policy, a denial of tenure mandated termination one year thereafter. The Supreme Court held that since termination flowed automatically and inescapably from a denial of tenure, i.e., that there was no separate decision-making process invoked relative to the termination decision, the decision to deny tenure was the only allegedly discriminatory act. The Court distinguished a decision from its effects, ruling that the continuing effects of past discriminatory acts do not constitute current violations; a doctrine that has played an important role in determining the date on which the limitations period begins to run.

This same doctrine previously had been employed by the Court in *United Air Lines, Inc. v. Evans*, 431 U.S. 553 (1997). There, a female flight attendant had been compelled to resign pursuant to the defendant's facially discriminatory policy prohibiting the employment of married female flight attendants. When the defendant subsequently abandoned that policy, it denied the plaintiff's request for reinstatement but did agree to rehire her as a new employee with no seniority credit for her prior service. The plaintiff never timely challenged the no-marriage policy. But after the employer denied her requests to be credited with that previously earned seniority, she filed a charge with the EEOC alleging that her employer had committed a continuing violation because the seniority system perpetuated the effects of the discriminatory no-marriage policy. The Supreme Court held that the plaintiff could not challenge the present day effect of the previously unchallenged (and therefore lawful) no-marriage policy. In so ruling, it rejected the plaintiff's allegation that the denial of seniority credit was simply a part of the employer's continuing violation that began with the no-marriage policy. Instead, it held, the continuing effects of past discrimination did not constitute a separate, present violation. Note, however, that if a plaintiff in a case like *Evans* could successfully challenge the lawfulness of the employer's seniority policy (which Evans could not—it was facially neutral since it denied credit to persons who were discharged or who resigned for any reason), §706(e)(2) now would be directly on point. It states that when a seniority system is alleged to have been adopted for an intentionally discriminatory purpose, the unlawful employment practice is deemed to have occurred either when the system was adopted, when an individual becomes subject to it, or when an aggrieved individual is injured by the application of that system.

The Supreme Court applied the *Evans* rationale to a wage discrimination claim in *Ledbetter v. Goodyear Tire & Rubber Co., Inc.*, 550 U.S. 618 (2007), when it held that the unlawful employment practice occurred when the employer made the pay-setting decision and rejected the plaintiff's contention that a new violation occurred every time she received payment pursuant to that initially unchallenged decision. Congress overturned this precise ruling by enacting the Lilly Ledbetter Fair Pay Act of 2009, which amended Title VII, the ADEA, the ADA, and the Rehabilitation Act to provide that a discriminatory compensation decision occurs each time compensation is paid pursuant to the initial discriminatory pay-setting decision. But since this statute applies only to compensation decisions, the *Evans* no-continuing-effects doctrine remains fully applicable to other alleged forms of discrimination. Additionally, the *Ledbetter* Court distinguished the case at bar from *Bazemore v. Friday*, 478 U.S. 385 (1986), in which the Court allowed an African American plaintiff to use the receipt of a paycheck as the predicate for an EEOC charge that challenged a previously unchallenged racially discriminatory compensation system. The *Ledbetter* Court, and subsequent lower court opinions, read *Bazemore* as allowing an individual to challenge the continuing implementation of a facially discriminatory systemic policy (i.e., date the running of the charge filing period) from the time that facially discriminatory policy initially applied to him.

But in *Lewis v. City of Chicago*, 560 U.S. 205 (2010), a unanimous Supreme Court limited the *Evans* distinction between a decision and its effect to Title VII claims alleging intentional discrimination. In *Lewis*, the Court ruled that where the plaintiff brings a *disparate impact* claim, the discriminatory event for determining the relevant charging period includes any "use" of an employment practice that produces a disparate impact upon a protected class. Consequently, the Court ruled, although the decision to adopt an impact-generating device would constitute a freestanding unlawful employment practice (which would have to be timely challenged), each separate use of that practice by the company constituted a separate violation. The Court distinguished *Evans* and *Ledbetter* as involving allegations of intentional discrimination.

The Supreme Court has recognized, albeit under very limited circumstances, a "continuing violation" doctrine that allows liability to be based on discriminatory conduct that occurred outside the filing period. In *National Railroad Passenger Corp. v. Morgan*, 536 U.S. 101 (2002), the Supreme Court held that the "unlawful employment practice" that must be timely challenged refers to a discrete act that occurred within the charging period. So, if a plaintiff is subjected to multiple acts of discrimination, s/he must file a timely charge with respect to each separate act in order to meet the requirements of §706(3)(1). However, the Court added, hostile environment–based sexual harassment claims are, by their very nature, serial violations. They comprise a series of separate acts, each of which may be individually non-actionable, but whose cumulative impact creates the actionable hostile working environment. Consequently, the Court held, in cases of a hostile environment claim, as long as one of the contributing acts occurred within the filing period, all the component parts of that violation, including those occurring outside the filing period, can be considered. This also means that the plaintiff can recover damages for that portion of the hostile environment that occurred outside the filing period. The Court also noted that the length of time over which a hostile environment claim will be permitted to extend can be circumscribed by the availability of equitable doctrines such as laches and estoppel, when the employer can demonstrate that the plaintiff unreasonably delayed in filing the charge. Note that the Court's decision in *Ledbetter* reflected the *Ledbetter* majority's decision not to extend the *Morgan* serial violation doctrine to a wage discrimination claim. Additionally, in *Mohasco*, *Ledbetter*, and *Morgan*, the Supreme Court expressly declined to rule on whether the filing period for EEOC charges is subject to a discovery doctrine, i.e., whether the filing period commences only when the aggrieved knows or should have known of the unlawful employment practice.

The fact that a prior act of discrimination that is not the subject of a timely filed charge is not actionable (absent waiver of the limitations affirmative defense by the defendant) does not mean that the fact of that prior act is inadmissible. The *Morgan* Court declared that these acts are admissible "as background evidence" of the timely challenged conduct.

Examples

Please Sir, I Need Some More

1. Fay Gin, manager of the customer service department at Artful Dodgers, Inc. (ADI), a sports equipment manufacturing firm, advised John Bumble, the company's president, to discharge Oliver Twist because Twist had repeatedly denied Gin's requests for a sexual liaison. On January 1, 2010, Bumble told Gin to fire Twist. Gin decided to inform Twist at the company picnic on March 1, 2010. Twist filed a charge with the EEOC on August 1, 2010, alleging that he had been discharged because of his sex. After obtaining a notice of right to sue on November 1, 2010, Twist filed a Title VII suit on November 15, 2010. ADI filed a motion to dismiss the suit on the ground that Twist had not filed a timely charge of discrimination with the EEOC. These events took place in a non-deferral state. How should the trial court rule on the defense motion?

2. Suppose that in the preceding example, Gin had informed Twist on January 1, 2010, that Twist had been discharged, and that the discharge would not take effect until March 1, 2010, in order to give Twist some time to find alternative employment. Twist filed his EEOC sex discrimination charge on August 1, 2010. After obtaining a notice of right to sue on November 1, 2010, Twist filed a Title VII suit on November 15, 2010. The company filed a motion to dismiss the suit on the ground that Twist had not filed a timely charge of discrimination with the EEOC. These events took place in a non-deferral state. How should the trial court rule on the defense motion?

3. Nancy Sikeslover, a shipping clerk at Artful Dodgers, Inc. (ADI), had been disciplined by her supervisor, Charley Bates, on several occasions. On January 1, 2010, Bates recommended to company president John Bumble that Sikeslover be terminated. Bumble fumbled around with the decision until March 1, 2010, when he informed Sikeslover that she was being discharged. Sikeslover filed an EEOC charge on August 1, 2010, claiming that she had been discharged because of her sex. After obtaining a notice of right to sue on November 1, 2010, Sikeslover filed a Title VII suit on November 15, 2010. ADI filed a motion to dismiss the suit on the ground that Sikeslover had not filed a timely charge of discrimination with the EEOC. These events took place in a non-deferral state. How should the trial court rule on the defense motion?

4. Suppose that in the preceding example, Bumble had immediately adopted Bates's recommendation and had told Sikeslover that she had been discharged on January 1, 2010. He also codified that decision in a letter, which was received at Sikeslover's address on March 1, 2010. Sikeslover filed her sex discrimination charge with the EEOC on August 1, 2010. After obtaining a notice of right to sue on November 1, 2010, Sikeslover

filed a Title VII suit on November 15, 2010. ADI filed a motion to dismiss the suit on the ground that Sikeslover had not filed a timely charge of discrimination with the EEOC. These events took place in a non-deferral state. How should the trial court rule on the defense motion?

5. Now suppose that in the preceding example, Bumble communicated the decision to discharge Sikeslover via letter that was received at her address on January 1, 2010. The letter also stated that as a unionized worker, Sikeslover had a right, under the governing collective bargaining agreement, to file a grievance challenging that decision. Sikeslover and her union filed a grievance that was finally denied on March 1, 2010. Sikeslover filed her sex discrimination charge with the EEOC on August 1, 2010. After obtaining a notice of right to sue on November 1, 2010, Sikeslover filed a Title VII suit on November 15, 2010. ADI filed a motion to dismiss the suit on the ground that Sikeslover had not filed a timely charge of discrimination with the EEOC. These events took place in a non-deferral state. How should the trial court rule on the defense motion?

6. Bill Sykes, an account manager at Artful Dodgers, Inc. (ADI), was discharged on July 1, 2009. Sykes always believed that he had been discharged because of his race, but for a variety of reasons never challenged that decision. On January 1, 2010, Sykes applied for re-employment with ADI. Pursuant to its policy, which ADI applied without exception, of refusing to rehire any individual who had been discharged for any reason, ADI declined to rehire Sykes. On March 1, 2010, Sykes filed a race discrimination charge with the EEOC, alleging that he had not been rehired because of his previously unlawful, racially based discharge. After obtaining a notice of right to sue on July 1, 2010, Sykes filed a Title VII suit on July 15, 2010. ADI filed a motion to dismiss the suit on the ground that Sykes had not filed a timely charge of discrimination with the EEOC. These events took place in a non-deferral state. How should the trial court rule on the defense motion?

7. Rose May Lee was hired as a sales manager at Artful Dodgers, Inc. (ADI) on July 1, 2009. Unbeknownst to her, Brown Lowe, a male sales manager hired on that same date, was paid $25,000 more than Lee for precisely the same job. On February 1, 2010, all the sales managers were in the staff lounge to receive their monthly paycheck. When Lee saw Lowe's paycheck, she discovered that his salary was significantly higher than hers. She filed an EEOC sex-based wage discrimination charge on July 1, 2010. After obtaining a notice of right to sue on November 1, 2010, Lee filed a Title VII suit on November 15, 2010. The company filed a motion to dismiss the suit on the ground that Lee had not filed a timely charge of discrimination with the EEOC. These events took place in a non-deferral state. How should the trial court rule on the defense motion?

8. Agnes Fleming, a salesperson at Artful Dodgers, Inc. (ADI), was subjected to a constant barrage of sexually demeaning remarks, offensive touchings, and unwanted sexual requests from her supervisor, Noah Claypole. This behavior was a weekly occurrence that began on January 1, 2009, but that appeared to end on August 1, 2009. But when Claypole recommenced his offensive behavior on January 1, 2010, by insisting that Fleming come to his home "for dinner and then something more intimate," Fleming decided to respond. On March 1, 2010, she filed a sexual harassment charge with the EEOC. After obtaining a notice of right to sue on July 1, 2010, Fleming filed a Title VII suit on July 15, 2010. The company filed a motion to dismiss the suit on the ground that Fleming had not filed a timely charge of discrimination with the EEOC with respect to any of Claypole's alleged conduct other than the remarks on January 1, 2010, and that this alleged statement, even if true, constituted nothing more than a single, stray remark that could not, as a matter of law, constitute sexual harassment. How should the court rule on that motion?

Explanations

Please Sir, I Need Some More

1. The motion will be denied. Since this is a non-deferral state, §706(e)(1) requires that the EEOC charge be filed within 180 days of the alleged unlawful employment practice. In *Ricks*, the Supreme Court ruled that this filing period begins on the day that the grievant was notified of the decision, not the day on which the decision was made. The fact that the decision was made by the company president on January 1 and the EEOC charge was filed seven months (or about 210 days) later on August 1 is irrelevant. The filing period began only when the grievant was notified of the decision, and Twist was not informed of the decision to terminate him until March 1, five months (or about 150 days) prior to the EEOC filing. So, since the EEOC charge was filed less than 180 days after the grievant's notification of the alleged unlawful employment practice, the charge was timely filed, and the defense motion will be denied.

2. The motion will be granted. Since this is a non-deferral state, §706(e)(1) requires that the EEOC charge be filed within 180 days of the alleged unlawful employment practice. In *Chardon*, the Supreme Court construed *Ricks* to mean that the EEOC filing period begins on the day that the grievant was notified of the decision, not the day on which the decision became effective. Twist filed his charge seven months (or about 210 days) after being notified of his termination. The fact that the charge was filed only five months (about 150 days) after the effective date of that decision is irrelevant. The charge was untimely filed, and so the defense motion will be granted.

3. The motion will be denied. Since this is a non-deferral state, §706(e)(1) requires that the EEOC charge be filed within 180 days of the alleged unlawful employment practice. In *Ricks*, the Supreme Court ruled that this filing period begins only at the moment of the final decision, not as of the date of an intermediary recommendation or preliminary decision made by a subordinate person in the company's decision-making hierarchy. Here, the final decision was made by company president Bumble on March 1, and so the filing period runs from that date. The EEOC charge was filed five months (or about 150 days) thereafter, and so it was timely filed. Accordingly, the defense motion will be denied.

4. The motion will be granted. Since this is a non-deferral state, §706(e)(1) requires that the EEOC charge be filed within 180 days of the alleged unlawful employment practice. The *Ricks* Court ruled that this filing period begins when the claimant is notified of the adverse decision. Sikeslover was notified verbally by the company president on January 1, which was seven months (about 210 days) before she filed her EEOC charge. The fact that she did not receive the official letter until March 1, 2010, i.e., five months (about 150 days) prior to the filing of her EEOC charge, is irrelevant. The filing period dates from the initial moment of notification, and an oral statement from the company president is sufficiently formal to constitute notification. Therefore, the charge was not timely filed, and the defense motion will be granted.

5. The motion will be granted. Since this is a non-deferral state, §706(e)(1) requires that the EEOC charge be filed within 180 days of the alleged unlawful employment practice. In *Ricks*, the Supreme Court ruled that this filing period begins when the claimant is notified of the adverse decision and that this period is not extended by either the availability or the pendency of an appeal through a grievance procedure. The grievance, the Court reasoned, is an attempt to overturn a decision that already has been made. So, the filing period began to run on January 1, 2010, when Sikeslover was notified of the decision, and not on March 1, 2010, when the grievance process was completed. Since the charge was filed seven months (about 210 days) after the date on which Sikeslover received notification of the termination decision, that charge was untimely, and so the company's motion to dismiss will be granted.

6. The motion will be granted. Since this is a non-deferral state, §706(e)(1) requires that the EEOC charge be filed within 180 days of the alleged unlawful employment practice. In determining the date of the alleged unlawful employment practice, the Supreme Court in *Evans* and *Ricks* distinguished between an unlawful act and its subsequent effects or ramifications. The continuing effects of a prior discrimination do not constitute a separate violation. Here, Sykes is not challenging the company's facially

neutral and consistently applied no-rehire policy. Rather, he is claiming that his racially discriminatory discharge is continuing to haunt him by making him subject to the nondiscriminatory no-rehire rule. Thus, he is challenging the lawfulness of a discharge decision that was made on July 1, 2009, eight months (or about 240 days) before Sykes filed his EEOC charge. The fact that the EEOC charge was filed only two months after Sykes was denied re-employment is irrelevant. The EEOC charge was filed in an untimely fashion, and so the defendant's motion will be granted.

7. The motion will be denied. Since this is a non-deferral state, §706(e)(1) requires that the EEOC charge be filed within 180 days of the alleged unlawful employment practice. The Lily Ledbetter Fair Pay Act of 2009 reversed the Supreme Court's ruling in *Ledbetter* so that a discrete discriminatory compensation decision now is deemed to have occurred not only at the time the level of compensation was set, but each time a worker receives compensation pursuant to that initial pay-setting decision. Each paycheck is now deemed a separate discriminatory act. Therefore, the fact that Lee did not file an EEOC charge until one year after her pay-setting decision is not fatal to the timeliness of that charge. Under the Fair Pay Act, her receipt of a paycheck on February 1, 2010, constitutes a new and discrete discriminatory act that starts a new filing period. Since Lee filed her EEOC charge on July 1, five months (or about 150 days) after receiving her paycheck, the EEOC charge will be deemed to have been timely filed, and so the court will deny the company's motion.

8. The motion will be denied. Since this is a non-deferral state, §706(e)(1) requires that the EEOC charge be filed within 180 days of the alleged unlawful employment practice. In *Morgan*, the Supreme Court applied the "continuing violation" doctrine to sexual harassment claims of a hostile working environment because such claims are, by their nature, serial violations. To prove the existence of a hostile environment, the plaintiff must establish that she had been subjected to severe or pervasive conduct. All but the most egregious individual acts cannot meet this standard; they are individually non-actionable. The violation can be established only when the cumulative impact of the component acts is assessed. Accordingly, the Court ruled, as long as one of the component acts occurred within the filing period (here, 180 days), all the contributing acts can be considered, including those that occurred outside the filing period. All of Claypole's actions can be considered since the final one occurred three months (about 90 days) before Fleming filed her EEOC charge. Therefore, the court will deny ADI's motion.

D. INDIVIDUAL SUITS: PERMISSIBLE SCOPE

Once a grievant has successfully negotiated the procedural hurdles antecedent to filing suit under Title VII, and assuming that the Title VII suit has been filed in a timely manner, another procedural issue often arises. This question concerns the permissible scope of that suit. Specifically, in light of the fact that suit was preceded by the filing of a charge with the EEOC (as well as the filing of a state law charge, where applicable), the courts have struggled with determining whether the scope of the lawsuit should be circumscribed by either the content of the grievant's EEOC charge or, if conducted, the scope of the agency's investigation of that charge. Recognizing that EEOC charges are often filed, and are designed to be filed, by lay persons, the courts have avoided imposing rigid pleading rules that would unnecessarily disadvantage claimants who proceeded through the initial administrative phase of the Title VII enforcement process without the benefit of legal counsel. Although the Supreme Court has not weighed in on this precise issue, the circuit courts have adopted the liberal standard articulated 40 years ago by the Fifth Circuit in *Sanchez v. Standard Brands, Inc.*, 431 F.2d 455 (5th Cir. 1970). Rather than limiting Title VII plaintiffs to the precise allegations contained in a summary EEOC charge, the courts link the scope of a Title VII plaintiff's complaint to "the scope of the EEOC investigation which can reasonably be expected to grow out of the charge of discrimination." But the fact that the courts apply the *Sanchez* standard does not mean that they apply that test the same way under similar circumstances. The circuits can vary on the critical determination of whether a particular basis (race, sex, etc.) or type (harassment, discharge, demotion, etc.) or incident of discrimination falls within the scope of an EEOC investigation that reasonably could be expected to grow out of the claimant's charge. But they generally agree that a charge alleging a particular act of discrimination can reasonably lead to an EEOC investigation of (and, therefore, suit challenging) post-charge conduct and violations. And where a plaintiff filed a specific EEOC charge and then believes that she was retaliated against for filing that charge, the courts do not require the grievant to file a separate retaliation charge with the EEOC as a precondition to including such a retaliation claim in the subsequent court suit. On the other hand, most courts do not allow a suit to contain allegations of a different base of discrimination (race, sex, etc.) than was contained in the EEOC charge. Nor can the plaintiff's complaint include a defendant who was not named in the EEOC charge or, at least, was not a subject of the agency's conciliation efforts.

Responding to the reality that a huge percentage of EEOC charges never result in an investigation since the claimant is entitled to obtain, by request, a notice of right to sue after the passage of 180 days from the date of filing, some circuits have expanded the *Sanchez* doctrine to allow the court in the

Title VII action to consider allegations that would fall within the scope of an investigation that could reasonably have been expected to grow out of the subject charge.

A somewhat related issue arises in multi-plaintiff or class action suits. In these actions, the courts have had to resolve whether an individual who did not file an EEOC charge can join as a plaintiff in a suit brought by someone who did comply, in a timely manner, with the administrative preconditions to suit. Again, the Supreme Court has not spoken. But the overwhelming majority of circuits have adopted, subject to a variety of conditions, a "single filing" or "piggybacking" rule. Under this doctrine, as long as one plaintiff has complied with the procedural preconditions to suit in a timely manner, additional individuals can join a multi-plaintiff or class action even if they did not file an EEOC charge or did not receive a notice of right to sue after filing an EEOC charge. Most courts, however, limit the piggybacking to claims that arise out of the series of events and occur within the same general time period as the claim that was properly filed with the EEOC. Some circuits go further and also require that the filed charge give notice to the employer that the allegations involve class-wide discrimination.

Finally, in *Yellow Freight Sys., Inc. v. Donnelly*, 494 U.S. 820 (1990), the Supreme Court ruled that Title VII actions fall within the concurrent subject matter jurisdiction of the federal and state courts. This means, of course, that the plaintiff can choose to file in state court, but that the defendant can also remove to federal court based on federal question subject matter jurisdiction. Section 706(f)(3) contains the venue provision for suits filed in federal court, permitting the plaintiff to file an action in any federal district in the state where the unlawful practice is alleged to have occurred, in the federal district where the relevant employment records are maintained, or in the federal district where the aggrieved would have worked in the absence of the alleged unlawful practice. And if the defendant cannot be "found" in any of these districts, venue will lie in the district where the defendant's principal office is located.

E. INDIVIDUAL SUITS: PRECLUSIVE EFFECT OF ADMINISTRATIVE AND STATE COURT RULINGS

The text of Title VII not only sets forth the scheduling of administrative filings with the EEOC and, where applicable, state or local enforcement authorities, it also addresses the level of deference that agency determinations should have on the courts in subsequent litigation. Specifically, §706(b) states that in making its reasonable cause determination, the EEOC should give "substantial weight" to findings and orders of the state or local enforcement entities in the antecedent proceedings under state law. On the other hand, as the Supreme Court noted in *McDonnell Douglas*, a Title VII suit is a *de novo* proceeding; i.e., although the EEOC's determinations are admissible and can be considered by the court, the court is not bound in any way by them. A separate issue, however, arises in deferral states, where the Title VII plaintiff is required to at least invoke the state or local law remedy in the appropriate state or local agency. In those situations where state law provides for state court review of state agency findings, to what extent, if any, is the state court's rulings entitled to preclusive effect in the subsequently litigated Title VII suit? In *Kremer v. Chemical Construction Corp.*, 456 U.S. 461 (1982), the Supreme Court ruled that although state *administrative* rulings have no preclusive effect on the court's *de novo* trial of the Title VII claim, traditional rules of preclusion do apply to rulings by a state court on the state law claim as required by the federal Full Faith and Credit Act, 28 U.S.C. §1738. This statute directs federal courts to give the same preclusive effect to state court judgments that a state court of the judgment-rendering state would give to that judgment under that state's rules of preclusion. Ultimately, this means that if a state agency decision is appealed to a state court, that state court's rulings can have preclusive effect on the court's trial of the Title VII action. And that is true regardless of whether it was the claimant or the defendant who initiated the appeal. And to reinforce the limited nature of its ruling in *Kremer*, the Court subsequently held in *Univ. of Tennessee v. Elliott*, 478 U.S. 788 (1986), that an *unreviewed* (by a state court) state administrative decision is not entitled to any preclusive effect on the Title VII claim, regardless of the procedural nature of those administrative proceedings. And *Elliott* has been construed to mean that an unreviewed state administrative ruling is not entitled to preclusive effect in a Title VII suit regardless of whether state preclusion law attaches any preclusive effect to administrative rulings.

F. THE IMPACT OF ARBITRATION AGREEMENTS ON LITIGATING TITLE VII CLAIMS

To an increasing extent, companies are requiring their employees to submit all employment-related disputes, whether of a contractual or statutory nature, to arbitration to the exclusion of all other enforcement mechanisms. Thus, where such arbitration agreements exist and are enforced, a worker has forfeited his right to have his statutory claim decided by a court. (However, enforceable arbitration clauses covering statutory disputes have not been held to preclude the individual from filing an *administrative* charge with the EEOC.) In *14 Penn Plaza LLC v. Pyett*, 556 U.S. 247 (2009), the Supreme Court held that so long as an arbitration agreement, whether contained in a collectively or individually bargained agreement, expressly applies to statutory claims, that agreement will be enforced pursuant to the terms of the Federal Arbitration Act (FAA), 9 U.S.C. §§1-14, 201-208 (1982). However, the FAA provides that the presumption of enforceability of any particular arbitration agreement is subject to rebuttal via defenses grounded in law or in equity, such as unconscionability, fraud, or lack of consideration. The most commonly asserted defense to the enforcement of an arbitration agreement is unconscionability. And this defense comes in two flavors — procedural and substantive unconscionability. Procedural unconscionability assesses the fairness of the manner under which the agreement was negotiated and focuses on such considerations as the comparative bargaining power of the parties, whether the agreement was offered on a "take it or leave it" basis by the employer, and whether it was a standardized form drafted by the employer with no opportunity for amendment. Substantive unconscionability refers to the fairness of the content of the arbitration promise and focuses on such factors as whether agreeing to arbitrate was a requirement of employment, whether the remedies available in arbitration were comparable to the remedies that would be available in court, whether the limitations period for arbitrable claims was comparable to the limitations period applicable to Title VII actions, or whether the costs of arbitration rendered it an ineffective or inadequate substitute for a judicial forum. And where an arbitration agreement contains a severability clause that permits the court to sever out the unenforceable portions of the agreement and enforce the rest, and even when it does not, the courts can sever the invalid provisions and enforce the rest, or choose to strike down the entire agreement on the ground that the invalid provisions rendered the entire agreement unenforceable.

When an arbitration agreement is challenged on the ground of unconscionability, the courts had been divided on whether that issue was to be resolved by a court or the arbitrator named in the agreement. In *Rent-A-Center, West, Inc. v. Jackson*, 130 S. Ct. 2772 (2010), the Supreme Court, by a 5-4 vote, held that when a party challenges the enforceability of an arbitration agreement that represents the entirety of the agreement between the parties, the threshold issue of unconscionability is to be resolved by the arbitrator when that agreement expressly and unambiguously delegates exclusive authority over that issue to the arbitrator. Previously, in *Prima Paint Corp. v. Flood & Conklin Mfg. Co.*, 388 U.S. 395 (1967), the Court had construed §2 of the Federal Arbitration Act (providing for the enforcement of written arbitration agreements subject to challenge under grounds recognized at law or in equity) to mean that a challenge to a contract as a whole, as opposed to a specific challenge to the arbitration provision within that contract, was to be resolved by the arbitrator and not a court. Extending that analysis to the instant case, the majority in *Rent-A-Center* reasoned that the entire contract before it was the arbitration agreement and that the employee had not specifically and independently challenged the unconscionability of the particular provision within that contract as a whole that delegated authority over unconscionability determinations to the arbitrator. Accordingly, it upheld the trial judge's decision to dismiss the employee's §1981 suit and to compel arbitration on the ground that, because the plaintiff former employee had challenged the validity of the contract as a whole, the unconscionability determination was for the arbitrator, and not a court, to decide. The four dissenters in *Rent-A-Center* rejected the majority's extension of *Prima Paint* to the instant facts. In their view, *Prima Paint* was "akin to a pleading standard, whereby a party seeking to challenge the validity of an arbitration agreement must expressly say so in order to get his dispute into court." 130 S. Ct. at 2784. They read *Prima Paint* to mean that the threshold question of enforceability can go to the arbitrator only when the challenge relates to the validity of the substantive contract "within which an arbitration clause is nested." On the other hand, where a party challenges the validity of the arbitration agreement, which is severable from the substantive terms, that issue is a matter for a court to resolve. The presence of the provision delegating unconscionability determinations to the arbitrator was "beside the point," the dissenters declared, because the essence of the former employee's claim was that he never consented to arbitrate in the first place because that agreement was procedurally and substantively unconscionable. And so, they concluded, the decision over whether the arbitration promise was enforceable had to be resolved by a court. Finally, the dissenters found *Prima Paint* to be inapposite to the case at bar because, in their view, the determination of whether the arbitration agreement was unconscionable was severable from the merits of the underlying employment discrimination dispute.

Virtually all arbitration agreements provide that the arbitrator's decision shall be "final and binding" upon the parties. This raises the question of whether arbitration decisions on statutory claims of discrimination are subject to judicial review. The FAA lists only four criteria for vacating arbitration awards, none of which go expressly to the merits of the decision: (1) the existence of fraud or other undue means in procuring the award; (2) partiality or corruption by the arbitrator; (3) arbitrator misconduct that prejudiced one of the parties; or (4) action by the arbitrator in excess of her delegated authority. In a non-employment case, *Hall Street Associates, LLC v. Mattel, Inc.*, 552 U.S. 576 (2008), the Supreme Court noted that several circuits traditionally had permitted the overturning of arbitration decisions that were in "manifest disregard" of applicable law, a criterion that was not expressly contained in the FAA. Some of these courts justified their use of the "manifest disregard" standard as fitting within the arbitrator misconduct or acting in excess of delegated powers criterion contained in the FAA. Without expressing any view on that practice, the Court held that the fact that an arbitration agreement contained a provision permitting judicial review for legal error was trumped by what it declared to be the exclusive bases for review contained in the FAA. In other words, the Court held that the statute preempted contractual attempts to expand the grounds for judicial review. But since the *Hall Street Associates* Court did not expressly rule on the availability of the "manifest disregard" standard of review, some circuits continue to review arbitration awards on that basis.

Examples

Tilting at Windmills

1. Alonso Quixano, a production worker at Cervantes Windmills, Inc. (CWI), a solar engineering firm in Toledo, Ohio, was given a two-week suspension on January 1, 2010, for reading on the job. He filed a charge of national origin discrimination on March 1, 2010, with the EEOC. On September 1, 2010, in response to Quixano's request and before it could investigate his allegations, the EEOC sent him a notice of right to sue. Quixano filed a Title VII action against CWI on September 15, 2010. The complaint alleged that Quixano had been suspended on January 1 and again on April 1, 2010 (also for reading on the job). In both instances, according to the complaint, the suspension was based on Quixano's national origin. CWI filed a motion to strike all allegations relative to the April 1 suspension on the ground that Quixano had failed to file an EEOC charge challenging that decision. How should the trial court rule on that motion?

2. Aldonza Lorenzo, an administrative assistant at Cervantes Windmills, Inc. (CWI), was denied a promotion to office manager on January 1, 2010. She filed an EEOC charge on February 1, 2010, claiming that she had been denied the promotion because of her sex. Two days after the president of CWI, Sancho Panza, learned of the EEOC filing, he fired Lorenzo. On August 1, 2010, one month after receiving her notice of right to sue, Lorenzo filed a Title VII suit against CWI, alleging that she had been denied a promotion because of her sex and that she subsequently had been discharged in retaliation for filing the EEOC charge challenging her promotion denial. CWI filed a motion to strike all allegations relative to the alleged retaliatory discharge on the ground that Lorenzo had failed to challenge the discharge in her EEOC charge. How should the trial court rule on the company's motion?

3. Della Mancha, a night manager at Cervantes Windmills, Inc. (CWI), was discharged on January 1, 2010. She filed an EEOC charge on February 1, 2010, alleging that she had been discharged because of her national origin. The EEOC investigated the case and found reasonable cause to believe that Mancha had been discharged because of her national origin

and also because of her sex. Conciliation efforts failed, and Mancha was sent a notice of right to sue on November 1, 2010. She filed suit on November 15, 2010, alleging that she had been discharged on the basis of sex and national origin. CWI filed a motion to strike all allegations of sex discrimination on the ground that Mancha had only alleged national origin discrimination in her EEOC charge. How should the court rule on the defense motion?

4. Della Mancha, a night manager at Cervantes Windmills, Inc. (CWI), was discharged on January 1, 2010. She filed an EEOC charge on February 1, 2010, alleging that she had been discharged by CWI because of her national origin. The EEOC investigated the case and found reasonable cause to believe that Mancha had been discharged because of her national origin. Conciliation efforts with CWI failed, and Mancha was sent a notice of right to sue on November 1, 2010. She filed suit on November 15, 2010, alleging that she had been discharged on the basis of her national origin. In her suit, she named as defendants both CWI and the labor union that represented all CWI employees, including Mancha, and which, she alleged, had colluded in the employer's decision. The union filed a motion to dismiss the complaint as to it. How should the court rule on the union's motion?

5. Miguel Saavedra, a night errand worker at Cervantes Windmills, Inc. (CWI), was denied a promotion to line supervisor on January 1, 2010. He filed an EEOC charge on February 1, 2010, alleging that the decision to deny him the promotion was based on CWI's unstated, but rigorously applied policy of not promoting Hispanic individuals to supervisory positions. The EEOC investigated the case and found reasonable cause to believe that Mancha had been denied the promotion because of his national origin. Conciliation efforts with CWI failed, and Saavedra was sent a notice of right to sue on November 1, 2010. On December 1, 2010, he and Don Quixote, a Hispanic co-worker of Saavedra's, filed a Title VII suit against CWI alleging that they had been denied promotions because of their national origin. Quixote claimed that he had been denied a promotion to line supervisor only three days after Saavedra. CWI filed a motion to dismiss Quixote's fanciful claim against it on the ground that he had never filed any EEOC charge challenging his promotion decision. How should the court rule on this motion?

6. In response to Miguel Saavedra's filing of a charge challenging CWI's denial of his application for promotion, the EEOC conducted a thorough investigation and found no reasonable cause to believe that a violation had occurred. Saavedra received a notice of right to sue and filed suit in a timely fashion against CWI. Subsequently, the company filed a motion to dismiss his complaint on the ground that pursuant to the doctrine of issue preclusion (collateral estoppel), the EEOC's no reasonable cause determination was final and binding on Saavedra and, therefore, CWI

was entitled to judgment as a matter of law that there had been no discrimination. How should the trial court rule on CWI's motion?

7. Equus Rocinante, a sales manager employed at Cervantes Windmills, Inc. (CWI), was fired on January 1, 2010. On February 1, 2010, he filed a charge with the Ohio Fair Employment Commission, alleging that he had been discharged because of his race. On April 1, 2010, the Ohio Commission informed all parties that it had found that Rocinante had been discharged for good cause. Disgusted with the unchivalrous findings of the state agency and dismayed by the whole state law process, on June 1, 2010, Rocinante trotted over to the local EEOC office and filed a charge alleging that he had been discharged because of his race. After waiting 180 days, Rocinante requested and received a notice of right to sue from the EEOC, which had not yet begun its investigation of his charge. One month thereafter, Rocinante filed suit against CWI, alleging that he had been discharged because of his race. CWI then filed a motion to dismiss the complaint on the ground that the Ohio Commission's finding that it had not discriminated against Rocinante was binding on the court and, therefore, that CWI was entitled to judgment as a matter of law. How should the court rule on the company's motion?

8. The union representing all Cervantes Windmill, Inc. (CWI) employees and the company had entered into a collective bargaining agreement that provided, *inter alia*, that all disputes, including statutory claims of employment discrimination, were to be resolved exclusively through the contractually provided grievance and arbitration process. Della Mancha, CWI's night manager, filed a timely EEOC charge and a timely Title VII action against CWI, alleging that she had been discharged because of her sex. CWI filed a motion to dismiss her complaint per the contractual arbitration clause. Mancha admitted that she failed to file a grievance or request for arbitration and that the arbitration clause is not unconscionable or otherwise unenforceable under state law. How should the trial court rule on CWI's motion?

Explanations

Tilting at Windmills

1. The motion will be denied. The circuit courts uniformly have adopted the *Sanchez* doctrine concerning the required relationship between Title VII and the preceding EEOC charge. Under that doctrine, the scope of the suit is linked to the scope of the EEOC investigation that reasonably could be expected to grow out of the EEOC charge. Here, the EEOC did not conduct an investigation; Quixano simply waited the required 180 days, requested a notice of right to sue, and received one. Most courts in these circumstances tie the scope of the ensuing suit to the scope of an

EEOC investigation that would reasonably have been expected to have flowed from the EEOC charge. And in doing so, the courts typically allow the suit to include allegations of conduct that postdated the filing of the charge, particularly where that subsequent conduct involves allegations similar to the one contained in the charge. Since that is the case here (both allegations are aimed at a suspension for reading on the job), the courts will allow the suit to proceed and, therefore, the defense motion will be denied.

2. The motion will be denied. In applying the *Sanchez* doctrine, the courts do not require a Title VII plaintiff to have previously filed a separate retaliation charge with the EEOC where the alleged cause of the retaliation was the filing of the charge that is the subject of the instant suit. Accordingly, this motion will be denied.

3. The motion will be granted. Here, the plaintiff alleged only national origin discrimination in her EEOC charge, but the EEOC investigation led to a finding of sex discrimination as well. And so the plaintiff's complaint alleged both sex and national origin discrimination. In applying the *Sanchez* doctrine, the circuit courts typically do not allow the suit to contain allegations of a form of discrimination (race, sex, national origin, etc.) that was not contained within the EEOC charge, even when the EEOC investigation led to a reasonable cause determination on that ground. They do so on the theory that the expanded EEOC investigation did not reasonably flow from the allegations in the charge. Thus, this motion will be granted.

4. The motion will be granted. Here, the plaintiff added a defendant who had not been named in the EEOC charge, who had not been part of the investigation or reasonable cause determination, and had not been involved in the agency's ultimately unsuccessful conciliation efforts. The courts have applied the *Sanchez* doctrine to bar a plaintiff from including in her Title VII complaint a defendant who was not named in the EEOC charge or, at least, was not a subject of the agency's conciliation efforts. Accordingly, the union's motion will be granted.

5. The motion will be denied. Here the issue is whether a plaintiff who never filed an EEOC charge can join in a suit filed by someone who did timely file with the EEOC. Pursuant to the *Sanchez* doctrine, the courts have adopted a "single filing" rule that permits "piggybacking" plaintiffs who did not file their own EEOC charge nevertheless to join in a multi-plaintiff or class action as long as one plaintiff had filed a timely charge with the EEOC, particularly where the additional plaintiff's claim arises out of the series of events and occur within the same general time period as the claim that was properly filed with the EEOC and where the filed charge had given notice to the employer that the allegations involved class-wide discrimination. Since all of these requirements are

met in this example, Quixote will be allowed to join in the suit and, therefore, the defense motion will be denied.

6. The motion will be denied. Although evidence of the EEOC's no reasonable cause determination would be admissible at trial, a Title VII plaintiff is entitled to a trial *de novo* on all issues. No finding or determination by the EEOC is binding on the court, which means that neither party can invoke either the doctrine of claim or issue preclusion. Consequently, the company's motion will be denied.

7. The motion will be denied. In *Elliott*, the Supreme Court ruled that an *unreviewed* (by a state court) state administrative decision is not entitled to any preclusive effect on the Title VII claim, regardless of whether state preclusion law attaches any preclusive effect to administrative rulings. Since Rocinante did not appeal the state agency decision to a state court, that administrative ruling is not entitled to any preclusive (binding) effect on the Title VII court. Accordingly, the company's motion will be denied. Note, however, pursuant to the Supreme Court's ruling in *Kremer*, that if Rocinante had appealed the state agency's decision to a state court, that state court judgment would have preclusive effect on the Title VII action to the degree required by state preclusion law.

8. The motion will be granted. In *14 Penn Plaza*, the Supreme Court held that arbitration agreements contained in collectively bargained agreements were enforceable under the Federal Arbitration Act. (The *Gilmer* Court previously had made the same ruling with respect to non-collectively bargained arbitration agreements.) Thus, since Mancha is not alleging that the arbitration agreement is unenforceable on state law grounds such as unconscionability, she will be bound to the arbitration agreement and be deemed to have waived her right to file suit under Title VII. Therefore, the court will grant the defense motion and dismiss the case.

G. SUITS BY THE EEOC

Section 706(f)(1) of Title VII authorizes the EEOC to file a civil suit against a nongovernmental respondent if it has been unable to obtain an acceptable conciliation agreement. But the statute does not contain any express time period within which suit must be filed by the agency. Nevertheless, in *Occidental Life Insurance Co. v. EEOC*, 432 U.S. 355 (1977), the Supreme Court acknowledged that EEOC suits are subject to the equitable doctrine of laches. Post-*Occidental Life* circuit court opinions demonstrate that a court can dismiss an EEOC suit upon finding that the defendant was materially prejudiced by the agency's inexcusable delay. The circuits are divided, however, on whether the filing of a private action terminates the EEOC's right to file suit based on that same charge. Some circuits limit the EEOC to permissive intervention, while others permit duplicative litigation. On the other hand, under §706(f)(1), the filing of suit by the EEOC cuts off the charging party's right to file suit, although that party can intervene as of right in the EEOC suit.

Recall that a grievant is only required to invoke, and not to exhaust, his administrative remedies. An individual can file suit without demanding any EEOC investigation or reasonable cause determination by simply demanding a notice of right to sue 180 days after filing her charge. But the courts condition the EEOC's right to bring suit on its exhaustion of the entire administrative process. This means that prior to filing suit, the EEOC must establish that it notified the respondent of the charge in a timely manner, investigated the charge, made a reasonable cause determination, and engaged in conciliation efforts with respect to every employment practice challenged in the charge and sought to be included in its complaint. These preconditions do not apply, however, when the EEOC seeks to intervene in the suit filed by the charging party, although the courts also hold that the EEOC is under a continuing duty to engage in conciliation efforts after it has chosen to intervene in a private suit.

Another important difference between suits brought by charging parties and those brought by the EEOC relates to the scope of the lawsuit. Because the EEOC suit is seen as vindicating a public interest, the agency is not treated as a proxy for the charging party and, therefore, is not limited to those claims or forms of relief that could be sought by that charging party.

Since an enforceable arbitration agreement covering statutory disputes only precludes the grievant from filing suit under Title VII and does not preclude her from filing a discrimination charge with the EEOC, an interesting question arises when an individual files a charge with the EEOC and the EEOC then decides to file suit on her behalf because the individual is precluded by an enforceable arbitration agreement from filing her own action. In *EEOC v. Waffle House, Inc.*, 534 U.S. 279 (2002), the Supreme Court held that since the EEOC was not a party to the arbitration agreement, it was not bound by that agreement and, therefore, was not precluded from filing suit (after making its reasonable cause determination and attempting conciliation), even when it was seeking only victim-specific relief.

H. PROCEDURAL REQUIREMENTS FOR FEDERAL EMPLOYEES

Title VII applies to most federal employees and virtually all state and local government workers. The substantive provisions, including the proof standards, applicable to private sector workers apply in the same fashion to those public employees who are covered by the Act. (In *Fitzpatrick v. Bitzer*, 427 U.S. 445 (1976), the Supreme Court upheld the constitutionality of the extension of Title VII rights and remedies to state and local government workers, ruling that Congress had validly abrogated the states' sovereign immunity from damage suits in federal court.) And nonfederal public sector employees are subject to the same procedural requirements that are imposed on private sector workers. But a separate provision, §717, governs federal employees. The *substantive* provisions of Title VII apply to employees or applicants for employment in all three branches of the federal government, except for those executive agency officers whose appointments are made with the advice and consent of the Senate. Uniformed members of the armed forces also are excluded from coverage. Yet while all of these covered federal employees enjoy the same substantive rights as private sector workers and state and local government employees, all covered federal employees are subject to a different set of procedures and available remedies than are provided for private and nonfederal public sector employees.

Any covered federal employee, other than one who works for the U.S. Congress, can file discrimination charges with the EEOC; but she does not have to do so as a precondition to filing suit. Such an employee is required initially to seek review of the challenged decision with the employing entity. Pursuant to the EEOC's procedural regulations, 29 C.F.R. §1613 (1979), this initial step with the employing agency's Equal Employment Opportunity Counselor must be taken within 45 days of the "matter alleged to be discriminatory." So, for example, in a discharge case, the 45-day limit begins to run from the date of the discharge. But the circuit courts had split for years on the appropriate timing period for cases alleging constructive discharge. Some said that the 45-day period commenced on the date of the defendant's last discriminatory act leading to the discharge. Others said that the period began to run only on the date of the plaintiff's resignation. The Supreme Court resolved this conflict in favor of the latter approach. In *Green v. Brennan*, 136 S. Ct. 1769 (2016), the Supreme Court concluded that the "matter alleged to be discriminatory" in a constructive discharge case included the date of the plaintiff's resignation, since that resignation was an element of the substantive claim of constructive discharge.

The employing agency is authorized to provide the employee with full relief. But if the aggrieved is not satisfied with the agency's internal decision, she can file a civil action in federal court or appeal the agency's decision to the EEOC's Office of Federal Operations (OFO). (In a few specified categories of cases involving particular employment decisions, the aggrieved is required to appeal the agency's decision to the Merit Systems Protection Board, with the right to appeal that Board's decision to the EEOC prior to filing suit.) If the claimant chooses to appeal the agency's decision to the EEOC rather than to go directly to court, §717(b) provides the EEOC with remedial authority, including the power to issue an order requiring reinstatement or hiring with or without back pay. And in *West v. Gibson*, 527 U.S. 212 (1999), the Supreme Court held that the EEOC also was authorized to award compensatory damages against federal agencies. If the complainant is dissatisfied with the agency's final decision and chooses to bypass the EEOC, suit must be filed no later than 90 days after receipt of notice of the employing agency's final decision. But as with private sector employees, federal employees are required to invoke, but not exhaust this administrative remedy. The individual has the right to file suit after waiting 180 days after filing the complaint with the agency, absent an earlier agency decision. Alternatively, where an individual appeals the agency's decision to the EEOC before filing suit, suit must be filed no later than 90 days after receipt of notice of the EEOC's final action. And again, to avoid burdening the complainant with a protracted EEOC proceeding, the federal employee, like a private sector employee, can file suit 180 days after the filing of the appeal with the EEOC if there has been no EEOC decision. The agency, however, cannot appeal the EEOC's final decision by filing suit. Finally, in *Irwin v. Department of Veterans Affairs*, 498 U.S. 89 (1990), the Supreme Court ruled that these limitations periods are subject to the same equitable tolling principles applicable to claims brought by private sector workers.

There is a more complicated process governing Title VII challenges by congressional employees. They are required initially to seek counseling from the federal Office of Compliance within 180 days of the unlawful practice. If the claimant is unsatisfied, he then must file a request for mediation. If mediation is unsuccessful, the individual, within 90 days after termination of mediation, can either request an administrative hearing with the Office of Compliance or file suit in federal court in either the district in which he works or the U.S. District for the District of Columbia. Any appeal from the Office of Compliance's final decision goes directly to the U.S. Courts of Appeals (federal circuit courts).

Acts of discrimination by federal employers can also be challenged as a violation of the equal protection guarantee of the Due Process Clause of the Fifth Amendment of the U.S. Constitution. But in *Brown v. G.S.A.*, 425 U.S. 820 (1976), the Supreme Court ruled that Title VII was the exclusive and preemptive federal remedy for employment discrimination claims brought by federal government employees. And on that same day, the Supreme Court decided *Chandler v. Roudebush*, 425 U.S. 840 (1976), in which it held that notwithstanding the more extensive administrative remedies available to federal workers, these employees enjoyed the same right to a trial *de novo* on their Title VII claims as private and state and local government workers. Some subsequent circuit court rulings indicate, however, that the right to trial *de novo* may extend only to cases where the individual lost before the EEOC and that *Chandler* was not intended to bar preclusion in cases where the EEOC had ruled in favor of the federal employee. Federal employees who are not covered by Title VII, according to the Supreme Court's ruling in *Davis v. Passman*, 442 U.S. 228 (1979), retain the right to file suit alleging a violation of their Fifth Amendment right to equal protection. Note, however, that in *Washington v. Davis*, 426 U.S. 229 (1976), the Supreme Court held that disparate impact analysis was inapplicable to claims brought under the Equal Protection Clause of the Fourteenth Amendment. This has been extended to equal protection claims brought by federal employees under the Fifth Amendment. To establish a constitutional violation, the plaintiff must prove the existence of intentional discrimination. And although the disproportionate impact of a facially neutral criterion is admissible evidence that is relevant to establishing discriminatory purpose, it simply is not sufficient, *per se*, to establish a prima facie constitutional violation.

The *Brown* rule of exclusivity has not been extended to state and local government workers. The circuit courts uniformly rule that a state or local government worker is not limited to proceeding under Title VII with his federal claim of employment discrimination. Such an employee can bring a claim under 42 U.S.C. §1983, as long as that suit alleges a violation of rights found elsewhere than Title VII, such as a claim that the defendant violated the plaintiff's Fourteenth Amendment right to equal protection.

I. CLASS ACTIONS: OVERVIEW

The possibility of bringing a class action often exists in Title VII cases, almost always in cases involving allegations of systemic intentional or disparate impact discrimination. As with all purported class actions filed in federal court, the court must determine that the case meets the various and frequently complicated requirements of Rule 23 of the Federal Rules of Civil Procedure. Additionally, however, since suit under Title VII must be preceded by some invocation of federal (and, where applicable, state or local) administrative remedies, Title VII class actions also raise unique issues concerning the applicability of these administrative preconditions to litigation.

With respect to this second consideration, the previously examined "single filing rule" has particular relevance. Specifically, as long as a representative plaintiff filed a timely charge with the EEOC, other individuals do not have to have filed their own administrative charge to become members of the class. In fact, the named plaintiff's EEOC charge does not even have to contain class allegations to support a class action. Additionally, the scope of the class action suit is subject to the same *Sanchez* rule applied to individual suits, i.e., the suit can encompass any form of discrimination reasonably implicated by the EEOC charge filed by the named plaintiff. However, any individual whose EEOC charge would have been time barred as of the date the named plaintiff filed his charge (i.e., because the unlawful practice suffered by that individual fell outside the EEOC filing period as of the date of filing of the predicate charge) cannot become a class member.

J. CLASS ACTIONS: RULE 23 ANALYSIS

Any class action filed in federal court must meet the four requirements of Rule 23(a): (1) numerosity (of members make standard multi-party litigation impracticable); (2) commonality (of some questions of law or fact across class claims); (3) typicality (of named plaintiff's claims vis-à-vis rest of the class); and (4) adequacy (of representation of class members' interest by named plaintiff). If any purported class action meets all of these requirements, it also must satisfy the terms of one of the three types of class actions enumerated in Rule 23(b) in order to be certified. The terms of Rule 12(b)(1) are rarely, if ever, relevant to employment discrimination cases. Consequently, Rule 23(b) inquiry in Title VII cases invariably focuses on the requirements of Rules 23(b)(2) and (3). A class action can be brought under Rule 23(b)(2) if the defendant acted on grounds generally applicable to the class and that equitable relief to the class as a whole is the predominant remedy sought. A class action can be certified under Rule 23(b)(3) if the questions of law or fact that are common to class members predominate over questions affecting only individual members and proceeding with a class action is a fairer and more efficient method of resolving the controversy than other alternatives in light of the interests of members in individually controlling the litigation, the existence and extent of pending litigation concerning the controversy, the desirability or undesirability of concentrating the litigation in the chosen forum, and the likely difficulties associated with managing a class action.

The circuit courts initially applied a liberal interpretation of the four requirements of Rule 23(a) in employment discrimination cases, allowing so-called "across-the-board" class actions in which the named plaintiffs were allowed to file suit on behalf of all similarly situated individuals who were subjected to the challenged employment practices in order to serve the statute's broad remedial objectives. These decisions rested primarily on the theory that all discrimination is, by definition, class based. Over time, however, the Supreme Court significantly circumscribed the availability of class actions in Title VII cases. In *East Texas Motor Freight System, Inc.* v. *Rodriguez*, 431 U.S. 395 (1977), for example, the Supreme Court reversed the circuit court's certification of a class composed of all African and Mexican American city drivers and applicants for line driver positions claiming discrimination on the basis of national origin in hiring and transfer. The named plaintiffs admitted that they had not been discriminated against at the time of their hiring to city driver positions and that they were not qualified to be line drivers. The Court reasoned that since the named plaintiffs were unqualified for line driver jobs, they could not have been the victims of discrimination and, therefore, were not eligible to represent a class composed of persons alleged to have been the victims of discrimination in connection with line driver positions. (The Court also noted that the named plaintiffs' failure to file a motion for class certification also demonstrated their inadequacy as representatives.) In *General Telephone Co. of the Southwest v. Falcon*, 457 U.S. 147 (1982), the named Mexican American plaintiff who alleged that he had been denied a promotion on the basis of his national origin sought to represent a class of Mexican American employees and job applicants alleging national origin discrimination in both promotion and hiring. Relying on *East Texas Motor Freight*, the Supreme Court reversed the trial court's certification of the class hiring claim. Since the named plaintiff had asserted only an individual promotion claim, the Court concluded that the Rule 23(a) commonality and typicality requirements were not satisfied, particularly since hiring and promotion decisions were not made pursuant to a uniform policy or by the same decision-maker.

Even if a class satisfies all the Rule 23(a) requirements, it also must fit within one of the three categories of actions set forth in Rule 23(b). The Rule 23(b)(1) class action is almost never invoked by plaintiffs in employment discrimination cases and so analysis invariably focuses on the (b)(2) and (b)(3) class actions. Since the text of Rule 23(b)(2) refers only to forms of equitable relief and has been construed to require, at a minimum, that equitable relief is the predominant remedy sought, the availability of compensatory and punitive damages in Title VII claims of intentional discrimination has persuaded most circuit courts to decline to certify such cases as (b)(2) class actions on the ground that equitable relief does not predominate. Some courts will certify a (b)(2) class action where monetary relief is determined to be only "incidental" to the requested equitable relief. If a class is certified under Rule 23(b)(2), however, there is no textual requirement of providing notice to class members of the right to opt out of the class (although the trial judge has the discretion to require notice and opt out rights). This requirement does exist, however, with respect to (b)(3) class actions, a category whose requirements are easier to satisfy than those of (b)(2).

Opting out is particularly important with respect to the issue of preclusion. Individuals who do not opt out are bound by the judgment in that case, whereas individuals who opt out are not precluded from bringing their own claims in the face of an adverse ruling on any class claim. However, if an unnamed member drops out, then she no longer will be covered by the single filing rule and will only be able to file suit, absent waiver by the defendant, if she has complied with the Title VII administrative preconditions to suit. Moreover, several circuits have ruled that members of a (b)(2) class action do not have a right to opt out. But the harshness of these rulings was reduced by the Supreme Court's decision in *Cooper v. Federal Reserve Bank of Richmond*, 467 U.S. 867 (1984). There, the Supreme Court ruled that the adjudication in a (b)(2) action alleging a pattern and practice of discrimination does not prevent an unnamed class member who did not opt out from filing suit as to issues that were not litigated in the class suit, i.e., their individual claims. The class action judgment, the *Cooper* Court held, only determined the existence (or not) of a pattern and practice of discrimination.

Where a class action is settled and that agreement is judicially approved as required by Rule 23(e), the settlement will bar dissatisfied unnamed class members from pursuing an individual claim encompassed within the settled class claims. Opting out is more likely to occur in (b)(3) class actions where providing notice of the right to opt out is mandatory. Finally, note that in *General Telephone Co. of the Northwest, Inc. v. EEOC*, 446 U.S. 318 (1980), the Supreme Court held that the EEOC can seek class-wide relief, including monetary damages, without satisfying any Rule 23 requirements or being certified as a class representative.

Examples

Making It a Federal Case

1. Max Aarons, a chemist employed by Federal Labs, Inc. (FLI), a private drug manufacturing company, was denied promotion on two separate occasions in 2009. He filed a charge with the EEOC on January 1, 2010, alleging that he had been the victim of sex discrimination. After investigating his allegations, the EEOC decided to file suit on Aarons's behalf against FLI on March 1, 2010. FLI thereafter filed a motion to dismiss the complaint on the ground that the EEOC's suit was barred by its failure to exhaust its administrative processes. How should the trial court rule on the defense motion?

2. Max Aarons, a chemist employed by Federal Labs, Inc. (FLI), a private drug manufacturing company, was denied promotion on two separate occasions in 2009. He filed a charge with the EEOC on January 1, 2010, alleging that he had been the victim of sex discrimination. After waiting 180 days, Aarons requested and received a notice of right to sue from the EEOC. One month later, on August 1, 2010, Aarons filed a Title VII sex discrimination suit against FLI. Two weeks later, the EEOC sought to intervene in Aarons's suit. FLI filed a motion in opposition to the EEOC's request to intervene on the ground that the EEOC had failed to exhaust

its own administrative processes to that point. How should the trial court rule on that motion?

3. Max Aarons, a chemist employed by Federal Labs, Inc. (FLI), a private drug manufacturing company, was denied promotion on two separate occasions in 2009. He filed a charge with the EEOC on January 1, 2010, alleging that he had been the victim of sex discrimination. After investigating his allegations, the EEOC decided to file a Title VII sex discrimination suit on Aarons's behalf against FLI on March 1, 2010. On August 1, 2010, Aarons filed his own Title VII sex discrimination action against FLI. FLI filed a motion to dismiss Aarons's complaint. How should the trial court rule on that motion?

4. Chloe Gabriel, a sales manager employed by Federal Labs, Inc. (FLI), a private drug manufacturing company, was discharged on August 1, 2007. As the company was located in a non-deferral state, Gabriel filed a charge with the EEOC on January 1, 2008, alleging that she had been fired because of her sex. On March 1, 2009, after a lengthy and complicated investigation, the EEOC found reasonable cause to believe that a violation had occurred. After extensive conciliation efforts, the EEOC determined on January 1, 2010, that further attempts at conciliation would not be successful. And on March 1, 2010, the EEOC filed a Title VII suit on Gabriel's behalf against FLI, alleging that she had been discharged because of her sex. FLI responded by filing a motion to dismiss the complaint on the ground that the suit was untimely filed. How should the trial court rule on this motion?

5. The union representing all Federal Labs, Inc. (FLI) employees entered into a collective bargaining agreement with FLI, which provided that all employment-related disputes, including statutory claims of discrimination, were to be resolved exclusively through the contractually created grievance and arbitration procedure. Alexa Erichs, an accountant employed by FLI, filed an EEOC charge on January 1, 2010, alleging that she had been the victim of sexual harassment by her supervisor. The EEOC investigated her charge, found reasonable cause to believe a violation had occurred, and unsuccessfully attempted to achieve voluntary compliance by FLI. Thereafter, on August 1, 2010, the EEOC filed suit on Erichs's behalf against FLI, alleging that she had been the victim of sexual harassment in violation of Title VII. FLI filed a motion to dismiss the complaint on the ground that the contractual arbitration clause precluded such a suit. How should the trial court rule on this motion?

6. Adam Kopolow, a systems analyst employed by the Federal Aviation Agency (FAA), believed that he had been denied a promotion on December 1, 2009, because of his religion. He filed suit against the FAA, a federal agency, alleging that its decision to deny him a promotion because of his religion violated his right to equal protection under the

law guaranteed by the Due Process Clause of the Fifth Amendment. The FAA filed a motion to dismiss the complaint. How should the trial court rule on this motion?

7. Adam Kopolow, a systems analyst employed by the Federal Aviation Agency (FAA), believed that he had been denied a promotion on December 1, 2009, because of his religion. On January 1, 2010, Kopolow challenged that decision by filing a charge with the EEOC, alleging that he had been discriminated against because of his religion by his employer, a federal agency. On August 1, 2010, one month after receiving a notice of right to sue from the EEOC, Kopolow filed a Title VII action against the FAA. The FAA filed a motion to dismiss the complaint based on Kopolow's failure to comply with the procedural preconditions to suit. How should the trial court rule on the FAA's motion?

8. Adam Kopolow, a systems analyst employed by the Federal Aviation Agency (FAA), believed that he had been denied a promotion on December 1, 2009, because of his religion. On January 1, 2010, Kopolow challenged that decision by filing a complaint with the FAA's Office of Equal Opportunity. On March 1, 2010, Kopolow was informed that the agency's final decision was to deny his complaint. He filed a Title VII suit against the FAA on May 1, 2010, claiming that he had been denied a promotion because of his religion. The FAA filed a motion to dismiss the complaint on the ground that the suit had not been preceded by the filing of an EEOC charge. How should the trial court rule on this motion?

Explanations

Making It a Federal Case

1. The motion will be granted. Although §706(f)(1) authorizes the EEOC to file suit against a private employer, the courts have required the EEOC to exhaust its own administrative processes as a precondition to filing suit. Suit cannot be filed by the EEOC until it has investigated the claim, made a reasonable cause determination, and attempted unsuccessfully to obtain an acceptable conciliation agreement. Here, the EEOC investigated but did not make a reasonable cause determination nor attempt voluntary conciliation. Accordingly, the defendant's motion will be granted and the complaint will be dismissed.

2. The motion will be denied. The requirement that the EEOC exhaust its administrative processes prior to filing suit does not apply when the EEOC seeks only to intervene in a suit brought by the charging party. Consequently, the company's motion will be denied. Note, however, that the courts require the EEOC to continue its processes, including engaging in conciliation efforts, after choosing to intervene in a private suit.

3. The motion will be granted. Once the EEOC files suit on behalf of the charging party, the individual's right to file suit is cut off. The individual's only recourse is to exercise his right to intervene in the EEOC suit. Consequently, since Aarons's right to bring a private cause of action was preempted by the EEOC suit, the defense motion will be granted and the complaint will be dismissed.

4. The motion will be denied. Although the EEOC is authorized to file suit on behalf of a charging party by §706(g)(1), Title VII does not contain any express time limit for such a suit. As long as the EEOC exhausts its administrative processes prior to filing suit, and as long as the defendant cannot persuade the court to invoke the equitable doctrine of laches on the ground that it was materially prejudiced by the EEOC's unreasonable delay, the EEOC suit is not subject to any maximum limitations period. Consequently, since an EEOC suit cannot be untimely filed, and there is no evidence to support a defense assertion of laches, the company's motion to dismiss the EEOC complaint will be denied.

5. The motion will be denied. Although the Supreme Court ruled in *14 Penn Plaza* that collectively bargained arbitration agreements were presumptively enforceable under the Federal Arbitration Act, that only precludes the individual employee from filing suit over a dispute covered by the arbitration clause. It does not preclude the employee from filing an EEOC charge. And in *Waffle House*, the Supreme Court held that the fact that the charging party was covered by an enforceable arbitration agreement did not preclude the EEOC (who was not a party to the arbitration agreement) from filing suit on that individual's behalf, even when it was seeking only victim-specific relief. Consequently, the company's motion will be denied and the EEOC suit will not be dismissed.

6. The motion will be granted. In *Brown*, the Supreme Court ruled that Title VII was the exclusive federal remedy for employment discrimination claims brought by federal employees. Thus, since Kopolow's suit consisted solely of a constitutional claim rather than a claim under Title VII, that complaint will be dismissed and the FAA's motion will be granted.

7. The motion will be granted. Non-congressional federal employees are required to seek review of a challenged employment practice with their employing agency prior to filing an EEOC charge or court suit. Here, Kopolow made no effort to invoke his agency's enforcement procedure, choosing instead to proceed initially with an EEOC charge. Since he failed to follow the proper procedure of seeking review initially from his employing agency, Kopolow's suit will be dismissed and the FAA's motion will be granted.

8. The motion will be denied. A federal employee who receives an adverse final decision from his employing agency has the option of either appealing that decision to the EEOC or directly filing suit. If the federal

employee files suit within 90 days after receiving notification of the employing agency's final decision, that suit will be timely. Thus, the fact that Kopolow failed to file an EEOC charge is not damaging to the viability of his suit. His suit was timely filed within 90 days of receiving notice of the FAA's final decision. Consequently, the FAA's motion will be denied and Kopolow's complaint will not be dismissed.

Enforcement: Remedies

A. OVERVIEW

As amended, Title VII authorizes the awarding of a variety of forms of relief upon a finding of a violation. Since its original enactment, §706(g) authorized the courts to issue equitable remedies, including reinstatement or hiring with or without back pay. And §706(k) provides the district courts with the discretion to award reasonable attorney's fees to a prevailing party in a Title VII action. Further, as a consequence of the amendments to Title VII contained in the 1991 Civil Rights Act (codified at 42 U.S.C. §1981a), plaintiffs asserting claims of intentional (but not disparate impact) discrimination can receive awards of a capped amount of compensatory and punitive damages (although punitive damages are not available against public sector employers). The 1991 Act (at 42 U.S.C. §1981a(c)) also provided any party with the right to request a jury trial where the plaintiff seeks compensatory or punitive damages for intentional discrimination. This provision also requires that the jury not be informed of the existence of a cap on damages. Over the years, a multitude of issues has arisen with respect to each form of remedy provided under the statute. We will now examine all of them as they relate to each of the three categories of available relief: equitable remedies, legal relief, and attorney's fees. In so doing, we will see how the courts have been guided by the Supreme Court's statements in *Albemarle Paper Co. v. Moody*, 422 U.S. 405 (1975), that in exercising their discretionary remedial authority, the district courts should be guided by the two principal objectives of the statute: (1) eliminating both future acts of discrimination and the effects of past acts of discrimination; and (2) compensating the victims of discrimination. These objectives, the Court declared, were best promoted by presumptively awarding "make whole" relief, i.e., relief that makes the plaintiff whole for injuries suffered. As previously mentioned, in 1991, Congress significantly expanded the range of available make whole remedies.

B. EQUITABLE RELIEF

Section 706(g) provides courts with broad authority to award equitable relief upon a finding of discrimination. Such relief can include an injunction barring further acts of discrimination, orders requiring reinstatement or hiring with or without back pay, "or any other equitable relief as the court deems appropriate." In light of its inclusion within this portion of §706(g), an award of back pay, although monetary in nature, is viewed as a form of equitable relief under Title VII as to which there is no constitutional or statutory right to jury determination. However, where identical factual issues arise in connection with a plaintiff's claim for both legal relief (where the statute provides for the right to a jury trial) and an equitable remedy such as back pay, a jury's findings of fact with respect to a claim for legal relief are binding on the judge's determination of the equitable claim. Finally, pursuant to the Supreme Court's ruling in *Albemarle*, a judge's equitable relief-granting authority is to be guided by the statute's twin objectives of deterrence and compensation, objectives that make presumptively proper the awarding of "make whole" relief.

1. Injunctive Relief

In addition to enjoining the defendant from continuing to discriminate, such as by terminating the use of a discriminatory policy or by forbidding the employer from retaliating against the plaintiff or class members in the future, the statute expressly authorizes the issuance of affirmative relief, such as an order of reinstatement or hiring. Pursuant to the Supreme Court's ruling in *Albemarle*, reinstatement is presumed to be an appropriate form of "make whole" relief in a discriminatory discharge case. The same is true for an order of instatement where the plaintiff has proved that she was denied employment because of her sex, race, etc. However, in *Firefighters Local Union No. 1784 v. Stotts*, 467 U.S. 561 (1984), the Supreme Court noted that an order requiring reinstatement or hiring will not be granted where it would require an otherwise innocent incumbent employee to be bumped out of that job. In such cases, however, the courts will issue an award of front pay. The circuit courts also have declined to issue orders of reinstatement or hiring where the existence of an extremely hostile relationship between the plaintiff and the employer (beyond the normal level of bad feeling created by any adverse litigation) was found to be incompatible with a satisfactory working relationship.

Another presumptively valid form of equitable relief is an award of retroactive seniority to make plaintiffs whole in cases where an employer's discriminatory hiring policy deprived them of both a job and the seniority that would have accrued from the date of the discriminatory rejection. In *Franks v. Bowman Transportation Co.*, 424 U.S. 747 (1976), the Supreme Court stated that in order to put the plaintiffs into their "rightful place," the district court's remedial order should require the defendant to hire applicants who had been denied employment because of their race with retroactive seniority dating from the time the plaintiffs would have been hired but for the defendant's racially discriminatory hiring policy. But since seniority is used by employers for both benefit (e.g., salary, fringe benefits) and competitive (e.g., layoff, promotion) purposes, the Supreme Court, in *International Brotherhood of Teamsters v. United States*, 431 U.S. 324 (1977), interpreted its prior ruling in *Franks* to mean that retroactive seniority for benefits purposes should be presumptively awarded, but that awards of competitive seniority (which put the plaintiffs in their rightful place but also can adversely affect the interests of incumbent workers) should be made after the trial judge has balanced all the relevant equities.

Recall that in "mixed motive" cases brought under §703(m), where the defendant establishes its same decision defense, §706(g)(2)(B) limits the plaintiff's recovery to declaratory and traditional injunctive relief, precluding the plaintiff from recovering either monetary damages or affirmative injunctive relief such as reinstatement, promotion, or hiring. This provision also provides that the court "may" award attorney's fees. The circuit courts are in disagreement as to precisely how this clause in §706(g)(2)(B) relates to the Supreme Court's ruling in *Farrar* (see below) concerning the availability of attorney's fee awards. Specifically, where the defendant has established its same decision defense, the plaintiff's recovery is limited; she will not recover much of the relief (positive injunctive relief and monetary damages) that was originally sought. Some courts have focused on the discretionary language of §706(g)(2)(B) as justifying the denial of attorney's fees in mixed motive cases where the plaintiff has obtained only partial success. Others have construed the provision to require virtual automatic awarding of fees for services that led to the partial success.

2. Back Pay

The *Albemarle* Court's declaration that "make whole" relief is presumptively awardable in Title VII cases expressly extended to the awarding of back pay. The Court stated that an award of back pay should be virtually automatic, but that a trial judge retained the discretion to deny back pay only for exceptional reasons that, if applied generally, would not frustrate the statute's remedial objectives. And this is true whether the plaintiff was the victim of a discriminatory discharge, failure to hire, denial of promotion, demotion, layoff, or other practice that affected her level of compensation. The Court has continued to adhere to this view except in rare cases of systemic discrimination where an award of back pay would be devastating to the employer's continued financial viability. Thus, for example, in *Los Angeles Department of Water & Power v. Manhart*, 435 U.S. 702 (1978), where the defendant's policy of requiring female employees to make higher premium contributions to a pension plan was held to constitute unlawful sex discrimination, the Court declined to require the employer to provide female employees with a refund of the excess payments because of the "devastating" impact such an order would have on the company's ability to fund future pension payments. Similarly, in *Arizona Governing Committee v. Norris*, 463 U.S. 1073 (1983), a case striking down as sex discriminatory a retirement plan that paid female employees a lower monthly retirement benefit than similarly situated male retirees, the Court refused to order make whole relief in the form of reimbursement for past unlawful benefit differentials in order to avoid the devastating financial impact such an award would have had on the pension fund, which would have adversely affected the plaintiff as well as all other plan beneficiaries.

Nevertheless, in the vast majority of cases, back pay (including fringe benefits such as forfeited bonuses, overtime and vacation pay, retirement plan benefits, and profit sharing) will be awarded in order to make the victim whole from the defendant's discriminatory practice. Under the terms of §706(g)(1), the defendant's liability for back pay cannot begin earlier than two years prior to the filing of the plaintiff's EEOC charge. (This two-year limit is rarely applicable since, per §706(e)(1), the plaintiff must file an EEOC charge within 300 days of the unlawful practice.) And it typically ends on the date of entry of judgment, unless the defendant can prove that the plaintiff has died, voluntarily retired, or become disabled before that date. Also, in *Ford Motor Co. v. EEOC*, 458 U.S. 219 (1982), the Supreme Court held that, absent special circumstances (undefined in *Ford Motor Co.*, but generally construed thereafter to apply only to situations where the rejection is deemed reasonable), back pay liability will end on the date that the plaintiff rejects an unconditional offer of reinstatement or hiring (i.e., not one tied to dismissing the Title VII action) to a position comparable to the one sought. Section 706(g)(1) also imposes a duty to mitigate by providing that interim earnings or "amounts earnable with reasonable diligence" will be offset from the otherwise allowable back pay award. Another fact that will terminate the employer's back pay liability is the emergence of "after-acquired evidence" of conduct on the part of the plaintiff that would have, if known at the time, justified the employer's decision. In *McKennon v. Nashville Banner Publishing Co.*, 513 U.S. 352 (1995), an ADEA (Age Discrimination in Employment Act) case, the Supreme Court ruled that while the post-decision acquisition of information justifying the defendant's challenged action is irrelevant to the issue of the defendant's motive (and, therefore, liability), such evidence is relevant to reducing the plaintiff's damage recovery. Where the defendant can demonstrate that it would have taken the challenged adverse action solely on the basis of the newly acquired evidence, the employer's back pay exposure will toll as of the date the evidence was discovered. Additionally, such evidence generally will preclude the awarding of reinstatement, instatement, and front pay.

3. Attorney's Fees

Attorney's fees are recoverable by a "prevailing party" in all but exceptional circumstances under the terms of §706(k). In *Hensley v. Eckerhart*, 461 U.S. 424 (1983) (a non–Title VII case construing the Civil Rights Attorney's Fees Awards Act of 1976, 42 U.S.C. §1988, which contains a "prevailing party" fee shifting provision identical to that in §706(k)), the Court declared that to qualify as a prevailing party, it is sufficient if the plaintiff "succeeds on any significant issue" in the case that results in the receipt of some of the benefits that the plaintiff had sought by filing suit. In *Texas State Teachers Assn. v. Garland Independent School District*, 489 U.S. 782 (1989), the Supreme Court amplified on its interpretation of "prevailing party," declaring that the plaintiff need not prevail on the central issue or obtain the primary relief sought in the suit. And though the extent of the plaintiff's overall success is a factor in setting the amount of the award, it is not a precondition to obtaining an award. Then, in *Farrar v. Hobby*, 506 U.S. 103 (1992), the Supreme Court explained that a plaintiff prevails when relief "materially alters the legal relationship between the parties by modifying the defendant's behavior in a way that directly benefits the plaintiff." This led the *Farrar* Court to conclude that an award of any amount of compensatory relief, or even an award of nominal damages, is a sufficient basis for some attorney's fee recovery because even a judgment for nominal damages modifies the defendant's behavior to the extent that it is compelled to pay money. But the *Farrar* Court also stated that the attorney's fee recovery would be zero in a situation where the plaintiff received only $1 in nominal damages because it failed to prove an essential element of the claim for compensatory relief. Moreover, in *Buckhannon*

Board & Care Home, Inc. v. West Virginia Dept. of Health & Human Resources, 532 U.S. 598 (2001) (a case construing identical "prevailing party" language in the Americans with Disabilities Act, whose ruling subsequently has been applied in Title VII cases), the Supreme Court concluded that a change in the defendant's behavior had to be the consequence of a judicial order—either a judgment on the merits or a consent decree. A voluntary change in behavior by the defendant, even when it results in precisely what the plaintiff initially sought by filing suit, does not qualify the plaintiff as a prevailing party. In so ruling, the Buckhannon Court rejected the previously endorsed (by the circuit courts) "catalyst" theory under which nearly all of the circuits had upheld an award of attorney's fees where the plaintiff established that its filing of suit was the "catalyst" that led the defendant voluntarily (e.g., unilaterally or through settlement not embodied in a consent decree or consent judgment) to change its behavior. Neither are attorney's fees awardable when the change in the defendant's behavior occurred prior to the filing of suit. But once suit is filed, the Supreme Court held, in New York Gaslight Club, Inc. v. Carey, 447 U.S. 54 (1980), that a plaintiff can obtain attorney's fees incurred in connection with the pursuit of those administrative proceedings (before the EEOC and a state or local agency in a deferral state) that are a precondition to filing suit under Title VII. And though Carey was a case where the plaintiff's claim for attorney's fees was part of a lawsuit involving a separate claim on the merits, some circuits have construed Carey to permit a plaintiff who obtained all desired relief in a mandated administrative proceeding to file suit solely for the purpose of obtaining attorney's fees incurred in those administrative proceedings per §706(k). Finally, where the plaintiff recovers only declaratory and injunctive relief, attorney's fees will be awarded only where the court concludes that the plaintiff's primary goal was limited to recovery of such non-monetary relief.

In determining the amount of awardable attorney's fees, the Supreme Court in Hensley adopted the "lodestar fee" as the starting point. This initial base amount is calculated by determining the number of hours reasonably expended multiplied by a "reasonable" hourly rate. This reasonable hourly rate is calculated, the Supreme Court held in Blum v. Stenson, 465 U.S. 886 (1984), by determining the prevailing market rate in the relevant community, whether the plaintiff's counsel is private or nonprofit. It is the plaintiff's obligation to establish the prevailing rate for attorneys of comparable experience and expertise in the relevant community, as well as to document the amount of hours expended by counsel. And in recognition of the fact that plaintiff attorneys in Title VII cases typically do not get paid until the conclusion of the case, the Supreme Court in Missouri v. Jenkins, 491 U.S. 274 (1989), ruled that the trial judge can increase the otherwise reasonable rate to account for this payment delay, typically by using the reasonable rate prevailing at the time of judgment rather than at the time the services were performed. On the other hand, the Court in City of Burlington v. Dague, 505 U.S. 557 (1992), ruled that the risk of loss is not a permissible basis for enhancing the market rate since the fact of contingency already was factored into that lodestar rate. The Court's most recent and most emphatic word on the subject of lodestar fee enhancement came in *Perdue v. Kelly*, 130 S. Ct. 1662 (2010), where it unanimously ruled that superior attorney performance and/or results are presumptively taken into account in making the lodestar calculation and, therefore, is not properly the basis for any enhancement. However, the Court also noted that it previously had recognized that the strong presumption of the reasonableness of the lodestar fee could be overcome in "rare" and "exceptional" cases where the lodestar fee did not adequately take into account a factor that properly could be considered in determining a reasonable fee. The Court indicated that enhancement might be appropriate, for example, in cases where the attorney had made an extraordinary outlay of expenses in extremely protracted litigation. It even acknowledged that enhancement for superior performance could be possible in a "rare" or "exceptional" case where the prevailing attorney tendered specific evidence that the lodestar fee would not have been "adequate to attract competent counsel." The Court split 5-4, however, in determining how this standard should apply to the instant case. The majority concluded that since the trial court's decision in the instant case to award a 75 percent enhancement was based on the trial judge's "impressionistic" view of the prevailing attorney's performance and result, the exceptional circumstances standard was not met. Enhancement based on a subjective assessment of performance, the majority explained, did not provide appellate courts with an objective reviewable basis for the fee determination. The four partial dissenters, on the other hand, concluded that the trial court had not abused its discretion in awarding the enhancement.

In *Blanchard v. Bergeron*, 489 U.S. 87 (1989), the Supreme Court ruled that a contingent fee agreement does not operate necessarily as a cap on the amount that can be awarded under a fee-shifting statute, so that where the contingent fee agreement provided a lower payment than a reasonable lodestar fee, the attorney was entitled to the lodestar fee. But in *Venegas v. Mitchell*, 495 U.S. 82 (1990) (another non–Title VII case construing identical "prevailing party" language in 42 U.S.C. §1988 whose ruling has been extended to Title VII cases), the Supreme Court rejected a prevailing plaintiff's argument that it should be relieved of its contractual duty to pay its attorney pursuant to a contingent fee agreement where counsel had been awarded a reasonable fee to be paid by the defendant. The Court held that the statutory fee-shifting provision affected only the relationship between the prevailing plaintiff and the defendant; it did not affect the deal made between the plaintiff and her attorney. Thus, it did not terminate the attorney's contractual right to a contingent fee. In keeping with that rationale, the *Venegas* Court also ruled that the lodestar fee did not operate as a cap on the amount owed under the contingent fee agreement.

Where the plaintiff alleges separable claims and prevails on only some of them, the circuit courts agree that the amount of the attorney's fees will be reduced. The amount of time expended by the attorneys on the unsuccessful claims will not be included in the calculation of the lodestar fee. Yet, where the plaintiff recovers on some, but not all, factually related claims, the courts typically do not reduce the fee amount.

Although §706(k) authorizes an award of attorney's fees to any prevailing party, in *Christianburg Garment Co. v. EEOC*, 434 U.S. 412 (1978), the Supreme Court ruled that the standard for awarding attorney's fees to a prevailing defendant was not coincident with the standard governing awards to prevailing plaintiffs. The Court declared that prevailing defendants should be awarded fees only to discourage non-meritorious litigation. Accordingly, it held that a trial court should exercise its discretion to award attorney's fees to a prevailing defendant only upon a finding that the plaintiff's suit was "frivolous, unreasonable, or without foundation, even though not brought in subjective bad faith." But the ruling in *Christianburg* did not answer the question of when a defendant is deemed to be a "prevailing party." For several decades, the circuit courts were divided on whether the defendant was required to win a favorable judgment on the merits (as opposed to a judgment based on a non-merits ground) to be deemed a prevailing party. The conflict was resolved by the Supreme Court in *CRST Van Expedited, Inc. v. EEOC*, 136 S. Ct. 1642 (2016). In this case, the Court unanimously ruled that it was not necessary for the defendant to succeed on the merits in order to be deemed a prevailing party for attorney's fee award purposes. All that is required is that the plaintiff's claim is rebuffed, regardless of the reason.

Additionally, in *Roadway Express, Inc. v. Piper*, 447 U.S. 752 (1980), the Supreme Court rejected a defendant's attempt to collect attorney's fees from the plaintiffs' *lawyers* in a Title VII case, ruling that only a party can be assessed attorney's fees under §706(k). However, the Court also noted that federal courts have inherent power in "narrowly defined circumstances" to assess attorney's fees against lawyers for engaging in abusive litigation practices. And under 28 U.S.C. §1927, where a federal court determines that an attorney has multiplied court proceedings unreasonably or vexatiously, that attorney can be ordered to pay the excess costs, expenses, and attorney's fees reasonably incurred because of that vexatious conduct.

Examples

My Fare Lady

1. Elisa Doolittle worked for Fare Collectors, Inc. (FCI), a private company that managed the fare collection booths at all subway stations in New London, Connecticut. Shortly after she was discharged and after she met all administrative preconditions to suit, Doolittle filed a Title VII action, alleging that she had been discharged because of her sex and seeking reinstatement with back pay. The trial court granted summary judgment

to the plaintiff on the merits of her claim. What standard should the trial court apply in determining whether or not to order reinstatement?

2. Elisa Doolittle was a supervisor employed by Fare Collectors, Inc. (FCI), a private company that managed the fare collection booths at all subway stations in New London, Connecticut. Doolittle supervised all fare collectors in New London. Shortly after she was discharged and after she met all administrative preconditions to suit, Doolittle filed a Title VII action, alleging that she had been discharged because of her sex and seeking reinstatement with back pay. The trial court granted summary judgment to the plaintiff on the merits of her claim. With respect to Elisa's request for reinstatement, the company offered uncontradicted discovery evidence that the supervisor's position had been filled and that no other comparable position was available. How should the trial court handle the plaintiff's request for reinstatement?

3. Elisa Doolittle worked for Fare Collectors, Inc. (FCI), a private company that managed the fare collection booths at all subway stations in New London, Connecticut. Shortly after she was discharged and after she met all administrative preconditions to suit, Doolittle filed a Title VII action, alleging that she had been discharged because of her sex and seeking reinstatement with back pay. The trial court granted summary judgment to the plaintiff on the merits of her claim. What standard should the trial court apply in determining whether or not to order back pay?

4. Elisa Doolittle worked for Fare Collectors, Inc. (FCI), a private company that managed the fare collection booths at all subway stations in New London, Connecticut. Shortly after she was discharged and after she met all administrative preconditions to suit, Doolittle filed a Title VII action, alleging that she had been discharged because of her sex and seeking reinstatement with back pay and an award of seniority retroactive to the date of her discriminatory discharge. The trial court granted summary judgment to the plaintiff on the merits of her claim. What standard should the trial court apply in determining whether or not to grant her request for retroactive seniority?

5. Emily Pearce, an accountant employed by Fare Collectors, Inc. (FCI), filed a Title VII action against FCI, alleging that she had been denied a promotion because of her sex. During the bench trial, Pearce offered evidence of statements by FCI president Henry Higgins asking "Why can't this woman be more like a man?" and declaring that the position in question was "not one that a woman could or should occupy." FCI offered evidence that Pearce had received numerous negative job evaluations over the past two years and had been disciplined on several occasions for unexcused absence and lateness. At the conclusion of the case, the trial judge ruled that sex had been a motivating factor behind the decision not to promote Pearce but that FCI had established that it would have made the same decision in the absence of its sex-based considerations. How

should the court rule on Pearce's request for an order seeking promotion and compensatory damages?

6. Zoltan Karpathy, a member of the public relations department of Fare Collectors, Inc. (FCI), filed a Title VII action against his employer, alleging that he had been discharged because of his Hungarian national origin. During the bench trial, Karpathy offered evidence of several demeaning and insulting statements by Cornell Pickering, FCI vice president for human relations, all of which made reference to Karpathy's national origin and the fact that Karpathy had occupied a position that was "too big for an ordinary Hungarian." FCI offered evidence that during discovery undertaken in connection with this action, it had learned that Karpathy had been stealing confidential customer lists and selling them to FCI's main competitor, Covent Garden, Inc. At the conclusion of the case, the trial judge ruled that Karpathy had been discharged because of his national origin but that FCI's discovery of his thievery was an independently justifiable basis for Karpathy's discharge. How should the court rule on Karpathy's request for back pay?

Explanations

My Fare Lady

1. Although §706(g)(1) is couched in discretionary terms, providing that a trial court "may" issue equitable relief upon a finding of an unlawful employment practice, applying the Supreme Court's teachings in *Albemarle*, all of the forms of equitable relief listed in §706(g)(1), including reinstatement, are presumptively valid forms of make whole relief designed to put the plaintiff in her rightful place. Thus, absent extraordinary circumstances, reinstatement will be awarded by the court since it already issued summary judgment in favor of the plaintiff on the merits.

2. The court will not order the company to reinstate Doolittle, but it will issue an award of front pay. In *Stotts*, the Supreme Court held that an order of reinstatement was not appropriate when it would require an otherwise innocent incumbent employee to be bumped from her position to accommodate the plaintiff. In such circumstances, the Court ruled, the trial court should issue an award of front pay.

3. In *Albemarle*, the Supreme Court held that, the discretionary language of §706(g)(1) notwithstanding, back pay is presumptively awardable upon a finding of discriminatory discharge. It stated that an award of back pay should be virtually automatic and that back pay should only be denied for exceptional reasons, which, if applied generally, would not frustrate Title VII's remedial objectives. Thus, in the absence of any suggestion of such extraordinary circumstances, since the trial court already ruled in favor of the plaintiff on the merits, it will grant her request for back pay.

4. In *Franks*, the Supreme Court held that an award of retroactive seniority, like an award of reinstatement with back pay, was presumptively
   appropriate upon a finding of discrimination in order to put the plaintiff
   in her rightful place. In *Teamsters*, however, the Court cut back a bit on
   this broad ruling. Where seniority is awarded for benefit purposes, it
   is presumptively proper. But where seniority is sought for competitive
   purposes, the *Teamsters* Court cautioned the trial courts to be a bit more
   circumspect and at least consider the consequences of such an award on
   innocent incumbent employees before granting the plaintiff's request.
5. The court will deny the request. Section 706(g)(2)(B) provides that in
   a mixed motive case, where the defendant establishes the same decision
   defense, the plaintiff's entitlement to relief is limited and the plaintiff
   cannot be awarded monetary damages or affirmative relief such as reinstatement or promotion. Since the trial judge ruled in favor of the defense
   on its same decision defense, the plaintiff will be unable to obtain monetary damages and/or an order requiring FCI to promote her.
6. The court will grant back pay, but only from the date of Karpathy's discriminatory discharge until the time it learned of Karpathy's thievery.
   In *McKennon*, the Supreme Court ruled that evidence discovered after a
   discharge was not relevant to a determination of liability. Since this information was not known at the time of the discharge, it could not provide
   an alternative, nondiscriminatory motive for that decision. However, the
   Court also ruled that this "after-acquired evidence" was admissible on
   the issue of remedies. It held that where the defendant, as here, can establish that this evidence independently justified its previous decision, such
   evidence ordinarily will cut off the defendant's back pay liability as of
   the date of discovery. Consequently, FCI will only be liable for back pay
   from the date of Karpathy's discharge to the date it discovered that he had
   stolen the documents and sold them to a competitor.

Examples

The Bright Side of Life

1. Brian F. Nazareth, sales manager for Monty's Python Sales, Inc. (MPS),
   a reptile supplier to zoos throughout the United States, filed a Title VII
   suit against his employer, alleging that he had been terminated because
   of his religion. He sought reinstatement with back pay and $250,000 in
   pain and suffering. The jury rendered a verdict in favor of Nazareth but
   awarded him only $150 in damages. MPS then filed a motion to strike
   Nazareth's prayer for reasonable attorney's fees on the ground that he was
   not a prevailing party since the jury had awarded such a small percentage of the compensatory damages sought in Nazareth's complaint. How
   should the court rule on the company's motion?

2. Mark Paltry filed an EEOC charge, alleging that he had been demoted by Monty's Python Sales, Inc. (MPS) because of his race. The EEOC conducted an investigation, made a reasonable cause determination, and succeeded in convincing MPS to reinstate Paltry to his former position. Nevertheless, Paltry proceeded to file a Title VII action, alleging that he also had been retaliated against for filing that EEOC charge. In this suit, Paltry sought an award of reasonable attorney's fees for the services his attorney provided during the EEOC phase of the proceedings. How should the court rule on that request?

3. Shortly after Brian F. Nazareth filed a Title VII suit against his employer, Monty's Python Sales, Inc. (MPS), alleging that he had been terminated because of his religion, the company president, Tory Gleam, reinstated Nazareth with back pay and lost seniority. Nevertheless, Nazareth pursued the case for the purpose of obtaining an award of reasonable attorney's fees. How should the court rule on Nazareth's prayer for attorney's fees?

4. When the Civil Liberties Foundation, a nonprofit organization that provides free legal counsel in civil rights cases, learned that Brian F. Nazareth had been discharged by his employer, Monty's Python Sales, Inc. (MPS), because of his religion, they offered the free services of one of their lawyers. Nazareth accepted the offer and ultimately obtained a judgment in his favor against MPS. MPS then filed a motion to strike Nazareth's prayer for an award of reasonable attorney's fees on the ground that Nazareth's attorney worked for a nonprofit organization that had provided Nazareth with free legal services. How should the court rule on this motion?

5. Harry D. Haggler, a maintenance worker employed by Monty's Python Sales, Inc. (MPS), entered into a contingent fee arrangement with his attorney whereby he agreed to pay the attorney 40 percent of any recovery received in his Title VII sexual harassment suit against MPS. The jury rendered a verdict in Haggler's favor and awarded him $100,000 in damages. During the hearing held in connection with Haggler's prayer for an award of reasonable attorney's fees, MPS moved that the court's attorney's fees award be capped at the $40,000 that Haggler had contractually agreed to pay his attorney. How should the court rule on this motion?

6. Grime Chipman, a reporter for *The Good Samaritan* (TGS), a weekly magazine, was assigned the job of writing a story on the life of Brian F. Nazareth after Nazareth won a $300,000 judgment against his employer. Shortly after receiving the assignment, however, Chipman was taken off the story by his editor, Derrick Isle. Chipman hired an attorney, Jaw Closed, and agreed to pay Closed 10 percent of any recovery that Chipman received from the Title VII suit that was filed against TGS, alleging that Chipman had been removed from this important assignment because of his religion. Chipman won a judgment in his favor, including an award of $300,000 in damages and $30,000 in attorney's fees. When Chipman refused to honor the contingent fee agreement on the ground

that Closed already had received $30,000 from the defendant, Closed sued Chipman for specific performance of the contingent fee agreement. How should that suit be resolved?

7. Stan Cheeky filed suit under Title VII against Flying Circus, Inc. (FCI), claiming that he had been denied several promotions because of his race. The court granted the defendant's motion to dismiss the case on the ground that the plaintiff had not timely filed his charge of discrimination with the EEOC prior to filing suit. When FCI moved for an award of reasonable attorney's fees, Cheeky moved to strike that prayer for relief on the ground that case had been dismissed on a procedural basis and, therefore, that the defense had not prevailed on the merits. How should the court rule on Cheeky's motion?

Explanations

The Bright Side of Life

1. The court will deny the motion. In *Farrar*, the Supreme Court held that the award of any amount of monetary damages, including nominal damages, was a sufficient basis for finding that the plaintiff was a prevailing party entitled to an award of reasonable attorney's fees under §706(k). And though the Court in *Farrar* decided that the plaintiff (who had been awarded $1 on a claim for $17 million) was entitled to zero amount of attorney's fees, that ruling was based on the Court's determination that the plaintiff had failed to recover compensatory damages because it failed to prove an essential element of his claim for compensatory relief. Here, the jury rendered a verdict in the plaintiff's favor on the merits and awarded some amount of compensatory damages. And though the amount is a small percentage of the damage amount sought in the complaint, the fact that some damages were awarded means that the jury determined that Nazareth had established all the elements of his damage claim. Accordingly, this case should be distinguished from *Farrar*, and the court should deny the defense motion to strike Nazareth's prayer for attorney's fees.

2. The court will grant the request. In *New York Gaslight Club*, the Supreme Court held that a plaintiff who prevails before the EEOC can obtain attorney's fees incurred in connection with those administrative proceedings since filing with the EEOC is a prerequisite to filing suit under Title VII. Here, Paltry prevailed before the EEOC, and his request for attorney's fees was asserted in a suit that was not limited solely to the recovery of attorney's fees. Consequently, the trial court will grant his prayer for reasonable attorney's fees.

3. The court will deny the prayer for attorney's fees. In *Buckhannon*, the Supreme Court held that a unilateral change in behavior by the defendant, even

one that provides a plaintiff in a pending suit with all his sought-after relief, does not render the plaintiff a "prevailing party" eligible to receive an award of reasonable attorney's fees under §706(k). The fact that the plaintiff's suit acted as a catalyst for the defendant's changed behavior does not make the plaintiff a prevailing party within the meaning of §706(k) when the changed behavior was not the consequence of a judicial order. Here, President Gleam acted unilaterally. He did not condition his action on Brian's dismissal of the suit. Nor did he act pursuant to any court order or settlement embodied in a consent decree. Consequently, Nazareth is not a prevailing party and is not entitled to an award of attorney's fees.

4. The motion will be denied. In *Blum*, the Supreme Court held that a prevailing plaintiff is entitled to an award of reasonable attorney's fees even when he is represented for free by a nonprofit organization. Accordingly, the court will deny the employer's motion to strike.

5. The motion will be denied. In *Blanchard*, the Supreme Court ruled that a contingent fee arrangement does not cap the lodestar amount a court can award to a prevailing plaintiff. The contingent fee agreement only affects the relationship between the plaintiff and his attorney; it does not impose any limit on how much the plaintiff's attorney can be paid by the losing defendant. Therefore, the court will deny the company's motion to limit the amount of statutorily awarded fees to the amount recoverable under the contingent fee agreement.

6. Closed will be allowed to obtain specific performance of the contingent fee agreement. In *Venegas*, the Supreme Court held that the fact that a prevailing party was awarded attorney's fees pursuant to a statutory fee-shifting provision does not relieve the client from the terms of his contingent fee agreement with counsel. The statutory fee-shifting provision, the Court reasoned, affects only the relationship between the prevailing plaintiff's attorney and the defendant; it does not affect the deal made between the plaintiff and his attorney. Moreover, the *Venegas* Court also ruled that the lodestar fee did not operate as a cap on the contractually entitled contingent fee. Thus, the statutory award of attorney's fees does not terminate the attorney's contractual right to a contingent fee.

7. The motion will be denied. In *CRST Van Expedited*, the Supreme Court ruled that a prevailing *defendant* can be deemed a "prevailing party" and therefore be eligible to obtain an award of reasonable attorney's fees regardless of whether it wins the case on the merits or on some procedural ground. Therefore, the plaintiff's motion to strike will be denied.

C. LEGAL RELIEF

Since the enactment of the Civil Rights Act of 1991, courts are authorized to award compensatory and punitive damages upon a finding that the defendant has engaged in intentional discrimination. Prior to that time, the statute said nothing about such relief, and the courts construed the statute as not authorizing the issuance of such awards. The 1991 amendments to Title VII changed that, but only with respect to claims of intentional discrimination. Neither compensatory nor punitive damages are recoverable upon a finding of disparate impact discrimination.

1. Compensatory Relief

Title VII (as codified at 42 U.S.C. §1981a(b)(3)) authorizes the trial court to issue an award of compensatory damages for both future pecuniary and non-pecuniary losses, including emotional pain and suffering, inconvenience, mental anguish, and loss of enjoyment of life. (In *West v. Gibson*, 527 U.S. 212 (1999), the Supreme Court held that the EEOC also is empowered to award compensatory damages in a case of intentional discrimination brought by a federal government employee.) In a non–Title VII case, *Carey v. Piphus*, 435 U.S. 246 (1978), where a plaintiff sought recovery of emotional harm caused by an alleged violation of his constitutional right to procedural due process, the Supreme Court held that damages for mental and emotional distress would not be presumed in discrimination cases. Rather, the plaintiff must offer competent evidence of the manifestation of such injuries, although a majority of the circuits also hold that such evidence does not have to take the form of expert medical testimony. This ruling has been extended to claims for emotional and mental distress damages in Title VII cases. The courts also agree that the plaintiff is under a duty to mitigate both consequential and other compensatory damages, although it is the defendant who must establish (burden of persuasion) that the plaintiff failed to exercise due diligence.

The statutory definition of compensatory relief (at §1981a(b)(2)) expressly excludes back pay (which was recoverable since the initial passage of the 1964 Civil Rights Act) and interest on back pay. This is important because the statute also imposes a cap on the amount of compensatory relief any individual plaintiff can receive. But by excluding back pay and the interest thereon from the definition of compensatory relief, awards of back pay plus interest do not count toward meeting the capped amount of recovery. Another important consequence of the exclusion of back pay and interest thereon from the definition of compensatory damages is that it retains the historic treatment of back pay as a form of equitable relief. This, in turn, is important because the 1991 Civil Rights Act's addition of the right to a jury trial in Title VII cases is limited to claims seeking compensatory or punitive damages. And the Seventh Amendment to the U.S. Constitution only provides a right to jury trial in actions at law. The combination of these two facts means that even where a plaintiff is seeking monetary damages, issues relating solely to the issuance of an award of back pay will be decided by the judge, and not by the jury.

In *Pollard v. E.I. Du Pont De Nemours & Co.*, 532 U.S. 843 (2001), the Supreme Court unanimously ruled that an award of front pay (an award of monetary damages from the date of judgment until or in lieu of reinstatement where the position in question is not presently available or where reinstatement is impractical) does not fall within the meaning of "future pecuniary losses" contained within the statutory definition of recoverable compensatory damages. Accordingly, the Court held, such an award is not subject to the statutory cap. Its holding was premised on the rationale that since the 1991 Civil Rights Act (which created the cap) was intended to provide plaintiffs with additional remedies not previously awardable, the cap should apply only to such previously unrecoverable forms of relief. Back pay was always awardable under Title VII. And the courts traditionally allowed it to cover the period dating from the occurrence of the unlawful practice through the date of judgment and beyond, up to the time of reinstatement. Damages past the time of judgment, the Court explained, are now called front pay. But this change in terminology does not change the fact, the Court held, that such awards are a form of §706(g)-authorized relief that was recoverable prior to the enactment of the 1991 statute. Accordingly, it held, such awards are not subject to the cap. Moreover, it continued, this holding also extended to front pay awards issued in lieu of reinstatement, i.e., where reinstatement was not a viable option.

The other consequence of the *Pollard* ruling that front pay is a form of previously recoverable equitable relief is that the determination of any front pay–related issues (e.g., liability for and amount of) is to be made by the judge and not the jury, even if front pay is sought in a claim alleging intentional discrimination. Note, however, that "future pecuniary losses," where awarded, do count within the cap and would be decided by the jury. This would apply to lost earning capacity from third parties, such as where the defendant's discriminatory discharge of the plaintiff discourages other employers from hiring that individual.

Examples

Heroes and Villains

1. Claire Bennet filed a Title VII sex discrimination suit against her employer, Primatech Paper Co. (PPC), alleging that she had been discharged because of her sex. The court issued a judgment in favor of the plaintiff on the merits and ordered the company to reinstate her with back pay in the

EXAMPLES

amount of $150,000. The jury also awarded her $250,000 in compensatory and $50,000 in punitive damages. The company moved to reduce Claire's recovery on the ground that the sum of the back pay, compensatory, and punitive damage awards exceeded the $300,000 cap on damages applicable to companies of its size. How should the court rule on this motion?

2. Matt Parkman, a member of Primatech Paper Co.'s security squad, filed a Title VII action against his employer, alleging that he had been discharged because of his race. He sought reinstatement, back pay, and compensatory and punitive damages. Will the judge or the jury decide those issues that relate solely to the availability and amount of back pay?

3. Mohinder Suresh, a scientist employed by Primatech Paper Co. (PPC), filed a Title VII action against his employer, alleging that he had been denied a promotion because of his national origin. The jury issued a verdict in favor of Suresh and awarded him $200,000 in compensatory and $100,000 in punitive damages. The judge also ordered Primatech to pay Suresh $100,000 in front pay because of the unavailability of the position that was discriminatorily denied to Suresh. PPC filed a post-trial motion asking the court to reduce Suresh's damage recovery on the ground that front pay, as a form of future pecuniary loss, falls within the statutory definition of compensatory relief and, therefore, is subject to the $300,000 cap on damages applicable to a company of its size. How should the court rule on this motion?

Explanations

Heroes and Villains

1. The motion will be denied. Back pay is a form of equitable relief that was available under §706(g) prior to the 1991 amendments to Title VII. It also is expressly excluded from the statutory definition of compensatory relief that is subject to a cap. Therefore, since a back pay award does not count toward satisfaction of the cap on legal relief awarded to the plaintiff, and the sum of compensatory and punitive damages awarded in this case does not exceed the applicable $300,000 cap, the defense motion will be denied.

2. The judge will decide all back pay–related issues. This suit involves a claim of intentional discrimination for which Matt is seeking compensatory and punitive damages. Consequently, either party is entitled to a jury trial. But the jury trial only extends to issues concerning the availability of legal relief. Back pay is a form of equitable relief, and so neither the statutory nor constitutional right to a jury trial attaches to issues relating solely to the availability or amount of back pay. Consequently, the judge will decide the back pay issues.

3. The motion will be denied. In *Pollard*, the Supreme Court held that front pay does not fall within the meaning of "future pecuniary losses" contained within the statutory definition of recoverable compensatory damages. Accordingly, the Court held, front pay awards are not subject to the statutory cap on damages. This means that the company's motion will be denied.

2.   Punitive Damages

A trial court is authorized (per §1981a(b)(1)) to issue an award of punitive damages, but only against nongovernment defendants and only upon a finding that the defendant discriminated "with malice or with reckless indifference" to the plaintiff's federally protected rights. Such awards are also subject to the damage cap that is linked to the respondent's number of employees. Although the circuit courts are not unanimous on the point, the prevailing view is that punitive damages are awardable in Title VII cases even in the absence of any award of compensatory or nominal damages.

To determine whether the plaintiff is entitled to an award of punitive damages, the court must address two questions. First, the plaintiff must establish that someone acted with the requisite malice or reckless indifference. Second, the plaintiff must establish that the employer is responsible for the acts of that actor.

Since legal relief is awardable only in Title VII claims alleging intentional discrimination, and since the statute limits the award of punitive damages to situations where the defendant acted with malice or reckless indifference to the plaintiff's statutory rights, the Supreme Court was called upon to elaborate on the meaning of the malice/reckless disregard standard. In *Kolstad v. American Dental Association*, 527 U.S. 526 (1999), the Court unanimously ruled that the plaintiff has to establish more than intentional discrimination, since that is a base requirement for the recovery of compensatory damages. The Court reasoned that Congress intended to impose a higher standard of culpability for the recovery of punitive damages. And the Court reasoned that by using the terms "malice" and "reckless disregard," Congress intended for the courts to focus on the employer's state of mind rather than on the egregiousness of the challenged conduct. Consequently, the plaintiff is not required to establish that the defendant engaged in egregious or outrageous conduct, although the level of egregiousness certainly is relevant to the amount of the damage award. Rather, the malice or reckless indifference standard is met by showing that the defendant had knowledge that it "may be" acting unlawfully. It is not enough, the Court stated, to show that the employer was aware that it was discriminating; the plaintiff must demonstrate that the employer discriminated "in the face of a perceived risk that its actions will violate federal law." So, for example, although nearly all employers will be aware of the terms of Title VII, an employer could be shielded from punitive damage liability based on its reasonable belief that its discriminatory conduct was not unlawful (e.g., based on the availability of a bona fide occupational qualification [BFOQ] or other statutory defense).

Additionally, since the employer typically is being charged with vicarious responsibility for the conduct of its agents, the plaintiff also must satisfy agency principles to impute liability for punitive damages to the defendant employer. An employer will be vicariously liable for punitive damages if the agent who engaged in the challenged conduct was an "important" manager (although he need not be a member of top management) acting within the scope of his employment. But the Court also provided employers with an affirmative defense to the imposition of a punitive damage award. To encourage companies to adopt antidiscrimination policies and to educate their personnel as to federal statutory requirements, the Kolstad Court stated that a defendant could avoid vicarious liability for punitive damages if it could prove that its conduct was taken in good faith compliance with its own antidiscrimination policy. Thus, if the company can prove that it had a written antidiscrimination policy, that it has enforced that policy, and that it made a good faith effort to educate its employees about the statutory requirements, it can avoid vicarious liability for punitive damages.

Judicial review of a jury's punitive damage award (as with compensatory damage awards) as excessive is not precluded by the Seventh Amendment as long as the court offers the plaintiff a remittitur, i.e., the option to have a new trial as an alternative to the reduced damage award. The presence of a damage cap, however, tends to operate as a de facto measure of reasonableness of punitive damage awards. Nevertheless, some circuits continue to apply an independent constitutional due process limit to such awards. In BMW of North America, Inc. v. Gore, 517 U.S. 559 (1996), the Supreme Court stated that the Due Process Clause of the Fourteenth Amendment precluded the imposition of a grossly excessive or arbitrary award of punitive damages by a state court. It instructed the lower courts to assess the excessiveness of punitive damage awards by considering (1) the level of egregiousness of the misconduct; (2) the disparity between the amount of compensatory and punitive damages awarded; and (3) the difference between the punitive damage award and the civil or criminal sanctions that could be imposed for comparable conduct. Subsequently, in State Farm Mutual Ins. Co. v. Campbell, 538 U.S. 408 (2003), the Supreme Court stated that with respect to the Gore-mandated comparison between the compensatory and punitive damage award, few punitive damage awards exceeding a single-digit multiplier would survive due process scrutiny.

3. Cap on Damages

The cap on damages (codified at §1981a(c)(3)) is a function of size of the employer's workforce. So, for example, the smallest cap—applicable to statutory employers with no more than 100 employees (remember that the employer must have 15 employees to be a statutory employer in the first place)—is $50,000, while a plaintiff working for an employer with more than 500 employees cannot recover more than $300,000. This cap applies to the sum of compensatory and punitive damages. It also is plaintiff-specific, i.e., it applies to the damages recoverable by a single plaintiff. Thus, in a multi-plaintiff or class action, the defendant's exposure extends to the capped amount for each aggrieved party. But, although the cap is plaintiff-specific, it is not claim-specific. In other words, the cap covers all Title VII claims that an individual plaintiff asserts against a single defendant; it does not apply separately to each individual claim. So, for example, where a plaintiff alleges that her employer engaged in multiple violations, such as sexual harassment, racially discriminatory discharge, and retaliation, the cap applies to the sum of the damages awarded for all of these claimed violations. However, this cap does not apply to an award issued with respect to a state law claim (although some state laws may impose a cap on such recoveries) or, for that matter, damages awarded in claims brought under §§1981, 1983, or 1985(3). Thus, as we will see, since both Title VII and §1981 prohibit intentional acts of racial discrimination, a plaintiff who brings race discrimination claims, as she can, under both Title VII and §1981, will have any recovery of compensatory damages assigned to the §1981 claim, which is not capped. But the language of §1981a(a)(1), stating that recovery of compensatory and punitive damages is available only when the plaintiff cannot recover under §1981, has been construed by the circuit courts to mean only that a plaintiff challenging the same practice under both Title VII and §1981 cannot obtain a double recovery, i.e., recovery under both statutory claims for the same act of discrimination. As construed by the circuit courts, this provision does not mean that a plaintiff must prove that he does not have a claim under §1981 in order to recover compensatory and/or punitive damages under Title VII.

A few courts that have considered the issue have ruled that the cap on damages does not infringe upon a plaintiff's Seventh Amendment right to jury trial by circumscribing the jury's fact-finding function. Even if the jury award is within the cap, the trial judge can review it for adequacy and excessiveness without violating the Seventh Amendment's ban on reexamination of facts determined by the jury. In *Hetzel v. Prince William County*, 523 U.S. 208 (1998), the Supreme Court held that judicial review of a jury's compensatory damage award as excessive is not precluded by the Seventh Amendment as long as the court offers the plaintiff a remittitur, i.e., the option to have a new trial as an alternative to the reduced damage award. The standard for reducing jury awards is whether the amount awarded was "grossly excessive" or "shocks the conscience," based typically on the egregiousness of the defendant's conduct and the amount awarded in comparable cases. At the same time, however, the statute (§1981a(c)) requires that the jury not be informed of the existence of the cap. So, if the jury issues an award that exceeds the cap, it is the court's obligation to reduce it in compliance with the cap.

4. Taxation of Monetary Damage Awards

Section 104(a) of the Internal Revenue Code excludes damage recoveries for "personal physical injuries or physical sickness" (other than punitive damages) that are either awarded or obtained via settlement from its definition of taxable gross income. This section also excludes "emotional distress" from the meaning of physical injury or physical sickness. Thus, both compensatory and punitive damages that are awarded by the court or recovered via settlement are taxable except in the unlikely event that a component of the compensatory damage award is related to physical injury. Similarly, since back and front pay represent recovery for lost wages, such amounts awarded or received in a settlement also constitute taxable gross income. In *Commissioner v. Banks*, 543 U.S. 426 (2005), the Supreme Court ruled that the total damage award is taxable to the plaintiff, including the amount that is diverted to the plaintiff's attorney pursuant to a contingent fee agreement. (The contingent fee payment is also taxable income to the attorney.) However, under the American Jobs Creation Act of 2004, 26 U.S.C. §§1 et seq., the plaintiff is entitled to deduct (but not exclude) the attorney's fee payment from gross income, and this deduction is not subject to the limitation on itemized deductions.

D. EQUITABLE AND LEGAL REMEDIES IN CASES INVOLVING SYSTEMIC DISCRIMINATION

As explained in Chapter 2, once a plaintiff in a multi-party or class action suit has established the existence of systemic intentional discrimination, the court must determine whether individual members of that group are entitled to relief as a result of that group-based finding. In *Teamsters*, the Supreme Court set forth a bifurcated approach toward systemic discrimination cases; with the first stage focusing on the existence of a violation (liability) and the second addressing the issue of the appropriate relief to be afforded individual members of the group or class.

A finding of systemic discrimination (the "liability phase") generates a *rebuttable* presumption that every member of the protected group who actually applied for an employment opportunity and was the victim of an adverse decision during the relevant time frame suffered that adverse result because of his or her membership in that group. In other words, all employment decisions of the type found to be a part of the employer's systemic pattern of discrimination are *rebuttably* presumed to have been the product of an unlawful motive. Consequently, upon a finding of liability, as explained in *Teamsters*, the trial court typically will convene a separate proceeding to determine the scope of individual relief. At this second stage (the "remedial phase"), the plaintiff (the government in a pattern or practice case) need establish only that the specific individual in question applied for some term or condition of employment that she did not receive. This, according to *Teamsters*, imposes upon the *defendant* the burden of *persuading* the trier of fact that the adverse decision was the product of a nondiscriminatory reason. Such reasons include the unavailability of the position sought by any particular plaintiff, the plaintiff's lack of qualifications, or the fact that the preferred candidate was more qualified than the plaintiff. Additionally, under *Teamsters*, relief may be obtained by protected class members who *never* applied for a position during the relevant time period, but only if they can sustain the difficult burden of proving that they were minimally qualified for the position *and* that they would have applied but for their reasonable belief that applying would be futile because of the employer's discriminatory reputation. And where the number of established victims is so large that it is impractical for the court to make individualized awards, the trial court has the discretion to issue a class-based award of back pay where the court assesses the total back pay accruing to the entire group or class and then divides that total amount among all members.

E. AFFIRMATIVE ACTION

I. Overview

Affirmative action — by which we mean some explicit consideration of an otherwise proscribed basis of classification — is a subject with which we have some passing acquaintance. We already have seen that both Title VII and the Americans with Disability Act (ADA) expressly mandate, to varying degrees, some form of affirmative action by requiring employers to make a reasonable accommodation to an individual's religious beliefs or practices and disability, respectively. And in *General Dynamics* (see Chapter 10, Section C), the Supreme Court, without saying it in so many words, construed the ADEA to permit, without limitation, affirmative action in favor of the more aged by declaring that discrimination in favor of older workers at the expense of younger workers does not fit within the statutory definition of forbidden age-based discrimination in the first place. Nevertheless, the more commonly used and most frequently challenged forms of affirmative action involve the overt use of race or sex as a factor in employment decision-making, and this aspect will be the subject of our discussion.

The implementation of affirmative action in the employment arena arises in two different contexts. It is crucial to recognize the particular context in which any instance of affirmative action is utilized because the use of affirmative action in these differing contexts raises different legal objections. Specifically, it is crucial to consider two different factors: (1) is the affirmative action voluntary or legally mandated (whether by statute, administrative regulation, or judicial decree); and (2) is the employer a public or private entity? Where an employer is compelled by law to engage in some form of affirmative action, or where a governmental employer engages in any form of affirmative action (whether voluntary or under force of law), the use of race or sex (or, for that matter, any other classification) raises a constitutional question under the equal protection guarantees of the Fifth and Fourteenth Amendments. On the other hand, the voluntary use of affirmative action by either a private or public employer is subject to challenge under the nondiscrimination provisions of Title VII. Thus, where a governmental employer engages in any form of affirmative action (i.e., voluntary or involuntary) that conduct must be examined under *both* the Constitution *and* Title VII. A private employer's use of affirmative action is only subject to statutory scrutiny unless the employer has acted under legal mandate, in which case such legally compelled affirmative action is subject to both constitutional and statutory attack. We begin with an examination of the constitutional limits on affirmative action.

2. The Constitutional Limits

Any use of race or sex as a basis for decision-making by the government raises an issue of a potential violation of the guarantees of equal protection under the law found in both the Fourteenth (with respect to state and local government action) and Fifth (with respect to federal governmental action) Amendments. The subject of the constitutionality of affirmative action has received a significant degree of attention from the Supreme Court. And though many of these Supreme Court rulings arose in non-employment cases, their teachings are directly transferrable to the employment context.

Race- and sex-based distinctions by the government are not accorded the same level of scrutiny. In *City of Richmond v. J.A. Croson Co.*, 488 U.S. 469 (1989), a case involving a constitutional equal protection challenge to a city ordinance that required prime contractors (other than minority-owned prime contractors) on city construction contracts to subcontract at least 40 percent of the dollar amount of such contracts to minority-owned businesses, a majority of the members of the Court agreed that *any* use of race by a state or local government entity, regardless of its motivation and regardless of the race whose members are accorded preferential treatment, is subject to the strict scrutiny reserved for governmental reliance upon a suspect classification. This means that employment decisions that involve state action and are based in any part on a consideration of race (1) must be designed to a compelling governmental interest that could not be achieved through non-racial means and (2) that use of race must be narrowly tailored to accomplish only that compelling governmental interest.

The *Croson* Court acknowledged that remedying the present effect of prior discrimination was a compelling governmental interest. However, the Court also stated that in order to be assured that the state or local government's use of race was designed to promote that legitimate remedial interest, the government had to identify its own prior involvement in identified instances of the type of discrimination that it intended to remedy. An intention to respond to generalized societal discrimination, the Court majority ruled, is not sufficient. Post-*Croson* rulings by the circuit courts demonstrate that although a judicial adjudication of the existence of prior discrimination is not essential to establish this factual predicate, the government must offer "a strong basis in evidence" of such prior discrimination, typically the kind of evidence sufficient to establish a prima facie case of a systemic pattern of discrimination.

And in determining whether the state or local government's use of race passed muster under the "narrowly tailored" means-oriented branch of this strict scrutiny, the Court traditionally has considered (1) the extent to which race-neutral means had been considered to accomplish the remedial objective; (2) the flexibility of the consideration of race (i.e., distinguishing an unlawful rigid numerical quota from a potentially lawful flexible goal); (3) the duration of the preference; and (4) the degree of the preference's adverse impact on non-members of the advantaged class. As a consequence of the Court's application of strict scrutiny and its requirement that the government establish the existence of identifiable prior discrimination in the affected market sphere to demonstrate the preference's remedial objective, most equal protection challenges to affirmative action in employment have been upheld and the preferences have been struck down.

Applying this analytical framework to the use of affirmative action in university student admission cases, the Supreme Court announced in *Grutter*

v. *Bollinger*, 539 U.S. 306 (2003), and *Gratz v. Bollinger*, 539 U.S. 244 (2003), that it was appropriate to defer to a state university's determination that the attainment of a diverse student body constituted a compelling state interest for equal protection purposes. In a subsequent case, *Fisher v. University of Texas at Austin*, 133 S. Ct. 2411 (2013), by a 7-1 vote (Justice Kagan did not participate), the Court added that such deference was not appropriate to the second half of the strict scrutiny standard applied to all governmental uses of race- or ethnicity-based criteria. In determining whether the use of race was narrowly tailored to achieve the compelling state interest of attaining a diverse student body, the Court declared, it was the judiciary's obligation to undertake "careful judicial scrutiny into whether a university could achieve sufficient diversity without using racial classifications." The majority quickly noted that such scrutiny does not require the university to establish that it exhausted every conceivable race-neutral alternative before explicitly relying on a racial classification. Rather, the Court continued, it was the judiciary's task to examine "with care, and not defer to" a university's "serious, good faith consideration of workable race-neutral alternatives." To meet the strict scrutiny standard, the university must convince the court that "no workable race-neutral alternatives would produce the educational benefits of diversity." If a race-neutral strategy could promote the diversity objective "about as well and at tolerable administrative expense," the Court continued, then the university's reliance on race would contravene the dictates of the Equal Protection Clause of the Fourteenth Amendment. The court of appeals in this case had limited its consideration to determining whether the university's use of race had been in "good faith" and, moreover, had presumed that the university acted in good faith and therefore required the plaintiff to rebut that presumption. This, the Court held, was inconsistent with its formulation of the "narrowly tailored" portion of the strict scrutiny standard applicable to all governmental uses of racial classifications. Accordingly, it vacated the lower court's grant of summary judgment in favor of the defendant and remanded for reconsideration by that court under the Supreme Court's articulated standard.

Although the Supreme Court's rulings in *Croson*, *Gratz*, *Grutter*, and *Fisher* dealt only with the Fourteenth Amendment equal protection challenge to the use of race by a state or local government, in *Adarand Constructors, Inc. v. Pena*, 512 U.S. 1288 (1995), the Supreme Court extended its application of strict scrutiny to the federal government's use of race as a factor in decision-making. It concluded that "all racial classifications, imposed by whatever federal, state, or local government actor, must be analyzed by a reviewing court under strict scrutiny."

Finally, this same constitutional analysis will apply to other forms of government mandated race-based affirmative action, such as a judicially ordered remedy in a case of proven discrimination or voluntarily implemented race-based affirmative action by a public employer.

Where affirmative action is based on considerations of sex, on the other hand, the courts employ a less rigorous form of equal protection scrutiny. Because a majority of the Supreme Court never has found sex to be a suspect classification, sex-based classifications need only pass an intermediate level of scrutiny. This means that the government must establish only that its use of sex is *substantially* related to the accomplishment of *important* governmental objectives.

3. Statutory Limits — Title VII Scrutiny of Affirmative Action

The use of race or sex as a factor in employment practices raises two distinct issues under Title VII. Most obviously, does affirmative action constitute "reverse discrimination" violative of §703(a)'s ban on discrimination in terms and conditions of employment? Second, does a court's exercise of its §706(f) remedial authority to award preferential relief on the basis of race or sex conflict with the anti–preferential treatment mandate of §703(j)?

In the context of voluntarily adopted affirmative action, the seminal Supreme Court opinion is *United Steelworkers of America v. Weber*, 443 U.S. 193 (1979). There, the Supreme Court held that §703(a) did not constitute a blanket prohibition against all voluntary uses of race by statutory employers. Focusing on the "spirit" and historical context, rather than the specific text, of §703(a), the Court concluded that Title VII did not prohibit the voluntarily adopted use of affirmative action that was designed to eliminate "manifest racial imbalances in traditionally segregated job categories." It also held that §703(j), which provides that nothing in Title VII shall "require" a covered entity "to grant preferential treatment to any individual or to any group because of the race . . . sex of such individual or group on account of an imbalance which may exist" in the employer's workforce or union's membership, was inapposite to cases involving the voluntary implementation of affirmative action. Since §703(j) referred only to what the statute did not *require*, the Court adopted the negative pregnant to conclude that Congress had chosen not to put a limit on what an employer was *permitted* to do in this context.

Having concluded that affirmative action was not forbidden by Title VII when designed to eliminate patterns of segregation in traditionally closed job categories, the Court declined to define in specific detail the boundary between forbidden and permitted degrees of affirmative action. However, the Court did indicate that this calculation should take into account the extent of the preference (whether it was dispositive or one of several factors), its duration (whether intended to attain or maintain racial balance), and the degree of its impact on the non-preferred (whether all or only some members of the non-preferred class were precluded from an employ-ment opportunity). Eight years later, in *Johnson v. Transportation Agency*, 480 U.S. 616 (1987), the Supreme Court extended its *Weber* analysis to a sex-based affirmative action program implemented by a public employer. Thus, voluntarily adopted affirmative action, whether sex- or race-based, and whether employed by a private or public employer, is subject to this unitary standard. This is particularly important in the context of public employ-ers because of the stark difference between the constitutional and statutory limits on affirmative action. Under *Croson*, affirmative action passes constitu-tional muster only if the implementing government actor establishes that it had engaged in previous identifiable acts of discrimination to establish the remedial objective of the preference. On the other hand, in *Weber*, the Court sanctioned the use of affirmative action in response to a manifest under-representation of a race or sex group in traditionally segregated job categories. Under this standard, it is unnecessary for the defendant to establish that it had been a part of that tradition of racial exclusion.

In *Ricci v. Stefano*, 129 S. Ct. 2658 (2009), the Supreme Court examined the dilemma confronted by a public employer who hoped to avoid poten-tial liability for disparate impact discrimination under §703(k)(1)(A) by engaging in a form of race-based affirmative action. The City of New Haven discarded the results of examinations used to choose candidates for promo-tion to lieutenant and captain positions within its fire department after it discovered that white candidates had outperformed minority candidates. Several white and Hispanic firefighters who probably would have received promotions based on their test results sued the City, alleging that its deci-sion to discard the results because of their disproportionate exclusionary impact upon minority candidates constituted intentional discrimination on the basis of race in violation of Title VII.

The Supreme Court agreed with the plaintiffs that choosing not to cer-tify test results (i.e., a change to an existing employment practice) because of their statistical disparity based on race was a prima facie form of Title VII–proscribed intentional race-based discrimination. However, it also ruled that the defendant City could avoid liability if its decision was justified by a valid defense. And it agreed with the City that avoiding impact-based liabil-ity was such a defense. Then, however, the Court compromised between the positions propounded by the two adverse parties with respect to the show-ing necessary to establish eligibility for this defense. It rejected the plain-tiff's claim that the employer had to prove that it would have been guilty of disparate impact discrimination. But it also held that the defendant's good faith belief that its actions were necessary to avoid impact liability would not suffice to justify race-conscious conduct. Instead, it ruled that the City had to present "a strong basis in evidence" that its selection device produced a sufficiently disparate impact and was not job-related and consistent with business necessity or that it had refused to adopt an equally valid, less discriminatory alternative selection device.

Based on its statutory ruling, the majority ordered the City to certify the test results and to make promotion decisions based on those results. But it also advised the City that:

> [i]f, after it certifies the test results, the City faces a disparate-impact suit, then in light of our holding today it should be clear that the City would avoid disparate-impact liability based on the strong basis in evidence that, had it not certified the results, it would have been subject to disparate-treatment liability.

Not surprisingly, after the City certified the test results and promoted some of the *Ricci* plaintiffs based on those results, an African American firefighter who had not been a party to the *Ricci* litigation and who had not been promoted brought a Title VII action against the City alleging that its promotion exams produced a racially disparate impact. The trial judge dismissed the complaint on the ground that it was precluded by the Supreme Court's judgment in *Ricci*. In *Briscoe v. City of New Haven*, 654 F.3d 200 (2d Cir. 2011), a Second Circuit panel vacated that decision and held that Briscoe, a nonparty to the *Ricci* litigation, was not precluded from filing the instant suit by that prior judgment. More importantly, however, the court also rejected the City's argument that the *Ricci* "strong basis in evidence" standard should also apply to the plaintiff's disparate-impact claim, i.e., that it could defeat the plaintiff's disparate-impact claim if it had a strong basis in evidence that it would have been subject to disparate-treatment liability if it had ignored the test results. The Second Circuit rejected this attempt to extend the *Ricci* Court's statement about avoiding disparate-treatment liability to an effort to avoid disparate-impact liability. This sort of symmetrical formulation, the court concluded, was neither mandated nor contemplated by the *Ricci* Court. For one thing, the court explained, the "strong basis in evidence" test is much more difficult to apply in the disparate-treatment (i.e., intentional discrimination) than the disparate-impact context. It is easier to assess whether there is a strong basis for believing that taking certain action will subsequently result in impact liability because the impact calculation involves quantitative metrics. But determining whether action will subsequently engender intentional discrimination-based liability is more challenging precisely because intent is a subjective concept for which consistent standards are impractical. Consequently, the court ruled that the plaintiff's claim could proceed. It also noted that the victorious plaintiffs in *Ricci* remained entitled to the promotions they had received as a result of the Supreme Court's order to certify and apply the promotion test results.

For nearly a quarter of a century, the Court's rulings in *Weber* and *Johnson* served as the analytic touchstone for all Title VII challenges to voluntary race-conscious decisions by employers. However the Supreme Court never cited either of these opinions in *Ricci*. This led some to suggest that perhaps some forms of race- or sex-based voluntary action undertaken by an employer would now be subject to the *Ricci* "strong basis in evidence" standard rather than the *Weber/Johnson* "manifest imbalance" and "no unnecessarily trammeling" criteria. In *U.S. v. Brennan*, 650 F.3d 65 (2d Cir. 2011), the Second Circuit examined this question in the context of a Title VII and Equal Protection Clause challenge to some terms of a settlement agreement entered into between the New York City Board of Education and the United States. The federal government had sued the City claiming, *inter alia*, that the City's civil service examinations results produced a disparate impact on the bases of race and sex. The settlement agreement provided permanent appointments and retroactive competitive seniority to a group of minority and female individuals. A group of incumbent employees brought a "reverse discrimination" suit against the City under Title VII. The trial judge, relying on *Weber* and *Johnson*, ruled that some of the retroactive seniority provisions violated Title VII and that many did not. The Second Circuit, in a lengthy opinion, ruled that the decision in *Ricci* "makes clear that at least some race- or sex-conscious voluntary employer actions are not subject to the 'affirmative action' analysis of *Weber* and *Johnson*." 650 F.3d at 98. The appellate panel concluded that *Weber* and *Johnson* involved challenges to employer action taken pursuant to an affirmative action plan and that the City's decision in the case at bar did not constitute affirmative action. Accordingly, it ruled, the defendant's action was not subject to the "more employer-favorable test of *Johnson* and *Weber*," but, instead, was subject to review under *Ricci*'s "strong basis in evidence" standard. In order to qualify as action taken pursuant to an affirmative action plan, the court explained, the employer must provide *ex ante* sex- or race-conscious benefits to all members of a protected class. But, the court reasoned, "where an employer, already having established its procedures in a certain way — such as through a seniority system — throws out the results of those procedures *ex post* because of the racial or gender composition of those results, that constitutes an individualized grant of employment benefits which must be individually justified, and not affirmative action." *Id.* at 102. So whereas the defendant in *Weber* had chosen to benefit "all members of the racially defined class in a forward-looking manner," the City had offered make whole relief, in the form of retroactive seniority, to a discrete group of individuals that it believed had been disadvantaged by its impact-generating selection procedure. Accordingly, the court concluded, since the City had not implemented an affirmative action plan, it had to show a strong basis in evidence that it was faced with disparate-impact liability at the time it decided to take race- or sex-conscious action (by showing (1) a strong basis in evidence of a prima facie case of impact discrimination, and (2) either (a) that its allegedly impact-creating selection device was neither job related nor consistent with business necessity, or

(b) that there was a less discriminatory alternative procedure that it refused to adopt that would have met its needs), and that such action was necessary to avoid or remedy that liability. Moreover, the court rejected the argument that the ruling in *Ricci* was limited to cases where the employer sought to avoid a current violation. Instead, it relied on language in *Ricci* stating that its core holding applies "whenever an employer takes race-conscious action for the asserted purpose of avoiding or remedying an unintentional disparate impact." *Id.* at 104. However, the court also emphasized that it was not ruling on whether *Ricci* had overruled *Johnson* and *Weber* in all cases involving race- or sex-conscious decision-making, i.e., it was not deciding that the "strong basis in evidence" standard also applied in instances where an employer took voluntary action pursuant to an affirmative action plan. But since the trial judge had decided the case under *Weber/Johnson* analysis, the court vacated the judgment and remanded for reconsideration under the *Ricci* "strong basis in evidence" standard.

The Title VII limitations placed on a trial court's §706(g) remedial authority to impose some form of affirmative action on a defendant adjudged to have violated the statute was addressed by the Supreme Court in *Local 28 of Sheet Metal Workers Intern. Assn. v. EEOC*, 478 U.S. 421 (1986). The specific statutory issue before the Court was whether a trial court's remedial authority under §706(g) authorized granting affirmative relief to individuals who were not identified victims of unlawful discrimination. The defendant union had been found to have engaged in a pattern and practice of excluding African Americans and Hispanics from union membership, and union leaders had been found in civil contempt for blatantly defying court orders to admit members on a nondiscriminatory basis. Based on that history of pervasive and egregious discriminatory conduct, the Supreme Court upheld the trial court's order requiring the defendant union to create and implement membership policies that would achieve a percentage of minority group membership equivalent to the percentage of minority individuals in the local labor pool, even though that would result in the preferential admission of minority individuals who had not previously been denied membership because of their race. The Court upheld this broad form of relief because it determined that it was necessary to remedy the union's prior sordid history of discrimination. However, the Court added that this relief could be made unavailable to minority members who had been denied membership for nondiscriminatory reasons.

When a class action suit is settled and the parties want to obtain a consent decree, the terms of the settlement must be approved by the trial judge. As part of that approval process, the court holds a hearing at which interested third parties can file objections to the terms of that proposed consent decree. In *Local Number 93, Int'l Assn. of Firefighters v. Cleveland*, 478 U.S. 501 (1986), a case decided on the same day as *Local 28*, the proposed consent decree included a race-based preference in promotions that was available to some minority firefighters who had not been found to be victims of discrimination. The union that represented most of the firefighters in Cleveland filed a third-party objection to these terms. The Supreme Court only addressed the narrow issue of whether the limitations on court-ordered relief contained in §706(g) of Title VII applied to consent decrees and ruled that a consent decree was not an "order" within the meaning of §706(g) and, therefore, that the only limit on the terms of the consent decree were the nondiscrimination mandate of §703(a) and the Equal Protection Clause of the Fourteenth Amendment. But the Court did not address these substantive issues. Neither did it resolve the question of whether third parties who had not intervened in the consent decree approval process could thereafter file a separate suit collaterally challenging the terms of that consent decree.

This latter issue was resolved by the Supreme Court in *Martin v. Wilks*, 490 U.S. 755 (1989). In *Wilks*, a group of white firefighters filed a civil action, claiming that they had been denied promotions on the basis of their race in violation of Title VII and the Constitution pursuant to a previously entered consent decree that contained goals for the hiring and promotion of minority firefighters. The plaintiffs had not participated in the consent decree approval process. The Supreme Court rejected the defense claim that individuals who chose not to intervene in the consent decree approval process were precluded from collaterally challenging the terms of that decree. Rather, the Court held that a judgment could not bind non-parties and that preclusive effect could not be predicated upon a failure to intervene. Joinder as a party, and not merely knowledge of the pending action and an opportunity to intervene, was a prerequisite to invocation of preclusion doctrine. The Court also held that the existence of the consent decree was not a defense to the plaintiffs' racial discrimination claims. Accordingly, the Court remanded the case for trial on the plaintiffs' substantive challenge to the terms of the decree. But *Wilks*, like several other Supreme Court rulings rendered in 1989, was a motivating factor behind the enactment by Congress of the 1991 Civil Rights Act. It amended Title VII to add §703(n), which significantly restricts the ability of potential intervenors to sit back and file a collateral challenge to the terms of a consent decree. This provision precludes a substantive challenge, under either the Constitution or federal statute, to a consent judgment by a non-party, non-class member, or non-intervenor who received actual notice of the opportunity to present objections to the terms of a proposed consent judgment and who was afforded a reasonable opportunity to make such objections. And it also precludes collateral challenges by individuals whose interests were adequately represented by someone who had challenged the terms of the decree on the same legal grounds and with a similar fact situation, unless there had been an intervening change in the law or facts. But the provision also permits collateral challenges where the plaintiffs allege either that the judgment was the result of collusion or fraud, was transparently invalid, or had been issued by a court lacking subject matter jurisdiction over the action.

Examples

Straighten Up and Fly Right

1. Nathan Cole, an employee of the Federal Aviation Agency (FAA), sued his employer under Title VII, alleging that he had been discharged because of his race with malice. His complaint sought reinstatement with back pay, $200,000 in compensatory damages, and $2 million in punitive damages. How should the court rule on the FAA's motion to strike Cole's prayer for punitive damages?

2. Ed E. Fisher, a flight attendant employed by Trans National Airlines, Inc. (TNA), filed a Title VII suit against his employer alleging that he had been the victim of sexual harassment by his supervisor and co-employees. The judge granted partial summary judgment in Fisher's favor as to the merits of his claim, leaving the issue of damages to be resolved at trial. In her ruling on the summary judgment motion, the trial judge held that Fisher had been the victim of intentional discrimination by his supervisor and co-employees. Thereafter, Fisher filed another motion for summary judgment, alleging that he was entitled to some amount of punitive damages as a matter of law since the court previously had found that the employer had engaged in intentional discrimination. How should the court rule on this motion?

3. Ed E. Fisher, a flight attendant employed by Trans National Airlines, Inc. (TNA), filed a Title VII suit against his employer, alleging that he had been denied several promotions because of his race. His complaint sought a court-ordered promotion and an award of compensatory and punitive damages. The judge granted partial summary judgment in Fisher's favor as to the merits of his claim, leaving the issue of relief to be resolved at trial. At the conclusion of a bench trial, the court ruled that TNA had discriminated against Fisher with malice because it knew that its decisions to not promote Fisher solely because of his race violated Title VII. The court also ruled, however, that these decisions were neither egregious nor outrageous. In light of these latter findings, TNA moved to strike Fisher's prayer for punitive damages. How should the court rule on that motion?

4. Edy Gourmet, a flight attendant employed by Trans National Airlines, Inc. (TNA), filed a Title VII suit against her employer alleging that she had been the victim of an unceasing pattern of sexual harassment by her supervisor, several members of upper management, and a few co-employees. Her complaint sought an award of $50,000 in compensatory

and $250,000 in punitive damages. At trial, Gourmet offered evidence that one of TNA's senior managers had maliciously chosen to harass Gourmet on multiple occasions and to encourage her supervisor and co-employees to do the same. TNA offered uncontroverted evidence that it had an anti-harassment policy that had been scrupulously enforced on every occasion in which a complaint had been asserted, and that it periodically trained all management officials on their statutory obligations. At the conclusion of the case, TNA moved the court to rule that TNA was not liable for punitive damages as a matter of law. How should the court rule on this motion?

Explanations

Straighten Up and Fly Right

1. The motion will be granted. Per 42 U.S.C. §1981a(b)(1), punitive damages are not recoverable against a governmental employer. So, this motion will be granted and the prayer for punitive damages will be stricken.

2. The motion will be denied. In *Kolstad*, the Supreme Court held that a plaintiff seeking punitive damages must prove more than the fact that the employer engaged in intentional discrimination. Rather, the plaintiff must prove that the employer had acted either with malice or in reckless disregard of the plaintiff's statutory rights. Consequently, since Fisher is alleging that he is entitled to punitive damages simply because the trial judge found that the defendant had engaged in intentional discrimination, the plaintiff's motion will be denied.

3. The motion will be denied. In *Kolstad*, the Supreme Court ruled that although the egregiousness of the defendant's conduct, or lack thereof, is a factor to be considered in determining the amount of punitive damages to be awarded, a Title VII plaintiff is not required to prove that the defendant had engaged in egregious acts of discrimination in order to be eligible for some award of punitive damages. Therefore, since establishing outrageousness is not a requirement for a punitive damage award, the defense motion will be denied.

4. The motion will be granted. In *Kolstad*, the Supreme Court ruled that even if, as here, the plaintiff can establish that (1) the employer's agents acted with malice or in reckless disregard of the plaintiff's statutory rights and (2) that the employer should be vicariously liable for punitive damages because the agent was an important manager acting within the scope of his employment, the employer can escape punitive damage liability by establishing an affirmative defense that it acted in good faith compliance with its own anti-harassment policy. To do this, the employer would have to prove that it had a formal anti-harassment policy, that it had enforced that policy, and that it had made good faith efforts to educate its

employees about their statutory obligations. As the employer has offered uncontroverted evidence of all elements of the affirmative defense, it will be held not vicariously liable for punitive damages. So, TNA's motion to strike will be granted.

Examples

You Can't Always Get What You Want

1. Michael Jagger filed a Title VII sex discrimination suit against his employer, Rolling Stones, Inc. (RSI), a land moving equipment manufacturer located in Oxford, Mississippi. The jury rendered a verdict in Jagger's favor and awarded him $250,000 in compensatory and $200,000 in punitive damages. RSI moved to have the award reduced in compliance with the $300,000 cap applicable to employers of its size. Jagger opposed the motion on the ground that neither award exceeded the cap. How should the court rule on this motion?

2. Kenneth Poor filed a Title VII action against his employer, Rolling Stones, Inc. (RSI), alleging that he had been denied a promotion because of his religion and had been retaliated against for filing an EEOC charge challenging the promotion denial. The jury returned a verdict in Keith's favor and awarded him $250,000 on the promotion claim and $200,000 on the retaliation claim. RSI moved to have the award reduced in compliance with the $300,000 cap applicable to employers of its size. Keith maintained that the cap had not been exceeded since each damage award related to a separate and independent claim against RSI. How should the court rule on RSI's motion?

Explanations

You Can't Always Get What You Want

1. The motion will be granted. The statutory cap on damages applies to the sum of punitive and compensatory damages recovered by a single individual against a single defendant. Thus, since the sum of the two awards exceeded the applicable cap, the defense motion will be granted.

2. The motion will be granted. The statutory cap on damages applies to the sum of punitive and compensatory damages recoverable on the totality of Title VII claims brought by a single plaintiff against a single defendant. Whether those multiple claims are related or not is irrelevant; the cap applies on a plaintiff-specific, and not a claim-specific, basis. Therefore, since the cap has been exceeded, the defense motion will be granted.

Other Federal Antidiscrimination Statutes

CHAPTER 9

The Reconstruction Civil Rights Acts — 42 U.S.C. §§1981, 1983, and 1985 — and the Equal Pay Act

A. THE CIVIL RIGHTS ACT OF 1866 — 42 U.S.C. §1981

1. Overview

Ever since the mid-1960s, a once-forgotten statute enacted during the Reconstruction Era has emerged as an important member of the group of federal antidiscrimination statutes. Enacted as part of a collection of Reconstruction Civil Rights Acts, §1981 is often used by plaintiffs as a supplement to Title VII because of a couple of important differences in coverage between these two statutes.

The bedrock substantive portion of §1981, contained in §1981(a), provides to "all persons" the same right "to make and enforce contracts" as is enjoyed by "white citizens." As amended by the Civil Rights Act of 1991, the right to make and enforce contracts is defined in §1981(b) to extend to the formation, performance, modification, and termination of contracts, as well as the enjoyment of all terms and conditions of the contractual relationship. This language was drafted expressly to ensure that §1981 applied, like Title VII, to discrimination with respect to all terms and conditions of employment, not just discrimination in the formation of the employment contract. The 1991 amendments also added §1981(c), which expressly extended the application of the substantive provisions to private and non-federal public sector workers. Federal government workers are not covered by §1981 pursuant to the Supreme Court's ruling in *Brown v. GSA* that Title

VII is the exclusive federal statutory remedy for employment discrimination claims brought by federal workers.

There are, however, important differences between §1981 and Title VII. Some of these differences make §1981 more comprehensive in coverage than Title VII. Specifically, §1981 contains no minimum employee requirement. Neither does it contain a cap on the recovery of damages. It also is subject to a longer statute of limitations than applies to suits filed under Title VII. Unlike Title VII, it does prohibit discrimination on the basis of citizenship. And since it applies in all contractual contexts, not only employment, it would provide a cause of action for independent contractors and others who do not have standing under Title VII because of the absence of an employment relationship. On the other hand, §1981 is significantly more limited in its applicability than Title VII in some regards. Most importantly, §1981 only prohibits discrimination on the basis of race and alienage. It also covers only claims of intentional discrimination; impact claims are not cognizable under this statute. And it does not have extraterritorial operation since it applies only to all persons "within the jurisdiction of the United States." One final important distinction between these two statutes is that a claimant seeking relief under §1981, unlike a Title VII plaintiff, has no recourse to, and therefore is not subject to the litigation precondition of, administrative remedies.

2. Coverage and Substantive Provisions

Although the courts agree that §1981 is limited to claims of racial or alienage discrimination, there remains some daylight between the ways in which different circuits define race. In a pair of companion cases, *Saint Francis College v. Al-Khazraji*, 481 U.S. 604 (1987), and *Shaare Tefila Congregation v. Cobb*, 481 U.S. 615 (1987), cases involving discrimination against an Arab professor and members of a Jewish congregation (*Shaare Tefila* involved a claim under 42 U.S.C. §1982, which parallels the terminology of §1981 but in the context of the right to buy, sell, and lease property), respectively, the Supreme Court looked to nineteenth century dictionaries for aid in defining the scope of the statutory ban on racial discrimination. Those sources, as well as the legislative history of §1981, led the Court to conclude that Congress intended to protect individuals from discrimination based on their "ancestry or ethnic characteristics." This merging of the concepts of ethnicity and race has required the circuit courts to define the meaning of ethnicity and to distinguish it from classifications such as religion and national origin, which are not covered by §1981. So, for example, while a plaintiff cannot state a §1981 claim if he alleges that he was discriminated against because he is a Muslim or observant Jew (religion), or because his ancestors came from Egypt or Israel (national origin), he can state a claim if he alleges that he was discriminated against because he is an Arab or an ethnic Jew. But some lower courts tend to blur the distinction between national origin and race/ethnicity by characterizing some national origin claims as racial in nature. For example, while the courts agree that §1981 applies to claims of discrimination on the basis of being Hispanic, some courts also have extended the application of the statute to claims of discrimination based on country-specific ethnicity on the theory that individuals from different countries share distinct ethnic and cultural characteristics.

The overwhelming majority of states recognize the existence of an employment-at-will relationship, i.e., one where the employer, in the absence of any specific agreement to the contrary, is permitted to terminate an employee for good cause, bad cause, or no cause at all. The circuits are in agreement that the federal courts must look to the state law definition of "contract" in construing §1981. Moreover, in each such case, the courts have held that an at-will arrangement is a "contract" as defined by the governing state law. Thus, an at-will employee who alleges that she was discharged on the basis of her race can state a claim under §1981.

In *General Building Contractors Association, Inc. v. Pennsylvania*, 458 U.S. 375 (1982), the Supreme Court ruled that since §1981 was enacted, at least in part, to enforce the equal protection guarantee of the Fourteenth Amendment, it should be construed consistently with that amendment. Accordingly, it ruled, §1981 is limited to claims of intentional discrimination; a demonstration of disparate impact is not sufficient to state a §1981 claim. And the courts typically apply the traditional Title VII *McDonnell Douglas/ Burdine* evidentiary paradigm. Yet, while the circuits agree that mixed motive analysis is available in §1981 cases, they do not agree on the impact of the fact that the 1991 amendments codifying mixed motive analysis and making it relevant only to the issue of damages did not expressly amend §1981. Some circuits rely on this fact to apply the pre-1991 mixed motive standard set forth by the Supreme Court in *Price Waterhouse* (where the same decision defense is an absolute defense to liability), while others read §1981 as incorporating this portion of the 1991 Civil Rights Act (where the same decision defense operates only to limit the plaintiff's recovery).

The availability of a retaliation claim under §1981 had a checkered history until the Supreme Court resolved the issue in *CBOCS West, Inc. v. Humphries*, 128 S. Ct. 1951 (2008). There, the Supreme Court held that notwithstanding the absence of any express anti-retaliation provision in §1981, the statute's ban on racial discrimination impliedly encompassed a claim of retaliation for protesting or opposing racial discrimination, regardless of whether that racial discrimination was suffered by the retaliation plaintiff or by somebody else. Thus, while an individual can bring a retaliation claim under §1981, such claims are limited to allegations of retaliation for challenging discrimination that itself is prohibited by §1981, i.e., racial or alienage discrimination.

3.   Procedures and Remedies

One of the most significant differences between §1981 and Title VII is that
there are no administrative preconditions to filing suit; a §1981 plaintiff has
immediate access to the courts. And although both statutes prohibit racial
discrimination in the private and public sectors, the Supreme Court held
in *Johnson v. Railway Express Agency, Inc.*, 421 U.S. 454 (1975), that these two
remedies are separate and independent rather than mutually exclusive. A
plaintiff does not have to engage in an election of remedies, she can pursue
either or both claims. However, in *Jett v. Dallas Independent School Dist.*, 491 U.S.
701, 109 S. Ct. 2702, 105 L. Ed. 2d 598 (1989), the Supreme Court held
that §1981 did not provide an independent cause of action against state and
local governmental units, and that the private cause of action for damages
provided in 42 U.S.C. §1983 was the exclusive federally created damages
remedy for violations of the terms of §1981 by state governmental units.
Two years later, §1981 was amended by the 1991 Civil Rights Act to add a
new §1981(c), which expressly extended the application of §1981 to discrimination under color of state law. The overwhelming majority of circuit
courts, though not all, that have addressed this issue have concluded that
Congress did not intend for the 1991 amendments to overrule the Supreme
Court's ruling in *Jett*. Therefore, they have ruled, §1981 does not create a
private right of action against state and local governmental units, including
municipalities. One circuit, on the other hand, has construed §1981(c) to
overrule *Jett* and to create a cause of action against municipalities and other
local governmental units, but not against "arms of the state" itself, i.e., state
actors such as state agencies. Federal government workers are not covered
by §1981 pursuant to the Supreme Court's ruling in *Brown v. GSA* that Title
VII is the exclusive federal statutory remedy for employment discrimination
claims brought by federal workers who are subject to its provisions.

Section 1981 does not contain any statute of limitations. In *Goodman v.
Lukens*, 482 U.S. 656 (1987), as modified by *Owens v. Okure*, 488 U.S. 235
(1989), the Supreme Court has decided that notwithstanding the contract-
related text of §1981, §1981 claims are subject to the general or residual
state statute of limitations applicable to personal injury tort claims. They
also are subject to state law doctrines of tolling or estoppel. However, the
enactment in 1990 of 28 U.S.C. §1658, a four-year residual statute of limitations for all federal laws enacted after December 1, 1990, also has a limited applicability to §1981 claims. In *Jones v. R.R. Donnelley & Sons Co.*, 541
U.S. 369 (2004), the Supreme Court unanimously held that the four-year
federal limitations period would apply to those §1981 claims that were
not cognizable prior to the amendment of §1981 by the 1991 Civil Rights
Act. Prior to the enactment of the 1991 amendments, §1981 had been
construed by the Supreme Court to apply only to discrimination in the
formation of employment contracts, not discrimination in the enforcement

or performance of extant agreements. This was one of Congress's targets in passing the 1991 Act. So any §1981 claim made possible by the 1991 amendments—such as discharge, failure to promote, demotion, and retaliation claims—will be subject to §1658's four-year federal limitations period. In *Johnson*, the Supreme Court held that the filing of a Title VII suit did not toll the limitations period applicable to §1981 claims. Similarly, state administrative decisions that are not reviewed by a state court have no preclusive effect on a related §1981 claim.

Although there was no specific language in the original version of §1981 relating to the recovery of damages, the statute historically was construed to permit the awarding of compensatory and punitive damages. The enactment of the 1991 Civil Rights Act, which, *inter alia*, provided for the recovery of such monetary relief under Title VII and other statutes, does not expressly apply to §1981. The consequence of this is that the cap contained in the 1991 Act does not apply to recoveries awarded in §1981 cases. However, a plaintiff challenging the same practice under both Title VII and §1981 will not be permitted to obtain a double recovery.

The Civil Rights Attorney's Fees Awards Act of 1976, 42 U.S.C. §1988, provides for an award of reasonable attorney's fees in §1981 cases to prevailing parties in precisely the same language as §706(k) of Title VII. Accordingly, in *Hensley*, the Supreme Court noted that the standards for awarding attorney's fees in §1981 cases were the same as in Title VII cases.

Title VII / §1981 Comparison Chart

Topic	Title VII	§1981
Minimum employee size	15	None
Proscribed classifications	Race, color, religion, sex, national origin	Race and alienage
Forms of discrimination	Intentional and impact	Intentional only
Extraterritorial effect	Yes	No
Administrative preconditions	Yes	No
Statute of limitations	90 days from receipt of letter	State personal injury limit or federal four-year limit for post-1990 recognized claims
Damage cap	Yes	No
Federal employees	Yes	No
Scope of coverage	Employment relationships	All contractual relationships

Examples

Riding Along on a Carousel

1. Julie Jordan was denied employment by National Carousels, Inc. (NCI). She filed a §1981 action, alleging that she had been rejected solely because of her sex. How should the trial court rule on NCI's motion to dismiss the complaint for failure to state a claim upon which relief can be granted?

2. Billy Bigelo, a barker employed at one of National Carousels, Inc.'s carousels, was fired when his supervisor discovered that Bigelow was a practicing Catholic from an old Italian family. When Bigelo filed a §1981 claim against NCI challenging his discharge, the defendant filed a motion to dismiss the complaint for failure to state a claim upon which relief can be granted. How should the trial court rule on this motion?

3. Graham Nash, an African American, is a member of National Carousels, Inc.'s international marketing team that operates out of a separate office in Paris, France. When Nash was denied a promotion to department manager by the general manager of the Paris office, he filed a §1981 claim of race discrimination against NCI. How should the trial court rule on NCI's motion to dismiss the complaint for failure to state a claim upon which relief can be granted?

4. Enoch Snow, an African American male who was the president and owner of Hammerstein Fishers, Inc. (HFI), sought to enter into a contract with Craigin Markets, Inc. (CMI), a company that owned several supermarkets in Maine, for the sale of his company's daily catch of tuna and all other fish off the coast of Maine. But after the parties could not agree on a deal, Snow discovered that Jigger Craigin, president of the supermarket chain, had told many people that he refused to enter into an agreement with any company owned by an African American. Snow filed a §1981 suit against CMI, alleging that CMI had refused to enter into an agreement with his company because of his race. CMI filed a motion to dismiss for failure to state a claim upon which relief can be granted. How should the trial court rule on that motion?

5. Allan Clarke was discharged by Boughs of Holly, Inc. (BHI), a New Hampshire corporation, on January 1, 2008. He filed a §1981 claim against BHI on January 1, 2011, alleging that he had been discharged because of his race. BHI moved to dismiss his complaint on the ground that it was time-barred. The New Hampshire general limitations period for filing personal injury claims is two years from the date of the alleged discrimination. How should the trial court rule on BHI's motion?

6. Allan Clarke was denied employment by Boughs of Holly, Inc. (BHI), a New Hampshire corporation, on January 1, 2008. He filed a §1981

claim against BHI on January 1, 2011, alleging that he had been rejected because of his race. BHI moved to dismiss his complaint on the ground that it was time-barred. The New Hampshire general limitations period for filing personal injury claims is two years from the date of the alleged discrimination. How should the trial court rule on BHI's motion?

7. Tony Hicks, a salesperson employed by Bus Stop, Inc. (BSI), a manufacturer of bus brakes, was disgusted by the pervasive incidence of sexual harassment inflicted upon female employees of BSI. After the company president learned that Hicks had been complaining about this in the company lunchroom, he fired Hicks. Hicks then filed a retaliation claim under §1981. How should the trial court rule on BSI's motion to dismiss the complaint for failure to state a claim upon which relief can be granted?

8. Corey Pipperidge, a ticket taker employed by National Carousels, Inc. (NCI), was upset when he learned that his two best pals, Billy Bigelo and Louis Jordan, had been fired. He vented his frustration in the company lunchroom on a daily basis by constantly accusing the company of firing these two African American employees because of their race. After the company president heard from several of Pipperidge's co-employees about these remarks, he fired Pipperidge. Pipperidge then filed a retaliation claim under §1981. How should the trial court rule on NCI's motion to dismiss the complaint for failure to state a claim upon which relief can be granted?

Explanations

Riding Along on a Carousel

1. The motion will be granted. Section 1981 only prohibits discrimination on the basis of race and alienage; it does not apply to acts of sex-based discrimination. Consequently, the employer's motion will be granted, and Jordan's complaint will be dismissed.

2. The motion will be granted. Section 1981 prohibits only discrimination on the basis of race or alienage. It does not apply to religion- or national origin–based claims. The Supreme Court has ruled that §1981's ban on racial discrimination applies to claims of ethnicity-based bias. So, the issue in cases like this is whether the plaintiff is claiming ethnic discrimination, which is covered by §1981, or religion or national origin discrimination, which is not. Although some lower federal courts have construed ethnicity to encompass country-specific claims in a way that clouds the distinction between ethnicity and national origin, unless a court would find that Italians share a unique set of ethnic and cultural characteristics, any allegation that Bigelo was fired because of his Italian

ancestry would not pass muster. Similarly, any claim that Bigelo was fired because he is a practicing Catholic clearly would fall into the category of statutorily unprotected religious discrimination. Therefore, the court will grant the defense motion and dismiss the plaintiff's complaint.

3. The motion will be granted. Section 1981 only applies to persons "within the jurisdiction of the United States." This language has been construed to bar any extraterritorial application of §1981. Since Nash is employed overseas and the decision to not promote him was made by an executive at the overseas office, he has no §1981 claim against the company, even though it is a U.S. company. The fact that the plaintiff is an American does not matter. Unlike Title VII, §1981 does not apply to either an American or an alien employed overseas by an American-incorporated company. Therefore, the motion will be granted, and the complaint will be dismissed.

4. The motion will be granted. In Domino's Pizza, Inc. v. McDonald, 546 U.S. 470 (2006), the Supreme Court unanimously ruled that the chief executive officer and sole shareholder of a company did not have standing under §1981 to bring a breach of contract claim alleging that another commercial entity had breached a contract with his firm because of racial animus toward him. The Court reasoned that §1981 only protected the right to enter contractual relationships in which the plaintiff would enjoy rights. Since the individual plaintiff—even though he was sole owner and chief operating officer and even when he alleged that he was the actual target of the racial discrimination—did not enjoy individual rights under the contract, he could not seek relief under §1981. It is worth noting, however, that the Court expressly reserved decision on whether a §1981 claim could be asserted by a third-party intended beneficiary of a contract.

5. The motion will be denied. Prior to the 1991 amendment to §1981, the statute was construed by the Supreme Court only to apply to discrimination in the formation of an employment contract. Acts of post-formation discrimination were not covered by §1981 until it was amended by the Civil Rights Act of 1991. Although the Supreme Court held in Goodman that §1981 claims are generally subject to the general or residual state statute of limitations governing personal injury tort claims, that state statute of limitations does not apply to those §1981 claims that were only cognizable after the enactment of the 1991 Civil Rights Act. Pursuant to 28 U.S.C. §1658, such "new" claims are subject to its federal four-year statute of limitations. Since Clarke filed a discriminatory discharge claim, such an action was not cognizable prior to the 1991 amendments to §1981 since it involves post-formation conduct. Since his claim is, therefore, subject to the four-year limitations period found in §1658, it is not time-barred. So, the trial court will deny the defense motion to dismiss.

6. The motion will be granted. The Supreme Court held in *Goodman* that §1981 claims are generally subject to the general or residual state statute of limitations governing personal injury tort claims. The federal four-year limitations period codified at 28 U.S.C. §1658 only applies to those §1981 claims that were not cognizable prior to 1991. But as denial of employment is a form of contract-formation conduct that always was proscribed by §1981, Clarke's claim is governed by the state limitations period. Therefore, since his complaint was filed more than two years after the alleged act of discrimination, his suit is time-barred, and the defense motion will be granted and the complaint will be dismissed.

7. The motion will be granted. Although the Supreme Court in *CBOCS West* held that retaliation claims were cognizable under §1981, it limited that holding to retaliation claims alleging retaliation in response to some protest or other opposition to an alleged act of racial discrimination. This ruling was predicated on the rationale that even though §1981 did not contain any express anti-retaliation language, its prohibition of racial and alienage discrimination encompassed claims of retaliation for complaining about acts which would be unlawful under §1981. Since §1981 does not prohibit sex-based discrimination, Hicks's termination for protesting alleged acts of sex discrimination is not the type of retaliation claim that is cognizable under §1981. Consequently, the defendant's motion will be granted, and the complaint will be dismissed.

8. The motion will be denied. In *CBOCS West*, the Supreme Court held that a plaintiff can state a claim under §1981 for retaliation as long as the claim alleges retaliation in response to protesting or otherwise opposing an alleged act of racial discrimination. Moreover, the Court stated that the plaintiff could state such a claim even when the target of the racial discrimination was someone else. Here, Clarke alleged that he was retaliated against for challenging the racially discriminatory discharge of other employees. That fits within the holding of *CBOCS West*, and therefore, he can state a claim. So, the company's motion to dismiss will be denied.

   But one word of caution. Remember that the key to analyzing retaliation claims under §1981 is keeping in mind that the statute only prohibits discrimination on the basis of race or alienage. So, there has to be some race or alienage component to the plaintiff's claim. Now, it is true that there was such a link in *CBOCS West* because the retaliation was taken in response to an accusation of racial discrimination. But suppose the defendant could establish that it retaliated against all individuals, regardless of race, who complained about racial discrimination against others. There is no express language in *CBOCS West* declaring that such a claim would not be cognizable, and the underlying rationale would appear to extend to such a situation since the retaliation was in response to the plaintiff's complaint about acts of racial discrimination. This same analysis can be applied to a plaintiff who complained about sex, or national origin, or religion discrimination and who then was fired pursuant to a policy of only firing African Americans who complained about any type of discrimination. In this latter situation, although the retaliation plaintiff was not complaining about racial discrimination, he was singled out for retaliation because of his race. The ruling in CBOCS West leaves this scenario unresolved.

B. THE CIVIL RIGHTS ACT OF 1871, SECTION ONE — 42 U.S.C. §1983

Originally enacted as part of the Ku Klux Klan Act of 1871, 42 U.S.C. §1983, commonly referred to as §1983, provides individuals with a private right of action for monetary damages and equitable relief for violations of their rights guaranteed by the federal Constitution and laws by persons acting under color of state law. This statute is the source of a huge amount of litigation challenging the lawfulness of a wide range of state and local governmental conduct and, as such, is often the subject of an entirely distinct course. On the other hand, it has a fairly limited role to play in the field of employment discrimination law — it is only available for state and local government workers and, as we will see, only with respect to claimed violations of constitutional and a very few independently created statutory rights.

Section 1983 is a remedial vehicle for state and local government workers that provides them with a cause of action for conduct taken by state actors (i.e., persons acting under color of state law) that violates substantive federal constitutional and some federal statutory rights found elsewhere. And its applicability to employment discrimination claims is further limited by a body of Supreme Court rulings dealing with the circumstances under which municipal and county governmental entities can be held vicariously liable for the acts of their agents and under which those agents are entitled to immunity from personal liability for their actions.

When a §1983 claim is predicated upon an underlying constitutional violation, typically involving the Equal Protection Clause of the Fourteenth Amendment, the Supreme Court held in Washington v. Davis, 426 U.S. 229 (1976), that the plaintiff must establish the existence of discriminatory intention as part of its prima facie case. And in Personnel Administrator of Massachusetts v. Feeney, 442 U.S. 256 (1979), the Court reaffirmed that any disparate impact produced by a facially neutral requirement is not independently sufficient to establish intent; that impact must be traced to a discriminatory purpose to compel the government to justify its reliance on a forbidden consideration such as, *inter alia*, race or sex. In establishing that link, the *Feeney* Court added, a plaintiff will have to prove more than the defendant's awareness of the foreseeable consequences of its voluntary actions. The state actor must be shown to have acted, at least in part, because of, and not merely in spite of, the adverse effects of its conduct upon an identifiable group.

If, however, the plaintiff establishes a prima facie case of intentional discrimination, the government then bears the burden of justifying that differential treatment. And the nature and extent of that showing depends, in equal protection cases, on the type of classification used to discriminate. Specifically, governmental use of race as a basis for decision-making is inherently suspect and will be subjected to the strictest level of scrutiny. The government will have to demonstrate that its use of race was narrowly tailored to accomplish a compelling governmental interest that could not be achieved through non-racial means. On the other hand, where the government discriminates on the basis of sex, it will be required to satisfy a somewhat lower standard. It will have to prove that its use of sex is substantially related to the accomplishment of important governmental objectives. All other bases of distinction, including age and disability, will be subjected only to rational basis scrutiny under which the government must establish merely that its reliance on that criterion was rationally related to furthering a legitimate government interest.

A plaintiff will *not* be able to assert an equal protection–based §1983 claim where she alleges that she was treated differently from all other similarly situated individuals without claiming that this difference was based on her membership in any particular group or class. In *Engquist v. Oregon Dept. of Agriculture*, 128 S. Ct. 2146 (2008), the Supreme Court rejected the use of a "class of one" claim in equal protection challenges to a decision by a public employer. Previously, "class of one claims" had been recognized in non-employment cases, which required the government to demonstrate a rational basis for treating one individual, for whatever reason, differently from all other similarly situated persons. But the *Engquist* Court concluded that employment decisions involved the use of individualized, subjective factors that did not lend themselves to equal protection analysis unless the differential treatment was alleged to have been based on membership in a particular group.

Sometimes, however, the §1983 plaintiff does not seek relief from a constitutional violation. In *Maine v. Thiboutot*, 448 U.S. 1 (1980), the Supreme Court construed the "Constitution and laws" language of §1983 to mean that this statute provided a remedy for actions taken under color of state law in violation of federal statutory law. Subsequently, however, the lower courts uniformly have limited the impact of that ruling by holding that a §1983 claim *cannot* be based on a violation of Title VII.

A §1983 plaintiff is not required to invoke any available administrative remedies as a prerequisite to suit. In *Patsy v. Board of Regents of State of Florida*, 457 U.S. 496 (1982), the Supreme Court rejected the notion that a plaintiff challenging a decision by a state actor was required to resort to grievance mechanisms supplied by the state, even where that mechanism could provide fully compensatory relief. Since there are no administrative prerequisites to filing suit under §1983, the courts reason that allowing a state or local government worker to bring a Title VII–based challenge to an adverse employment decision under §1983 would permit that worker to circumvent Title VII's administrative processes. Thus, Title VII is the exclusive remedy for a state or local government worker alleging a violation of its provision. For the same reason, a §1983 claim cannot be brought to enforce rights created by the Age Discrimination in Employment Act (ADEA) or Americans with Disabilities Act (ADA). However, a state or municipal worker can state a claim under §1983 based on an alleged equal protection or other constitutional violation, even when that plaintiff also could challenge that same employment decision under Title VII, the ADEA, or the ADA. Section 1983 claims also are available when the federal statute relied upon for the predicate substantive violation does not impose administrative prerequisites to suit. Thus, for example, in *Fitzgerald v. Barnstable School Committee*, 129 S. Ct. 788 (2009), the Supreme Court ruled that a §1983 claim was cognizable where the plaintiff alleged sex-based discrimination by a public school in violation of Title IX of the Education Amendments of 1972 since there were no administrative prerequisites to a private right of action for damages under that statute. And in *Jett*, the Supreme Court stated that plaintiffs not only can, but must, bring a claimed violation of §1981 rights by state actors under §1983. As previously noted, the amendment to §1981 expressly extending it to discrimination under color of state law has been construed by the overwhelming majority of circuit courts not to override the Court's ruling in *Jett*.

Another significant limitation of §1983 relates to the impact of its language providing a cause of action against every "person" (who acted under color of law to deprive someone of federal constitutional or statutory rights) on the nature of the defendants who are subject to suit under its terms. In *Monroe v. Pape*, 365 U.S. 167 (1961), the Supreme Court construed this terminology to mean that only individual agents, and not governmental entities, were proper defendants under §1983. But this ruling was overruled in *Monell v. Department of Social Services*, 436 U.S. 658 (1978), where the Supreme Court held that municipal and county governments, but not a state or state agency, were suable "persons" within the meaning of §1983, but only where the plaintiff demonstrated that the unlawful action was taken by its agents pursuant to a "policy or custom" of that governmental unit. This means that the plaintiff will have to prove either that the agent who committed the unlawful act possessed final policymaking authority to perform that action, or that the governmental entity either ratified that conduct after the fact or acted with reckless indifference by failing to oversee the conduct of that actor in a manner that would have prevented the challenged conduct.

Where a §1983 plaintiff cannot meet the proof requirements for imposing vicarious liability on the municipal or county unit, he may choose to file suit against the individual actor in his individual capacity. On the one hand, it is substantially easier to establish personal rather than vicarious liability, since the plaintiff need only establish that the state actor acted under color of state law when engaging in conduct that was unlawful under the Constitution or federal statutes that will support a §1983 claim. However, where the plaintiff seeks monetary damages from the individual state actor, it must also deal with immunity defenses that the governmental unit cannot assert. The complete immunity from liability for monetary damage awards accorded to legislators, judges, and prosecutors for actions taken pursuant to their legislative, judicial, or prosecutorial functions, respectively, does not arise in employment discrimination cases.

But in *Harlow v. Fitzgerald*, 457 U.S. 800 (1982), the Supreme Court set forth the standard that still governs the availability of qualified immunity for other governmental officials. Under this standard, a public official who performs a discretionary function enjoys qualified immunity in a civil action for damages, where the individual can prove that her conduct does not violate clearly established federal statutory or constitutional rights of which a reasonable person would have known. A governmental official is entitled to qualified immunity, the *Harlow* Court declared, unless his "act is so obviously wrong, in the light of preexisting law, that only a plainly incompetent officer or one who was knowingly violating the law would have done such a thing." This is an objective standard; the subjective intention of the actor is irrelevant. Consequently, the defendant does not have to prove that he acted in subjective good faith. Qualified immunity is not only immunity from liability, it also shields the state actor from being sued, even where a constitutional violation may have occurred.

Where the state actor cannot invoke qualified immunity, the plaintiff can recover an uncapped award of compensatory and punitive damages, with judicial review of such awards subject to the same standards discussed in connection with Title VII. Compensatory damages are recoverable against municipalities and counties who are subject to vicarious liability under §1983 because Eleventh Amendment sovereign immunity against the recovery of monetary damages in federal court does not apply to such political subdivisions of a state. However, punitive damages cannot be recovered against these political subdivisions since the Supreme Court ruled in *City of Newport v. Fact Concerts, Inc.*, 453 U.S. 247 (1981), that public employers enjoy common-law immunity from punitive damage awards.

Section 1983 actions, like those brought under §1981, are subject to the relevant state's general or residual statute of limitations governing personal injury tort actions.

Examples

Ships of State

1. Edward Ships was an accountant employed by the City of Sheboygan, Wisconsin. When he was denied a promotion, he filed a §1983 action against the City, alleging that he had been discriminated against because of his race in violation of Title VII. How should the trial court rule on the City's motion to dismiss the complaint for failure to state a claim upon which relief can be granted?

2. Suppose that Mr. Ships's §1983 complaint alleged that the decision not to promote him was based on his race in violation of the Equal Protection Clause of the Fourteenth Amendment. How should the trial court rule on the City's motion to dismiss the complaint for failure to state a claim upon which relief can be granted?

3. Elaine Boate, a social worker employed by the City of Topeka, Kansas, was the only city employee who was fired for engaging in an unauthorized work stoppage in which hundreds of city workers had participated. She filed a §1983 claim against the City, alleging that singling her out violated her rights under the Equal Protection Clause of the Fourteenth Amendment. How should the trial court rule on the City's motion to dismiss the complaint for failure to state a claim upon which relief can be granted?

4. Margaret Ships, an accountant working for the State of Wisconsin, filed a §1983 claim seeking monetary damages against the State of Wisconsin after she was discharged from her position. She claimed that she had been discharged because of her race in violation of the Equal Protection Clause of the Fourteenth Amendment. How should the trial court rule on the state's motion to dismiss her complaint for failure to state a claim upon which relief can be granted?

5. Cruz Liner was denied employment by Acme Shipyards, Inc., a private shipbuilding company that sold all of its products to private cruise line operators. Liner filed a §1983 claim against Acme, alleging that he had been denied employment in violation of his constitutional and federal statutory rights. How should the trial court rule on the state's motion to dismiss his complaint for failure to state a claim upon which relief can be granted?

Explanations

Ships of State

1. The motion will be granted. Section 1983 is a purely remedial statute providing state and local government employees with a cause of action for damages for violations of substantive rights found in the federal Constitution and a few other federal statutes. But Title VII is not one of the federal statutes whose substantive provisions can form the predicate of a §1983 claim. To do otherwise, the courts reason, would allow the plaintiff to eschew Title VII's administrative processes since suit under §1983, unlike Title VII, does not require the invocation of any administrative remedies. Title VII is the exclusive remedy for claimed violations of its provisions brought by state and local government workers. Thus, the motion will be granted, and the complaint will be dismissed.

2. The motion will be denied. Here, the §1983 plaintiff is seeking redress for a violation of the Constitution and is not seeking to enforce rights guaranteed by Title VII. This is true even though Ships could have asserted a Title VII claim challenging that same promotion decision. As long as the §1983 claim is based on an alleged constitutional violation, the plaintiff can state a claim.

3. The motion will be granted. The plaintiff here is attempting to assert a "class of one" equal protection claim on the ground that she was treated differently from all other similarly situated individuals without alleging that the adverse action was based on her membership in any particular group or class. Although recognized in non-employment related equal protection claims, the Supreme Court in *Engquist* held that "class of one" constitutional equal protection claims cannot be asserted in employment cases unless the plaintiff alleges that the differential treatment was based on class membership. Since Boate's complaint did not contain any such allegation, the motion will be granted, and her complaint will be dismissed.

4. The motion will be granted. The Supreme Court has held that a state is not a suable "person" under §1983. Section 1983 claims can only be brought against either the individual acting under color of state law or a municipal or county entity. Accordingly, the motion will be granted, and the complaint will be dismissed.

5. The motion will be granted. A §1983 claim will only lie against a person who violates someone's constitutional or statutory rights acting under color of state law. The defendant here is a purely private company that could not be said to have acted under color of state law. Accordingly, regardless of whether or not any federal statute would be a proper vehicle for a §1983 claim, this plaintiff cannot assert any §1983 claim against this private defendant. So, the motion will be granted, and the complaint will be dismissed.

C. THE CIVIL RIGHTS ACT OF 1871, SECTION TWO — 42 U.S.C. §1985(3)

The third and least commonly used of the package of Reconstruction Civil Rights Acts is §1985(3), which provides a private right of action for damages caused by private (i.e., nongovernmental) conspiracies to deprive individuals of the equal protection of the laws or of equal privileges and immunities under the laws. A trio of Supreme Court decisions has further limited the impact, and therefore significance, of this statute in the employment discrimination context.

In *Griffin v. Breckenridge*, 403 U.S. 88 (1971), the Supreme Court ruled that §1985(3) only reached conspiracies that were motivated by "some racial, or perhaps otherwise class-based, invidiously discriminatory animus." Subsequently, in *United Brotherhood of Carpenters & Joiners of America, Local 610 v. Scott*, 463 U.S. 825 (1983), the Court construed *Griffin* to mean that §1985(3) did not reach conspiracies motivated by economic or commercial, as opposed to racial, animus. And though the Supreme Court has not ruled on these issues, the lower courts have agreed that §1985(3) does apply to conspiracies to discriminate on the basis of sex, religion, national origin, and age. The prevailing, though not uniform, position taken by the circuit courts is that §1985(3) does not outlaw conspiracies motivated by disability animus.

The most important Supreme Court ruling construing §1985(3) is *Great American Federal Savings & Loan Assn. v. Novotny*, 442 U.S. 366 (1979). There, the Supreme Court concluded that, like §1983, §1985(3) was only a remedial statute that conferred no substantive rights of its own. And since §1985(3), like §1983, does not impose any administrative prerequisites to filing suit, the *Novotny* Court relied on the anti-circumvention rationale to hold that a plaintiff cannot state a claim under §1985(3) based on a claimed violation of rights guaranteed under Title VII, at least where the defendant could have been sued under Title VII. Thereafter, the lower federal courts have ruled that §1985(3) does not apply to conspiracies to violate rights guaranteed under the ADEA, the ADA, and the Equal Pay Act, all statutes that were enacted after §1985(3) and that require the invocation of administrative remedies prior to filing suit. However, most of the few courts that have ruled on the issue have concluded that §1985(3) would support a claim alleging a conspiracy to deprive someone of rights guaranteed by §1981, since that statute both predates the enactment of §1985(3) and does not require pre-litigation invocation of administrative remedies.

The *Novotny* Court expressly declined to rule on whether the conspiracy requirement of §1985(3) could be satisfied by "intracorporate" conspiracies, i.e., conspiracies between several agents of the same employing entity. Post-*Novotny*, most of the circuits refuse to recognize intracorporate conspiracies, reasoning that actions taken by the agents of a corporation within the scope of their employment constitute conduct by a single entity, thereby failing to meet the statutory "two or more persons" requirement. However, some courts deviate from this rule where the individual employees, rather than the company, are named as defendants.

Examples

King of the Mountain

1. Edward Grieg, a driver employed by Peer Gynt Movers, Inc. (PGM), was denied a promotion to inter-city driver. He brought suit against PGM under §1985(3), alleging that several of his supervisors had conspired to deny him this position because of his national origin in violation of Title VII. How should the trial court rule on PGM's motion to dismiss for failure to state a claim?

2. After the management of Peer Gynt Movers, Inc. (PGM) denied Edward Grieg's request for a transfer to an inter-city driving position, they discharged his best friend and co-employee, Henry Ibsen. Ibsen, an African American, alleged that he had been discharged because of his race and filed suit against PGM under §1985(3). His complaint alleged that the president of the union that represented all PGM employees had conspired with the president of PGM to discharge him in violation of his §1981 rights. How should the trial court rule on PGM's motion to dismiss for failure to state a claim?

Explanations

King of the Mountain

1. The motion will be granted on two different bases. First, as the Supreme Court held in *Novotny*, a claim alleging a conspiracy to violate rights guaranteed by Title VII is not cognizable under §1985(3). Additionally, §1985(3) requires the existence of a conspiracy, and although the *Novotny* Court did not rule on this question, the prevailing view among the circuit courts is to reject the concept of an intracorporate conspiracy on the theory that a corporation cannot conspire with itself and that its agents are viewed as part of the corporation, at least when the individual actors are not sued in their individual capacity. Here, since the plaintiff sued the company, the Court would not recognize the existence of an intracorporate conspiracy. Consequently, for both of these reasons, the motion will be granted, and the complaint will be dismissed.

2. The motion will be denied. Here, the plaintiff is alleging a conspiracy between two separate entities, the union and the company. Thus, the "two or more persons" requirement of §1985(3) has been met; this is not an intracorporate conspiracy. The remaining issue is whether §1985(3) supports a claim based on a violation of rights guaranteed by §1981. Since §1981 was enacted before §1985(3) and since there are no administrative prerequisites to suit under §1981, the circumvention of administrative processes rationale behind Novotny does not apply. That is why the prevailing view of the courts, post-Novotny, is that a §1981-based claim is cognizable under §1985(3). Accordingly, the defense motion to dismiss will be denied.

D. THE EQUAL PAY ACT

1. Overview

The Equal Pay Act (EPA), 29 U.S.C. §206(d), is the only twentieth-century federal statute dealing with employment discrimination that predates Title VII. Enacted in 1963, the EPA is a statute of very limited application that has largely been supplanted by the more expansive terms of Title VII. The EPA targets only one kind of employment practice — it prohibits discrimination on the basis of sex with respect to wages. Specifically, it requires employers to pay members of both sexes equal wages for "equal work on jobs the performance of which requires equal skill, effort, and responsibility, and which are performed under similar working conditions." It also prohibits unions from causing or attempting to cause an employer to violate the Act. Finally, the equal pay mandate is subject to four statutory defenses that immunize an employer from liability for implementing a sex-based wage differential pursuant to (1) a seniority system; (2) a merit system; (3) a system linking wages to quantity or quality of production; or (4) factors other than sex. Most litigation under the EPA turns on the issue of the meaning of the statute's equal work requirement, the scope of the four statutory exceptions, and/or its relationship to Title VII.

2. Coverage and Substantive Provisions

Since the EPA was enacted as an amendment to the Fair Labor Standards Act (FLSA), its coverage is tied to the coverage provisions of the FLSA. Unlike Title VII, the FLSA does not contain any minimum employee requirement. Instead, the statute extends coverage under two different standards — one of which focuses on the individual, and the other of which relates to the nature of the employer. Under its "employee" test, statutory protection is accorded to any employee who is engaged in interstate commerce or in the production of goods for interstate commerce. Any employee meeting this standard is covered, regardless of whether or not her employer meets the employer-focused standard. Alternatively, the statute's "enterprise" standard extends statutory protection to all workers, regardless of their connection to interstate commerce, if they are employed by an enterprise that (1) is engaged in interstate commerce or the production of goods for interstate commerce; (2) has two or more employees; and, with the exception of a few exempted industries like fishing and agriculture, (3) generates at least $325,000 in annual gross income. There is also language specific to the EPA that several circuits have construed to extend coverage to any employer with two or more employees of different sexes who engage in or produce goods for interstate commerce, regardless of whether that employer meets the FLSA "enterprise" standard. Additionally, the EPA applies to federal, state, and local government workers.

In order to determine whether a man or woman has been denied equal pay on the basis of sex, the court must determine whether the plaintiff is (a) receiving unequal wages for the performance of (b) "equal work" (c) on the basis of sex. The classic articulation of the EPA's equal work requirement is found in *Corning Glass Works v. Brennan*, 417 U.S. 188 (1974). There, the Supreme Court emphasized that the statutory equal pay standard did not require precise identity between the jobs held by a man and a woman. Rather, the Court focused on the "skill, effort, responsibility, and performed under similar work conditions" modifier contained in that provision. It held that the jobs must be "substantially equal" in terms of these four criteria. Thereafter, the circuits have construed this to require only that the jobs be "substantially similar." The *Corning* Court construed the "working conditions" factor to refer to those hazards or surroundings that influence the manner in which a job is performed. So, the Court noted, whether a person worked the day or night shift did not constitute a "working condition" within the meaning of the EPA.

Applying the *Corning* standard, the circuit courts do not give anything like determinative effect to job descriptions or titles; they focus on a comparative assessment of actual job requirements (and not the quality of an individual employee's performance) in determining whether the jobs in question are substantially similar. It is the skill and effort required to do the job, not a comparative evaluation of the plaintiff's abilities, that is relevant to this determination. A finding of substantial similarity will not be negated by the presence of some extra or different job duties involving different skill, effort, responsibility, or working conditions, unless the wage differential is occasioned and justified by these job differences. Job differences also will not justify wage differentials where the disparate job duties do not involve differences in skill, effort, responsibility, or working conditions. Accordingly, each case involves a detailed examination of the particular personnel practices and an *ad hoc* application of the equal work standard to those facts.

The EPA only requires covered entities not to discriminate on the basis of sex with respect to its rate of "wages." Although the EPA does not define "wages," this term is defined in the FLSA, the parent statute to which the EPA was enacted as an amendment. Under the FLSA, wages include not only salary but "the reasonable cost to the employer of furnishing such employee with board, lodging, or other facilities, if such board, lodging, or other facilities are customarily furnished by such employer to his employees."

If an EPA plaintiff establishes that she has been paid an unequal wage for equal work, she still must prove that this differential is based on her sex. Normally, this is accomplished by comparing the wage received by the plaintiff to a person of the opposite sex who is performing substantially similar work. This raises a problem in a sex-segregated working environment where there is no opposite-sex comparator available. Note, however, that the EPA states that the employer shall not engage in sex-based wage discrimination within any "establishment." Thus, as long as the comparator (who can be a contemporary, a predecessor, or a successor) is employed within the same "establishment," his or her wages can be used as the basis for establishing the claim. The EPA does not define "establishment" in this context. But the courts focus on a physical location rather than the entirety of the defendant's operations. In most cases, then, an employer with multiple locations will have each location viewed as a separate establishment for EPA purposes.

The EPA also contains four affirmative defenses. Three of these are specific; they permit wage-based differentials pursuant to seniority, merit, or incentive (quality or quantity of production) systems. They also are rarely invoked. Most of the litigation concerning the defenses has focused on the more generally phrased "factor other than sex" defense. This defense poses an analytic problem. In some sense, a defendant's argument that the alleged wage differential was not sex-based constitutes a form of denial of the plaintiff's prima facie case and, therefore, is an issue as to which the defendant only bears the burden of coming forward. But it is listed among the statutory affirmative defenses. And affirmative defenses are not denials but explanations or justifications and, therefore, are issues as to which the defendant bears the burden of persuasion. Having said this, the fact of the matter is that the courts treat this as an affirmative defense and saddle the defendant with the burden of persuasion. Among the criteria that have been held to fall within this defense are prior salary considerations, economic benefit derived by the employer (e.g., where lawfully sex-segregated sales jobs resulted in female or male sales personnel generating higher revenue because of the relatively higher profits generated by the sale of sex-linked products), and lesser experience. On the other hand, reliance on market forces (including evidence that women are prepared to work for less pay than men at a particular job), as well as a difference in the time of day of a work shift (i.e., day versus night shift), has not been accepted as legitimate "other than sex" factors.

3. Relationship to Title VII

Since the payment of wages is a term or condition of employment, any sex-based wage differential that would violate the EPA also would violate Title VII (assuming the Title VII statutory employer would also fall within the coverage of the EPA). On the other hand, since Title VII, unlike the EPA, does not contain an equal work standard, it has potentially broader application to sex-based wage claims. The seminal case addressing the relationship between these two statutes is *County of Washington v. Gunther*, 452 U.S. 161 (1981). In *Gunther*, the Court was asked to determine whether the proof requirements of EPA actions applied to sex-based wage claims brought under Title VII. The Court limited its ruling to claims of intentional sex-based wage discrimination, declaring that plaintiffs asserting such claims do *not* have to satisfy the equal work requirement of the EPA. The Court, however, did not explain which proof formula would apply to such Title VII claims of intentional sex-based wage discrimination. The circuit courts have not agreed on this issue; some require direct evidence of a facially discriminatory wage system, while others invoke the *McDonnell Douglas* circumstantial evidence scheme.

The *Gunther* Court did address, however, the issue of the impact of the last sentence of §703(h) of Title VII, also known as the Bennett Amendment, on Title VII sex-based wage claims. This sentence provides that it is not unlawful under Title VII for an employer to engage in sex-based wage discrimination when such discrimination is not unlawful under the EPA. The *Gunther* Court interpreted this sentence to incorporate all four EPA affirmative defenses into Title VII in connection with intentional claims of sex-based wage discrimination. But it did not comment directly on the way in which the EPA's "factor other than sex" defense should be applied in Title VII cases in light of the fact that under traditional Title VII jurisprudence, it is the *plaintiff* who has to prove that sex was at least a motivating factor for any allegedly discriminatory act. Circuit court decisions subsequent to *Gunther* have not provided a uniform answer to this question, with some applying the standard *McDonnell Douglas* formulation and others requiring the defendant to establish that the decision was based on a factor other than sex. One issue, however, on which the circuits agree is that Title VII is not amenable to a claim of comparable worth, i.e., a situation where a member of one sex alleges that she was paid less than a male doing a different job, but one that provided the employer with comparable worth.

4. Procedure and Remedies

Since the EPA was enacted as an amendment to the FLSA, its enforcement is tied to the provisions of the FLSA, which, in several regards, differs from the procedures governing Title VII claims. Unlike Title VII plaintiffs, for example, an individual with an EPA claim can proceed immediately with a suit, although such individuals have the option of filing a charge with the EEOC prior to bringing suit. The EEOC is also authorized to bring suit on behalf of an aggrieved individual, and its exercise of this authority cuts off the individual's right to file an independent suit. And, unlike under the Title VII regime, the EEOC does not have to have attempted conciliation before filing suit. But unlike a Title VII plaintiff, an EPA claimant cannot intervene as of right in an EEOC-initiated action.

The two-year statute of limitations governing other FLSA suits also applies to claims brought under the EPA, except that any suit involving an allegation of a willful violation (i.e., that the defendant knew or should have known that its conduct was proscribed by the EPA) is subject to a three-year limitations period.

The FLSA (and therefore the EPA) authorizes recovery of back wages, liquidated damages, and attorney's fees. Recovery of unlawfully depressed wages can date back no longer than two years prior to the filing of the complaint, or three years where the employer is found to have engaged in a willful violation. An award of liquidated damages is discretionary, and the employer can avoid the imposition of this remedy by establishing that it had a (subjectively) good faith and (objectively) reasonable belief that its conduct was not unlawful. Although the Supreme Court in *Garcia v. San Antonio Metropolitan Transit Authority*, 469 U.S. 528 (1985), upheld the constitutionality of the application of the FLSA's *substantive* provision to state and local governments, it has not ruled on the constitutionality of the statute's *remedial* provision. However, the circuit courts have upheld the constitutionality of the EPA provision providing a private right of action for damages to state government workers as a constitutionally effective abrogation of the states' Eleventh Amendment sovereign immunity from damage claims in federal court.

Examples

School's Out

1. Alice Copper and Ozzie Osborn were tenured faculty members of the economics department of Rock Island University (RIU), which operated campuses in three different cities in California. Copper and Osborn had identical resumes and had started their employment at RIU on the same day. Copper works at the Los Angeles campus of RIU, while Osborn teaches at the school's San Francisco campus. Each campus has its own administrative structure. Copper was paid $80,000 and Osborn was paid $100,000. When she discovered that she was being paid less than Osborn, Copper filed suit under the EPA. How should the court rule on RIU's motion to dismiss the complaint for failure to state a claim upon which relief can be granted?

2. Would your answer to the preceding question be different if Alice had filed suit under Title VII?

3. Rock Island University (RIU) pays the same salary to all of its similarly situated faculty members, regardless of sex. However, it also provides faculty members with a professional development allowance that can be used to pay for the costs of attending academic conferences. But under the terms of that allowance, female professors are required to share double rooms with other conference-attending female professors, while male professors are permitted to stay in single rooms. Professor Sharon Osborn filed suit against RIU, challenging this policy as violative of the EPA. How should the court rule on RIU's motion to dismiss the complaint for failure to state a claim upon which relief can be granted?

4. Rock Island University (RIU) operates a campus store in which it sells RIU-embossed apparel. No more pencils, no more books, just clothing. The campus store employs only women in the women's clothing department and only men in the men's clothing department. Because the store is able to charge significantly higher prices for women's apparel, it pays its saleswomen more than its salesmen of equal seniority. When David Bohee, a salesman at the RIU campus store, filed suit against RIU challenging this policy under the EPA, the school responded with affidavits demonstrating that all its female sales personnel generated higher revenues than all of its salesmen. How should the trial court rule on RIU's motion for summary judgment?

5. Rock Island University (RIU) employs part-time cashiers in its campus store during the heavy sales period of the holiday season. It offered Alice Copper $15 per hour at the same time that it offered Ozzie Osborn $20 per hour to do the same job. Alice filed suit under the EPA. In its answer, RIU asserted that it paid Alice less than Ozzie because women were willing to work part-time at a lower salary than males would accept for the

same part-time position. How should the court rule on RIU's motion for summary judgment?

Explanations

School's Out

1. The motion will be granted. The plaintiff has alleged that she is receiving unequal pay for equal work. The issue here is whether or not the fact that the female and male professors work on different campuses is fatal to her claim. This raises two separate considerations. First, are the two campuses separate "establishments"? If so, the salaries of a female at one campus must be compared to the salary paid to a similarly situated male at that campus. Most, though not all, circuits have defined "establishment" to be restricted to a single physical location, particularly where each location is independently managed, as here. Accordingly, each campus would be deemed a different establishment and, therefore, Copper's reliance on the salary paid to Osborn would be insufficient as a matter of law to state a claim, and the court should dismiss the complaint. On the other hand, if the court found that the entire university was one establishment, we would be left with the matter of whether the different locations constitute different working conditions within the meaning of the EPA's equal work standard. As to this, the courts are in agreement. Working conditions relate to the hazards encountered in the working environment and do not extend to the physical location. Accordingly, the fact that the plaintiff and her comparator work on different campuses would not mean that they work under different working conditions. Thus, the plaintiff would have satisfied the equal work standard. But, on balance, because the courts will find that the two campuses are different establishments, the motion will be granted, and the complaint will be dismissed.

2. Yes, the answer would be different. Unlike the EPA, Title VII does not contain any "same establishment" requirement. Thus, it would be sufficient for the plaintiff to compare her salary to someone employed at the same defendant's other location. In this case, the motion to dismiss would be denied.

3. The motion will be denied. The EPA prohibits discrimination in wages, and the FLSA defines "wages" to include "the reasonable cost to the employer of furnishing such employee with board, lodging, or other facilities, if such board, lodging, or other facilities are customarily furnished by such employer to his employees." Since payment for traveling and lodging expenses is customarily furnished by the university, this policy would appear to fall within the statutory definition of "wages." Some courts have added a gloss to the statute that only includes such

payments when they are provided for the benefit of the employee. But even under this test, furnishing a single room rather than requiring employees to share rooms is a concession made primarily for the employee's convenience and comfort. Thus, the policy will fall within the purview of the EPA, and so the motion will be denied.

4. The motion will be denied. Although the plaintiff has stated a prima facie case, the defense has asserted a recognized "factor other than sex" affirmative defense. The courts have recognized that economic profitability is a legitimate factor other than sex. Since the plaintiff is not challenging the sex-segregated assignment of sales personnel, which would not be covered in any case by the EPA, that issue is not relevant. The defense motion for summary judgment will be granted.

5. The motion will be denied. The courts have ruled that market forces do *not* fit within the EPA's "factor other than sex" affirmative defense. So, the defense motion for summary judgment will be denied.

The Age Discrimination in Employment Act

A. OVERVIEW

Enacted within four years of the passage of Title VII and amended several times thereafter, the Age Discrimination in Employment Act of 1967 (ADEA), 29 U.S.C. §§621 et seq., is the exclusive *federal statutory* remedy (most states also have enacted statutes proscribing age discrimination in employment, and public sector workers can challenge age-based decisions under the equal protection guarantees of the Fifth and Fourteenth Amendments) for age-based employment discrimination. As we will see, the ADEA was patterned directly after Title VII, with most, though not all, of its substantive and procedural (though not remedial) provisions tracking the analogous portions of Title VII. But there are a few significant differences, all of which will be examined in this chapter.

B. COVERAGE

The ADEA, like Title VII, applies to employers, unions, and employment agencies. With respect to statutory employers, there are three key things to remember. First, the minimum employee size is 20 (as opposed to 15 under Title VII); second, the statute applies to U.S. citizens employed abroad by American corporations or their subsidiaries unless application of the ADEA would violate the domestic laws of the foreign nation in which the American citizen was employed; and third, the statute covers federal, state, and local government workers as well as private sector employees. Elected officials are excluded from protection, as are, as under Title VII, uniformed members of the armed forces. The ADEA's coverage of unions and employment agencies is identical to that found in Title VII, except that the ADEA requires unions without hiring halls to have 25 members, while only 15 are required under Title VII. Unions, however, are not subject to suits for damages under the ADEA because the ADEA, like the Equal Pay Act, incorporates the remedial scheme of the Fair Labor Standards Act (FLSA) and not that of Title VII, and the FLSA only authorizes damage suits to be brought against an "employer" and excludes unions from the definition of that term. The statute contains a blanket exemption from coverage for state and local law police officers and firefighters who have attained the age of hiring or retirement in effect under applicable state or local law.

The constitutionality of the application of the statute's *substantive* provisions to state and local government workers was upheld against a Tenth Amendment challenge in EEOC v. Wyoming, 460 U.S. 226 (1983). However, in Kimel v. Florida Board of Regents, 528 U.S. 62 (2000), the Supreme Court struck down a remedial provision of the ADEA, ruling that in expressly providing state and local government workers with a private cause of action for monetary damages, Congress had not constitutionally abrogated the states' Eleventh Amendment sovereign immunity from private suits for monetary awards in federal court. Invoking the doctrine it had enunciated in Seminole Tribes of Florida v. Florida, 517 U.S. 44 (1996), the Kimel Court concluded that this provision could not be justified as an exercise of Congress's enforcement power under §5 of the Fourteenth Amendment because the statute failed its "congruence and proportionality" test. Under that standard, the courts (1) compare the scope of the statutory proscription against the degree of conduct that would violate constitutional norms; and (2) examine the legislative history for evidence that Congress had acted in response to a demonstration of prior discrimination by the states. Applying that test, the Kimel Court concluded that (1) since age discrimination receives only rational basis scrutiny under the Equal Protection Clause, the broad statutory prohibition against age discrimination far exceeded the limited protection against age discrimination that is afforded under the Fourteenth Amendment; and (2) since there was no legislative record identifying a pattern of age-based employment discrimination by the states, Congress's remedial response could not be justified as an exercise of its §5 authority to enforce the provisions of the Fourteenth Amendment. The combination of the Court's rulings in Wyoming and Kimel means that state and local government workers can still bring suit for equitable relief to challenge acts of age discrimination by state actors under the ADEA, but they cannot collect monetary damages. But don't forget that states can waive their Eleventh Amendment right to immunity from monetary damage awards in federal court either expressly (by statute or judicial ruling) or indirectly (by failing to assert this immunity on a case-by-case basis). Also, keep in mind that pursuant to the Supreme Court's declaration in *Alden v. Maine*, 527 U.S. 706 (1999), a state's sovereign immunity to suits for monetary damages does not apply to actions brought against them by the federal government, and the circuit courts permit the Equal Employment Opportunity Commission (EEOC) to sue state and local government employers for make whole monetary relief for aggrieved individuals.

C. THE MEANING OF AGE DISCRIMINATION

In language taken in *haec verba* from Title VII, the ADEA prohibits discrimination with respect to all terms and conditions of employment because of someone's age. However, there is one crucial limitation on the statute's nondiscrimination mandate. It only applies to individuals 40 years of age and older. Persons under the age of 40 cannot state a claim under this statute. Additionally, in *General Dynamics Land Systems, Inc. v. Cline*, 540 U.S. 581 (2004), the Supreme Court ruled that notwithstanding (a) the absence of any textual modifier to "age," and (b) an EEOC guideline to the contrary, the statute's "social history" demonstrated that Congress was concerned only with protecting relatively older workers from discrimination that worked to the advantage of their relatively younger competitors. Thus, it concluded, when Congress used the word "age" it really meant "old" or "older" age, i.e., it intended only to prohibit discrimination where the victim is older than the preferred. As Justice Souter explained in a phrase that encapsulates his opinion for the Court, "the enemy of 40 is 30, not 50."

Four years later, the Supreme Court revisited the meaning of "age" in *Kentucky Retirement Systems v. EEOC*, 128 S. Ct. 2361 (2008), where it held that a dual-track retirement system that provided larger benefit payments to workers who retired because of disability than to employees who retired at the plan's standard retirement eligibility age of 55 was not age-based on its face because it calculated retirement benefits on the basis of the chosen type of retirement rather than the age of the retiree.

D. PROVING AND DEFENDING INTENTIONAL AGE-BASED DISCRIMINATION CLAIMS

Throughout the first 40-plus years after their enactment, the substantive provisions of the ADEA and Title VII were almost always accorded identical treatment. This was a function of two factors: (1) the overwhelming textual similarity between the two statutes; and (2) the fact that they both addressed the same topic — employment discrimination — and were enacted only four years apart. So, for example, the Supreme Court's Title VII rulings creating the proof formulation for the use of circumstantial evidence in intentional discrimination claims, from *McDonnell Douglas* through *Burdine* and *St. Mary's*, consistently have been applied to ADEA claims. Similarly, the Court's final statement on that proof scheme, *Reeves*, is an ADEA case that uniformly has been transplanted to the Title VII context. And the circuit courts have held that the Supreme Court's ruling in *Gross* (see below), that impact analysis is unavailable in ADEA cases, does not cast doubt on the continued viability of the *McDonnell Douglas/Burdine* proof scheme for single motive claims of intentional discrimination.

Unlike the Title VII protected categories, age is not a discrete characteristic that permanently separates members from nonmembers of the protected group. Rather, it is a continuum along which relative distinctions can be made. This has raised the issue of whether it is fatal to an ADEA plaintiff's claim that he or she was adversely treated in favor of another member of the protected (i.e., 40 and over) age group. In *O'Connor v. Consolidated Coin Caterers Corporation*, 517 U.S. 308 (1996), the Supreme Court unanimously ruled that the fact that a statutorily protected plaintiff was replaced or otherwise passed over in favor of someone who also was within the protected class "lacks probative value" and is "utterly irrelevant." The Court emphasized that the relevant issue was whether the decision was based on the plaintiff's age and not on whether the favored individual was or was not within the statutorily protected class. The Court explained that "the fact that a replacement is substantially younger than the plaintiff is a far more reliable indicator of age discrimination than is the fact that the plaintiff was replaced by someone outside the protected class." Of course, after *General Dynamics*, we know that the plaintiff must be older than the preferred candidate. How much older is a fact that goes to the strength of the inference that the decision was motivated by the plaintiff's age.

Keep in mind, also, that the "after-acquired" evidence doctrine that we explored in the Title VII materials was first enunciated in *McKennon*, which was an ADEA case. Such evidence, you recall, is admissible only to limit the plaintiff's recovery; it is irrelevant to the finding of liability since it is not probative of the employer's intention at the time it made the challenged employment decision.

Consistent with the general trend of transplanting jurisprudence back and forth across the Title VII/ADEA frontier, for more than two decades after the Court's creation of mixed motive analysis in *Price Waterhouse*, the circuit courts extended that doctrine to ADEA cases. But after the *Price Waterhouse* analysis was codified in part and reversed in part through the enactment of the 1991 Civil Rights Act, an issue was raised as to which mixed motive analysis should apply in age cases since the 1991 amendments did not refer, in this context, to the ADEA. Finally, there also was some dispute as to whether the Supreme Court's ruling in *Desert Palace,* which recognized the applicability of mixed motive analysis to claims involving either direct or circumstantial evidence of the presence of an unlawful motivating factor, applied to ADEA cases.

All of these issues were resolved by the Supreme Court's ruling in *Gross v. FBL Financial Services, Inc.,* 129 S. Ct. 2343 (2009). Although the sole issue raised in the petition for the writ of certiorari in *Gross* was whether *Desert Palace* should apply to ADEA cases, the majority went beyond that to rule that mixed motive analysis was totally unavailable in ADEA cases. The majority relied on the fact that the 1991 Act's provision codifying mixed motive claims amended only Title VII and not the ADEA. Since the 1991 amendments did amend the ADEA in other areas, the majority concluded that Congress did not intend for the mixed motive provision to apply to age cases. Moreover, the majority rejected the plaintiff's claim that the pre-1991 Title VII ruling in *Price Waterhouse* should extend to cases brought under the ADEA. It offered four reasons for this conclusion: (1) that the "because of" language in the ADEA was not properly amenable to an interpretation that allowed claims to be based upon a showing that age was "a" as opposed to "the" motivating factor; (2) that the Court's approach to interpreting the ADEA in light of Title VII has not been uniform; (3) the fact that Congress chose in 1991 to incorporate "motivating factor" liability into Title VII and not into the ADEA; and (4) that even if the ruling in *Price Waterhouse* was doctrinally sound (which the majority strongly implied might not be the case), the problems that the trial courts had experienced in crafting jury instructions to explain its burden-shifting framework "have eliminated any perceivable benefit to extending its framework to ADEA claims." In light of its ruling that mixed motive claims were not cognizable at all under the ADEA, the Court declined to rule on the *Desert Palace* issue.

Section 4(d) of the ADEA contains a separate antiretaliation provision that, like §704(a) of Title VII, protects individuals from retaliation for engaging in acts of either opposition or participation.

The ADEA, like Title VII and the EPA, also contains affirmative defenses to claims of intentional discrimination, which are set forth at §4(f). The statute permits age-based distinctions (1) where age is a bona fide occupational qualification (BFOQ) defense; or (2) pursuant to the terms of either a bona fide seniority system not intended to evade the purposes of the Act or of a bona fide employee benefit plan.

The text of the ADEA's BFOQ provision is identical to §703(e)(1) of Title VII. But whereas the BFOQ exception is most frequently accepted by the courts in Title VII cases when it is based on considerations of authenticity and privacy, the courts are most likely to apply it in age cases on the basis of safety concerns. Otherwise, the rules governing the BFOQ defense in Title

VII cases have been transplanted to the ADEA context. Thus, for example, in *Western Air Lines, Inc. v. Criswell*, 472 U.S. 400 (1985), the Court held that an employer must demonstrate that the qualification used to justify the age requirement is reasonably necessary to the essence of its business and then prove that it was compelled to rely on age as a proxy for this qualification by establishing either that all or substantially all individuals over a particular age lack the qualification or that it is impracticable or impossible to treat persons over this age on an individualized basis. Then, in *Johnson v. Mayor and City Council of Baltimore*, 472 U.S. 353 (1985), decided the same day as *Western Air Lines*, the Court stated that the existence of a federal statute establishing a mandatory retirement policy for a class of federal firefighters did not automatically establish a BFOQ defense to a state or local government rule imposing an identical mandatory retirement age on analogous state and local government workers. The *Johnson* Court concluded that Congress's decision to implement a mandatory retirement policy was not based on a legislative determination that age was a BFOQ for the subject class (federal firefighters), but, rather, on the idiosyncratic problems of federal civil servants and Congress's desire to create an image of a "young man's service." Accordingly, the Court stated that the federal statute authorizing mandatory retirement was not relevant to the question of whether age was a BFOQ for firefighters.

The circuit courts typically reject reliance on economic considerations as a basis for a BFOQ since the practice of refusing to employ older workers because of their higher relative cost was one of the evils the ADEA was designed to eliminate. Moreover, §4(a)(3) of the ADEA expressly prohibits an employer from attempting to accommodate its interest in minimizing costs and the plaintiff's interest in retaining his job by offering to employ the older worker only at the lower wage level offered to the younger applicant.

The bona fide seniority and employee benefit plans defenses of §4(f)(2) are frequently invoked in ADEA, particularly §4(f)(2)(i), which instructs employers on how to handle the increased cost of providing certain fringe benefits, such as medical or life insurance, to older workers when the cost of such benefits is a function of age. Section 4(f)(2)(i) allows employers to pay either (a) equal fringe benefits to all employees regardless of age, or (b) unequal fringe benefits to older workers as long as the cost incurred by the employer on behalf of older workers is at least equal to the cost borne by that employer for younger workers. Additionally, an employer is allowed to prevent an employee from receiving multiple benefits by §4(l)(1)(B), which permits employers to coordinate benefit payments with Social Security and Medicare. An EEOC regulation that permits employers to reduce or eliminate employer-sponsored health benefits for retirees when retirees become Medicare-eligible (i.e., when they reach the age of 65) was upheld as within the agency's §9 authority to establish "such reasonable exemptions" to the Act as it finds "necessary and proper in the public interest." Section 4(l)(3) authorizes employers to reduce the amount of a former worker's long-term disability benefits by the amount of pension payments that individual will receive at age 62 or retirement, whichever comes later.

As in Title VII cases, the federal courts recognize a "ministerial exception" in ADEA cases that precludes the application of this statute to any employment discrimination claim between a "church" and a "minister." The federal courts also construe the ban on age discrimination to include cases of alleged age-based harassment. The courts once again have applied the relevant Title VII jurisprudence governing both the quid pro quo and hostile environment forms of harassment claims.

Examples

The Age of Aquarius

1. James Rado was denied a position as a stylist with Hair Care, Inc. (HCI), a tonsorial establishment located in New York City. HCI employs 18 individuals, including the person hired instead of Rado. During his interview, Rado was told by the company representative that the company was looking for a stylist "who could relate to our young, hip, rich clientele." Rado was 60 years old with 30 years of haircutting experience when his application for employment was rejected, and Gerome Ragni, a 37-year-old, was hired. After fulfilling all his administrative preconditions to suit, Rado sued HCI, alleging that he had been denied employment because of his age. HCI filed a motion to dismiss the complaint for failure to state a claim upon which relief can be granted. How should the trial court rule on this motion?

2. After he was denied a position with Hair Care, Inc., James Rado applied for a marketing position with the New York State Tourism Office. His application was rejected. During his job interview, the interviewer asked if Rado was "young and energetic enough" to handle the job and indicated that the office was looking for "new young blood." After fulfilling all administrative prerequisites, Rado filed suit against the Tourism Office in federal district court, seeking injunctive and declaratory relief and compensatory and punitive damages in the amount of $250,000. How should the trial court rule on the defendant's motion to dismiss Rado's complaint?

3. On January 1, 2010, the president of HCI announced that all HCI employees over the age of 60 would be given a $5,000 bonus in honor of the company's sixtieth year in business. Galt MacDermott, a 55-year-old stylist, filed suit against HCI under the ADEA, alleging that the bonus policy constituted unlawful discrimination on the basis of age. How

should the trial court rule on HCI's motion to dismiss the complaint for failure to state a claim upon which relief can be granted?

4. Fiff Dimension, a 65-year-old male, was denied a position as office manager by Hair Care, Inc. (HCI). The job was given to Marilyn McCoo, a 42-year-old woman. After fulfilling all administrative prerequisites, Dimension filed an ADEA claim against HCI, alleging that he had been denied employment because of his age. HCI filed a motion for summary judgment, claiming that since McCoo, like Dimension, was a member of the age group protected by the ADEA, it was entitled to judgment as a matter of law that it had not violated the statute. How should the trial court rule on this motion?

5. Dee Ageuv, a 53-year-old glass grinding technician employed by Aquarius Visions, Inc. (AVI), a telescope manufacturer, unsuccessfully applied for a promotion that was awarded to Dawn Ning, a 65-year-old co-employee of Ageuv's. The company told Ageuv that it had chosen Ning over her because of Ning's greater level of experience, better judgment, and because the company felt it needed to have a more aged person at the helm of the department. Her golden living dreams of visions dashed by this disappointing turn of events, Ageuv fulfilled all of her administrative preconditions to suit and then filed suit against AVI, alleging that she had been denied a promotion because of her age. How should the trial court rule on AVI's motion to dismiss the complaint for failure to state a claim upon which relief can be granted?

6. William Davis, Jr. was discharged from his position as sales manager for Aquarius Visions, Inc. (AVI). After Davis filed suit against AVI under the ADEA, alleging that he had been terminated because of his age, AVI discovered that Davis had demonstrated a distinct lack of harmony and understanding of the company's best interests as well as a lack of sympathy and trust for his colleagues by leaking company secrets to the press and spreading falsehoods and derisions about the company's top leadership to officials of AVI's main competitor. After learning of Davis' various treacherous and disloyal acts, AVI filed a motion for judgment as a matter of law. How should the trial court rule on this motion?

7. When Florence LaRue was demoted from office manager to file clerk at Aquarius Visions, Inc. (AVI), she filed suit against the company under the ADEA, alleging that the demotion decision had been based on her age. At trial, the undisputed evidence established that LaRue had been consistently absent or late without permission and that the supervisor who made the demotion decision had told several of LaRue's workers that "LaRue was just too old in the tooth to do this high profile job." At the conclusion of the case, AVI's attorney asked the trial judge to give the jury a mixed motive instruction to the effect that even if they concluded that LaRue's age had been a motivating factor in the demotion decision,

she could not be awarded damages or be reinstated to her management position if the jury also believed that LaRue would have been demoted simply because of her record of absenteeism and tardiness. How should the court rule on AVI's request?

8. When Florence LaRue was demoted from office manager to file clerk at Aquarius Visions, Inc. (AVI), she filed suit against the company under the ADEA, alleging that the demotion decision had been based on her age. At trial, the undisputed evidence established that LaRue had been consistently absent or late without permission and that the supervisor who made the demotion decision had told several of LaRue's workers that "LaRue was just too old in the tooth to do this high profile job." At the conclusion of the case, AVI's attorney asked the trial judge to give the jury a mixed motive instruction to the effect that even if they concluded that LaRue's age had been a motivating factor in the demotion decision, they must render a verdict in favor of AVI if they also determined that LaRue would have been demoted simply because of her record of absenteeism and tardiness. How should the court rule on AVI's request?

9. LaMonte McLemore was a salesman with 30 years of seniority at Aquarius Visions, Inc. (AVI). When the company's revenues took a nose dive as a result of the national recession, its president, Crystal Revelation, decided that the company needed to cut expenses to the bone. McLemore, as the salesman with the greatest seniority, was also the company's highest paid non-management employee at an annual salary of $75,000. The parties agree that Revelation went to McLemore and told him that the company had to cut its payroll and that there were dozens of entry level applicants willing to work in the company's sales department for $30,000. It is also undisputed that Revelation told McLemore that McLemore could keep his job only if he agreed to have his salary cut to $30,000, the amount it would pay his replacement, if necessary. McLemore refused and filed suit against AVI, alleging that he had been discriminated against on the basis of his age. The company claimed that the decision was based on financial exigency and not age. How should the court rule on McLemore's motion for judgment as a matter of law?

10. Jupiter A. Lines decided to attend law school after a successful career as a screenwriter. By the time he graduated, Lines was 57 years old. He applied for a position with the law firm of Love, Will, Steer, & Destars (LWS&D). The managing partner of LWS&D informed Lines during the job interview that all entry-level associates were put on an 8-year partnership track, at which point they began to reach a high level of professional and economic productivity. Because of Lines's age, he was informed, it was economically nonviable to hire him since the

firm could not anticipate receiving many additional years of that level of productivity, even assuming me made it through the 8-year training period for associates. Consequently, the firm did not hire Lines. Lines then filed suit under the ADEA, alleging that he had been denied employment because of his age. LWS&D filed a motion for summary judgment on the ground that the economics of law practice made age a BFOQ for the entry-level associate attorney position. How should the court rule on this motion?

11. The Church of the Fifth Dimension (CFD) interviewed several candidates to replace its minister when she retired. Dr. Ron Towson, a 60-year-old ordained minister, applied for, but was denied, the position. He was told by the chairman of the board of CFD that the church was looking for a young, dynamic, recently ordained minister to attract young families to its membership. Towson had always received a great deal of satisfaction from serving as a minister, and he particularly enjoyed officiating at life cycle events such as marriages. But after singing the wedding bell blues, Towson followed up on his disappointment by filing an ADEA suit against CFD, alleging that he had been denied employment because of his age. CFD filed a motion to dismiss the complaint for failure to state a claim upon which relief can be granted. How should the trial court rule on that motion?

Explanations

The Age of Aquarius

1. The motion will be granted. The trick here is that unlike Title VII, which only requires an employer to employ 15 individuals, the ADEA contains a minimum employee requirement of 20. Since HCI employs only 18 individuals, it is not subject to the requirements of the ADEA, and so the complaint will be dismissed since the defendant timely asserted this otherwise waivable affirmative defense.

2. The motion will be granted in part and denied in part. The issue here is the constitutional validity of the ADEA provision providing state workers with a private right of action for money damages against a state employer. Although the Supreme Court in *Wyoming* upheld the extension of the ADEA's substantive provisions to states, the Court in *Kimel* struck down the ADEA provision giving state and local workers a private right of action for the recovery of monetary damages as a constitutional ineffective abrogation of the states' Eleventh Amendment immunity from monetary damage claims in federal court. Consequently, the plaintiff will be able to retain his claim, including the prayer for declaratory and equitable relief, against the state department. But his prayer for

monetary relief in the form of compensatory and punitive damages will be stricken.

3. The motion will be granted. Under the Supreme Court's ruling in *General Dynamics*, the ADEA's prohibition against discrimination on the basis of age only applies when the company discriminates against older workers in favor of younger employees. Although it is true that the plaintiff is a member of the statutorily protected class, since he is over the age of 40, the company's bonus policy discriminates in favor of older workers to the detriment of younger workers. Since, under the ruling in *General Dynamics*, the employer's policy does not discriminate on the basis of age, the defense motion will be granted, and the plaintiff's complaint will be dismissed. To paraphrase Justice Souter, the enemy of 55 is 35, not 60.

4. The motion will be denied. The Supreme Court held in *Consolidated Coin Caterers* that the fact that the plaintiff was passed over in favor of a candidate who was also within the statutorily protected age group was not fatal to the plaintiff's claim. The issue is not whether or not the preferred candidate was within the protected class, but whether the decision to reject the plaintiff was based on his age. Consequently, the defense is not entitled to judgment as a matter of the law, and its motion will be denied.

5. The motion will be granted, but be careful of two red herrings. The reason the motion will be granted and the complaint will be dismissed is because the plaintiff is younger than the person chosen for the job. Under the Court's ruling in *General Dynamics*, a decision that favors an older person over a younger person on the basis of age does not constitute unlawful age-based discrimination. Now for red herring #1. The facts indicate that the company had several explanations for its promotion decision, one of which was age-based. So, if this is viewed as a mixed motive case, the Court's ruling in *Gross* tells us that mixed motive analysis is unavailable under the ADEA. Nevertheless, this would not be a reason for dismissing the complaint for failure to state a claim because, the *General Dynamics* problem aside, the plaintiff's complaint certainly alleges enough to at least state a prima facie claim of age-based discrimination. Red herring #2 is the fact that the chosen candidate, like the plaintiff, is a member of the statutorily protected group. This would not be a reason to dismiss the complaint, per the Court's ruling in *Consolidated Coin Caterers*. The reason this complaint will be dismissed is because of the application of the Court's definition of age-based discrimination in *General Dynamics*.

6. The motion will be denied. This is a classic example of "after-acquired evidence," i.e., evidence obtained after the challenged employment practice. In *McKennon*, the Supreme Court ruled that although such evidence is admissible, it is admissible only for the purpose of limiting the plaintiff's recovery. It is irrelevant to the issue of liability since it is not probative

of the employer's intention at the time it made the discharge decision. Consequently, the motion for summary judgment will be denied. Note that if this evidence is determined to constitute an adequate, independent, nondiscriminatory reason for discharge, the plaintiff's recovery of back pay will be cut off as of the date of discovery, and he will not be awarded the promotion or front pay.

7. The request will be denied. Even though this appears to be a classic example of a mixed motive case, the Supreme Court in *Gross* ruled that mixed motive analysis is unavailable under the ADEA. Consequently, the trial court will deny the request for a mixed motive instruction.

8. The request will be denied. Do not be fooled by the fact that in this case, as compared with the prior example, the defense is asking for a *Price Waterhouse* version of the mixed motive instruction, i.e., with the same decision defense going to liability rather than to damages. In *Gross*, the Supreme Court held that no version of the mixed motive analysis was available in any ADEA case. So, a judge can never give a mixed motive instruction in any ADEA case and, therefore, this request will be denied.

9. The motion will be granted. Section 4(a)(3) of the ADEA is directly on point and expressly prohibits an employer from reducing the wage rate of an older worker in order to avoid violating the statute. Accordingly, since the facts are undisputed, the plaintiff is entitled to judgment as a matter of law, and his motion will be granted.

10. The motion will be denied. As in cases brought under Title VII, the BFOQ defense is narrowly construed in ADEA cases. Here, the plaintiff has clearly established a prima facie claim of age discrimination. The issue is whether or not the employer can establish a BFOQ defense based on a cost justification. The courts uniformly reject such a cost justification basis for the BFOQ defense, principally on the ground that avoiding the higher cost of older workers was precisely one of the employment decisions that the statute was designed to forbid. Consequently, even though there is no genuine issue of material fact, the defense is not entitled to judgment as a matter of law on its BFOQ defense, and so its motion will be denied.

11. The motion will be granted. As they have done in Title VII cases, the courts uniformly have read a ministerial exception into the ADEA, precluding the application of the ADEA from any decision involving the selection of a "minister" by a "church." Since that is precisely the type of employment decision being challenged in this suit, the defense motion will be granted, and the plaintiff's complaint will be dismissed.

E. PROVING AND DEFENDING DISPARATE IMPACT CLAIMS

Hazen Paper Co. v. Biggins, 507 U.S. 604 (1993), was another ADEA case in which the plaintiff asserted a claim of intentional discrimination. Nevertheless, in her opinion for the unanimous Court, Justice O'Connor mentioned that the Supreme Court never had decided whether ADEA liability could be based on a showing of *Griggs*-styled disparate impact, even as she acknowledged that since the plaintiff had alleged only disparate treatment discrimination, the Court did not have to decide that question in this case. But three Justices joined in a concurring opinion for the sole purpose of emphasizing that the Court's opinion should not be read as incorporating disproportionate impact theory into the ADEA context and suggesting that impact analysis should not carry over to the ADEA context. This language led to a conflict among the circuits as to the viability of impact analysis in ADEA cases, a split that was resolved by the Supreme Court in *Smith v. City of Jackson*, 544 U.S. 228 (2005). In *City of Jackson*, five Justices (four in a plurality opinion of the Court and one in a concurring opinion) agreed that impact analysis was available in ADEA cases.

The plurality opinion offered several reasons for its conclusion that impact analysis was available in ADEA cases: (1) the fact that Congress used the same language in the substantive provisions of two statutes with similar purposes that were enacted within four years of one another justified indulging in the presumption that Congress intended that text to have the same meaning in both statutes; (2) since the Court's ruling in *Griggs* was supported by the text of Title VII and that text was identical to the corresponding provision in the ADEA, it was appropriate to extend the ruling in *Griggs* to the ADEA context; (3) post-*Griggs*, the federal circuit courts uniformly had construed the ADEA to recognize impact claims, at least until the Supreme Court's decision in *Hazen v. Biggins*, a case that did not address that issue and, therefore, whose holding did not preclude the extension of *Griggs*; (4) the fact that the ADEA contained a provision that did not appear in Title VII—the provision stating that otherwise unlawful conduct is not prohibited where it is based on a reasonable factor other than age (RFOA)—was consistent with the recognition of impact claims under the ADEA since that provision was redundant in *McDonnell Douglas* intent cases; and (5) recognizing impact claims in ADEA cases was consistent with the EEOC's construction of the ADEA. Justice Scalia joined the four members of the plurality solely on the ground that the Court should defer to the EEOC's reasonable interpretation of the ADEA.

Having concluded that a prima facie case of age discrimination could be established by showing that a facially neutral criterion produced a disparate impact on those over the age of 40, the City of Jackson Court then addressed the nature of the defendant's response to an impact claim. Recall that in Title VII cases, once a plaintiff has established disparate impact, the defendant can escape liability by shouldering the burden of persuasion on the job-relatedness/business necessity affirmative defense. But the nature of a defendant's burden is quite different in an impact claim brought under the ADEA. In City of Jackson, the Court focused on the portion of §4(f)(2) establishing a "reasonable factor other than sex" affirmative defense to age discrimination claims. It reasoned that since a RFOA defense was inapplicable to claims where the plaintiff was alleging intentional age-based discrimination, it could only apply in cases where the plaintiff was not alleging that age was not the reason for the allegedly unlawful employment practice, i.e., where the plaintiff was challenging the disparate impact of a facially neutral requirement. Thus, the Court reasoned, the only reason for the existence of the RFOA provision was to serve as an affirmative defense to an impact claim. Once an ADEA plaintiff has established that an identified employment practice produced a disparate impact, the defendant can escape liability merely by showing that its impact-producing criterion was a "reasonable" factor. This is a significantly lower threshold than a Title VII defendant is required to meet. And if there was any doubt in City of Jackson as to the nature of the defendant's burden of proof on this question, it was resolved in Meacham v. Knolls Atomic Power Laboratory, 128 S. Ct. 2395 (2008). There, the Court held that this was an affirmative defense as to which the defense bore the burden of persuasion by a preponderance of the evidence. The Meacham Court also reemphasized its statement in City of Jackson that the business necessity defense played no role in age-based impact claims.

F. VOLUNTARY AND INVOLUNTARY RETIREMENT

Section 4(f)(2)(A) of the ADEA prohibits involuntary retirement at any age if the retirement decision is made on the basis of age. This provision, however, is subject to the statutory BFOQ defense. So, if a plaintiff is involuntarily retired either because of a non-age factor or where age is a BFOQ, that retirement will not be unlawful. There is an exemption allowing involuntary retirement of a limited category of highly paid, bona fide executive or high policy-making officials who have attained the age of 65.

The statutory ban on involuntary retirement does not prohibit an employer from offering employees the option of voluntary retirement, even when this option is offered on the basis of the employee's age. Under General Dynamics, a voluntary retirement offer made to persons over a particular age would not constitute discrimination on the basis of age as a prima facie matter because the discrimination would be in favor of, and not against, the older workers. Plus, pursuant to amendments to the ADEA contained in the 1990 Older Workers Benefit Protection Act (OWBPA), voluntary early retirement incentive plans are lawful as long as the employer can establish that the plan is consistent with promoting the employment of older workers based on ability rather than age, prohibiting arbitrary age-based discrimination in employment, and assisting employers and employees in addressing problems associated with the impact of age on employment.

The OWBPA also lists some requirements that must be met in order for the court to enforce an agreement where an employer secures a waiver of ADEA claims as a condition for a worker's receipt of early retirement or severance pay. Such agreements are only enforceable if the waiver of statutory rights is deemed to be knowing and voluntary. Among these requirements are that the waiver (1) be written in a manner calculated to be understood by the average worker; (2) specifically refer to rights or claims arising under the ADEA; (3) not include a waiver of rights or claims that may arise after the date of execution of the waiver; (4) be made in exchange for consideration beyond anything to which the individual already was entitled; (5) contain a written statement advising the individual to consult with an attorney prior to executing the agreement; and (6) provide the individual with at least 21 days within which to consider the agreement (or 45 days where the waiver is part of an exit incentive or other employment termination program offered to a group of employees) and with another seven days after the execution of the agreement to revoke the agreement. A waiver agreement that meets these requirements is enforceable, but only after the revocation period has expired.

The burden of proving that the waiver is enforceable (i.e., knowing and voluntary) is on the party asserting its validity. Note, in this regard, that the statute requires the employer to prove that the waiver was written in a manner calculated to be understood by the average worker. This suggests that the employer may not satisfy its burden of persuasion merely by demonstrating that the plaintiff understood the meaning of the waiver. The statutory text indicates that the employer must prove that the waiver would be understood by the average worker who would be subject to its terms. But even an otherwise effective waiver agreement does not cut off the EEOC's right to bring an ADEA claim on behalf of an individual who has accepted such an agreement, or its authority to investigate a charge filed with it by that individual. Consequently, any attempted waiver of an individual worker's right to file an age discrimination charge with the EEOC (as opposed to filing suit) cannot be enforced. But where an agreement includes both a purported (and unenforceable) waiver of the right to file an EEOC charge as well as a waiver of ADEA causes of action, the presence of the unenforceable portion of that agreement does *not* invalidate the waiver of the individual's right to file a lawsuit.

If a worker signs an otherwise enforceable voluntary retirement agreement containing a release and waiver of ADEA claims and then accepts and retains the benefits paid pursuant to that agreement, but subsequently decides to challenge the agreement for failure to meet the OWBPA requirements, the retention of benefits will not cure any defects in the agreement and bar her from pursuing the purportedly waived statutory claims. In *Oubre v. Entergy Operations, Inc.*, 522 U.S. 422 (1998), the Court held that regardless of whether a party's retention of benefits would operate to ratify an otherwise voidable contract under general common law principles, the circumstances that make a release of ADEA-protected rights enforceable are limited solely to those contained within the OWBPA's list of requirements for enforceable waivers. And since retention of benefits is not listed as a basis for enforcing a waiver, if the waiver agreement does not meet the statutorily listed requirements, it cannot be enforced. To rule otherwise, the Court reasoned, might tempt employers to risk noncompliance with the OWBPA waiver requirements on the assumption that most of their former employees will be unable to repay the monies and thus be subject to this ratification defense. Having said that, however, the *Oubre* Court also expressly left the door open for an employer to attempt to recover those retained benefit payments through a claim for restitution, recoupment, or setoff against whatever award the plaintiff might receive on her underlying claim.

G. PUBLIC EMPLOYEES AND CONSTITUTIONAL CHALLENGES TO AGE DISCRIMINATION

Government employers are subject not only to the requirements of the ADEA but to the equal protection requirements of the Fifth and Fourteenth Amendments as well. *Massachusetts Board of Retirement v. Murgia*, 427 U.S. 307 (1976), involved an equal protection constitutional challenge to a Massachusetts statute that required uniformed state police officers to retire at age 50. The Supreme Court ruled that an age-based classification need only pass rational basis, rather than strict scrutiny under the Equal Protection Clause of the Fourteenth Amendment. It then found that mandatory retirement at age 50 rationally furthered Massachusetts's interest in protecting the public by assuring the physical preparedness of the uniformed police. Similarly, in *Vance v. Bradley*, 440 U.S. 93 (1979), a federal statute mandating retirement at age 60 of Foreign Service personnel was upheld in the face of an equal protection challenge. The Supreme Court held that the retirement provision rationally furthered Congress's legitimate objective of maintaining a competent Foreign Service.

Examples

King of the World

1. Titanic Productions, Inc. (TPI), a movie making company, had always provided its employees with very generous paid vacation benefits. Specifically, new employees received three weeks of paid vacation, workers with 15 years of seniority received four weeks of paid vacation, and employees with 25 years of seniority received six weeks of paid vacation. But when its business boomed, the company decided that it needed to increase each worker's productivity and that it no longer could afford to have so many workers on vacation for such long periods of time. Accordingly, it announced that all employees thereafter would receive only three weeks of paid vacation leave. The 30 Titanic employees with more than 15 years of seniority joined together to file an ADEA suit against TPI, alleging that the reduction in paid vacation leave discriminated against them on the basis of their age. TPI contends that its decision was based on economic, and not age, considerations. How should the trial court rule on TPI's motion to dismiss the complaint for failure to state a claim upon which relief can be granted?

2. Titanic Productions, Inc. (TPI), a movie making company, had always provided its employees with very generous paid vacation benefits. Specifically, new employees received three weeks of paid vacation, workers with 15 years of seniority received four weeks of paid vacation, and employees with 25 years of seniority received six weeks of paid vacation. But when the company fell on hard times as a result of the nationwide recession, it announced that all employees thereafter would receive only three weeks of paid vacation leave. All of these facts are undisputed. The 30 Titanic employees with more than 15 years of seniority joined together to file an ADEA suit against TPI, alleging that the reduction in paid vacation leave discriminated against them on the basis of their age. TPI acknowledged that its decision had a disparate impact on its more senior workers, but maintained that its decision was not based on age, but was necessary in order to increase worker productivity without increasing its salary and fringe benefit expenses. How should the court rule on TPI's motion for judgment as a matter of law?

3. Rose Bukater had been employed as a film director for Titanic Productions, Inc. (TPI) since 1960. It is undisputed that during the filming of her most recent movie, Bukater often missed production and other meetings because she forgot about the appointments, and she frequently gave incoherent instructions to her videographers and assistant directors. It is

also undisputed that based on these and other performance deficiencies, the president of TPI, Cal Hockley, told Bukater that it was time for her to retire. At the retirement party, a visibly disappointed and hurt Bukater told those assembled that she never wanted to retire, that she no longer felt like the king of the world, and that she had decided to file an ADEA suit against TPI. In its answer, TPI stated that although it did not have any mandatory retirement policy, Bukater's retirement had been involuntary. It subsequently filed a motion for judgment as a matter of law. How should the trial court rule on TPI's motion?

4. For a variety of economic reasons, Titanic Productions, Inc. (TPI) offered all employees over the age of 60 the opportunity to take early retirement and receive a one-time payment of $100,000 as well as monthly retirement benefits. Spicer Lovejoy, a 50-year-old TPI employee, filed suit under the ADEA against TPI, alleging that he had been denied the opportunity for voluntary retirement because of his age. How should the trial court rule on TPI's motion to dismiss the complaint for failure to state a claim upon which relief can be granted?

5. In exchange for releasing his employer, Titanic Productions, Inc. (TPI), from liability for any and all pre-existing ADEA claims, Brock Lovett, a cinematographer, agreed to take an early retirement incentive package consisting of a one-time severance payment of $250,000. The day after receiving this payment, Lovett used the money to purchase a blue diamond necklace for his wife. Two months later, Lovett filed an ADEA action against TPI, alleging that he had been denied a promotion on the basis of his age one week before signing the release and early retirement agreement. In its answer, TPI admitted that the release agreement was unenforceable because it did not contain any language advising Lovett to consult with an attorney before signing it or informing Lovett that he had four weeks within which to revoke the agreement. But in its answer, TPI also contended that Lovett's acceptance and retention of the severance payment cured any defect in that agreement and thereby rendered the agreement enforceable, including its provision releasing TPI from liability for all pre-existing ADEA claims, such as Lovett's claim of a discriminatory denial of promotion. Based on those contentions, TPI filed a motion for judgment as a matter of law. How should the trial court rule on TPI's motion?

6. After Alexander D. Great, a social worker employed by the State of Missouri, was discharged, he filed suit under §1983 against the state, alleging that he had been fired because of his age in violation of the ADEA. He alleged that his termination letter stated that "the State has decided that you are just too old to relate to the population that we serve." The state filed a motion to dismiss the complaint for failure to state a claim upon which relief can be granted. How should the trial court rule on that motion?

Explanations

King of the World

1. The motion will be denied. Since the employer's decision discriminates against employees with significant amounts of accumulated seniority, and since seniority is linked to age, the plaintiffs will be able to state a claim of disparate impact discrimination. In *City of Jackson*, the Supreme Court ruled that disparate impact claims were cognizable under the ADEA. Consequently, the motion will be denied, and the complaint will not be dismissed.

2. The motion will be granted. The issue here is different from the one posed in the preceding example. Here, the defense is not claiming that the plaintiff has failed to state a prima facie claim upon which relief can be granted. Rather, it has asserted that it is entitled to judgment as a matter of law based on its defense that its use of a facially neutral criterion—seniority—that generates a disparate impact on older workers is a reasonable method of attaining its legitimate business objectives. In *City of Jackson*, the Court held not only that disparate impact claims were cognizable under the ADEA, but that the statutory "reasonable factor other than age" was an affirmative defense to such a claim. And in *Meacham*, the Court reinforced this decision, adding that this was an issue as to which the defendant bore the burden of persuasion. Since the facts are undisputed, the issue is whether relying on seniority as the criterion for cutting the cost of operating the business is a reasonable factor other than age. This is a much lesser threshold to meet than the job-relatedness/business necessity defense that would be applicable to an impact-based claim brought under Title VII. The court will find that the use of seniority meets this low threshold of justification, and so the defense motion will be granted.

3. The motion will be granted. The ADEA prohibits mandatory retirement, but only when that retirement is based on the employee's age. Here, the undisputed facts reveal that Bukater was involuntarily retired for cause and not because of her age. Consequently, the defense is entitled to judgment as a matter of law, and so its motion will be granted.

4. The motion will be granted. But notice the trick here. An employment opportunity was limited to those workers over the age of 60. Under the Supreme Court's ruling in *General Dynamics*, discrimination in favor of older workers and against younger workers does not constitute unlawful age-based discrimination within the meaning of the ADEA. Consequently, for this reason, the defense motion will be granted, and the complaint will be dismissed. The fact that this is a voluntary retirement option is irrelevant. The plaintiff cannot state a prima facie claim, and so there is no need to consider the applicability of any affirmative defense.

5. The motion will be denied. In *Oubre*, the Supreme Court ruled that voluntary retirement agreements containing a release and waiver of pre-existing ADEA claims are only enforceable if they meet the requirements set forth under the OWBPA amendments to the ADEA. And since acceptance and retention of severance benefits is not among the statutory bases for enforcing such agreements, it does not operate to validate an otherwise defective agreement. Accordingly, since the waiver agreement is unenforceable, Lovett is not precluded by its terms from challenging his loss of the promotion. This means that the company is not entitled to judgment as a matter of law, and its motion will be denied.

6. The motion will be granted. This is another trick question. Notice that suit here was filed against the state under §1983. As we explained in Chapter 9, a §1983 claim cannot be brought to enforce rights created by the ADEA. So, the defense motion will be granted, and this complaint will be dismissed. Note, however, that if the plaintiff had based his §1983 claim on a violation of the Equal Protection Clause of the Fourteenth Amendment, he could have stated a claim. But as the Supreme Court held in *Murgia*, such a claim of age-based discrimination would be subjected only to rational basis scrutiny, where the state would have to prove only that it had a rational basis for basing its decision on the plaintiff's age.

H. PROCEDURE AND REMEDIES FOR NONFEDERAL EMPLOYEES

The procedural scheme governing ADEA suits is similar, though not identical, to that applicable in Title VII proceedings. For example, as under Title VII, §7(d) of the ADEA requires all but federal employee grievants, as a precondition to filing suit, to file a charge with the EEOC within 180 days after the alleged unlawful practice, or within 300 days of the alleged unlawful practice where a state or local deferral agency exists, or within 30 days after receipt of notice of termination of proceedings under state law, whichever comes first. And §14(b) provides that in a deferral state, an aggrieved cannot file suit under the ADEA until after she has filed an age discrimination complaint with the state or local enforcement agency and waited for 60 days, unless those administrative proceedings are earlier terminated. However, because the passage of time is often more prejudicial to an ADEA plaintiff than to someone who is pursuing a Title VII claim, the ADEA contains a few terms that are intended to expedite the pre-litigation enforcement process. For example, as the Supreme Court acknowledged in *Oscar Mayer & Co. v. Evans*, 441 U.S. 750 (1979), an individual intent on pursuing her ADEA cause of action can pursue both her state and federal administrative remedies concurrently, not serially as required by Title VII. Moreover, as the Supreme Court authorized in *Oscar Mayer*, if a plaintiff files suit before invoking his state administrative remedy, the federal trial court will simply stay its proceedings, permit the plaintiff to file his state charge, and wait 60 days before reviving the lawsuit. Another concession to the typical ADEA plaintiff's need for an expedited administrative process is the provision in §7(d) of the ADEA that permits an ADEA claimant to file suit as early as 60 days after the filing of an age charge with the EEOC without waiting 180 days (as under Title VII) for the agency to issue a notice of right to sue. On the other hand, if the grievant chooses to wait for the EEOC to send a right to sue letter, then §7(e) of the ADEA requires, like §706(f)(1) of Title VII, that he file suit no later than 90 days after receiving either that letter or notice that the agency has concluded or terminated its proceedings. However, in contrast to the Title VII regime, once a plaintiff files suit under the ADEA, all state proceedings are superseded.

Although §7(d) states that an aggrieved cannot file a civil action until 60 days after a "charge" has been filed with the EEOC, it does not explain what is sufficient to constitute a "charge." In *Federal Express Corp. v. Holowecki*, 128 S. Ct. 1147 (2008), an ADEA suit had been preceded by the plaintiff's filing only an intake questionnaire with the EEOC, accompanied by a signed affidavit describing the alleged discriminatory practices in greater detail. The Court adopted the EEOC's position that a filing would meet the statutory requirement where—in addition to an allegation of age discrimination and the name of the charged party—"the document reasonably can be construed to request agency action and appropriate relief on the employee's part."

The preclusive effect of state administrative rulings on a court's disposition of an ADEA suit mirrors the practice applicable to Title VII cases. In *Astoria Federal Savings & Loan Assn. v. Solimino*, 501 U.S. 104 (1991), the Supreme Court ruled that a judicially *unreviewed* state or local administrative ruling on a state age discrimination charge is not entitled to any preclusive effect on suit filed under the ADEA.

The EEOC is empowered to file suit under the ADEA, but §7(b) requires the EEOC to engage in conciliation efforts prior to filing suit. And an EEOC-filed action on behalf of a worker or workers, under §7(c)(1), terminates the individual right of action. But since §7(c) refers only to the termination of the individual's right to "bring" as opposed to "maintain" a civil action, this provision does not require a court to dismiss a previously filed individual action once the EEOC determines to file suit on that person's behalf. And the few circuits that have considered the question have construed §7(c) to mean that a first-filed individual suit does not preclude the EEOC from subsequently filing suit on behalf of the aggrieved.

The remedial provisions of the FLSA govern ADEA actions, as they do claims brought under the Equal Pay Act. Section 7(b) of the ADEA authorizes the awarding of injunctive relief, back pay (called "unpaid wages" and subject to the same mitigation obligation imposed in Title VII cases), liquidated damages, and attorney's fees. The courts consistently have construed their authority to issue equitable relief to include the awarding of front pay where instatement or reinstatement is not practicable. The awarding of liquidated damages is subject to the same strictures that apply to claims under the Equal Pay Act. They are awarded only in cases of willful violations and in an amount equal to the back pay (but not a front pay) award, resulting in an award of "double damages." In *Trans World Airlines, Inc. v. Thurston*, 469 U.S. 111 (1985), the Supreme Court ruled that a violation is willful for liquidated damages purposes under the ADEA if "the employer either knew or showed reckless disregard for the matter of whether it conduct was prohibited by the ADEA." And in *Hazen*, the Supreme Court added that it was insufficient for the plaintiff to prove that the employer knew it was making a decision based on age, i.e., that it engaged in intentional discrimination; the plaintiff must also demonstrate that the employer knew or recklessly disregarded the fact that its consideration of age was unlawful. Significantly, however, a victorious ADEA plaintiff cannot recover compensatory or punitive damages. Consequently, there is no cap on those damages that are recoverable in ADEA actions. Attorney's fees awards are only available to a prevailing ADEA plaintiff. But unlike the rule in Title VII cases, awarding attorney's fees to a prevailing ADEA plaintiff is mandatory, not discretionary.

In *Lorillard v. Pons*, 434 U.S. 575 (1978), the Supreme Court held that recovery of unpaid wages under the ADEA was a form of legal relief, thereby invoking the Seventh Amendment right to a jury trial, where such relief was sought in an ADEA action. Subsequently, the ADEA was amended to include §7(c)(2), which expressly makes jury trials available with respect to any factual issue, including those relevant to the recovery of equitable relief, back pay, or liquidated damages, as long as the complaint includes a request for relief in the form of unpaid wages. However, there is one exception to this rule. In *Lehman v. Nakshian*, 453 U.S. 156 (1981), the Supreme Court held that federal employees are not entitled to a jury trial in ADEA cases. Finally, in *Commissioner of IRS v. Schleier*, 515 U.S. 323 (1995), the Supreme Court held that liquidated damages awarded in an ADEA action are taxable income because they are punitive in nature and therefore not intended to serve as compensation for personal injury.

I. FEDERAL EMPLOYEES

Pursuant to §15 of the ADEA, federal employees and applicants for federal employment are subject to a different remedial scheme than is prescribed for nonfederal employees. Specifically, they are not required to invoke any state or federal administrative remedy prior to instituting suit. As under Title VII, a federal employee has the option of seeking administrative resolution of a claim by the employing agency (with an appeal to the EEOC from a final agency decision) before filing suit, or bypassing the administrative mechanism entirely and directly filing suit. However, if the second option is chosen, the federal employee, like all other claimants, must file a notice of intent to sue with the EEOC at least 30 days prior to instituting suit. Additionally, as the Supreme Court held in *Stevens v. Department of Treasury*, 500 U.S. 1 (1991), §15(d) requires the claimant to file this notice with the EEOC within 180 days of the alleged discriminatory occurrence and then to wait at least 30 days from said filing before bringing a federal civil action. The *Stevens* Court also noted that the ADEA does not contain an express limitations period within which federal employees and job applicants must file their suit. But the Court declared that it would "assume that Congress intended to impose an appropriate period borrowed either from a state statute or from an analogous federal one." However, since the Court determined that the plaintiff in *Stevens* had filed suit "well within whatever statute of limitations might apply," it declined to rule on which limitations period was applicable. Post-*Stevens*, the prevailing view among the circuit courts is that where a federal employee resorts to the administrative process prior to filing suit under the ADEA, the appropriate limitations period to borrow is the one contained in Title VII, i.e., 90 days from the termination of the administrative process. But there is no consensus among the circuits with respect to the applicable limitations period for federal employees who elect to bypass the administrative process and to proceed directly with their civil action. Some circuits apply the FLSA limitations period, others the timing requirements contained in Title VII.

Section 15(a) does not contain any express reference to retaliation, unlike §4(d), which expressly prohibits retaliation by private employers. In *Gomez-Perez v. Potter*, 128 S. Ct. 1931 (2008), the Supreme Court declared that notwithstanding the absence of such explicit terminology, the general prohibition on age-based discrimination should be read to include claims of retaliation taken in response to the filing of an age discrimination charge. As it did in the §1981 context in *CBOCS West*, a case decided on the same day as *Gomez-Perez*, the majority reasoned that retaliating against a person for complaining of age discrimination is another form of intentional age-based discrimination. The Court also noted that the private sector antidiscrimination provision contained a specific list of forbidden employment practices, whereas the federal employee provision contained merely a broad prohibition of "discrimination." Thus, the Court explained, although Congress might have concluded that it was necessary to include a reference to retaliation in the list of proscribed practices in the private sector, such detail was unnecessary with respect to federal employees. Having concluded that the text of the ADEA's federal employee provision encompassed retaliation claims, the Court also ruled that this provision waived the federal government's sovereign immunity against age-based retaliation claims.

Title VII / ADEA Comparison Chart

Topic	Title VII	ADEA
Minimum employee size	15	20
Proscribed classifications	Race, color, religion, sex, national origin	Age
Mixed motive claims	Yes	No
Defense to impact claim	Job-relatedness/business necessity	Reasonable factor other than age
Administrative preconditions	State or local agency (where applicable) charges must be filed before EEOC filing; must obtain right to sue letter	State or local agency and EEOC filings can be concurrent; can file suit 60 days after EEOC filing without waiting for right to sue letter
Statute of limitations	90 days from receipt of letter	90 days from receipt of letter
Damages awardable	Compensatory and punitive	No compensatory or punitive; only liquidated damages in cases of willful violations
Attorney's fees	Prevailing parties	Only to prevailing plaintiffs

Examples

The Times They Are a Changin'

1. Robert Zimmerman, a 43-year-old reporter for the Sun Valley Times who prophesized with his pen, believed that he had been discharged because of his age on January 1, 2010. He filed an age discrimination charge with the EEOC on June 1, 2010, and an identical charge with the California

Fair Employment Commission on September 1, 2010. He filed an ADEA suit against the newspaper on December 1, 2010. Under the governing California law, all age discrimination charges must be filed with the California Fair Employment Commission no later than 100 days after the alleged unlawful employment practice. The newspaper filed a motion to dismiss Zimmerman's complaint for failure to file his state administrative charge in a timely fashion. How should the court rule on that motion?

2. Robert Zimmerman, a 43-year-old reporter for the *Sun Valley Times*, believed that he had been discharged because of his age on January 1, 2010. He filed an age discrimination charge with the EEOC on June 1, 2010, and an identical charge with the California Fair Employment Commission on September 1, 2010. He filed suit in California state court under the relevant California antidiscrimination statute on December 1, 2010. Under that state law, all age discrimination charges must be filed with the California Fair Employment Commission no later than 100 days after the alleged unlawful employment practice. The newspaper filed a motion to dismiss Zimmerman's complaint for failure to file his state administrative charge in a timely fashion. How should the court rule on that motion?

3. Robert Zimmerman, a 43-year-old reporter for the *Sun Valley Times*, believed that he had been discharged because of his age on January 1, 2010. He filed an age discrimination charge with the EEOC on June 1, 2010, and an identical charge with the California Fair Employment Commission on October 1, 2010. He filed an ADEA suit against the newspaper on December 1, 2010. Under the governing California law, all age discrimination charges must be filed with the California Fair Employment Commission no later than 100 days after the alleged unlawful employment practice. The newspaper filed a motion to dismiss Zimmerman's complaint for failure to file his EEOC charge in a timely fashion. How should the court rule on that motion?

4. Gather Roundpeople, a 50-year-old male, was denied a promotion by his employer, the *Sun Valley Times*, on January 1, 2010. He was confident that the decision was based on his age. Since the newspaper was located in a non-deferral state, Roundpeople filed an age discrimination charge with the EEOC on February 1, 2010. Intent on doing something that would shake the windows and rattle the walls of the newspaper, Roundpeople decided not to wait for the EEOC to send him a notice of right to sue before proceeding with his case. Instead, he filed an ADEA suit against the newspaper on May 1, 2010. The *Times* filed a motion to dismiss the complaint on the ground that Roundpeople had failed to wait for 180 days and obtain a notice of right to sue from the EEOC before bringing this civil action. How should the court rule on that motion?

5. Gather Roundpeople, a 50-year-old male, was denied a promotion by his employer, the *Sun Valley Times*, on January 1, 2010. He was confident

that the decision was based on his age. Since the newspaper was located in a non-deferral state, Roundpeople filed an age discrimination charge with the EEOC on February 1, 2010. He received a notice of right to sue on August 1, 2010, and filed suit under the ADEA against the *Times* on December 1, 2010. The newspaper moved to dismiss his complaint as time-barred. How should the court rule on this motion?

6. Battle Rajun was a seriously unhappy and disgruntled employee of the *Sun Valley Times*. Throughout his tenure, he was constantly complaining about imaginary acts of discrimination to co-employees who, in his opinion, did not keep their eyes wide open to a chance to hurt the newspaper that might not come again. He also filed multiple charges of race, age, and sex discrimination with the EEOC, all of which were dismissed as non-meritorious. On January 1, 2010, he filed his twentieth age discrimination charge against the *Times* with the EEOC, claiming that he had been denied a promotion because of his age. The EEOC investigated, found no reasonable cause to believe a violation had occurred, and transmitted a right to sue letter on March 1, 2010. Rajun filed an ADEA civil action on March 3, 2010. Neither side requested a jury trial. At the conclusion of the court trial, the judge granted judgment as a matter of law to the defense, finding that the record did not contain a scintilla of evidence of age discrimination. The newspaper then filed a motion seeking attorney's fees. How should the trial court rule on this motion?

7. Sam Hunter, a 62-year-old accountant employed by the Federal Aviation Agency (FAA), was discharged after he filed his twentieth baseless age discrimination charge against the federal agency with the EEOC. In response, Hunter filed an ADEA civil action against the FAA, alleging that he had been the victim of a retaliatory discharge. The agency filed a motion to dismiss for failure to state a claim based on the absence of any applicable antiretaliation provision in the ADEA. How should the court rule on this motion?

Explanations

The Times They Are a Changin'

1. The motion will be denied. In *Oscar Mayer*, the Supreme Court ruled that while an ADEA plaintiff must invoke his state administrative remedy prior to filing suit, that state administrative filing does not have to be timely under state law to preserve the federal statutory remedy. As long as the ADEA plaintiff files with the state agency and waits for 60 days before filing suit, the obligation under §14(b) to resort to appropriate state administrative remedies has been met. Since Zimmerman filed with the state agency on September 1 and filed suit three months later, he has

met the §14(b) requirement, and so the defense motion will be denied and the complaint will not be dismissed.

2. The motion will be granted. This example differs from the preceding example in that it asks whether a timely state administrative filing is a prerequisite to preserving the right to file suit under *state* law. The answer to that question is yes. So since Zimmerman's administrative charge was filed in an untimely manner, the defendant can successfully assert this as an affirmative defense to the state substantive law claim. Accordingly, the motion will be granted, and the state law complaint will be dismissed.

3. This motion will be denied. Here, the issue is whether a timely filed state administrative charge is a prerequisite for an ADEA claimant to be eligible for the extended 300-day period for filing an EEOC charge in a deferral state. The Supreme Court's ruling in *Oscar Mayer* did not address this issue. *Oscar Mayer* involved the relationship between state limitations periods and the filing of a federal *suit*, whereas this example addresses the relationship between state limitations periods and the filing of a charge with the federal administrative agency. In the few cases examining this question, the circuit courts have read *Oscar Mayer* to imply that the state limitations period is similarly irrelevant in determining whether the 180- or 300-day period applies to the filing of EEOC charges. Thus, they conclude that a grievant can take advantage of the 300-day filing period in deferral states regardless of when the state charge was filed. Since Zimmerman filed his EEOC charge nine months after the alleged unlawful practice, that charge is timely filed, and so the court will deny the defense motion to dismiss.

4. The motion will be denied. Although a Title VII plaintiff does have to wait 180 days to obtain a right to sue notice from the EEOC (unless the EEOC terminates its proceedings earlier than that date), §7(d) of the ADEA allows plaintiffs to file suit only 60 days after the filing of an EEOC charge, regardless of whether or not they have obtained any notice of the termination of the EEOC's proceedings or a notice of right to sue. Consequently, this complaint is timely filed, and the motion to dismiss will be denied.

5. The motion will be granted. If an ADEA plaintiff decides to wait for the EEOC to send a notice of right to sue, then suit must be filed no later than 90 days after receipt of that notice. The plaintiff here waited four months after receiving the notice before filing suit. So, his claim is time-barred, and the defense motion to dismiss the complaint will be granted.

6. The motion will be denied. Unlike Title VII, which *permits* an award of attorney's fees to a prevailing "party," the ADEA *mandates* an award of attorney's fees, but only to the prevailing "plaintiff." The courts have construed this text to preclude the awarding of attorney's fees to a prevailing

defendant in an ADEA action, regardless of whether or not the court finds the suit was frivolous or unreasonable. The motion, therefore, will be denied.

7. The motion will be denied. It is true that there is no express antiretaliation provision in §15 of the ADEA, the provision providing substantive rights to federal employees. However, in *Gomez-Perez*, the Supreme Court ruled that notwithstanding the absence of such explicit terminology, the general prohibition on age-based discrimination contained in §15 as applied to federal employees should be read to include claims of retaliation against federal employees taken in response to the filing of an age discrimination charge. Since the plaintiff here is alleging that he was retaliated against in response to filing an age discrimination charge with the EEOC, he has a cognizable claim under the ADEA. So, the defense motion will be denied.

Discrimination on the Basis of Disability

A. THE AMERICANS WITH DISABILITIES ACT (ADA)

I. Overview

Two federal statutes prohibit employment discrimination on the basis of disability—the Federal Rehabilitation Act of 1973 and the Americans with Disabilities Act (ADA). The Rehabilitation Act is an enactment of narrow scope, prohibiting discrimination by only three categories of employers: the federal government (and the U.S. Postal Service), entities receiving federal financial assistance, and federal contractors. The ADA was passed in large measure to fill the huge gap in coverage with respect to private and nonfederal governmental workers. It extended the Rehabilitation Act's prohibition of disability-based discrimination to employers, unions, and employment agencies covered by Title VII. To accomplish that objective, Congress chose to incorporate the substantive provisions of the Rehabilitation Act and the proof standards, coverage, procedural, and remedial provisions of Title VII into the ADA. By including in the ADA much of the precise terminology used in the substantive terms of the Rehabilitation Act, Congress signaled its intention for courts to be guided by Rehabilitation Act jurisprudence in construing comparable provisions in the ADA. But in terms of coverage, proof standards, procedures, and remedies, Congress intended for the courts to look to Title VII case law for guidance in enforcing the ADA.

In this section of the chapter, we focus on the ADA. The second section of this chapter more briefly examines the now less frequently invoked Rehabilitation Act.

Like the Civil Rights Act of 1964, the ADA is a comprehensive statute that proscribes disability-based discrimination in a variety of contexts. Title I of the ADA, like Title VII of the 1964 Act, focuses on discrimination in employment and is the Title that we examine in this chapter. The class of entities covered by the ADA is nearly identical to those covered by Title VII. Like Title VII, the ADA applies to private employers with 15 or more employees, state and local government employers, unions, and employment agencies, and is inapplicable to Indian tribes and bona fide private membership clubs. Similarly, under both statutes, American citizens employed by U.S. companies, or foreign subsidiaries controlled by U.S. companies, are covered when working outside the territorial limits of the United States, except where compliance with the requirements of the ADA would compel the defendant to violate foreign domestic law. And the "ministerial exception" read into Title VII in order to avoid conflict with the requirements of the First Amendment has been incorporated into ADA case law. And as under Title VII, the agents of a statutory employer are not suable in their individual capacity. The major difference in coverage between the two acts is that the ADA does not apply to federal employees, other than those employed by the U.S. Senate, the House of Representatives, and congressional instrumentalities.

In its simplest terms, the ADA prohibits covered entities from

- discriminating against
- a disabled individual
- who is otherwise qualified for the position
- because of that individual's disability
- in the absence of an affirmative defense.

But four of these five components of an ADA claim must also be parsed out into their individual subcomponents to gain an accurate representation of an ADA claim. So, taking them in order:

1. The prohibition against discrimination is composed of two elements:
   - The duty not to take adverse action; and
   - The duty to make a reasonable accommodation to an individual's known disability that does not impose an undue hardship upon the covered entity
2. A "disabled" individual is someone who:
   - Presently has, has a record of (i.e., previously had), or is regarded as having
   - a physical or mental impairment

- that substantially limits
- one or more major life activities

3. A disabled individual is otherwise qualified for the position in question if she:
   - can perform the essential job functions
   - with or without the assistance of a reasonable accommodation

4. A covered entity can escape liability for an otherwise unlawful act of disability discrimination where it can establish any of these affirmative defenses:
   - employment of a disabled individual poses a direct threat to the health or safety of that person or others in the workplace;
   - being non-disabled is a bona fide occupational qualification;
   - a facially neutral criterion that produces a disparate impact on disabled individuals is justified as job-related and consistent with business necessity; or
   - the entity acted pursuant to the terms of a bona fide insurance plan

Let's turn now to an examination of each of these elements of an ADA claim. We begin by examining the class of persons protected by the ADA, i.e., persons who are "disabled" within the meaning of the Act.

2. The Meaning of "Disability"

As noted at the outset of this chapter and by the Supreme Court in *Bragdon v. Abbot*, 524 U.S. 624 (1998), the proper framework for resolving whether a plaintiff is "disabled," as that term is defined in §3(2) of the ADA, is to determine whether that person (a) has or had or is regarded as having (b) a physical or mental impairment (c) that substantially limits (d) a major life activity. There is rarely an issue over the meaning of "has" or "has a history of." The courts uniformly agree that Congress intended to protect both those who are currently disabled and those with a history of prior disability in order to promote its core objective of proscribing conduct that is predicated on stereotyped views of disabilities and the disabled. On the other hand, there has been substantial litigation, and subsequent congressional reinvolvement, with respect to when a plaintiff is "regarded as" disabled. We begin our discussion of the meaning of disability with an examination of the "regarded as" prong of the definition of "disability," followed by a discussion of the three other components of that crucial statutory term.

a. "Regarded As"

In *Sutton v. United Air Lines*, 527 U.S. 471 (1999), the Supreme Court construed the meaning of the "regarded as" terminology of the ADA in a case involving a pair of severely myopic twin sisters who were rejected for employment as pilots by the defendant airline because they did not satisfy its visual acuity requirements. In that context, the Court ruled that where a plaintiff was neither presently nor previously disabled, she could only be "regarded as" disabled if the employer operated under one of two erroneous premises. Either the employer operated under the mistaken belief that the plaintiff had a physical or mental impairment that was substantially limiting, or the employer correctly believed that the plaintiff was impaired but was mistaken about its impact on one or more major life activities, i.e., the employer believed that a non-limiting impairment was substantially limiting.

Congress passed, and President Bush signed, the ADA Amendments Act of 2008 for the express purpose of reversing this and a few other Supreme Court decisions that had, in Congress's judgment, misconstrued various provisions of the ADA. In this context, the 2008 Act's Findings and Purposes section states that the amendments were designed, inter alia, "to reject the Supreme Court's reasoning in Sutton with regard to coverage under the ["regarded as"] definition of disability and to . . . set forth a broad view" of that term. To that end, the Act added new §3(3) to the definition of "disability," which states that a plaintiff can establish that she is "regarded as" being impaired simply by proving that the defendant's challenged conduct was motivated by the plaintiff's actual or perceived (by the employer) impairment, irrespective of the impairment's actual or perceived limiting impact upon a major life activity. As a consequence of this amended language, a plaintiff no longer needs to establish that the defendant believed, correctly or not, that the impairment had a substantially limiting impact upon a major life activity. The plaintiff only has to establish a causal link between the adverse action and an actual or perceived impairment. At the same time, however, the 2008 Act also provides that "regarded as" status will not attach when the impairment is merely "transitory or minor," with transitory being defined as "an actual or expected duration of six months or less."

b. Physical or Mental Impairment

The ADA does not contain either an exhaustive or illustrative list of covered physical or mental impairments. In Bragdon, where the Supreme Court held that asymptomatic HIV-infected status was a physical impairment that could substantially impair an individual's major life activity of reproduction, the Court instructed the lower courts to make an individualized evaluation of any asserted condition guided by considerations that now are set forth in Equal Employment Opportunity Commission (EEOC) interpretative regulations. These regulations provide that a "physical impairment" includes "any physiological disorder, or condition, cosmetic disfigurement, or anatomical loss affecting one or more of the following body systems: neurological, musculoskeletal, special sense organs, respiratory (including speech organs), cardiovascular, reproductive, digestive, genitourinary, hemic and lymphatic, skin, and endocrine." However, the ADA does expressly exclude certain listed conditions from the definition of disability. Sections 509, 511, and 512, for example, provide that the following do not fall within the protected group of physical or mental impairment: homosexuality, bisexuality, transvestism, current illegal drug use, transsexualism, pedophilia, exhibitionism, voyeurism, gender identity disorders not resulting from physical impairments or other sexual behavior disorders, compulsive gambling, kleptomania, pyromania, and psychoactive substance use disorders resulting from current illegal use of drugs. But with respect to drug users, §104(b) provides that someone who is participating in or has successfully completed a supervised drug rehabilitation program and is not currently using illegal drugs does meet the statutory definition of presently or previously having a history of a physical or mental impairment.

c. Substantially Limiting

The ADA, as originally enacted, did not offer any textual standard to assist the courts in determining when an impairment "substantially" limits one or more major life activities. But in a trio of opinions, all of which were released on the same day, the Supreme Court attempted to put some meat on the bare bones of this important statutory concept. In *Sutton*, the Court declared that an impairment would be found to substantially limit the major life activity of working (based on the assumption that working is a major life activity) when, at a minimum, it rendered the plaintiff unable to work "in a broad class of jobs." The Court agreed with the EEOC's view that the inability to perform a single, particular job did not constitute a substantial limitation. Rather, the Court explained, the plaintiff's disability must preclude him from more than one type of job, a specialized job, or a particular job of choice. This meant, the Court added, that a plaintiff would not be substantially limited in working where positions utilizing his skills (but perhaps not his unique talents) were available, or where a host of different types of jobs for which he was qualified were available. Since the plaintiffs in *Sutton* had alleged that their visual disability precluded them from working only as global airline pilots, the Court found that they had not met the "substantially limiting" threshold, particularly where there were other available positions for which they were qualified, such as regional pilot and pilot instructor. Similarly, in *Murphy v. United Parcel Service, Inc.*, 527 U.S. 516 (1999), the Court held that a claim that a plaintiff with high blood pressure was regarded as unable to perform the single job of UPS mechanic was insufficient, as a matter of law, to prove that he was regarded as substantially limited in the major life activity of working. And in *Albertsons, Inc. v. Kirkingburg*, 527 U.S. 555 (1999), the Court reversed the circuit's ruling that a plaintiff with monocular vision had a physical impairment that substantially limited the major life activity of seeing because individuals with monocular vision (the ability to see only out of one eye) saw objects differently from normally sighted individuals. The Supreme Court stated that "difference" was not equivalent to "substantially limited" as a matter of law and ruled that the lower court had erred in not making an individualized determination of whether the impact of monocular vision on this plaintiff was substantial.

The most important ruling by the Supreme Court with respect to the meaning of "substantially limiting" came in *Toyota Manufacturing, Kentucky v. Williams*, 534 U.S. 184 (2002). There, in a case involving an employee who suffered from carpal tunnel syndrome, which prevented her from performing some of her job duties involving manual labor, but which did not prevent her from performing manual tasks at home, the Court declared that "substantially limiting" needed to be "interpreted strictly to create a demanding standard for qualifying as disabled." Accordingly, it ruled that an impairment is substantially limiting only if it "prevents or severely restricts" the individual from performing one or more major life activities.

Both of these portions of the *Toyota* Court's construction of "substantially limiting" were repudiated by Congress in its 2008 amendments to the ADA. The Findings and Purposes section of the 2008 Act states that the *Toyota* Court "interpreted the term 'substantially limits' to require a greater degree of limitation than was intended by Congress" and, therefore, that one of the purposes of the Amendments is to "reject the standards enunciated by the Supreme Court in *Toyota* . . . that the terms 'substantially' and 'major' in the definition of disability . . . 'need to be interpreted strictly to create a demanding standard for qualifying as disabled.'" The Findings and Purposes section of the 2008 amendments also "rejects" the "prevents or severely restricts" standard set forth in *Toyota* as creating an "inappropriately high level of limitation necessary to obtain coverage under the ADA." Additionally, the "Rules of Construction" now codified at §3(3) provide, *inter alia*, that "the definition of disability . . . shall be construed in favor of broad coverage of individuals . . . to the maximum extent permitted by the terms of this Act" and that the definition of "substantially limits" "shall be interpreted consistently with the findings and purposes of the ADA Amendments Act."

The *Toyota* Court had further defined "substantially limits" to mean that the impact of the plaintiff's impairment must be "permanent or long-term." The 2008 amendments replace this standard with a broader definition that includes impairments that are episodic or in remission if that condition would substantially limit a major life activity when active. This means that the courts now will be asked to divine the impact of conditions from which the plaintiff is not presently suffering ill effects.

One aspect of the Court's ruling in *Toyota* was left untouched by the 2008 amendments. After agreeing with the plaintiff that performing major life activities was a major life activity and noting that the parties agreed that her carpal tunnel syndrome was a physical impairment, the Court held that to determine whether that impairment substantially limited the plaintiff's ability to perform manual tasks, the circuit court had erred in considering only the impact of her carpal tunnel syndrome on her ability to perform job-related manual tasks. The Court held that to meet the statutory definition of disability, the plaintiff had to establish that her impairment substantially limited those manual tasks that were central to daily life, i.e., those that occurred both on and off the job. This ruling has been construed by the circuit courts to require assessment of the impact of an impairment on both job-related and non–job-related aspects of a variety of major life activities beyond performing manual tasks. The 2008 amendments do not address this issue, thereby leaving this ruling in *Toyota* untouched.

Perhaps the single most controversial interpretative issue concerning "substantially limiting" arises in the context of an individual who attempts to ameliorate the impact of a physical or mental impairment through the use of corrective or mitigating devices such as prosthetics, medication, or glasses. In *Sutton*, the Supreme Court ruled that the courts must consider the effect of such mitigating devices in assessing the impact of the plaintiff's physical or mental impairment. A person whose physical or mental impairment is corrected by medication or other measures, the Court concluded, does not have an impairment that presently "substantially limits" a major life activity. The Court's ruling was based in significant part on its view that adopting the alternative, broader definition would expand the coverage of the ADA way beyond the 43 million Americans identified as disabled in the findings section of the ADA as originally enacted. And the Court extended this ruling in *Albertsons* to cases where the mitigation was undertaken, whether consciously or not, with the body's own system, as well as with artificial aids or medications.

These rulings, and most particularly the holding in *Sutton*, were directly targeted by Congress when it passed the ADA Amendments Act of 2008. The amendments overturned the Court's ruling regarding the impact of mitigating devices, declaring in its Findings and Purposes section that the decision in *Sutton* "narrowed the broad scope of protection intended to be afforded by the ADA" and that one of the purposes of the Act was "to reject the requirement enunciated by the Supreme Court in *Sutton* and its companion cases that whether an impairment substantially limits a major life activity is to be determined with reference to the ameliorative effects of mitigating measures." To that end, the ADA now contains a new §3(4), which sets forth "Rules of Construction" providing, *inter alia*, that "the determination of whether an impairment substantially limits a major life activity shall be made without regard to the ameliorative effects of mitigating measures" and also including a non-exclusive list of such measures. However, the Act also expressly creates an exception to this general rule for two mitigating measures — "ordinary eyeglasses" and contact lenses. Consistent with the ruling by the *Sutton* Court, the ameliorative impact of these two items "must" be considered in making the "substantially limits" assessment. But the Act now also provides that if an employer utilizes an employment criterion based on an individual's uncorrected vision, the employer must prove that this criterion is job-related and consistent with business necessity.

d. Major Life Activities

The meaning of "major life activity" was also left undefined in the ADA as originally enacted. But the 2008 amendments added new §3(2), which defines major life activity by reference to a non-exclusive list of major life activities, including working, reading, and communicating, as well as a non-exclusive list of major bodily functions. Additionally, in §3(4)'s "Rules of Construction," Congress codified the general understanding that a plaintiff need only show that an impairment substantially limits one major life activity.

ADA Prima Facie Case

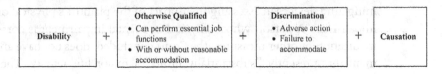

Definition of Disability

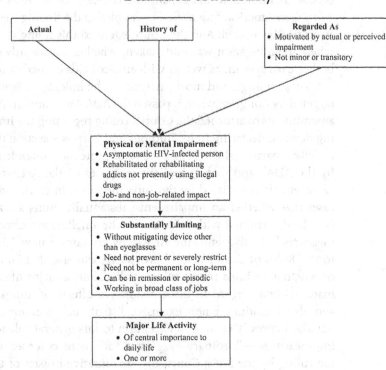

Examples

Only Twenty-Four Hours in a Day

1. Jack Bauer unsuccessfully applied for a software developer position with Computer Technology Unit, Inc. (CTU), a software engineering and development company. After fulfilling all relevant administrative preconditions to suit, Bauer filed an ADA civil action against CTU, alleging that he had been discriminated against because he was regarded as being disabled. His complaint alleged that he had been rejected for the position because the company president, David Palmer, believed that Bauer suffered from a mental disorder that prevents individuals from engaging in highly advanced abstract thinking and visualizing. The complaint further alleged that although Palmer never discussed the matter with Bauer and did not seek to have Bauer tested in any way, Palmer had a son who suffered from that disorder and was very familiar with its manifestations. CTU filed a motion to dismiss the complaint on the ground that Bauer had failed to state a claim upon which relief can be granted. It based this motion on the argument that Bauer had failed to allege an essential element of his prima facie claim, i.e., that he was or had been erroneously regarded as having an impairment that substantially limited a major life activity. How should the trial court rule on the defense motion?

2. Jack Bauer unsuccessfully applied for a software developer position with Computer Technology Unit, Inc. (CTU), a software engineering and development company. After fulfilling all relevant administrative preconditions to suit, Bauer filed an ADA civil action against CTU, alleging that he had been discriminated against because he was regarded as being disabled. The complaint alleged that during his job interview, Bauer had informed the company president, David Palmer, that he was presently having trouble concentrating for more than one hour at a time as the result of a recent automobile accident, but that his doctors had assured him that the problem would disappear within about two months. How should the court rule on CTU's motion to dismiss Bauer's ADA complaint on the ground that he failed to state a claim upon which relief can be granted?

3. Chloe O'Brian was denied a position as a computer systems analyst with Computer Technology Unit, Inc. (CTU) when she informed the company president, David Palmer, during her job interview that she had suffered from a congenital gender identity disorder. On that basis alone, Palmer informed O'Brian that she could not work at CTU. After fulfilling all administrative preconditions, she filed suit against CTU under the ADA. In response, CTU filed a motion to dismiss her complaint for failure to state a claim upon which relief can be granted. How should the trial court rule on that motion?

4. When Tony Almeida's application for a security position with Computer Technology Unit, Inc. (CTU) was rejected, he fulfilled all administrative preconditions to suit and then filed a civil action against CTU, alleging that he had been rejected for employment because of his disability in violation of the ADA. His complaint alleged that when Almeida informed company president, David Palmer, during his job interview that he was addicted to gambling, Palmer informed Almeida that the company would never employ anyone who gambled, let alone a compulsive gambler. How should the trial court rule on CTU's motion to dismiss the complaint for failure to state a claim upon which relief can be granted?

5. Bill Buchanan had been employed by Computer Technology Unit, Inc. (CTU) for 20 years as its chief developer of three-dimensional sports video games. After he was terminated, Buchanan filed an ADA action against CTU, alleging that he had been discharged because of a mental impairment that substantially limited his ability to engage in the major life activity of working. His complaint alleged that he recently had been stricken with a permanent mental disorder that prevented him from engaging in the complex three-dimensional thinking and visualization necessary to continue to develop three-dimensional sports video games. How should the trial court rule on CTU's motion to dismiss the complaint for failure to state a claim upon which relief can be granted?

6. Audrey Raines had been employed on the production line at Computer Technology Unit, Inc. (CTU) for 15 years before she was discharged. After fulfilling all administrative preconditions, Raines sued CTU, alleging that she had been discharged because of her disability in violation of the ADA. Her complaint alleged that she had suffered permanent neurological damage to her hand as the result of an automobile accident that substantially limited her ability to perform manual tasks of the types that her production job required. In its answer, CTU admitted the truth of all of Raines's allegations but alleged that she was able to perform manual tasks at home, including matters of personal hygiene, housecleaning, and child care. In her deposition, Raines admitted all of these facts. Thereafter, CTU filed a motion for judgment as a matter of law on the ground that Raines was, as a matter of law, not disabled within the meaning of the ADA. How should the trial court rule on that motion?

7. Mike Novick was hired as a computer programmer by Computer Technology Unit, Inc. (CTU). On his initial day on the job, Novick informed his supervisor, Charles Logan, that he suffered from epilepsy, but that all of his symptoms could be controlled as long as he was allowed to take a 15-minute break every two hours to inject himself with the proper medication. Logan denied the request, stating that all programmers were entitled to only two breaks per nine-hour shift. After fulfilling all administrative prerequisites, Novick filed an ADA action against

CTU, alleging that he was disabled as a result of his epilepsy and had been denied a reasonable accommodation. CTU filed a motion to dismiss the complaint on the ground that Novick was not disabled within the meaning of the statute because his epileptic symptoms, which, CTU acknowledged, constitute a physical impairment that substantially limits more than one major life activity, are under control as a result of his medication. How should the trial court rule on that motion?

8. Aaron Pierce was denied employment as a night watchman by Computer Technology Unit, Inc. (CTU) because he admitted during his job interview that he was functionally blind without the use of his eyeglasses, although he could see perfectly when wearing his glasses. Pierce filed an ADA action against CTU, alleging that he had been denied employment because of his visual disability. CTU filed a motion to dismiss the complaint on the ground that Pierce was not disabled within the meaning of the statute because his glasses completely ameliorated the effects of his visual disability. How should the trial court rule on that motion?

9. Renee Walker suffered from anemia. She applied for a job at Computer Technology Unit, Inc. (CTU) as a member of the warehouse packing staff. These jobs required extended amounts of heavy lifting throughout the day. Walker was rejected because the company president, David Palmer, concluded that someone with anemia would just not have the physical strength and endurance required of this job. Walker filed an ADA suit against CTU, alleging that she had been denied the position because of her anemia, a physical impairment that substantially limited her ability to engage in physical activity and perform manual tasks. CTU filed a motion to dismiss the complaint on the ground that she was not disabled because her anemia, an admitted physical impairment, did not prevent or severely restrict her from engaging in all physical activities or performing manual tasks. How should the trial court rule on that motion?

Explanations

Only Twenty-Four Hours in a Day

1. The motion will be denied. The issue here is whether or not Bauer is disabled. Under the statute, the plaintiff has to establish that he has, had, or is regarded as having a mental or physical disability that substantially impairs his ability to perform at least one major life activity. But the 2008 amendments to the ADA specifically addressed the issue of what is required to state a claim when the plaintiff alleges that he is "regarded as" disabled. Rejecting the Supreme Court's construction of that term in *Sutton*, Congress provided in the 2008 amendments that a "regarded as" plaintiff need only allege and prove that the defendant's challenged conduct was motivated by the plaintiff's actual or perceived

(by the employer) impairment, irrespective of the impairment's actual or perceived limiting impact upon a major life activity. As a consequence of this amended language, a plaintiff no longer needs to establish that the defendant believed, correctly or not, that the impairment had a substantially limiting impact upon a major life activity in order to fit within the "regarded as" standard. The plaintiff only has to establish a causal link between the adverse action and an actual or perceived impairment. Since Bauer has made that allegation, the defense motion will be denied, and his complaint will not be dismissed.

2. The motion will be granted. As part of the 2008 amendments to the definition of "regarded as" disabled, Congress provided that "regarded as" status will not attach when the impairment is merely "transitory or minor," with transitory being defined as "an actual or expected duration of six months or less." Thus, since the complaint alleges that the plaintiff's impairment was transitory, he cannot state a "regarded as" claim under the ADA, and so the motion will be granted and his complaint will be dismissed.

3. The motion will be granted. Section 512 of the ADA expressly excludes gender identity disorders not resulting from physical impairments from the definition of disability. Since the plaintiff's gender identity disorder was congenital, and, therefore, not resulting from a physical impairment, she is not covered by the ADA. Consequently, the defense motion will be granted, and the complaint will be dismissed.

4. The motion will be granted. Section 512 expressly excludes compulsive gambling from the definition of disability. Since the plaintiff is not protected by the statute, the court will grant the defense motion and dismiss the complaint.

5. The motion will be granted. The issue here is whether the plaintiff has sufficiently alleged that his mental impairment substantially limits the major life activity of working. The 2008 amendments expressly include working within the list of covered major life activities. But in cases such as Sutton, Albertsons, and Murphy, the Supreme Court, in opinions left undisturbed by the 2008 amendments, held that where the plaintiff alleges that his impairment substantially limited the major life activity of working, the plaintiff must allege and prove that the impairment substantially limited his ability to work in a "broad class of jobs," not just the specific position that he currently held. Here, as in Murphy, the plaintiff alleged only that his impairment substantially limited his employment in a particular job that matched his unique skills. That is not sufficient. So, the motion will be granted, and the complaint will be dismissed.

6. The motion will be granted. This issue was resolved by the Supreme Court in Toyota and was unaffected by Congress's subsequent passage of the 2008 ADA amendments. In Toyota, the Court held that where the plaintiff alleges that her impairment substantially limited her ability to

perform manual tasks, it was an error for the court to limit its analysis to whether the impairment substantially limited the ability to perform those manual tasks associated with the plaintiff's job and not also to evaluate whether the plaintiff was similarly limited in the ability to perform manual tasks unrelated to her job that were central to daily life. Here, the plaintiff admitted that she was not substantially limited in performing manual tasks central to daily life that were not associated with her job. Consequently, under the Court's ruling in *Toyota*, she is not disabled and, therefore, cannot state a claim under the ADA. So, the defense motion will be granted, and her complaint will be dismissed.

7. The motion will be denied. The issue here is whether the plaintiff is disabled. That, in turn, depends upon whether his physical impairment (epilepsy) substantially limits a major life activity. The only issue there is whether the plaintiff's limitation should be assessed with or without consideration of the impact of his medication. If the medication is considered, the plaintiff will not be deemed to be disabled since in his medicated state he suffers no symptoms of the disease. The opposite would be true if the plaintiff was evaluated without consideration of this mitigating factor. As a consequence of the 2008 amendments, which reversed the Supreme Court's ruling on this issue in *Sutton*, under §3(4)(E)(i), an ADA plaintiff is assessed without consideration of any mitigating factor or device. Consequently, the plaintiff fits the statutory definition of disabled and the defense motion will be denied.

8. The motion will be granted. Although the 2008 amendments reversed the Supreme Court's ruling in *Sutton* and provided that the determination of whether an impairment substantially limits a major life activity shall be made without regard to the ameliorative effects of mitigating measures, the amendment contains an express exception to this general rule for eyeglasses and contact lenses. Now, §3(4)(E)(ii) provides, consistent with the ruling by the *Sutton* Court, that the ameliorative impact of these two items "must" be considered in making the "substantially limits" assessment. Consequently, when considered in light of the fact of the plaintiff's admission that he does not suffer from any visual impairment when wearing his glasses, the plaintiff would not be deemed disabled. So, the defense motion will be granted.

9. The motion will be denied. Although the Supreme Court in *Toyota* construed the meaning of "substantially limiting" to require that the plaintiff allege and prove that his physical impairment "prevents or severely restricts" the ability to engage in at least one major life activity, Congress rejected this interpretation in the 2008 amendments, stating that it created an "inappropriately high level of limitation necessary to obtain coverage under the ADA." And though Congress did not provide an alternative interpretation, it clearly intended for the courts to apply a more liberal standard. Since the defense motion here is based only on

the argument that the plaintiff was not prevented from engaging in a major life activity by her admitted physical impairment, it has misstated the statutory requirement for demonstrating "substantially limiting." Accordingly, the motion will be denied.

3. The Meaning of "Otherwise Qualified"

Section 102 of the ADA prohibits discrimination against any "qualified individual with a disability." This latter term is defined in §101(8) to include any individual with a "disability" who, with or without reasonable accommodation, can perform the "essential functions" of the job held or sought by that individual. It further provides that in determining what constitutes an "essential function," the employer's judgment on this matter, including any written job description prepared before advertising or interviewing applicants for the particular job, must be considered. For ease of language, we will refer to this requirement as the "otherwise qualified" requirement. (The Rehabilitation Act used this "otherwise qualified" language and it was replaced in the ADA with "qualified individual with a disability." The latter terminology was meant by Congress to be synonymous with the Rehabilitation Act's use of "otherwise qualified.")

Although the circuit courts have not reached consensus on this question, the prevailing view is that the "otherwise qualified" criterion is an element of the plaintiff's prima facie case, which means that the plaintiff must persuade the trier of fact that she can perform the essential job functions with or without the benefit of a reasonable accommodation.

Among the most common situations in which the "qualified individual" factor comes into play is where a plaintiff brings an ADA action claiming that she is still qualified to do the job notwithstanding her disability *after* she applied for and received disability benefits from the federal Social Security Administration (SSA). Does an SSA disability application containing an allegation that the claimant was permanently disabled estop that individual from subsequently claiming in an ADA suit that she is qualified to do a job, thereby rendering her not a "qualified person with a disability" as a matter of law? In *Cleveland v. Policy Management Systems Corp.*, 526 U.S. 795 (1999), the Supreme Court unanimously ruled that the ADA and the Social Security Disability Insurance (SSDI) program contained enough differences to make it inappropriate to utilize the doctrine of judicial estoppel against an ADA claimant who previously had filed for SSDI benefits. Specifically, since the SSDI definition of disability does not include the applicant's ability to perform job functions with the help of a reasonable accommodation, and because the SSA determines the existence of a disability on the basis of presumptions that preclude assessments of individual circumstances, the

Court ruled that to defeat a defense motion for summary judgment, an ADA plaintiff must explain or attempt to resolve the disparity between the previous sworn statements made to the SSA and the allegations in the subsequent ADA action. This explanation must be "sufficient to warrant a reasonable juror's concluding that, assuming the truth of . . . the earlier statement, the plaintiff could nonetheless perform the essential functions of her job with or without reasonable accommodation." Merely filing a subsequent affidavit that contradicted the prior statements, the Court added, would not be enough to create a genuine issue of fact to survive summary judgment. Otherwise, summary judgment could never be granted. Subsequent rulings by the circuit courts indicate that it will be sufficient to avoid estoppel for the plaintiff to establish that while statements made at the time of the SSA disability application were correct when made, his physical situation had changed by the time the ADA action was filed.

A question that has divided the circuits is how to deal with the "qualified" requirement in the case of a former employee who alleges post-employment discrimination, typically with respect to fringe benefits such as insurance or pension benefits. Some of the circuits have reasoned that since the statute defines a qualified individual as one who "can perform" essential job functions, this use of the present tense reflects Congress's intent to limit the application of the statute to individuals who are able to perform the job functions *at the time of the alleged discrimination*. Other circuits require only that the plaintiff establish that he *had been able* to perform the essential functions of the job while employed and, on that basis, had earned the post-employment fringe benefit. Since the fringe benefit was earned for actual service, these courts reason, whether a former employee could still perform the essential functions of the former job after termination of employment is beside the point. To rule otherwise, they explain, would encourage employers to engage in wholesale discrimination against disabled retirees the moment they no longer can perform the essential functions of their former jobs, a result that would conflict with the legislative purpose to provide comprehensive protection from disability-based discrimination in the provision of fringe benefits.

Examples

Rock Around the Clock

1. William Haley applied for employment with Comet Cleaners, Inc. (CCI). Every job at CCI requires the lifting and moving of heavy cleaning machinery on a continuing basis. When Haley revealed during his job interview that he had coronary artery disease that prevented him from engaging in strenuous activity, his application was rejected. After fulfilling all administrative prerequisites to suit, Haley filed a civil action

against CCI, alleging that he had been denied employment because of his disability in violation of the ADA. CCI filed a motion to dismiss the complaint for failure to state a claim upon which relief can be granted. How should the court rule on this motion?

2. Johnny Clifton had been employed as a personal trainer by Shake, Rattle & Roll, Inc. (SRR), a regional chain of exercise clubs. After a tragic fall from the roof of his house, Clifton suffered severe spinal cord injury, which left him paralyzed from his shoulders to his feet. He resigned from his job at SRR and filed a sworn claim for disability benefits with the Social Security Administration, claiming that he was totally and permanently disabled. About six months later, he applied for reinstatement as a personal trainer with SRR. His application was rejected on the ground that he was no longer qualified to do that job. After fulfilling all administrative prerequisites to suit, Clifton brought a civil action against SRR, alleging that he had been denied employment because of his disability in violation of the ADA. SRR filed a motion for summary judgment, arguing that Clifton was estopped from alleging that he was a qualified individual with a disability by virtue of the claimed total and permanent disability status set forth in his application with the SSA. In his response to the motion, Clifton attached his own affidavit averring that he was qualified to do the job. How should the trial court rule on that motion?

3. Johnny Clifton had been employed as a personal trainer by Shake, Rattle & Roll, Inc. (SRR), a regional chain of exercise clubs. After a tragic fall from the roof of his house, Clifton suffered severe spinal cord injury, which left him paralyzed from his shoulders to his feet. He resigned from his job at SRR and filed a sworn claim for disability benefits with the Social Security Administration, claiming that he was totally and permanently disabled. About six months later, he applied for reinstatement as a personal trainer with SRR. His application was rejected on the ground that he was no longer qualified to do that job. After fulfilling all administrative prerequisites to suit, Clifton brought a civil action against SRR, alleging that he had been denied employment because of his disability in violation of the ADA. SRR filed a motion for summary judgment, arguing that Clifton was estopped from alleging that he was a qualified individual with a disability by virtue of the claimed total and permanent disability status set forth in his application with the SSA. In his response to the motion, Clifton attached his own affidavit averring that in the period between his SSA application and his application for reemployment with SRR, he had just successfully undergone surgery that gave him partial use of his extremities and that with a reasonable accommodation, he could perform the essential job duties of a personal trainer. How should the trial court rule on that motion?

Explanations

Rock Around the Clock

1. The motion will be granted. In order to fall within the statutorily protected class of qualified individual with a disability, the plaintiff must
   establish that he is able to perform the essential functions of the job in
   question with or without a reasonable accommodation. An employer is
   not required, as part of its duty to accommodate, to change the essential
   nature of a job. Here, the essential job requirements include the ability
   to engage in strenuous activity. And since all of the jobs require strenuous activity, there is no possible accommodation short of changing the
   nature of the job. Consequently, since the plaintiff is not "otherwise
   qualified" for the job, i.e., able to perform the job's essential job functions with or without a reasonable accommodation, he cannot state a
   prima facie claim, and so the defense motion will be granted and the
   complaint will be dismissed.

2. The court will grant the motion. The Supreme Court in *Policy Management
   Systems* acknowledged that sufficient differences existed between the SSA
   disability and ADA disability regimes to automatically invoke judicial
   estoppel against an ADA plaintiff who previously had alleged the existence of a permanent disability in an SSA disability benefits application.
   However, the Court also stated that to defeat a defense motion for summary judgment, an ADA plaintiff must explain or attempt to resolve the
   disparity between the previous sworn statements made to the SSA and
   the allegations in the subsequent ADA action. This explanation must be
   "sufficient to warrant a reasonable juror's concluding that, assuming the
   truth of . . . the earlier statement, the plaintiff could nonetheless perform
   the essential functions of her job with or without reasonable accommodation." Merely filing a subsequent affidavit that contradicted the prior
   statements, the Court added, would not be enough to create a genuine
   issue of fact to survive summary judgment. Since that is all the plaintiff did in this situation, the court will find that he has not sufficiently
   explained any difference to defeat the invocation of judicial estoppel
   and the granting of the defense motion. So, the defense motion will be
   granted, and the complaint will be dismissed.

3. The court will deny the motion. Here, the plaintiff has at least alleged
   a sufficient explanation for the disparity between the previous sworn
   statements made to the SSA and the allegations in the subsequent ADA
   action to defeat the invocation of judicial estoppel and to defeat the
   defense motion for judgment as a matter of law. Accordingly, the court
   will deny the motion to dismiss, and it will be up to the plaintiff to
   convince the trier of fact that either his physical condition has changed

or that his disability notwithstanding, he can perform the essential job functions with the aid of a reasonable accommodation.

4. The Dual Meaning of Discrimination

Title I of the ADA imposes two analytically separate types of nondiscrimination obligations on covered entities. The first, and most obvious, is the mandate not to take adverse action on the basis of an individual's disability. And Congress codified in Title I both the intentional and disparate impact forms of this type of discrimination. But §102(b)(5) defines unlawful discrimination to include failure to make a reasonable accommodation to the known physical or mental limitations of an otherwise qualified individual with a disability unless that covered entity can prove that the accommodation would impose an undue hardship upon the operation of its business. We begin our discussion with an examination of the prima facie and defense components of the duty not to take adverse action on the basis of disability and then examine the duty to accommodate.

a. Proving Adverse Action–Based Discrimination: Intentional and Disparate Impact Claims and Retaliation

Section 102(a) sets forth the basic nondiscrimination commandment of the ADA in language strikingly parallel to that found in §703(a) of Title VII. It provides that a covered entity shall not discriminate against a qualified individual with a disability with respect to all terms and conditions of employment. And in §102(b), in terminology that also tracks the text of Title VII, it describes a range of employment practices and policies that could result in forbidden intentional discrimination. Moreover, the ADA, like Title VII, codifies the disparate impact form of discrimination. Section 102(b)(1) defines unlawful discrimination to include the treatment of an applicant or employee in a manner "that adversely affects the opportunities or status" of that individual because of his or her disability. And §102(b)(3) includes within the definition of proscribed discrimination the use of standards or criteria "that have the effect of discrimination on the basis of disability." Not surprisingly, the courts in ADA cases lean heavily on Title VII jurisprudence in analyzing both types of claims, including the recognition of harassment claims brought by individuals who allege that they have been harassed because of their disability. Similarly, the prevailing view in the circuits is that the Price Waterhouse version of mixed motive analysis (because the mixed motive provisions of the 1991 Civil Rights Act did not expressly amend the ADA) is available and applicable to ADA claims.

However, after the Supreme Court held, in *Gross v. FBL Financial Services, Inc.*, 557 U.S. 167 (2009), that mixed motive claims are not cognizable under the Age Discrimination in Employment Act (ADEA), an issue arose as to whether that ruling should be extended to ADA claims. In *Serwatka v. Rockwell Automation, Inc.*, 591 F.3d 957 (7th Cir. 2010), the Seventh Circuit read *Gross* to mean that with respect to claims brought under any employment statute that was not expressly amended to codify mixed motive analysis, a mixed motive claim is not viable and the plaintiff must establish but-for causation. And as to the language in §107 of the ADA linking it to the enforcement provisions of Title VII, the court emphasized that the pertinent language of §107 referred only to the "remedies" available under §706 and not to liability established under §703. Consequently, it held, this linkage provision did not incorporate the codification of mixed motive analysis found in §703(m) of Title VII as amended by the 1991 Civil Rights Act. Accordingly, it ruled that mixed motive claims were not cognizable under the ADA and vacated a mixed motive judgment that the trial court had entered in favor of the plaintiff based on the jury's answers to a special verdict form and directed the court to enter judgment in favor of the defendant. The underlying rationale of this ruling subsequently was adopted by the Supreme Court in *University of Texas Southwestern Medical Center v. Nassar*, 133 S. Ct. 2517 (2013), where the Court ruled that mixed motive similarly was unavailable to a plaintiff asserting a retaliation claim under §704(a) of Title VII.

Sometimes, however, the line of demarcation between claims of intentional and impact-based discrimination are blurred, and the Supreme Court has insisted that the lower courts recognize this distinction. In *Raytheon Co. v. Hernandez*, 540 U.S. 44 (2003), an employee with 25 years' seniority was fired for violating company rules when he tested positive for cocaine. Two years later, after regularly attending Alcoholics Anonymous meetings, he applied for reinstatement. The company followed a blanket policy of refusing to rehire any former employee who previously had been discharged for violating any company rule. Pursuant to that policy, the plaintiff was not rehired, and so he brought a civil action under the ADA against the company, alleging intentional discrimination, i.e., that he had been denied reemployment because of his record of past drug use. In response to a defense motion for summary judgment, the plaintiff alleged, for the first time, that the company's reliance on its no-rehire policy would disproportionately disadvantage rehabilitated former drug users whose discharge was based on their prior drug use. A unanimous Supreme Court agreed with the trial court (which had granted the defense motion for summary judgment on the intentional discrimination claim) that the plaintiff had waived his right to bring an impact claim by failing to plead it in a timely fashion.

But it reversed the Ninth Circuit's ruling that the plaintiff's intentional discrimination should not be dismissed because the company's no-rehire rule explanation had a disparate impact on recovering drug users. The Supreme Court concluded that after ruling that the plaintiff had waived his impact claim, the Ninth Circuit nevertheless had let impact analysis in through the back door by incorporating impact analysis into its treatment of the defendant's legitimate, nondiscriminatory response defense to the plaintiff's disparate treatment claim of disability-based discrimination. The proper approach, the Supreme Court explained, would have been to use the traditional *McDonnell Douglas/Burdine* formula for claims of intentional discrimination. Under that rubric, the Court instructed, the lower court should have ruled that the no-rehire policy constituted a legitimate, nondiscriminatory explanation, and then should have examined whether or not the defendant actually relied on this policy or whether this purported explanation was merely a pretext for discrimination.

The ADA also contains an anti-retaliation provision codified at §503, which mirrors the provisions of §704(a) of Title VII.

b. Causation

An ADA plaintiff must establish that the discrimination was linked to her disability. A particularly vexing aspect of this causation element arises in cases where the plaintiff suffers an adverse employment action because of conduct that is linked to, if not directly caused by, his disability. In these cases, the courts attempt to distinguish between discrimination based on one's status as a disabled person and adverse action taken in response to conduct that is, in some fashion, a consequence of the plaintiff's disability. Where the conduct happens also to be criminal, such as driving under the influence of drugs or alcohol, the courts are most apt to distinguish between the disability and its consequences and find that adverse action targeted at such consequences does not violate Title I.

c. Associational Discrimination

Title I of the ADA also prohibits a form of discrimination that is not covered by Title VII or any of the other antidiscrimination statutes. Section 102(b)(4) prohibits discrimination against a qualified individual because of the known disability of someone else with whom that qualified (non-disabled) individual is known to have a relationship or association. But the statute does not define the kind of relationship or association to which this provision was intended to apply. However, the EEOC's interpretive guidelines declare that the purpose of this provision is to prevent conduct based on stereotypical attitudes toward persons who associate with disabled individuals. These guidelines also include a non-exclusive list of examples of proscribed associational discrimination, not all of which are limited to familial relationships.

Most associational discrimination claims fall into one or more of three categories: (1) expense claims—where the employer is alleged to have discriminated against an employee because that employee's association (typically familial) with a disabled individual imposed significant costs (usually in connection with an employer's health or disability plan) on the employer; (2) distraction claims—where the employer is alleged to have discriminated against an employee out of concern that this employee would be distracted from work by obligations (such as providing care) to a disabled person with whom the employee is associated; or (3) disability by association claims—where the employer is alleged to have discriminated against an employee because the employer is concerned that this employee would develop a disabling condition (such as an infection or disease) because of her relationship to a disabled individual. Of course, irrespective of which form of associational claim is advanced by the plaintiff, she must establish causation, i.e., that she was disadvantaged because of her association with a disabled person.

d. Defending Adverse Action–Based Discrimination Claims

i. Direct Threat

Section 103 of Title I, entitled "Defenses," sets forth several defenses to both intentional and disparate impact claims of discrimination. Section 103(b) provides that an employer can require that an employee not pose a direct threat to the health or safety of others in the workplace. Two Supreme Court cases shed important light on the meaning of this provision. In *Bragdon*, a non-employment case brought under Title II of the ADA against a dentist who had refused to treat an asymptomatic HIV-infected patient in his office, the defendant claimed that providing this treatment would have posed a direct threat to the health and safety of others. The Supreme Court ruled that the subjective good faith belief of the defendant was not dispositive. Rather, the Court said that it needed to examine the objective reasonableness of the defendant's judgment, even when the defendant, as in the instant case, was a health care professional. And that objective assessment should be rendered, the Court held, in light of the available medical evidence, with particular focus on the views of public health authorities such as the U.S. Public Health Service, the National Institutes of Health, and the Centers for Disease Control. Subsequently, in *Chevron v. Echazabal*, 536 U.S.

73 (2002), the Court unanimously construed the textual reference to the health and safety of "others" to embrace a defense claim that the plaintiff's disability posed a direct threat to his or her own health or safety.

The prevailing, though not universally accepted view among the circuit courts is that the existence of a "direct threat" is an affirmative defense as to which the defendant bears the burden of persuasion. And they point primarily to the fact that this provision is contained in a section entitled "Defenses." However, in a few instances where the essential functions of the job in question necessarily implicated the health and safety of others in that workplace, such as cases involving police officers, some circuits have ruled that the plaintiff was required to persuade the trier of fact that she could perform these essential functions without endangering others as part of her prima facie obligation to prove that she was qualified for the job despite her disability.

Note also that §101(3) defines "direct threat" to mean a significant risk to the health or safety of others *that cannot be eliminated by reasonable accommodation*. It is not sufficient, therefore, for the court to determine only that the plaintiff creates a risk in the abstract; it must evaluate whether that risk can be "eliminated" by a "reasonable" accommodation.

ii. Bona Fide Insurance Plans

Section 501(c) contains a safe harbor provision covering the insurance industry as well as those employers that provide insurance coverage for their employees with respect to any insurance policy containing a disability-based distinction. Section 501(c)(1) permits employers, insurers, and plan administrators to establish and implement the terms of an "insured" (i.e., purchased from someone else, such as an insurance company) health insurance plan based on underwriting, classifying, or administering risks that are neither inconsistent with state law nor used as a subterfuge to evade the purposes of the Act. And under §501(c)(2), employers can create, or observe the terms of, a bona fide *self-insured* health insurance plan that is not used as a subterfuge to evade the purposes of the Act. Thus, where a plaintiff alleges that an employer's health insurance plan contains a disability-based distinction, in order to fall within the protection of §501(c), the employer must establish that this provision is part of either a bona fide insured plan that is not inconsistent with state law or a bona fide self-insured plan and, in either case, that the plan is not being used as a subterfuge to evade the purposes of the ADA.

In response to a split in the circuits over whether the ADA required employers who provided health benefits to provide equal benefits for mental and physical conditions, Congress passed the Mental Health Parity

Act of 1996, 42 U.S.C. §300gg-5 (1996). This statute requires employers who offer mental health benefits in a health insurance plan to provide the same level of coverage for mental health care as is provided for physical illnesses. The Act prohibits any group health plan or health insurance company from establishing a lesser annual or lifetime limit for mental health care than it does for any other condition. There are, however, major exceptions contained in the law that will limit its impact on most employer-sponsored health plans. For example, the statute does not require parity with respect to number of inpatient or outpatient care days, it expressly excludes employers with less than 50 employees, and health plans and health insurance companies are permitted to provide different annual and lifetime caps for mental health care than for other covered services. Most importantly, perhaps, the Act exempts "disability income insurance" from its coverage, thereby not requiring parity for mental and physical disabilities in employer-provided disability (as opposed to health insurance) plans. Additionally, group health plans may also be exempted from this Act if the application of the "leveling-up" provision results in a cost increase to the plan of at least 1 percent.

iii. Job-Relatedness and Business Necessity

Section 103(a) of Title I of the ADA provides defendants in disparate impact cases with the opportunity to escape liability by establishing that the impact-generating device is job-related and consistent with business necessity and that successful performance under that challenged criterion cannot be attained by a reasonable accommodation on its part. And the circuit courts have heeded the warning sounded by the Supreme Court in *Raytheon*, in which the Court underscored the importance of asserting the proper defense against the proper form of prima facie case.

iv. Religious Entities

Title I of the ADA contains an exemption for religious entities that parallels the §702 exemption contained in Title VII. Section 103(d) provides that a religious organization may discriminate on the basis of religion with respect to anyone connected with its activities. Additionally, the courts have engrafted the blanket "ministerial exception" onto the terms of Title I in the same manner, and for the same First Amendment reasons they relied upon in Title VII cases.

Forms of Proscribed Discrimination

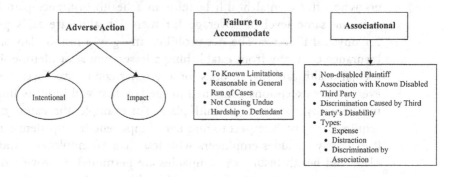

Defenses

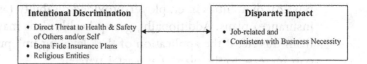

Examples

Expecting a Lot

1. Philip Pirrip, a lifelong fan of Gladys Knight & the Pips, applied for a job in the mail room of Havisham & Associates, Inc. (HAA), a talent management firm specializing in the representation of rock and roll artists. Havisham required applicants for all positions with the company to pass a speed-reading test that required them to read a very long passage and answer detailed questions under extreme time pressure. Pirrip, who suffered from dyslexia, failed the test and was denied the job. After fulfilling all administrative prerequisites, Pirrip filed an ADA suit against HAA, alleging that the use of the speed-reading test discriminated against him and others with dyslexia. In its answer, HAA claimed that it had no intention to discriminate against anybody, but that it simply wanted to boast to its competitors that all of its employees were speed readers. Based on that argument, HAA filed a motion seeking judgment as a matter of law. How should the court rule on this motion?

2. Joe Gargery, a talent agent employed by Havisham & Associates, Inc. (HAA), was arrested by the police when he refused to take a breath analyzer test after being stopped for driving his car while under the influence of alcohol. After Gargery pleaded guilty to the charge, he lost his driver's license and his job. He filed suit against HAA, alleging that he had been discharged on the basis of his disability—alcoholism. Although HAA

does not deny that alcoholics fall within the class of disabled individuals covered by the ADA, it nevertheless filed a motion for judgment as a matter of law on the ground that it had not discriminated against Gargery because of his disability. How should the trial court rule on this motion?

3. Havisham & Associates, Inc. (HAA) provides health insurance for its employees and their dependents under a self-insured plan. Herbert Pocket, a bookkeeper employed by HAA, had a young son who developed a severe case of leukemia. This tragedy was well known to everyone at HAA. After Pocket submitted a request for reimbursement of $15,000 for his son's initial medical bills, he was discharged. Pocket filed suit against HAA under the ADA, claiming intentional discrimination on the basis of his son's disability. His complaint alleged that he had been terminated because his employer wanted to be relieved of the obligation under its self-insured health insurance plan to pay for the medical costs incurred by his cancer-infected son. In its answer, HAA disclosed that it had a well-publicized policy of discharging any employee who sought more than $12,000 in annual medical insurance benefits for a dependent. All of these facts are undisputed. How should the court rule on the parties' cross-motions for summary judgment?

4. Clara Barley applied for a position as courier with Havisham & Associates, Inc. (HAA), a job that required her to drive a company car to deliver contracts and other items to clients throughout the city. Barley informed the company during the job application process that she suffered from aortic stenosis, a cardiovascular disease that causes individuals to suffer unpredictable blackouts. HAA rejected her application because of that condition. Barley sued HAA under the ADA, claiming that she had been discriminated against because of her disability. In its answer, HAA claimed that it was justified in rejecting her because her disability rendered Barley a direct threat to her own safety since she could suffer an unanticipated blackout while driving the car in the course of her employment. Barley filed a motion to strike that defense on the ground that she did not pose a threat to anyone else's health or safety. How should the court rule on that motion?

Explanations

Expecting a Lot

1. The court will deny the motion. The plaintiff's complaint states a claim of impact-based discrimination, which is expressly recognized in §102(b) of the ADA. The relevant defense to an impact-based claim is the job-relatedness/business necessity defense codified at §103(a). But here, the defendant is only asserting a nondiscriminatory explanation for its speed-reading policy. As the Supreme Court noted in *Raytheon*, it is crucial for the defense to assert the proper defense to a prima facie claim under

the ADA. And since the defense did not assert the relevant defense to the plaintiff's impact claim, its motion will be denied.

2. The motion will be granted. As part of his prima facie claim, the plaintiff must allege that he was discharged because of his disability. The courts distinguish between a disability and its consequences, particularly where the consequences involve criminal behavior. Here, the plaintiff was fired for driving under the influence of alcohol, not for being an alcoholic. His alcoholism may have compelled the plaintiff to drink, but it did not compel him to drive while under the influence. Accordingly, since the plaintiff has not established causation, the defense motion for judgment as a matter of law will be granted.

3. The court should grant the defense motion. This is a tricky case. The plaintiff is alleging associational discrimination, i.e., discrimination against him because of his association with a person known by the defendant to be disabled. The plaintiff can establish that he has a relationship with someone (his son) who is known by the company to be disabled. But the issue here is whether the discrimination occurred because of the son's disability. The company alleges that it has a nondiscriminatory policy of terminating anyone who asks for more than $12,000 in annual medical benefits for a dependent, regardless of whether or not it is incurred because of a disability. Thus, it would seem that this is not a policy that discriminates intentionally because of the disability of someone with whom the plaintiff has a relationship. Accordingly, since the plaintiff is only alleging intentional discrimination, and has not alleged that this policy has a disparate impact on individuals who have a relationship with a disabled person, the defense should receive judgment as a matter of law.

4. The court will deny the plaintiff's motion. Section 103(b) of the ADA permits an employer to discriminate on the basis of disability where employing the disabled individual will pose a direct threat to the safety and health of *others* in the workplace. However, in *Echazabal*, the Supreme Court construed that defense to extend to instances where the plaintiff poses a direct threat to her own health or safety. Consequently, this defense is available to the defendant in this case, and so the plaintiff's motion will be denied.

e. The Duty to Accommodate

In addition to the more obvious adverse action form of discrimination, §102(b)(5) of Title I includes within the definition of unlawful discrimination the failure to make (a) a *reasonable* accommodation (b) to the *known* physical or mental limitations (c) of an otherwise qualified individual (d) unless the defendant can prove that the accommodation would impose an undue hardship on the conduct of its business. Thus, unlike the other anti-discrimination statutes, the ADA requires, under appropriate circumstances, that a covered entity do more than treat disabled individuals the same as non-disabled persons; it must engage in some form of preferential treatment on behalf of disabled individuals. In cases where a reasonable accommodation exists that would render a disabled person qualified to perform the job in question, and that accommodation does not impose an undue hardship upon the defendant, the defendant is obliged to provide that preferential treatment/accommodation.

It is true that the two anchor concepts of this obligation—(1) reasonable accommodation and (2) undue hardship—are also found in the religious accommodation duty codified at §701(j) of Title VII. But, as we saw when we examined the duty to engage in religious accommodation, that obligation has been extremely narrowly construed by the Supreme Court in *Hardison*, primarily because of the First Amendment Religion Clause complications that arise when the government compels differential treatment on the basis of religion. A much broader obligation to accommodate is mandated by the ADA where, obviously, the First Amendment concerns are inapposite. For example, these two terms are explicitly defined in the ADA, which is not the case in Title VII. Section 101(9), for example, defines "reasonable accommodation" by listing a non-exclusive collection of responses including (1) redesigning physical facilities to make them accessible to and usable by individuals with disabilities; (2) restructuring various aspects of the work environment, such as job requirements and assignments, work schedules, working equipment and devices, examinations, and training materials; and (3) providing qualified readers or interpreters. And in language clearly more expansive than the standard read into Title VII by the Supreme Court in *Hardison*, §101(10)(A) defines "undue hardship" to mean a response that requires "significant difficulty or expense" when considered in light of the list of factors set forth in §101(10)(B). Notice, by the way, that these factors refer not only to the nature and cost of the requisite accommodation, but also to the financial resources of the particular facility at which the accommodation is sought, as well as to the resources, size, and structure of the defendant's overall business.

Where the plaintiff alleges that he has been discriminated against because the defendant failed to fulfill its duty to accommodate, the plaintiff must establish (1) that the employer knew of the plaintiff's need for an accommodation; (2) that the plaintiff was otherwise qualified; and (3) that the defendant failed or refused to fulfill its duty to make a reasonable accommodation that did not result in an undue hardship. The prevailing rule in the circuits is that the plaintiff bears the initial burden of informing her employer that she is disabled and requesting an accommodation that will render her "otherwise qualified" for employment. At that point, the employer must initiate an "informal interactive process" with the employee to determine whether an appropriate reasonable accommodation exists. If the employer fails to make a good faith effort to engage in this interactive process, it will be found to have violated the Act unless it can prove that no reasonable accommodation was possible. But where the employer does not persuade the trier of fact that no reasonable accommodation was possible, its failure to commence the interactive process will result in *per se* liability under the ADA. Moreover, in attempting to establish that no reasonable accommodation was possible, it is not enough for the employer to assert that the employee did not come forward with a proposal that constituted a reasonable accommodation. Conversely, if the plaintiff rejects a reasonable accommodation, she no longer will be considered to be a qualified individual with a disability and, therefore, forfeit her protected status. At least one circuit court, however, has emphasized the importance of distinguishing between an employer's knowledge of an employee's disability and an employer's knowledge of the need for an accommodation to respond to the limitations produced by that disability. In *Taylor v. Principal Financial Group, Inc.*, 93 F.3d 155 (5th Cir.), *cert. denied*, 519 U.S. 1029 (1996), the Fifth Circuit stated that an employer should not be held to assume that every disabled individual suffers from a limitation that needs accommodation. To the contrary, it concluded, the statute embodied the opposite presumption by prohibiting employers from evaluating the capabilities of disabled individuals on the basis of stereotypes and myths. Accordingly, it found that since the plaintiff had not informed his employer of his need for an accommodation, the employer was under no obligation to participate in the interactive process of determining one.

In *US Airways, Inc. v. Barnett*, 535 U.S. 391 (2002), the Supreme Court explained the respective evidentiary burdens borne by the adverse parties with respect to proving "reasonable accommodation" and "undue hardship." The plaintiff bears the burden of persuading the court that a particular accommodation is reasonable. To meet this burden, the Court declared, the plaintiff must establish that a particular accommodation seems reasonable on its face, i.e., that it would be reasonable "in the run of cases." And an employer is only required to make *a* reasonable accommodation; there is no duty to make the most reasonable accommodation, or the accommodation preferred by the plaintiff. Once the plaintiff has made this showing, the burden of persuasion shifts to the employer to demonstrate that this accommodation would impose an undue hardship upon it in light of its particular circumstances. Thus, "reasonable accommodation" is an objectively determined standard calculated by balancing the impact of this alteration on the plaintiff's ability to perform essential job functions against its effect upon the conduct of business in the general run of situations. "Undue hardship," on the other view, is an economic safe harbor for the particular employer, i.e., it requires an evaluation of the specific defendant's ability to sustain the cost of an otherwise reasonable accommodation, regardless of whether a different employer might be required to adopt that same proposed accommodation.

However, the *Barnett* Court also threw an additional consideration into the mix, at least with respect to proposed accommodations that would violate the terms of either a unilaterally implemented or collectively bargained seniority system. In such situations, the Court explained, the employer is entitled to the benefit of a rebuttable presumption that such an accommodation is *unreasonable* in the general run of cases. But the plaintiff can rebut that presumption by establishing the existence of "special circumstances" in its particular situation that justify a finding that the requested accommodation is reasonable. And the Court offered two examples of circumstances that would justify the rebuttal of this presumption of unreasonableness: (1) where the employer's retention and "fairly frequent" exercise of the right to make unilateral changes to its seniority system suggested that one more departure, designed to accommodate a disabled individual, would not likely make a difference; and (2) where the seniority system already contained exceptions so that one further exception was unlikely to cause significant damage to its ability to conduct its operations.

Remember also that the duty to accommodate only exists to the extent that a reasonable accommodation will result in the disabled individual's being able to perform the essential functions of the job. Accordingly, modifying or eliminating an essential job function would not constitute a reasonable accommodation. However, the circuits have not agreed on which party has the burden of persuading the trier of fact that the accommodation in question would render the plaintiff able to perform the job's essential functions. Some courts require the defendant to prove that the employee could not perform the essential functions of the job even with the proposed accommodation that the plaintiff has established to be otherwise reasonable in the general run of cases. On the other hand, some circuits insist that the defendant bears the burden of persuasion only with respect to establishing undue hardship. They require the plaintiff to prove both that an accommodation is generally reasonable *and* that it would render him capable of performing essential job functions.

Section 101(9)(B) of the ADA expressly recognizes "reassignment to a vacant position" as a form of reasonable accommodation. Two frequently litigated issues arise in cases involving this particular form of accommodation. One of these issues arises when a plaintiff's disability renders him unable to perform the functions of his present job, but would not prevent him from performing the functions of an available alternative position. The issue in such cases is not whether reassignment is a reasonable accommodation, but whether the plaintiff's inability to perform the functions of his present position renders him *not* "otherwise qualified" and, therefore, not entitled to any statutory protection, including the right to a reasonable accommodation. The prevailing view among the circuit courts is that since the statutory definition of "otherwise qualified" includes the ability to perform the essential functions of a job that the plaintiff holds "or desires," this language should be read to mean that a disabled employee is covered under the statute if she is able to perform the essential functions of a reasonably available alternative position, even if she is no longer able to fulfill the essential functions of her present position.

Another problem associated with requests of reassignment is whether, assuming that reassignment is reasonable and that a position is available, the disabled plaintiff enjoys an absolute right to that position or only the right to be considered along with other applicants for the position. Again, the courts are split. Some take the position that if the duty to accommodate is construed to require nothing more than the obligation to consider the disabled employee on an equal basis with other candidates, the duty would become superfluous since it would add nothing to the obligation not to discriminate. These courts also make the textual point that the statutory list of reasonable accommodations refers to "reassignment" and not "consideration of a reassignment." Accordingly, under this view, if an employer concludes that no reasonable accommodation could be made to keep the disabled employee in her current position, it is obliged to award the reassignment to a disabled individual who was qualified for that position, even if there are other more qualified non-disabled applicants. Other circuits, however, take the position that the ADA does not require that degree of preferential treatment, and they do not compel an employer to reassign a qualified disabled employee to a vacant position in violation of its nondiscriminatory policy of hiring the most qualified candidate.

Prior to the enactment of the 2008 amendments, the circuit courts were split on the question of whether a plaintiff who establishes that she was "regarded as" being disabled by her employer was entitled to a reasonable accommodation to this perceived, but nonexistent disability. While some circuits express incredulity at the notion that an employer could be required to make an accommodation to a disability that did not exist, other than in its own mind, others insist that Congress intended to offer the same level of protection to a "regarded as" worker as an actually disabled employee because being perceived as disabled can be as disabling as an actual disability. Congress resolved the matter in §6(a)(1) of the ADA Amendments Act of 2008 by providing that a covered entity need not make a reasonable accommodation to an individual who is "regarded as" being disabled.

The Duty to Accommodate

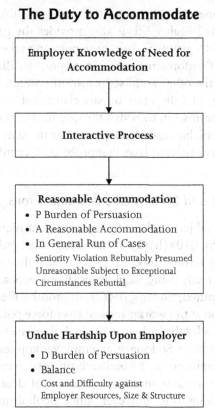

Employer Knowledge of Need for Accommodation

↓

Interactive Process

↓

Reasonable Accommodation
- P Burden of Persuasion
- A Reasonable Accommodation
- In General Run of Cases
  Seniority Violation Rebuttably Presumed
  Unreasonable Subject to Exceptional
  Circumstances Rebuttal

↓

Undue Hardship Upon Employer
- D Burden of Persuasion
- Balance
  Cost and Difficulty against
  Employer Resources, Size & Structure

i. *A Few Words About Genetic Testing*

The development of genetic testing for predisposition to various diseases and conditions has raised the issue of whether employment practices based upon the discovery that an employee or applicant is genetically predisposed to a disabling condition are subject to scrutiny under the ADA. There is no specific reference to genetic testing in the ADA. But ADA regulations promulgated by the EEOC, while not referring expressly to genetic testing, state that a "characteristic predisposition to illness or disease" does not constitute an impairment and, therefore, cannot be the basis for being considered a disability under the statute. However, the Genetic Information Nondiscrimination Act of 2008 (GINA), Pub. L. No. 110-233, 122 Stat. 881 (2008), prohibits employers, employment agencies, and unions from using genetic information (other than information about the sex or age of any individual) of employees and job applicants (or their family members) in connection with decisions concerning any term or condition of employment. Like Title VII, GINA provides plaintiffs with a private cause of action for compensatory and punitive damages subject to the caps set forth in the 1991 Civil Rights Act. It also provides the parties with the right to a jury trial. GINA plaintiffs, like those pursuing relief under Title VII, must invoke the EEOC enforcement machinery prior to filing suit. However, unlike Title VII and the other antidiscrimination statutes, GINA expressly precludes the bringing of a disparate impact claim. But it does require Congress to create a commission to revisit the question of the availability of impact claims for genetic bias claims six years after the statute's enactment. More than 30 states have enacted laws that prohibit discrimination based on genetic data.

ii. Drug Testing and Other Medical Examinations

Entities subject to the nondiscrimination requirements of Title VII are permitted by §104(b)(3) to use "reasonable policies or procedures," including drug testing, to ensure that a rehabilitated or rehabilitating individual is not currently using illegal drugs. Employers and other covered entities also are permitted, under §104(c), to prohibit illegal drug use and alcohol consumption at the workplace and to enforce policies requiring that employees not be under the influence of alcohol or be engaged in using illegal drugs at the workplace. So long as an employer applies its no-drug or alcohol policy to all employees in a nondiscriminatory manner, it can discipline an alcoholic for working under the influence of alcohol or for drinking on the job. At the same time, however, since alcoholism is uniformly viewed by the courts to constitute a covered disability, alcoholics (unlike current users of illegal drugs) are entitled to a reasonable accommodation that would render them otherwise qualified to perform their job as long as it does not impose an undue hardship upon the employer. But that accommodation does not include the right to appear at the worksite in an inebriated condition.

There are a separate collection of rules governing the employer's use of medical examinations, since such examinations could disclose the existence of a qualifying disability. Section 102(d) prohibits the use of medical examinations and inquiries that are designed to ascertain the existence, nature, or severity of a disability. But the statute sets forth different rules depending upon who is being examined. The three different categories are (1) job applicants (subject to "pre-employment exams"); (2) individuals who have been offered a job but whose offer is conditioned upon the results of the examination (subject to "employment entrance examinations"); and (3) incumbent employees.

Section 102(d) prohibits employers from requiring job applicants to undergo medical examinations or inquiries (other than tests for the presence of illegal drugs) for the purpose of determining the presence, nature, or severity of a disability. However, the employer can inquire about the applicant's ability to perform relevant job functions. A similar rule applies to exams and inquiries given to incumbent employees; they cannot be given for the purpose of determining the presence, nature, or severity of a disability unless shown to be job-related and consistent with business necessity.

But a very different set of rules applies to employment entrance examinations. An employer is permitted to require a medical exam *after* the offer has been made but before employment has begun. And the employer can condition that offer on the results of the examination as long as (1) the test is given to all new employees; (2) the results of the exam are treated confidentially and segregated from other employment files and records; and (3) the results are used in accordance with the statute. However, there is no requirement, as in the other two situations, that the test be restricted to matters related to job performance. The only limitation relates to the use to which the employer can put the resulting information and the confidential and segregated manner in which it is kept. The courts are very careful, however, to emphasize that these conditional employment entrance exams be given *only* after a "real offer" has been made, i.e., they can be given only after the employer has completed all of the non-medical components of its selection process.

Examples

Escaping a Dickens of a Situation

1. David Copperfield was employed as a painter by Blunderstone Rookery, Inc. (BRI), a company that renovates blighted housing, until he developed a severe back injury from repeated falls from painting ladders. When the pain from his injury prevented him from continuing as a painter, Copperfield asked his supervisor if he could be reassigned to a job installing sinks, which would not be taxing on his back but would allow him to stay out in the field renovating blighted properties. The supervisor declined that request but offered Copperfield a reassignment, with no loss of pay or benefits, to the company's home office dealing with customer requests for renovations. Copperfield declined that offer and sued BRI, alleging that he had been discriminated against in violation of the ADA by the company's failure to meet its duty to accommodate his disability. Copperfield admitted that the company's offer was reasonable but alleged that his proposal also was reasonable and that the company's failure to adopt his proposal violated the ADA. BRI admitted that Copperfield's proposal was reasonable but nevertheless filed motion for judgment as a matter of law. How should the court rule on BRI's motion?

2. James Steerforth was employed as a carpenter by Blunderstone Rookery, Inc. (BRI), a company that renovates blighted housing. He developed carpal tunnel syndrome, which made it more difficult for him to utilize

many of his tools. In order to keep his job, Steerforth asked the company to provide him with a new set of specially designed ergonomically enhanced tools. The company refused on the ground that it was not obliged to make such an accommodation since that accommodation would involve more than a *de minimis* cost. How should the court rule on BRI's motion for judgment as a matter of law?

3. Wilkins Micawber, a floor refinisher employed by Blunderstone Rookery, Inc. (BRI), a company that renovates blighted housing, developed pleurisy and other pulmonary diseases from years of inhaling the fumes emitted by chemicals used to refinish flooring. Although he never complained, Micawber eventually started missing work because of the ill effects of his inhalation of the fumes. Eventually, he was discharged. Micawber filed suit under the ADA, claiming that the company had failed to meet its statutory duty to accommodate his disability by providing him with a gas mask or other air filtration device. The company moved for judgment as a matter of law. How should the trial court rule on its motion?

4. Margaret (Peg) Gotty was a recently hired accountant at the main office of Blunderstone Rookery, Inc. (BRI), a company that renovates blighted housing. Within a few days of her joining the company, Gotty began displaying extremely eccentric behavior, frequently jumping on office furniture or opening the darkened second floor windows and claiming that she needed to see sunlight so she would not feel trapped in darkness. The company's office manager, Edward Murdstone, began to think that Gotty was mentally imbalanced. When Gotty asked Murdstone to replace the darkened windows with clear glass, he said, "You are one mentally imbalanced woman," and refused. She subsequently filed an action against BRI under the ADA, claiming that in refusing her reasonable request to replace the window glass, the company had regarded her as mentally disabled and refused to make a reasonable accommodation. BRI responded with a motion to dismiss the complaint for failure to state a claim. How should the court rule on this motion?

5. David Kotkin applied for a sales job with Houdini Enterprises, Inc. (HEI), a manufacturer of magician's supplies and illusions. After passing an employee motivation test and a background check, Kotkin was offered a job contingent upon passing a physical examination. Concerned that the exam would reveal a congenital heart defect and result in his rejection, Kotkin refused to take the exam and sued HEI, claiming that the medical exam requirement violated his rights under the ADA. In its answer, HEI admitted that it had not yet conducted its mandatory reference check of Kotkin before requesting that he take the medical exam. Nevertheless, it filed a motion for judgment as a matter of law on the ground that it had made him a conditional offer. How should the trial court rule on that motion?

Explanations

Escaping a Dickens of a Situation

1. The court will grant the motion. The duty to accommodate is limited to a duty to make a reasonable accommodation, not the most reasonable accommodation, nor the accommodation preferred by the plaintiff. Since the plaintiff admitted that the company's proposal was a reasonable accommodation, the company has satisfied its statutory duty to accommodate. Therefore, its motion will be granted.

2. The court will deny the motion. Unlike Title VII's duty to accommodate religious beliefs and practices, the duty to accommodate provided in the ADA requires the employer to assume more than a de minimis cost before a proposed accommodation will be viewed as imposing an undue hardship. Section 101(10) of the ADA establishes the factors to be considered in determining whether a proposed accommodation imposes an undue hardship upon the employer. It defines undue hardship as an action requiring "significant difficulty or expense" based on the defendant's particular economic situation. But here, the employer has asserted only that the cost would be greater than de minimis, and that is not enough to establish undue hardship as a matter of law. Thus, the defense motion will be denied.

3. The motion will be granted. Section 102(b)(5) defines discrimination to include not making a reasonable accommodation to the known limitations of an otherwise qualified individual with a disability. The courts have construed this to require the plaintiff to inform the employer of both the existence of an impairment and the need for an accommodation. The plaintiff here did neither of these, and this is not a situation of a manifest impairment with a self-evident need for accommodation. Consequently, the plaintiff has not established the elements of his prima facie claim of accommodation-based discrimination, and so the defense motion will be granted.

4. The court will grant the motion. Although the circuit courts have split on this issue, the ADA Amendments Act of 2008 states that a "regarded as" disabled plaintiff is not entitled to a reasonable accommodation. Therefore, the defense motion will be granted, and the complaint will be dismissed.

5. The court will deny the motion. Section 102(d) permits employers to require job applicants to undergo medical exams after an offer has been made, even if the offer is conditioned on the results of the examination. But the courts only permit this when the exam is required after the giving of a "real offer," by which they mean that all of the non-medical components of the application process have to have been satisfactorily completed by the applicant before he can be required to take the medical

exam. Since the company had not yet conducted its mandatory reference check prior to requiring Kotkin to submit to a medical exam, it would not fall within the "real" conditional offer requirements of §102(d). Consequently, the court will deny the defense motion for judgment as a matter of law.

5. Procedures and Remedies

Since §107(a) of the ADA incorporates by reference the enforcement mechanism of Title VII, nearly all of the rules and issues concerning the procedure for asserting claims of employment-related disability claims under Title I of the ADA, as well as the remedies available in such actions, parallel those governing Title VII actions. This includes the right to recover a capped amount of compensatory and punitive damages in all discrimination cases, including cases involving a claimed breach of the duty to make a reasonable accommodation. Recovery of compensatory and punitive damages under the ADA is subject to the same rules that apply to Title VII cases, except that these damages are unavailable under the ADA where the defendant establishes that it made a good faith effort, after consulting with the plaintiff, to make a reasonable accommodation. And because §107(a) provides for the recovery of punitive and compensatory damages in actions brought to enforce §102, and retaliation is proscribed by §103, the circuit courts have concluded that these forms of relief are not available in ADA retaliation cases.

Section 502 of the ADA explicitly removes a state's Eleventh Amendment immunity from suit for monetary damages in federal court under Title I by providing state employees with the same right to sue their employer for equitable and legal damages that is available to employees of private and non-state public entities. Recall that in *Kimel*, the Supreme Court struck down an analogous provision in the ADEA on the ground that it did not meet the "congruence and proportionality" test for determining the constitutionality of Congress's attempted abrogation of sovereign immunity. The Court reached the same conclusion with respect to §502 of the ADA as applied to Title I cases in *Board of Trustees of Univ. of Alabama v. Garrett*, 531 U.S. 356 (2001). The Court determined that Congress could not be deemed to have been enacted pursuant to its authority under §5 of the Fourteenth Amendment in light of the fact that the legislative record of the ADA did not sufficiently identify a history and pattern of unconstitutional disability-based employment discrimination by the states. It also found that the statute failed the congruence and proportionality test because its duty of accommodation and prohibition against standards that produced a disparate impact far exceeded constitutional requirements.

B. THE FEDERAL REHABILITATION ACT OF 1973

As noted at the outset of this chapter, the substantive obligations contained in the ADA were patterned after the preexisting terms of the Rehabilitation Act. Consequently, the courts typically apply the same legal analysis to claims made under both statutes including, for example, issues such as whether a plaintiff is "disabled." The major difference between these two statutes, of course, is that the Rehabilitation Act applies only to the federal government (and the U.S. Postal Service), recipients of federal financial assistance, and federal contractors.

The Rehabilitation Act contains three substantive provisions, located at §§501, 503, and 504. Section 501 requires federal agencies and departments to create affirmative action programs for their employment of disabled individuals. Section 503 imposes a similar affirmative action obligation on parties to a contract in excess of $2500 with a federal agency or department. Neither of these two provisions contains an express prohibition against discriminating on the basis of disability. Section 504, on the other hand, prohibits entities receiving federal financial assistance, the U.S. Postal Service, and the federal government from discriminating against disabled individuals. Thus, since §504 provides federal employees with the right to be free from disability-based discrimination that is absent from §501, the only category of covered employees without an express right to be free from disability-based discrimination under the Rehabilitation Act are employees of federal contractors.

The procedural and remedial terms of the Rehabilitation Act are contained in §505. Section 505(a) subjects complaints brought under §501 to the "remedies, procedures, and rights" provided to federal employees by §717 of Title VII, while §505(b) subjects employees of federal funding recipients who allege a violation of §504 to the remedial and procedural provisions of Title VI. Consequently, §501 and §504 claimants can assert a private cause of action to enforce their substantive right to be free from disability-based discrimination in employment by the federal government, the U.S. Postal Service, and federal grantees. The courts permit federal employees to assert claims under either §501 or §504. But §501 claims are enforced under the Title VII regime, and §504 claims are subject to the procedures used to enforce Title VI. To avoid unnecessary confusion and to promote uniform treatment of federal employee disability claims, the circuits agree that disability claims by federal employees, whether brought under §§501 or 504, are subject to the procedural requirements applied to federal employees by §717 of Title VII. This means that all such claims are subject to the limitations period applied to federal employee Title VII claims and that these plaintiffs are required to invoke administrative remedies prior to filing suit. On the other hand, damages are recoverable in

§501 claims (because they are tied to the remedial provisions of Title VII), but are not recoverable if the federal employee brings suit under §504. In *Lane v. Pena*, 518 U.S. 187 (1996), the Supreme Court ruled that Congress had not waived the federal government's immunity against monetary damages awards in §504(a) violations.

C. CONSTITUTIONAL CLAIMS

In addition to the availability of the ADA for claims by state and local government employees and the Rehabilitation Act's availability for federal employees, government employees also can look to the Equal Protection Clause of the Fourteenth Amendment for redress from employment discrimination on the basis of disability. However, governmental distinctions on the basis of disability, like those that discriminate on the basis of age, are subjected only to rational basis scrutiny.

Examples

This Land Is Your Land

1. John E. Appleseed, a census taker employed by the U.S. Census Bureau, was discharged when the government discovered that he suffered from a rare blood disease. He filed a civil action against the federal government under the ADA, claiming that he had been discharged because of his disability. The government filed a motion to dismiss for failure to state a claim upon which relief can be granted. How should the court rule on that motion?

2. Wood E. Guthry was an accountant employed by the Nevada State Gaming Commission. He was discharged when the government discovered that he suffered from a congenital heart defect. After fulfilling all administrative prerequisites to suit, Guthry filed suit in federal district court against the State of Nevada under the ADA, claiming $100,000 in compensatory and $100,000 in punitive damages. The state filed a motion to strike the requests for monetary relief. How should the trial court rule on that motion?

3. Wood E. Guthry was an accountant employed by the Nevada State Gaming Commission. He was discharged when the government discovered that he suffered from a congenital heart defect. He filed suit in federal district court against the State of Nevada under the ADA, seeking an injunction and reinstatement. The state filed a motion to dismiss the complaint for failure to state a claim upon which relief can be granted

based on its claim of sovereign immunity. How should the trial court rule on that motion?

4. Peter Cigar was an orderly employed by the Old Folks Singer Center (OFS). He was discharged when the company discovered that he suffered from a congenital heart defect. Two days after being terminated, Cigar filed suit in federal district court against OFS under the ADA, claiming that he had been discharged because of his disability. The state admitted that it had discharged Cigar because of his disability

Explanations

This Land Is Your Land

1. The motion will be granted. The ADA does not apply to federal government workers. They must bring disability-based claims under either §501 or §504 of the Rehabilitation Act. Since this complaint was filed under the ADA, the motion to dismiss will be granted.

2. The motion will be granted. Although the ADA expressly provides state government workers with a private cause of action for monetary damages against a state employer, the Supreme Court held in *Garrett* that Congress had not constitutionally abrogated the states' sovereign immunity from claims for monetary relief in federal court. Consequently, it struck down that portion of the ADA that provided state employees with a right to collect monetary damages from the state employer. As a result of that decision, the defense motion will be granted, and the plaintiff's prayer for damages will be stricken.

3. The court will deny the motion. In *Garrett*, the Supreme Court only struck down that portion of the ADA that provided state government workers with a cause of action for monetary damages against a state. It did not strike down the ADA's substantive provisions relative to state employees, including the right to bring a right of action for injunctive relief of the sort requested here. Accordingly, the motion will be denied.

4. The motion will be granted. The ADA is governed by the procedural and remedial provisions of Title VII, including the requirement of filing administrative charges with the EEOC and, if applicable, the state or local enforcement agency. This plaintiff did not comply with any of those requirements, and so the defense motion will be granted and the complaint will be dismissed.

Index

Note: *Page locators in italics refer to figures*

Ability testing
  professionally developed, 41, 98, 102-105
Abortion
  discharge of worker for, 88, 147
Absolute immunity, 122, 127
Abuse of discretion, 7, 13
Accommodations. *See* Reasonable
    accommodations
Actionable discrimination/harassment,
    106-114, 142, 172, 177
Actuarial tables
  sex-based, 151-152, 155, 202
ADA. *See* Americans with Disabilities Act (ADA)
ADA Amendments Act of 2008, 292, 294-295,
    318. *See also* Americans with Disabilities
    Act (ADA)
ADEA. *See* Age Discrimination in Employment
    Act (ADEA)
Adequacy requirement, 192, 218
Administrative Procedure Act, 125
Administrative proceedings, 122, 180, 204,
    211, 280
Administrative remedies, 286-287, 325
  enforcement: procedures, 158, 188, 190-191
Reconstruction Civil Rights Acts, 236, 246,
    249-250
Admissibility, 6-7, 12-13, 107
Adverse action, 20-21, 78, 249
  ADA and, 290, 292, 300, 306-314
  defending claims, 309-312
  "paramour" cases, 108
  proving, 306-308
  remedies, 203
  retaliation, 121-124, 123, 127, 127, 131-132
  specific issues involving five protected
    classifications, 150, 155
Affirmative action, 28, 116, 121, 220-232
  constitutional limits, 221-224
  non-preferred class, 224-225
  overview, 220-221
  public or private employers, 221
  "reverse discrimination," 224
  sexual harassment cases, 116, 121
  statutory limits—Title VII scrutiny, 224-230
  voluntary, 28, 226-228, 245

Affirmative defenses, 5, 25
  disparate impact, 54-62, 57, 279, 284
  Equal Pay Act, 254-255
  examples, 104-105
  explanations, 105
  "factor other than sex" defense, 254-255
  individual intentional discrimination, 5, 15,
    16, 19, 25
  seniority or merit systems, 102-105
  systemic claims of intentional discrimination,
    28, 35, 39, 40
  untimely filing, 161, 165-167, 183. *See also*
    Bona fide occupational qualification
    (BFOQ); professionally developed tests;
    "same decision" affirmative defense
After-acquired evidence, 22-23, 93, 209
  ADEA and, 264
  "after-after acquired evidence," 25
  examples, 23-24
  explanations, 24-25
"After-after acquired evidence," 25
Age Discrimination in Employment Act
    (ADEA), 4, 121, 157, 246, 250,
    261-288, 307
  affirmative action, 221
  age-based harassment, 267
  back pay, 203
  BFOQs, 265-266, 272, 274
  burden of proof, 274
  coverage, 261-263
  deferral states, 280, 287
  disparate impact, 41, 130, 272-274, 277,
    279, 284
  examples, 267-270, 277-278, 284-286
  explanations, 270-272, 278-279, 286-288
  federal employees, 283-288
  Federal Express Corp. v. Holowecki, 159, 167
  jury trials, 7
  McKennon v. Nashville Banner Publishing Co., 22,
    203, 209, 264, 271-272
  meaning of age discrimination, 263
  mixed motive analysis, 127, 130, 264-265,
    271-272
  non-deferral states, 285-286
  overview, 261

Age Discrimination in Employment Act
(ADEA) (continued)
procedure and remedies for nonfederal
employees, 280-282
proving and defending disparate impact
claims, 272-273
proving and defending intentional claims,
263-272
reasonable factor other than age (RFOA),
273-274
Reeves v. Sanderson Plumbing Products, Inc., 5, 7, 14,
264
retaliation and, 127, 130
retirement, voluntary and involuntary,
274-276
Title VII comparison chart, 284
Agency doctrine, 69
Alabama, 28
Alienage, 88, 138, 236-237, 239, 241, 243
Aliens employed in the United States, 85, 86,
138
Alito, Samuel, 83, 84
Amendments to the Constitution
First, 81-83, 91, 134, 149, 315
Fifth, 3, 149, 190-191, 221, 261
Seventh, 218, 282
Tenth, 262
Eleventh, 247, 256, 262-263, 270, 324
Thirteenth, 4
Fourteenth, 3, 4, 148-149, 191, 217, 221,
229, 237, 261, 262, 276, 324
Fifteenth, 4
American Jobs Creation Act of 2004, 219
Americans employed abroad, 85, 86, 242
Americans with Disabilities Act (ADA), 4, 121,
157, 246, 250, 289-327
ADA Amendments Act of 2008, 292, 294-
295, 318
affirmative action, 220
alcohol and drug use, 293, 307-308, 312,
314, 320
associational discrimination, 308-309, 312,
313, 314
bona fide insurance plans, 310-311, 312
"broad class of jobs," 293, 300
burden of persuasion, 316-317, 319
categories of employers, 289
causation, 306-309, 314
constitutional claims, 326
direct threat, 309-310, 312
disability, meaning of, 291-302, 296

disparate impact, 41, 206, 291, 308-309,
311, 314, 320, 324
drug testing and medical examinations, 320-
321, 323-324
dual meaning of discrimination, 306-324
"essential functions," 302-303, 305, 310,
317-318
examples, 297-299, 303-304, 321-322,
326-327
explanations, 305-306, 323-324, 327
genetic testing, 319-320
informal interactive process, 316, 319
jury trials, 6-7
major life activities defined, 296, 296
mitigation, 295, 301
mixed motive analysis, 306-307
nonoccupational disability, 146-147
"otherwise qualified" individual, 302-306,
314, 315, 317-318
overview, 289-291
physical or mental impairments, 292-293,
296, 297, 298, 300-301
post-employment fringe benefits, 303
pregnancy and, 146-147
"prevailing party" language, 204
procedures and remedies, 324
prohibition against discrimination, 290
reasonable accommodations, 290, 296, 297-
298, 301, 310, 312, 314-324
"regarded as" prong, 291-292, 296, 297,
299-300, 318
religious exemption case, 83
Social Security Administration (SSA) benefits,
302-303, 305-306
substantially limiting, defined, 293-296, 296,
301-302
Title I, 306
Title VII cases, 69
undue hardship, 290, 306, 314-317
Appeals, 158-159
Applicant flow data, 31, 34, 35, 38-39
Aptitude tests, 42-43
Arbitration agreements, 180-183, 187, 188,
195
Associational discrimination, 308-309, 312,
313, 314
Atheism, 134, 137
Attorney's fees, 199, 201, 203-206, 209-212
ADEA, 282, 287-288
Attorney General, 162
Authenticity, 35-36, 95-99, 98, 101-102, 139

Back pay, 23, 24, 200, 202-203, 206-210,
    213-214
  ADEA and, 282
Bennett Amendment, 255
BFOQ. *See* Bona fide occupational qualification
    (BFOQ)
Binomial distribution analysis, 32, 38
Bona fide occupational qualification (BFOQ),
    19, 28, 35-36, 94-102, 98
  ADEA and, 265-266, 272
  authenticity, 35-36, 95-99, 98, 101-102,
    139
  cost justification-based defense, 96
  customer preference, 19, 35, 96-97,
    100-101
  examples, 98-100
  explanations, 100-102
  national origin cases, 139
  pregnancy, 148
  privacy, 96-97
  race and color cases, not available, 141
  seniority or merit systems, 102-105
  sex-based discrimination, 143
Bottom line, employer's, 46, 49-50, 53-54
Burden of persuasion
  ADA, 316-317, 319
  ADEA, 273-274
  disparate impact cases, 55
  individual claims of intentional
    discrimination, 5-6, 8, 15, 19-20, 23,
    25, 121-122
  non-intentional discrimination, 55-56, 60-61
  remedies, 213, 220
  retaliation, 122
  sexual harassment and retaliation, 93-94
  systemic claims of intentional discrimination,
    29, 40
  Title VII, special proof issues under, 93, 100,
    103, 113, 122
Burden of proof
  ADEA, 274
  defendant, 5
  individual claims of intentional
    discrimination, 5-6, 8, 15, 19-20, 23,
    25, 121-122
  nondiscriminatory explanation, 5, 6-7, 8, 10,
    12, 220
  "not onerous," 5, 6
  plaintiff, 5
  systemic claims of intentional discrimination,
    28

Business necessity. *See* Job-relatedness and
    business necessity
"But-for" causation standard, 126-127, 127,
    307

Cap on damages, 199, 215, 218-219
"Capable of separation," 46, 50, 53-54
"Catalyst" theory, 204
"cat's paw" or "rubber stamp" cases, 18, 21-22
Causation, 126-127, 127, 155
  ADA and, 306-309, 314
  "but-for" standard, 126-127, 127, 307
  "paramour" cases, 108
  retaliation cases, 126-127, 127, 131
  sex-linked, 150, 307
"Charge," 281
Charges, 157-169
Chilling effect standard, 124-125
Circuit courts, 71, 82, 127
  Second Circuit, 107, 227
  Fifth Circuit, 150, 178, 316
  Sixth Circuit, 124, 125, 163
  Seventh Circuit, 107
  Ninth Circuit, 97, 118, 143-144, 154, 308
  Eleventh Circuit, 126
  facially neutral policies and, 139
  retaliation cases, 124
Circumstantial evidence, 93
  individual claims of intentional
    discrimination, 5, 19
  pattern or practice cases, 28
Citizenship, 44, 86, 138. *See also* National
    origin-based discrimination
Civil Rights Act of 1866—42 U.S.C. §1981,
    14, 42, 239
  coverage and substantive provisions,
    236-237
  examples, 240-241
  explanations, 241-244
  federal limitations period, 238-239, 242
  overview, 235-236
  procedures and remedies, 238-239
Civil Rights Act of 1871, Section One—42
    U.S.C. §1983, 244-249
  "Constitution and laws" language, 245
  examples, 248
  explanations, 249
Civil Rights Act of 1871, Section Two—42
    U.S.C. §1985(3), 250-252
  examples, 251
  explanations, 251-252

Civil Rights Act of 1964, 67, 213, 290. *See also* Title VII (1964 Civil Rights Act)
Civil Rights Act of 1991, 7, 15, 16, 20, 95, 127, 199, 214, 229, 235, 238-239, 242, 306, 320
  ADEA and, 264-265
  disparate impact and, 43, 45-47, 52, 54, 56, 57, 146
  retaliation and, 127, 130
Civil Rights Attorney's Fees Awards Act of 1976, 203, 239
Class actions, 28, 179, 218, 228-229
  opting out, 193-194
  overview, 191-192
  Rule 23 analysis, 192-194. *See also* Systemic claims of intentional discrimination
Collective bargaining agreements, 133-134
Color discrimination. *See* Race and color discrimination
Commerce Clause, 68
Commonality requirement, 192
Commonlaw agency doctrine, 69
Compensatory relief, 213-216, 213-219, 230-232, 239, 246, 284
"Complaining party," 43-44
Conciliation, 161-162
Congress, 4, 46, 81, 238, 289
"Congruence and proportionality" standard, 148, 262
Consent decrees, 204, 212, 228-229
Conspiracies, 250-252
Constitution, 3, 42, 221
Construct validation, 55
Constructive discharge, 116, 119, 120, 121, 189
Content validation, 55
Contracts, right to make and enforce, 235-236
  employment-at-will relationship, 237
Covered practices, 78-80
Criterion validation, 55
Customer preference, 19, 35, 96-97, 100-101, 139

De minimis costs, 134-135, 322-323
Decision-maker, 21-22
Defamation action, 129, 131
Defendant, burden of proof, 5-6
Deferral states, 158, 160, 164, 168-169, 180, 204
"Demonstrate," defined, 56
Direct evidence, 5, 15
Direct threat, 309-310, 312, 313

Disability, meaning of, 290-302
Disability-related discrimination, 144. *See also* Americans with Disabilities Act (ADA)
Discrimination, two constructs, 4
Disparate impact (non-intentional discrimination), 4, 27, 41-63
  ADA, 41, 206, 291, 306-308, 308-309, 311, 314, 320, 324
  ADEA, 41, 130, 272-274, 277, 279, 284
  affirmative defenses, 54-62, 57, 94, 279
  applying impact analysis to multi-factored decisions and subjective criteria, 45-47, 139
  constitutional challenges, 62-63
  defending impact claims, 54-62
  enforcement: procedures, 171-172, 191
  enforcement: remedies, 199, 213, 225-228
  establishing prima facie case, 42-45
  examples, 47-48, 50-52, 58-60
  explanations, 48-50, 52-54, 60-62
  facially neutral policies, 41-43, 48-49, 57-58, 103
  four-fifths rule, 45, 49
  Griggs v. Duke Power Co., 41-44, 46, 53, 54-55, 273
  job-relatedness and business necessity, 54-57, 57, 60-62, 225-226
  less discriminatory alternative, 56-58, 61-62
  multi-component selection process, 45-47, 53
  national origin cases, 139, 140
  "norming," 57-58
  professionally developed ability tests, 102-105
  quantum not decided, 45
  race and color discrimination, 46, 225-226
  Reconstruction civil rights acts, 237, 244
  seniority/merit systems, 102-105
  special proof issues under Title VII, 94, 98, 100, 102-103
  specific issues involving five protected classifications, 138-140, 145-148
  state and local government workers, 244-249
  subjective criteria, 45-47, 52-53, 57. *See also* Systemic claims of intentional discrimination; individual claims of intentional discrimination
District of Columbia, U.S. District for, 190
Drug testing and medical examinations, 320-321, 323-324
Due diligence, 213
Due process guarantee, 3, 42, 149-150, 190, 196, 217

Index

Education Amendments of 1972, 246
EEOC. *See* Equal Employment Opportunity Commission (EEOC)
Elected officials, 68
Eleventh Circuit: *Underwood v. Dept. of Financial Services State of Florida*, 126
Eligibility requirements, 11
Employees
 defined, 68-70
 former employees and job applicants, 69
 payroll rule, 69
Employer-initiated investigations, 122, 123, 130-131
Employers
 employer-initiated investigations, 122, 123, 130-131
 sexual harassment and liability, 114-121
 statutory employer, 68, 70, 72, 74-78, 85, 89, 218, 261-262
 as suable defendants, 68-72
Employment agencies, 72-74
Employment Nondiscrimination Act (ENDA), 149
Employment-at-will relationship, 237
Enforcement: procedures, 157-198
 amended charges, 165, 167
 arbitration agreements and, 180-183, 187, 188, 195
 charges, 157-169
 class actions: overview, 191-192
 class actions: Rule 23 analysis, 192-194
 deferral states, 158, 160, 164, 168-169, 180, 204
 duty to conciliate, 161-162
 East Texas Motor Freight System, Inc. v. Rodriguez, 192-193
 EEOC, suits by, 187-188
 examples, 164-166, 173-175, 183-185, 194-196
 explanations, 167-169, 175-177, 185-187, 196-198
 federal and state administrative charges, 157-169
 federal employees, 188-191
 filing requirements, 163, 164
 individual suits: permissible scope, 178-179
 individual suits: preclusive effect of administrative and state court rulings, 179, 184-185, 187, 190, 193-194
 multi-plaintiff or class action suits, 179, 191-194
 non-deferral states, 160, 163, 164-165, 167, 173-177, 195

nonfederal employees, 157-158
retaliation, 178, 183, 186
review required, 189, 197, 281
timely filing of charges, 158-161
work sharing agreements, 160, 164, 165, 167, 168
Enforcement: remedies, 199-232
 affirmative action, 220-232
 attorney fees, 199, 201, 203-206, 209-212
 back pay, 199, 200, 202-203, 206-210, 213-214
 cap on damages, 199, 215, 218-219
 equitable remedies, 199, 200-214
 examples, 206-208, 230-231
 explanations, 208-209, 211-212, 231-232
 Franks v. Bowman Transportation Co., 201, 209
 injunctive relief, 200-201
 legal relief, 199, 200, 213-219
 "make whole" relief, 200, 202, 208, 227, 263
 overview, 199-200
 reinstatement, 16, 22-23, 189-190, 199-200, 207-208, 230
 three categories of available relief, 199
 twin objectives of deterrence and compensation, 199-200, 228. *See also* Remedies
EPA. *See* Equal Pay Act (1963)
Equal Employment Opportunity Commission (EEOC), 73
 age-based claims and, 281-282
 "deferral" policy, 160
 enforcement and, 158-159, 187-188
 federal employees and, 188-191
 filing requirements, 163, 164
 interpretive regulations, disability-related, 292-293
 Office of Federal Operations (OFO), 189
 reasonable cause determination, 158, 161, 166, 179-180, 183-188, 195-196
 religious exemption case, 83
 retaliation cases, 122, 123
 right to sue letter, 162-163
 suits brought by, 187-188, 194-197
 supervisor, definition, 116-117
 systemic claims of intentional discrimination, 27, 29
Uniform Guidelines on Employee Selection Procedures (EEOC), 45
validation of scored test guidelines, 55
"work sharing agreement," 160. *See also* Bona fide occupational qualification (BFOQ); enforcement: procedures

Equal Employment Opportunity Counselor, 189
Equal Pay Act (1963), 4, 250, 252-259, 282
   coverage and substantive provisions, 252-255
   examples, 257-258
   explanations, 258-259
   jury trials, 6
   procedure and remedies, 256
   Title VII, relationship to, 255-256
Equal protection guarantees, 3, 42, 149-150,
      191, 227, 229
   ADEA and, 262, 276
   affirmative action, 221-223
   Reconstruction Civil Rights Acts, 244
"Equal treatment" language, 145-146
Equitable remedies, 199, 200-214
Establishment Clause, 81-83, 134
"Establishment," defined, 254
Ethnicity, 236-237
Evidence
   after-acquired, 22-25
   alternative approaches, 15-22, 56
   circumstantial, individual claims, 5, 12, 16,
      16, 19, 20
   direct, individual claims, 6, 15-16, 16,
      19-20, 24
   prima facie case, 5-7
   statistical, 28
Exceptions and exemptions
   overview, 80-81
   religious discrimination for religious
      institutions, 81-84
"Expected" vs. "observed" composition of
      workforce, 30-31, 31, 34, 37-38

Facially neutral policies, 41-43, 48-49, 57-58,
      103
   ADA, 291
   ADEA, 273-274
   national origin cases, 139
   no-rehire policy, 176-177
   race and color discrimination, 171
   sex-based discrimination cases, 142-143
   sexual orientation and, 150
Fair Labor Standards Act (FLSA), 252-253, 256,
      262, 282
Family and Medical Leave Act of 1993 (FMLA),
      148-149
Federal and state administrative charges,
      157-169
Federal Arbitration Act (FAA), 181, 187, 197
Federal employees, 3, 68
   ADEA and, 283-288

Civil Rights Act of 1991 and, 245-246
   enforcement: procedures, 188-191
   remedies, 199
Federal Rules of Civil Procedure, 70, 73
   12(b)(6) motion for dismissal, 70, 73, 75,
      155-156
   Rule 23, 191-194
Federal statutes, 3-4
Fifth Circuit Court
   Sanchez v. Standard Brands, Inc., 178-179, 185-
      186, 191
   Taylor v. Principal Financial Group, Inc., 316
First Amendment, 91
   Establishment Clause, 81-83, 134
Foreign Service, 276-277
Four-fifths rule, 45, 49
Franchises, 70, 72
Free Exercise Clause, 81-83
Front pay, 214
Full Faith and Credit Act, 180
Fundamental/immutable rights, 143-144
"Future pecuniary losses," 214

Gambling disorder, 298, 300
Gender identity, 149
   ADA and, 293, 297, 300
Genetic Information Nondiscrimination Act of
      2008 (GINA), 319-320
Genetic testing, 319-320
Good faith, 84, 134, 247, 256, 309, 316, 324
   remedies, 217, 223, 231-232
Government, claims brought by, 27, 40
Government Employee Rights Act (GERA), 68
Grooming codes, 143-144, 152, 154

Health insurance, 310-311
High customer-contact positions, 36
Hostile environment, 90, 106-107, 111-113,
      117, 120, 137
   reasonable person standard, 107, 111-112
   serial violation doctrine, 172, 177

Immigrants, 138
Immigration Reform and Control Act of 1986
      (IRCA), 138-139, 140-141
Immunity
   absolute, 122, 127
   sovereign, 148, 247, 256, 270, 324,
      326-327
Impact-based discrimination. *See*
      Disparate impact (non-intentional
      discrimination)

Independent contractors, 77
Individual claims of intentional discrimination, 3-25, 93
  ADA and, 307-308, 312
  after-acquired evidence, 22-25
  burden of proof, 5-6
  direct and indirect motive, 6, 8, 13, 15
  examples, 9-11
  explanations, 11-14
  McDonnell Douglas/Burdine (single motive) proof framework, 8, 121-122, 273
  mixed motive cases, 15-22
  proving pretext, 6-8
  tripartite analytical framework, 4-6, 121-122
Individuals, as plaintiffs, 70, 76-78
"Inexorable zero," 28-29, 36
Infertility cases, 147
Injunctive relief, 200-201
Insurance policies, disability distinctions, 310-311
Intentional discrimination. *See* Systemic claims of intentional discrimination; individual claims of intentional discrimination
Internal Revenue Code, 219
Interracial relationships, 141-142
Interstate commerce, 253
"Invoke," defined, 158
IRCA. *See* Immigration Reform and Control Act of 1986 (IRCA)

Job differences, 253-254
Job title, 84
Job-relatedness and business necessity, 54-57, 57, 60-62, 95, 225-226
  ADA and, 291, 311, 312
Judicial order, 204, 212
Jurisdictional objections, 70
Jury trial, right to, 213, 214, 215, 282
  enforcement: remedies, 199, 200
Jury trials, 6-7

Kagan, Elena, 83, 84, 124, 223
Ku Klux Klan Act of 1871, 244

Labor organizations
  duty to accommodate and, 133, 135
  race-based discrimination, 228-229
  as suable defendants, 74-76
Laches, doctrine of, 163, 172, 197
Law school placement offices, 73-74
Legal relief, 199, 200, 213-219
  cap on damages, 218-219

compensatory relief, 213-219, 230-232, 239, 246, 284
punitive damages, 216-217, 230-232, 239, 247
taxation of monetary damage awards, 219, 282
Less discriminatory alternative, 56-58, 61-62
Liability, 5, 15-16, 16
  absolute, 115, 117, 120, 121
  absolute defense, 19, 237
  ADA and, 291
  back pay, 202-203
  retaliation, 127
  supervisorial discrimination, sexual harassment, 106, 109-111, 114-120, 117
  systemic claims of intentional discrimination, 28, 40
Licensing agencies, 73, 74
Lilly Ledbetter Fair Pay Act of 2009, 171, 177
Limitations periods
  ADEA, 283, 284
  Civil Rights Act of 1866, 238-239, 242
"Lodestar fee," 204-206
"Longstanding and gross disparity" standard, 38
"Lurking in the record" situation, 7, 14

"Make whole" relief, 200, 202, 208, 227, 263
"Malice" and "reckless disregard," 216-217, 230-231, 282
"Manifest imbalance," 227
Marital status requirements, 143, 170-171
Marshall, Thurgood, 95, 143
McDonnell Douglas/Burdine formula, 8, 15, 121-122, 180, 237, 255, 264, 308
"Me too" evidence, 7, 12-13
Mental Health Parity Act of 1996, 310-311
Merit Systems Protection Board, 189
Ministerial exception, 82-84, 118
  ADA and, 290
  ADEA and, 267, 270, 272
Mixed motive cases, 15-22, 201, 237
  ADA, 306-307
  ADEA, 127, 130, 264-265, 271-272, 284
  examples, 16-22
  proof framework, 16
  retaliation, 126-127, 127, 129-130
Monetary damages, 219, 244, 247
"Most favored nation" status, 146-147
Motive
  direct and indirect, 6, 8, 13, 15
  mixed motive cases, 15-22

Multi-component selection process, 45-47, 53
Multi-plaintiff or class action suits. *See* Class
    actions

"National origin," interpretations, 138
National origin-based discrimination, 44,
    138-141, 193-194, 236-237, 284
  BFOQ defense, 95
  examples, 139-140, 208, 215, 241-242, 251
  explanations, 140-141
  Title VII cases, 76-77
Native American tribes, 138
New York State Antidiscrimination Act, 165
Ninth Circuit Court, 154, 308
  Elvig v. Calvin Presbyterian Church, 118
  Fernandez v. Wynn Oil Co., 97
  Jesperson v. Harrah's Operating Co., Inc., 143-144
"No unnecessarily trammeling" criteria, 227
No-continuing-effects doctrine, 171
Non-deferral states, 160, 163, 164-165, 167,
    173-177, 195
Nondiscriminatory explanation, 5, 6-7, 8, 10,
    12, 20, 220
  "lurking in the record" situation, 7, 14
Nonfederal employees
  ADEA and, 280-282
  enforcement: procedures, 157-158
Non-intentional discrimination, 41-63. *See
    also* Disparate impact (non-intentional
    discrimination)
"Norming," 57-58
Numerosity requirement, 69-70, 192

Objective criteria, 46-47, 52-53, 57
  hostile environment, 106-107, 112-113,
    137
O'Connor, Sandra Day, 15-16, 273
Office of Compliance, 190
Older Workers Benefit Protection Act
    (OWBPA), 275-276
Opposition, acts of, 122-125, 127, 130-131

Pattern or practice of conduct, 27, 94. *See
    also* Systemic claims of intentional
    discrimination
Pension plans, 145, 151-152
Performance requirements, 11
Performing arts, 97
"Person," defined, 68, 246
Plaintiff
  burden of proof, 5

proper plaintiffs: "employees" and
    "individuals," 76-78
rightful place, 201, 208-209. *See also* Class
    actions
Post-Act hiring, 29, 30, 36
Pre-Act hiring, 29
Preclusion, rules of, 179-180, 184-185, 187,
    190, 193-194
Pregnancy Discrimination Act (PDA) of 1978,
    104, 144-146
Pregnancy-based discrimination, 104, 144-
    148, 152-153
Pretext, proving, 6-8
  examples, 10-14
  explanations, 14-15
Prevailing party, 203-205, 209, 211-212
  ADEA, 282, 287-288
Prima facie case, 8, 16, 143
  Civil Rights Act of 1871 and, 244-245
  establishing disparate impact, 42-45
  evidence, 5-7
  intentional discrimination, individual claims,
    5-15, 8, 16, 19
  intentional discrimination, systemic claims,
    28-29, 31-39
  statistics, 28-29
Privacy, 96-97
  sexual orientation, 149-150
Private property rights, 3
Probability theory, 29
Procedural unconscionability, 181
Professionally developed tests, 41, 98, 102-104,
    102-105
Protected classifications, 4, 15, 36
  non-members, 12. *See also* Specific issues
    involving five protected classifications;
    systemic claims of intentional
    discrimination
Protected conduct, 68, 121-127, 127, 131
Public employers, 30
Punitive damages, 216-217, 230-232, 239,
    247

Qualifications
  superior, 8, 10, 14-15
Quid pro quo claim, 106, 115, 117, 120

Race and color discrimination, 141-142
  Civil Rights Act of 1886 and, 240-244
  disparate impact, 46, 225-226
  ethnicity, 236-237

examples, 11, 17-18, 20-21, 23
facially neutral policies, 42-43, 171
interracial relationships, 141-142
labor organizations, 228-229
non-intentional, examples and explanations,
    59-60
race-neutral alternatives, 223
seniority and, 227
Title VII cases, 73-74, 75. *See also* Affirmative
    action
"Rare" or "exceptional" case, 205
Rational basis scrutiny, 149
Reasonable accommodations
ADA, 290, 296, 297-298, 301, 310, 312,
    314-324
duty to accommodate, 133-137, 314-324,
    319
"reassignment to a vacant position," 317-
    318, 321
religion-based discrimination, 133-137, 315
Reasonable cause determination, 158, 161,
    166, 179-180, 183-188, 195-196
Reasonable factor other than age (RFOA),
    273-274
Reasonable person standard, 137, 247
hostile environment, 107, 111-112
retaliation, 127, 131
Reconstruction Civil Rights Acts, 141, 235
disparate impact, 237, 244. *See also* Civil
    Rights Act of 1866— 42 U.S.C. §1981;
    Civil Rights Act of 1871, Section
    One— 42 U.S.C. §1983; Civil Rights
    Act of 1871, Section Two— 42 U.S.C.
    §1985(3)
Reconstruction Era, 4, 235
Reexamination of facts, ban on, 218
Rehabilitation Act of 1973, 4, 289, 290, 302,
    325-326, 327
Reinstatement, 16, 22-23, 189-190, 199-200,
    230
"Relation back" rule, 159, 167
Religion-based discrimination
BFOQ defense, 95
duty to accommodate, 133-135
examples, 87-88, 89, 136
explanations, 88-90, 137
ministerial exception, 82-84, 118
for religious institutions, 81-84
Remedies, 16, 159
ADA, 324
after-acquired evidence and, 22-23, 93
declaratory relief, 15, 16, 19-20, 201

injunctive relief, 15, 16, 19-20, 200-201
reinstatement, 16, 22-23, 189-190, 199-
    200. *See also* Enforcement: remedies
Remittitur, 218-219
Retaliation, 94, 106, 114, 120
absolute immunity, 122, 127
ADEA, 283-284, 284, 286, 288
adverse action, 121-124, 127, 127, 131-132
"but-for" causation standard, 126-127, 127
Civil Rights Act of 1886 and, 237, 239, 241,
    243
enforcement procedures and, 178, 183, 186
examples, 128-129
explanations, 129-132
against former employees, 123-124
IRCA and, 139
for letter to editor, 131-132
mixed motive analysis, 126-127, 127, 129-130
opposition, acts of, 121-125, 127
participation, 121-125, 127, 130
protected conduct, 68, 121-127, 127, 131
reasonable person standard, 127, 131
"same decision" affirmative defense, 129-130
status-based discrimination, 126-127
temporal proximity of protected conduct,
    127, 132
third-party claims, 124-126, 132
Retirement, 262
dual-track system, 263
employer-sponsored health benefits, 266-267
mandatory policies, 266
voluntary and involuntary, 274-276,
    277-278
waiver of rights or claims, 275-276, 278
Roberts, John, 83
Rules of evidence, 7, 13, 107

"Same decision" affirmative defense, 237, 272
intentional discrimination, individual claims,
    93, 237, 272
remedies, 201, 207, 209
retaliation, 129-130
Title VII, special proof issues under, 93,
    129-130
Same-sex harassment actions, 108
Scalia, Antonin, 124, 148-149
Second Circuit Court: *U.S. v. Brennan*, 227
Selection process
multi-component, 45-47, 53
religious exemption, 90, 91
Uniform Guidelines on Employee Selection
    Procedures (EEOC), 45

Self-care provision (FMLA), 148-149
Seniority or merit systems, 102-105
 ADA and, 317, 319
 ADEA and, 277
 Equal Pay Act and, 254
 examples, 207
 marital status requirements, 170-171
 pension plans, 145
 pregnancy discrimination, 144-145
 race and color discrimination, 227
 religion-based discrimination, 133-134
 remedies, 201, 207, 209
 retroactive, 201
Serial violation doctrine, 172, 177
Severability clause, 181
Sex-based discrimination, 142-156
 actuarial tables, 151-152, 155, 202
 "because of sex," 142, 147
 examples, 9-14, 16-17, 152-154, 194-195,
  206-208
 explanations, 154-156
 facially neutral policies, 43, 142-143
 flight attendants, 95-96
 FMLA and, 148-149
 grooming codes, 143-144, 152, 154
 infertility cases, 147
 marital status requirements, 143, 170-171
 non-intentional, examples and explanations,
  58-62
 pregnancy-based discrimination, 104, 144-
  148, 152-153
 "sex-plus" doctrine, 142-144, 154
 sexual orientation, 149-151, 155-156
 stereotype analysis, 19-20, 97, 143-144,
  150-151, 154, 156
 Title VII examples, 70-71. See also Bona
  fide occupational qualification
  (BFOQ); Equal Pay Act (1963); sexual
  harassment
Sex-based wage discrimination, 4. See also Equal
 Pay Act (1963)
"Sex-plus" doctrine, 142-144, 154
Sex-segregated working environment, 254-255
Sexual harassment, 142
 actionable discrimination, 106-114, 142,
  172, 177
 anti-harassment policy must be used, 115-
  116, 118-120, 128, 231-232
 by co-employee, 114, 116, 117
 constructive discharge, 116, 119, 120, 121
 examples, 109-111, 118-119, 128-129
 explanations, 111-114, 120-121, 129-132

hostile environment, 90
 liability of defendant employer, 114-121
 "paramour" cases, 108, 110-111, 113-114
 religious exemption and, 90
 same-sex harassment, 108, 150-151
 "severe or pervasive" standard, 106, 111
 supervisorial harassment, 106, 109-111,
  114-117, 117
 tangible employment action, 115-118, 117,
  120-121
 "unwelcomed" element, 106, 107, 111,
  113, 117
Sexual orientation, 108, 149-151, 155-156
Similarity of jobs, 253-254
"Single filing" or "piggybacking" rule, 179,
 186-187, 191, 193-194
"Snapshot" of entire workforce, 30, 34, 36
Social Security Disability Insurance (SSDI)
 program, 302
Souter, David, 263, 271
Sovereign immunity, 148, 247, 256, 270, 324,
 326-327
Specific issues involving five protected
 classifications
adverse action, 150, 155
disparate impact (non-intentional
 discrimination), 138-140, 145-148
State action requirement, 3
State agency, 158-160
State and local government workers, 244-249
State law
 discrimination under color of, 238
 enforcement, 158-163, 163, 164, 179-180
 work sharing agreements, 160, 164, 165,
  167, 168
State sovereign immunity, 148, 247, 256, 270,
 324, 326-327
Statistical analysis, 28, 94
 applicant flow data, 31, 34, 35, 38-39
 binomial distribution analysis, 32, 38
 "snapshot" of entire workforce, 30, 34, 36
 standard deviation analysis, 30-31, 38, 45
 systemic claims of intentional discrimination,
  30-38, 34
Statutory fee-shifting provision, 205, 212
Strict scrutiny standard, 222-223, 245, 276
"Strong basis in evidence" standard, 222,
 225-228
Subject matter jurisdiction, 70, 179, 230
Subjective criteria, 45-47, 52-53, 57
 hostile environment, 106-107, 112-113, 137
Subsidiaries, 70, 71

Substantive unconscionability, 181
Superior qualifications, 8, 10, 14-15
Supervisorial discrimination, 21-22
    sexual harassment, 106, 109-111, 114-117, 117
Supreme Court cases, 4
    14 Penn Plaza, 187, 197
    Adarand Constructors, Inc. v. Pena, 223
    Albemarle Paper Co. v. Moody, 54-55, 57, 98, 103,
        199-200, 202, 208-209
    Albertsons, Inc. v. Kirkingburg, 293-294, 295, 300
    Alden v. Maine, 263
    American Tobacco Co. v. Patterson, 103
    Ansonia Board of Education v. Philbrook, 135
    Arbaugh v. Y&H Corp., 70
    Arizona Governing Committee v. Norris, 151-152,
        202
    Ash v. Tyson Foods, Inc., 5, 8, 13
    Astoria Federal Savings & Loan Assn. v. Solimino, 281
    AT&T Corp. v. Hulteen, 104, 145
    Bazemore v. Friday, 32, 171
    Blanchard v. Bergeron, 205, 212
    Blum v. Stenson, 204, 212
    BMW of North America, Inc. v. Gore, 217
    Board of Trustees of Univ. of Alabama v. Garrett, 324,
        327
    Bragdon v. Abbot, 291, 292, 309
    Briscoe v. City of New Haven, 226
    Brown v. GSA, 190, 191, 197, 235-236, 238
    Buckhannon Board & Care Home, Inc. v. West Virginia
        Dept. of Health & Human Resources, 203-204,
        211-212
    Burlington Industries, Inc. v. Ellerth, 115-116, 120,
        121
    Burlington Northern & Santa Fe Railway Co. v. White,
        123-126
    Burns v. McGregor Electronic Industries, Inc., 113
    California Brewers Assn. v. Bryant, 103
    California Federal Savings & Loan Assn. v. Guerra, 146
    Carey v. Piphus, 213
    CBOCS West, Inc. v. Humphries, 237, 243-244,
        283-284
    Chandler v. Roudebush, 190
    Chardon v. Fernandez, 170, 175
    Chevron v. Echazabal, 309-310, 314
    Christianburg Garment Co. v. EEOC, 206
    City of Burlington v. Dague, 204-205
    City of Newport v. Fact Concerts, Inc., 247
    City of Richmond v. J.A. Croson Co., 222, 225
    Clackamas Gastroenterology Associates v. Wells, 69
    Clark County School District v. Breeden, 127
    Cleveland Newspaper Guild, Local 1 v. Plain Dealer
        Publishing Co., 163

Cleveland v. Policy Management Systems Corp., 302,
    305
Coleman v. Court of Appeals of Maryland, 148
Commissioner of IRS v. Schleier, 282
Commissioner v. Banks, 219
Connecticut v. Teal, 46, 53
Consolidated Coin Caterers, 271
Cooper v. Federal Reserve Bank of Richmond, 194
Corning Glass Works v. Brennan, 253
Corporation of Presiding Bishop of the Church of Jesus
    Christ of Latter-Day Saints v. Amos, 82
County of Washington v. Gunther, 255
Crawford v. Metropolitan Government of Nashville and
    Davidson County, 122, 123, 130-131
Crown, Cork & Seal Co. v. Parker, 161
CRST Van Expedited, Inc. v. EEOC, 206, 212
Davis v. Passman, 191
Delaware State College v. Ricks, 169-170, 175, 176
Desert Palace, Inc. v. Costa, 16, 20, 265
Domino's Pizza, Inc. v. McDonald, 242
Dothard v. Rawlinson, 28, 43, 46, 96
Edelman v. Lynchburg College, 159, 167
EEOC v. Abercrombie & Fitch Stores, Inc., 134-135
EEOC v. Commercial Office Products Co., 160, 168
EEOC v. Waffle House, Inc., 188, 197
EEOC v. Wyoming, 262, 270
Engquist v. Oregon Dept. of Agriculture, 245
Espinoza v. Farah Manufacturing Co., 44, 46, 88,
    138, 140
Faragher v. City of Boca Raton, 115, 116
Farrar v. Hobby, 201, 203, 211
Federal Express Corp. v. Holowecki, 159, 167, 281
Firefighters Local Union No. 1784 v. Stotts, 200-201,
    208
Fisher v. University of Texas at Austin, 223
Fitzgerald v. Barnstable School Committee, 246
Fitzpatrick v. Bitzer, 189
Ford Motor Co. v. EEOC, 202
Garcia v. San Antonio Metropolitan Transit Authority,
    256
General Building Contractors Association, Inc. v.
    Pennsylvania, 237
General Dynamics Land Systems, Inc. v. Cline, 221,
    263-264, 271, 274-275, 279
General Electric Co. v. Gilbert, 144
General Telephone Co. of the Northwest, Inc. v. EEOC,
    194
General Telephone Co. of the Southwest v. Falcon, 193
Gilmer, 187
Gomez-Perez v. Potter, 283, 288
Goodman v. Lukens, 238, 242, 243
Gratz v. Bollinger, 223

Great American Federal Savings & Loan Assn. v. Novotny, 250-252
Green v. Brennan, 189
Griffin v. Breckenridge, 250
Griggs v. Duke Power Co., 41-44, 46, 53, 54-55, 273
Gross v. FBL Financial Services, Inc., 126-127, 271, 272, 307
Grutter v. Bollinger, 222-223
Hall Street Associates, LLC v. Mattel, Inc., 182-183
Harlow v. Fitzgerald, 247
Harris v. Forklift Systems, Inc., 106, 107
Hazelwood School District v. U.S., 29, 30-31, 31, 36, 37, 38
Hazen Paper Co. v. Biggins, 273, 282
Hensley v. Eckerhart, 203, 204, 239
Hetzel v. Prince William County, 218-219
Hosanna-Tabor Evangelical Lutheran Church and School v. E.E.O.C., 82-84, 90
International Brotherhood of Teamsters v. U.S., 29, 30, 31, 36, 37, 40, 103, 201, 209, 219-220
International Union, U.A.W. v. Johnson Controls, 95, 147
Int'l Union of Electrical, Radio & Machine Workers, Local 790 v. Robbins & Myers, Inc., 161
Irwin v. Department of Veterans Affairs, 190
Irwin v. Veterans Administration, 162
Jett v. Dallas Independent School Dist., 238, 246
Johnson v. Mayor and City Council of Baltimore, 266
Johnson v. Railway Express Agency, Inc., 238, 239
Johnson v. Transportation Agency, 225, 226-228
Jones v. R.R. Donnelley & Sons Co., 238
Kentucky Retirement Systems v. EEOC, 263
Kimel v. Florida Board of Regents, 262, 324
Kolstad v. American Dental Association, 216, 231
Kremer v. Chemical Construction Corp., 180, 187
Lane v. Pena, 326
Ledbetter v. Goodyear Tire & Rubber Co., Inc., 171, 172, 177
Lehman v. Nakshian, 282
Lewis v. City of Chicago, 171-172
Local 28 of Sheet Metal Workers Intern. Assn. v. EEOC, 228
Local Number 93, Int'l Assn. of Firefighters v. Cleveland, 228-229
Lorillard v. Pons, 282
Los Angeles Department of Water & Power v. Manhart, 151, 155, 202
Love v. Pullman, 160
Mach Mining, LLC v. E.E.O.C., 161
Maine v. Thiboutot, 245

Martin v. Wilks, 229-230
Massachusetts Board of Retirement v. Murgia, 276, 280
McDonald v. Santa Fe Trail Transportation Co., 141
McDonnell Douglas Corp. v. Green, 5, 8, 11, 14, 121-122, 180, 255, 264, 273
McKennon v. Nashville Banner Publishing Co., 22, 203, 209, 264, 271-272
Meacham v. Knolls Atomic Power Laboratory, 274, 280
Meritor Savings Bank, FSB v. Vinson, 106, 107, 111, 114-115
Missouri v. Jenkins, 204
Mohasco Corp. v. Silver, 160, 172
Monell v. Department of Social Services, 246
Monroe v. Pape, 246
Murphy v. United Parcel Service, Inc., 293, 300
Nashville Gas Co. v. Satty, 144-145
National Railroad Passenger Corp. v. Morgan, 172, 177
Nevada Dept. of Human Resources v. Hibbs, 148
New York City Transit Authority v. Beazer, 44, 46
New York Gaslight Club, Inc. v. Carey, 204, 211
Newport News Shipbuilding & Dry Dock Co. v. EEOC, 145, 154
Occidental Life Ins. Co. v. EEOC, 163
Occidental Life Insurance Co. v. EEOC, 187
O'Connor v. Consolidated Coin Caterers Corporation, 264
Oncale v. Sundowner Offshore Services, Inc., 108, 150
Oscar Mayer & Co. v. Evans, 280-281, 286, 287
Oubre v. Entergy Operations, Inc., 276, 279
Owens v. Okure, 238
Patsy v. Board of Regents of State of Florida, 246
Patterson v. McLean Credit Union, 14-15
Penn Plaza LLC v. Pyett, 180-181
Pennsylvania State Police v. Suders, 116, 121
Perdue v. Kelly, 205
Personnel Administrator of Massachusetts v. Feeney, 244-245
Phillips v. Martin Marietta Co., 95, 142-143, 154
Pollard v. E.I. Du Pont De Nemours & Co., 214, 216
Price Waterhouse v. Hopkins, 15-16, 19, 20, 127, 130, 144, 150, 156, 237, 272, 306
Prima Paint Corp. v. Flood & Conklin Mfg. Co., 181-182
Pullman-Standard v. Swint, 103
Raytheon Co. v. Hernandez, 307, 313
Reeves v. Sanderson Plumbing Products, Inc., 5, 7, 14, 264
Rent-A-Center, West, Inc. v. Jackson, 181-182
Ricci v. Stefano, 225-228

Roadway Express, Inc. v. Piper, 206
Robinson v. Shell Oil Co., 76, 123-124
Saint Francis College v. Al-Khazraji, 236
Seminole Tribes of Florida v. Florida, 262
Serwatka v. Rockwell Automation, Inc., 307
Shaare Tefila Congregation v. Cobb, 236
Smith v. City of Jackson, 42, 273-274, 279
Sprint/United Management Co. v. Mendelsohn, 7
St. Mary's Honor Center v. Hicks, 5, 6, 7, 12, 14
State Farm Mutual Ins. Co. v. Campbell, 217
Staub v. Proctor Hospital, 21
Stevens v. Department of Treasury, 283
Sutton v. United Air Lines, 291-292, 293,
    295-296, 299-300, 301
Taylor v. Principal Financial Group, Inc., 316
Texas Department of Community Affairs v. Burdine, 5,
    6, 8, 13
Texas State Teachers Assn. v. Garland Independent School
    District, 203
Thompson v. North American Stainless, LP, 124-126,
    132
Toyota Manufacturing, Kentucky v. Williams, 294-
    295, 300-301
Trans World Airlines, Inc. v. Hardison, 133-134,
    135, 315
Trans World Airlines, Inc. v. Thurston, 282
UAW v. Johnson Controls, Inc., 95, 96
United Air Lines, Inc. v. Evans, 170-171
United Brotherhood of Carpenters & Joiners of America,
    Local 610 v. Scott, 250
United Steelworkers of America v. Weber, 224, 225,
    227-228
Univ. of Tennessee v. Elliott, 180, 187
University of Texas Southwestern Medical Center v.
    Nassar, 126, 307
US Airways, Inc. v. Barnett, 316-317
Vance v. Ball State University, 116-117
Vance v. Bradley, 276
Venegas v. Mitchell, 205, 212
Walters v. Metropolitan Educational Enterprises, Inc., 69
Wards Cove Packing Co., Inc. v. Atonio, 55-56
Washington v. Davis, 191, 244
Watson v. Fort Worth Bank & Trust, 46-47, 52-53,
    55-56
West v. Gibson, 190, 213
Western Air Lines, Inc. v. Criswell, 266
Yellow Freight Sys., Inc. v. Donnelly, 179
Young v. United Parcel Service, Inc., 146-147
Zipes v. Trans World Airlines, Inc., 161. See also
    Ninth Circuit Court
Systemic claims of intentional discrimination,
    27-40, 93

affirmative defenses, 28, 35, 39, 40
Bazemore v. Friday, 32
burden of proof, 28
equitable and legal remedies, 219-220
examples, 32-35, 34
"expected" vs. "observed" composition of
    workforce, 30-31, 31, 34, 37-38
explanations, 35-39
Hazelwood School District v. U.S., 29, 30-31, 31,
    36, 37, 38
liability and remedial stages, 28, 40, 219-220

"Temp" agencies. See Employment agencies
Third-party retaliation claims, 124-126, 132
Thomas, Clarence, 83, 84
Title VII (1964 Civil Rights Act), 3-4, 10, 14
    §703(m), 15, 19, 127, 201, 207
    ADA cases, 69
    ADEA comparison chart, 284
    age or disability discrimination not covered,
        122
    amendments, 1991, 42
    coverage, 85
    covered practices, 78-80
    EEOC, 27
    employers as suable defendants, 68-72
    employment agencies as suable defendants,
        72-74
    Equal Pay Act, relationship to, 255-256
    examples, 70-71, 73, 75, 76-77, 86-88
    exceptions and exemptions, overview, 80-81
    explanations, 71-72, 73-74, 75-76, 77-78,
        88-90
    general overview, 67-91
    jury trials, 6-7
    labor organizations as suable defendants, 74-76
    McDonnell Douglas/Burdine formula, 8, 15,
        121-122, 180, 237
    non-Title VII cases, 21
    Price Waterhouse ruling, 15-16, 19, 20, 127,
        130, 144, 150, 156, 237, 272, 306
    professional workers, 69
    proper plaintiffs: "employees" and
        "individuals," 76-78
    public employers, 30
    religious discrimination exemption, 81-84,
        85, 87-90
    special proof issues, 93-94
    threshold issues, 70
    unpaid volunteers, 69, 70
Title IX of the Education Amendments of 1972,
    246

Totality of the circumstances test, 69
"Two or more persons" requirement, 251, 252
Typicality requirement, 192, 193

Unconscionability, 181-182, 185
Undercover law enforcement assignments, 97
Undocumented aliens, 138
"Unequal treatment," 134
Uniform Guidelines on Employee Selection
    Procedures (EEOC), 45
Unions. *See* Labor organizations
Unlawful employment practices, 62, 68
    ADEA, 274, 285

enforcement: procedure, 158-160, 165, 169,
    171-172, 175-177
enforcement: remedies, 208
special proof issues under Title VII, 122,
    127

Vacation leave, 277
Validation, 55
Voluntary compliance, 106, 158, 161-162,
    166, 195
Volunteers, unpaid, 69, 70

"Wages," as term, 254